1 MONTH OF
FREE READING

at

www.ForgottenBooks.com

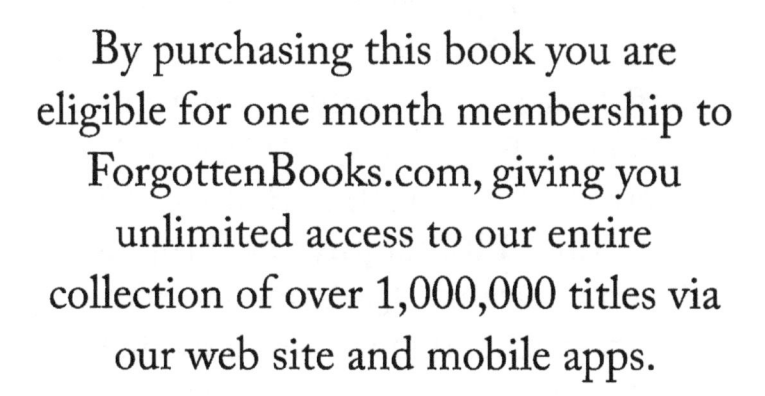

By purchasing this book you are eligible for one month membership to ForgottenBooks.com, giving you unlimited access to our entire collection of over 1,000,000 titles via our web site and mobile apps.

To claim your free month visit: www.forgottenbooks.com/free513679

*Offer is valid for 45 days from date of purchase. Terms and conditions apply.

English
Français
Deutsche
Italiano
Español
Português

www.forgottenbooks.com

Mythology Photography **Fiction** Fishing Christianity **Art** Cooking Essays Buddhism Freemasonry Medicine **Biology** Music **Ancient Egypt** Evolution Carpentry Physics Dance Geology **Mathematics** Fitness Shakespeare **Folklore** Yoga Marketing **Confidence** Immortality Biographies Poetry **Psychology** Witchcraft Electronics Chemistry History **Law** Accounting **Philosophy** Anthropology Alchemy Drama Quantum Mechanics Atheism Sexual Health **Ancient History Entrepreneurship** Languages Sport Paleontology Needlework Islam **Metaphysics** Investment Archaeology Parenting Statistics Criminology **Motivational**

1,000,000 Books
are available to read at

Forgotten Books

www.ForgottenBooks.com

Read online
Download PDF
Purchase in print

ISBN 978-1-333-51138-8
PIBN 10513679

This book is a reproduction of an important historical work. Forgotten Books uses state-of-the-art technology to digitally reconstruct the work, preserving the original format whilst repairing imperfections present in the aged copy. In rare cases, an imperfection in the original, such as a blemish or missing page, may be replicated in our edition. We do, however, repair the vast majority of imperfections successfully; any imperfections that remain are intentionally left to preserve the state of such historical works.

Forgotten Books is a registered trademark of FB &c Ltd.
Copyright © 2018 FB &c Ltd.
FB &c Ltd, Dalton House, 60 Windsor Avenue, London, SW19 2RR.
Company number 08720141. Registered in England and Wales.

For support please visit www.forgottenbooks.com

LETTERS OF FARADAY AND SCHŒNBEIN

WHAT! ONLY ONE?

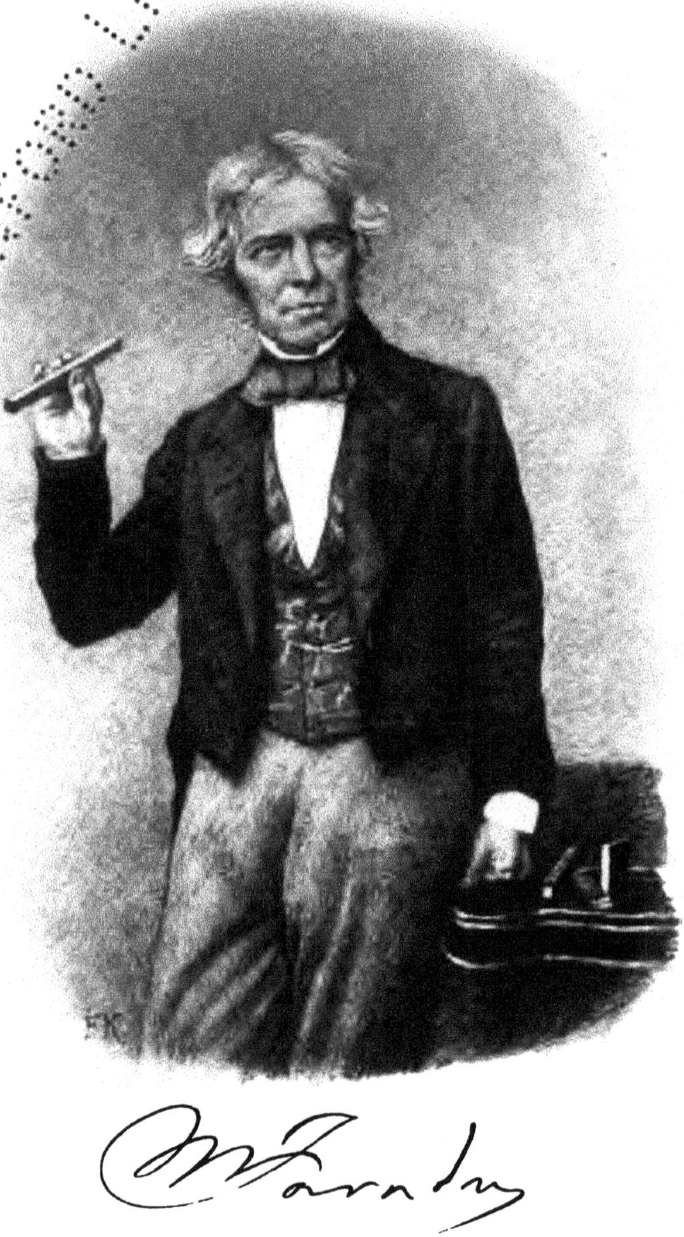
M. Faraday

LETTERS

FARADAY AND SCHÖNBEIN
1836 to

WITH NOTES

ENCES TO

GEORG W. A. K

FRANCIS V. DARBY

BÂLE   LO

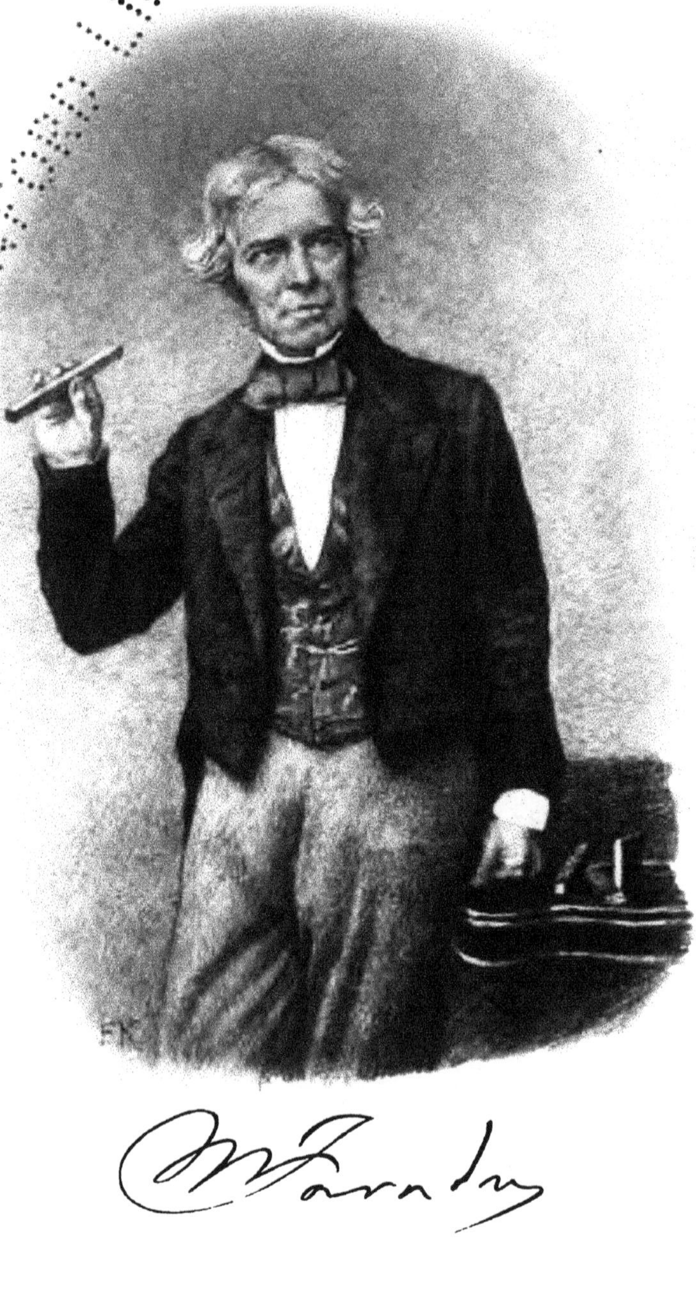
M. Faraday

1836

G. W. A.

W. D.

THE
LETTERS
OF
FARADAY AND SCHŒNBEIN

1836—1862

WITH NOTES, COMMENTS
AND
REFERENCES TO CONTEMPORARY LETTERS

EDITED BY

Georg W. A. Kahlbaum

AND

Francis V. Darbishire

"C'est un chéri et grand plaisir que cette correspondence avec un homme comme vous."
Oct. 20. 1838.
AUGUSTE DE LA RIVE TO SCHOENBEIN.

| BÂLE | 1899 | LONDON |
| BENNO SCHWABE | | WILLIAMS & NORGATE |

All rights reserved.

194995

PRINTED BY M. WERNER-RIEHM, BÂLE

DEDICATED

TO

SVANTE ARRHENIUS

AND

WALTHER NERNST

Preface

THE publication of historical documents, and letters are such documents, should be controlled by two principles. In the first place they should be set forth in exact agreement with the original, and in the next place provided with as many suitable comments as possible, to explain their meaning.

In preparing these letters for publication we have laid down these two rules as a guide for our conduct, remaining innocent of the smallest change, printing them with all their many imperfections, faults and errors. Only when we were satisfied that, to prevent a mistaken interpretation, alterations could not well be neglected, we yielded. We have however enclosed such additions in brackets.

But why all this? Because any change of that kind is a willfull misrepresentation of the original text; though for the most part, perhaps invariably, done from quite disinterested motives, it is nevertheless an inaccuracy. How are we to determine whether the writer did not make a point of constantly employing some form of speech, which now sounds strange, nay incorrect? It would not even be the first time that misprints were deliberately included in printed copies; how much more should we keep unchanged the pardonable slips in confidential messages. Who is to decide whether sixty years ago a different sense was not attached to what at the present time strikes us as irregular? Moreover what is to be the limit for legitimate changes? In short we have avoided all alterations.

As regards punctuation however, we have made bold to introduce some emendations. Faraday was not given to introducing these signs: dashes and commas are sometimes, but rarely, met with, full stops never. In order to save the readers of this book the annoyance which it caused the readers of the originals, we have transferred Schœnbein's more or less superfluous punctuation to Faraday's letters, and we venture to believe that we have lessened the difficulties of understanding their meaning.

With regard to the second point one should surely aim, as far as possible, at placing one's self in the position of the writer or the receiver of the letter. Faraday writes, for example: "Since my unfortunate letter to my late friend M. Hachette hurried Nobili into such mistakes." Now this information is of no value, so long as you are unacquainted with the particulars concerning this incident, and I hold it to be the duty of an editor to enlighten one on all such points.

To perform this duty was an arduous task, and these explanations, notes, and marginal comments involve more labour than the reader fancies. However we never shrunk from the undertaking, and so we made brief notes on anything that impressed us as deserving notice, our intention being to bring the reader, as it were, into close fellowship with the two writers. To what extent we have accomplished what we attempted the reader must decide. I am however most happy to acknowledge the services rendered by Mr. Francis V. Darbishire, who joined me when a considerable amount of the work had been carried out, and who, following up the subject with the greatest skill, also added many a valuable comment to the part already finished.

The story of the origin and progress of this publication is as follows. These letters were among the first material I received for the life of Schœnbein which I am now in the act of compiling. Miss Jane Barnard, Faraday's niece, very kindly sent me that portion of the correspondence which was in her possession, and to this Schœnbein's family added the share written by Faraday. This took place in the autumn of the year 1897. On glancing over these letters and finding out what a really important part they played in the development of the history of science in the middle of our century, I immediately decided on publishing them in full. To this end copies of the letters had to be taken, and it was Dr. Friedrich Tschopp-Müller, professor of Mathematics and Physics at the Academy here, and for many years my fellow-worker, who took upon himself this tedious work, and carried it through with so much care and indefatigable attention that I must express to him my heartiest gratitude. Without such assistance, owing to my numerous professional duties, the edition could not have been completed at the appointed time. To ascertain the correctness of the reading, I read the original and Dr. Tschopp followed his copy, comparing word for word. It required much perseverence on the part of us two Germans in order to decipher Faraday's all but illegible scrawls. What an Englishman can make out without much effort, is very perplexing to a foreigner, who has only acquired the native idiom artificially. The comparative facility with which Schœnbein's letters were read is quite worthy of notice; it is due to the fact that, though written in English, they were thought in German, from which they are in fact a translation.

In this manner the whole correspondence was read and explored, notes being added whenever they were considered to be essential. These additions were in German, for I had at first thought of bringing out a German as well as an English edition. It was at the beginning of the year 1899, when about one half had been provided with explanations, that I resolved to invite one of my English acquaintances to take charge of the English edition, in as much as my own knowledge of English is not fully sufficient for the requirements of such a case; preface and introduction were, for the same reason, written by me in German and translated by Mr. Darbishire. However, before settling the preliminaries of this undertaking in the manner intended, Mr. Darbishire, during the Christmas holidays, applied to me for the right of translating my edition of the letters of Berzelius and Schœnbein. I readily gave my consent and thus our friendly relations began.

Unhappily Mr. Darbishire was otherwise occupied at that time, so that, during the summer term, we had to continue our work without his aid. When the first sheets were in the press he came to Bâle and took up his work with great eagerness, and in so doing he rendered the greatest service in bringing these letters before the public, and has earned for himself my sincerest gratitude. After consulting with my publisher the idea of a separate German edition was abandoned.

Miss Jane Barnard in addition to placing these letters at my disposal has, at my request, most generously made a gift of them to the Library of the University of Bâle, under the condition that access may be had to them at any future time. In consequence of this genuine act of kindness the complete series of these valuable and important documents are now to be preserved at Schœnbein's scene of activity, for Schœnbein's daughters have also renounced their claim in favour of the University Library.

The artistic supplement added to the book, is the work of the young and promising artist F. Kraus of Bâle, who drew it from the photograph, kindly lent me by Miss Barnard, taken in 1857 by Maull and Polybank. It is the one serving as frontispiece to Dr. Bence Jones' Life of Faraday and we must not omit to express our obligation to Messrs. Longmanns, Green & Co. for kindly offering to consent to its reproduction here. The portrait of Schœnbein is drawn after a statuette from the year 1855 by the late Mr. Breikle of Munich, and some contemporary photographs.

The number of misprints is unfortunately very large, but it must be borne in mind that the printers were dealing with a foreign language.

Together with these letters I am, jointly with Dr. E. Thon, bringing out the correspondence of Schœnbein with Liebig; it will be published in Leipsic and is to form the fifth part of the Monographs from the History of Chemistry.

GEORG W. A. KAHLBAUM.

Bâle, *September* 15th, 1899.

INTRODUCTION

THESE letters reveal to the reader's mind the likeness of two persons, who became acquainted with each other under the influence of science, and who all their lifetime continued in undiminished friendship and mutual esteem. Though as dissimilar from each other in thought and conduct as one could well conceive, they harmonized in their implicit obedience to science, which held possession of their entire lives, in their pure love of truth and in their steadfast and unshaken confidence in each other.

One of these, Schœnbein, in a paper, which however he did not publish till he was in his thirty-sixth year, describes a most remarkable observation he was led to make, when studying the relation of iron to nitric acid. Even at the present day we have not succeeded in gaining clear insight into the cause from which this phenomenon proceeds. Such a want of knowledge in relation to this point worried him; and so he hastened to impart his observations to the foremost leaders in the domain of science.

He wrote a precise and critical letter to Berzelius, the venerable patriarch of Stockholm, he wrote to Poggendorff at Berlin, the editor of the most widely circulating continental journal, and he wrote to Faraday. Nearly ten years previously, during a brief sojourn in the English metropolis, he had had the extreme satisfaction of being present at one of his world-famed Friday Evening Lectures; but he did not take advantage of his opportunity to converse with him. Schœnbein was constrained to take this somewhat unusual step of making a communication to an entire stranger, by a keen desire on his part, to reason with his fellow-workers in the same branch of science, upon what at that moment occupied his time and thoughts. He worked heart and soul at whatsoever he took in hand, and was inspired by the significance of his research to such an extent, that he would take for granted a corresponding active interest on the part of other scientific men.

As to Faraday this turned out to be true. He printed the first letter in the Philosophical Magazine, and upon a second communication, also published in the Philosophical Magazine, he made remarks and criticisms, in a letter to one of the editors of the said journal, to illustrate, as it were, the opinion he had formed on the value of Schœnbein's results. With this the intercourse between the Englishman and the Swabian was established — Schœnbein continued a staunch and loyal Swabian.

He was born at Metzingen in Swabia in 1799, and was accordingly eight years junior to Faraday, and a similarity existed between the two, in as much as Schœnbein also was of humble parentage. He was the son of a dyer.

In 1813 he entered a chemical factory at Böblingen, as an apprentice to Bonz' and Son, at that time Metzger and Kaiser. After serving his term of seven years apprenticeship, he was articled to the chemical factory of Dr. Dingler at Augsburg, the editor of the well known Polytechnical Journal. In 1821 he entered at the University of Erlangen, where the great thinker Schelling exerted a powerful influence upon him; but he removed to Tübingen University in the same year, returning once more to Erlangen (during the winter term of 1822 to 1823), to finish his studies, after which he received an appointment at Friederich Fröbel's renowned school. In 1825 he became a teacher at Dr. Mayo's institute at Epsom, on the recommendation of his friend C. F. Wurm. For two years he remained in England, where the conditions of living and the character of the people were very much to his mind, particularly when contrasted to France, where he went later. He had just returned to England, in the autumn of the year 1828, when he was invited to take, temporarily, the place of Peter Merian at Bâle, who had fallen ill; and then in 1835 he was appointed full professor of Chemistry and Physics at the latter University.

In January 1836 his correspondence with Faraday commenced. The reading of these letters is in truth a great delight. For, apart from their historical value, they bring before our minds these two eminent men, with all their feelings, sympathies, and individual dispositions, and involuntarily produce in us a sense of kindly feeling towards them. To effect this is one of the duties, and not the least, of the biographer. Appreciating the importance of letters for the just valuation of a person's merit and worth, Dr. Bence Jones gave to his well known book the title of: "Life and Letters of Faraday."

We offer letters only, and nothing more, but with this complete collection, which continued in existence for a life time, we share the secrets and inclinations of two men, who are reckoned among the noblest of their race.

Georg W. A. Kahlbaum.

Bâle, *September*, 15th, 1899.

SYMBOL [REV.]

C. F. Schoenbein

1

Schœnbein to Faraday.[1]

SIR,

As our continental and particularly German periodicals are rather slow in publishing scientific papers, and as I am anxious to make you as soon as possible acquainted with some new electro-chemical phaenomena lately observed by me, I take the liberty to state them to you by writing. Being tempted to do so only by scientific motives, I entertain the flattering hope, that the contents of my letter will be received by you with kindness. The facts, I am about laying before you seem to me not only to be new, but at the same time deserving the attention of chemical philosophers. *Les voici.*[2]

If one of the ends of an iron wire be made red hot, and after cooling be immersed in nitric acid, spec. gr. 1.35, neither the end in question nor any other part of the wire will be affected, whilst the acid of the said strength is well known to act rather violently upon common iron. To see how far the influence of the oxidized end of the wire goes, I took an iron wire of 50′ in length and 0′′′.5 in thickness, heated one of its ends about 3′′ in length, immersed it in the acid of the strength above mentioned, and afterwards put the other end into the same fluid. No action of the acid upon the iron took place.

---

[1] This letter is published in the Phil. Mag. S. 3. vol. 9. 1836. p. 53 under the following title: "On a peculiar voltaic condition of Iron, by Professor Schœnbein, of Bâle." It is, although the original is not in our possession, reprinted here for the sake of completeness.

[2] Schœnbein also describes these results in his first letter to Berzelius, dated April 22, 1836. Kahlbaum Briefwechsel Berzelius-Schœnbein. Basel. 1898. p. 13.

From a similar experiment made upon a cylindrical iron bar of 16″. in length and 4‴ diameter the same result was obtained. The limits of this protecting influence of oxide of iron with regard to quantities I have not yet ascertained; but as to the influence of heat, I found that above the temperature of about 75° the acid acts in the common way upon iron, and in the same manner also, at common temperatures, when the said acid contains water beyond a certain quantity, for instance, 1, 10, 100, and even 1000 times its volume. By immersing an iron wire in nitric acid of sp. gr. 1.5 it becomes likewise indifferent to the same acid of 1.35.

But by far the most curious fact observed by me is, that any number of iron wires may be made indifferent to nitric acid by the following means. An iron wire with one of its ends oxidized is made to touch another common iron wire; both are then introduced into nitric acid of sp. gr. 1.35, so as to immerse the oxidized end of the one wire first into the one fluid, and to have part of both wires above the level of the acid. Under these circumstances no chemical action upon the wires will take place, for the second wire is, of course, but a continuation of that provided with an oxidized end. But no action occurs, even after the wires have been separated from each other. If the second wire, having become indifferent, be now taken out of the acid and made to touch at any of its parts not having been immersed, a third wire, and both again introduced into the acid so as to make that part of the second wire which had previously been in the fluid enter first, neither of the wires will be acted upon either during their contact or after their separation. In this manner the third wire can make indifferent or passive a fourth one, and so on.

Another fact, which has as yet, as far as I know, not been observed, is the following one. A wire made indifferent by any of the means before mentioned is immersed in nitric acid of sp. gr. 1.35, so as to have a considerable part of it remaining out of the fluid; another common wire is put into the same acid, likewise having one of its ends rising above the level of the fluid. The part immersed of this wire will, of course, be acted upon in a lively manner. If the ends of the wires which are out of the acid be now made to touch one another, the indifferent wire will instantly be turned into an active one, whatever may be the lengths of the parts of the wires not immersed. (If there is any instance of chemical affinity being transmitted in the form of a current by means of conducting bodies, I think the fact just stated may be considered as such.) It is a matter of course that direct contact between the two wires in question is not an indispensably necessary condition for communicating chemical activity from the active wire to the passive one; for any metal connecting the two ends of the wires renders the same service.

Before passing to another subject, I must mention a fact, which seems to be one of some importance. An iron wire curved into a fork is made to touch at its bend a wire provided with an oxidized end; in this state of contact both are introduced into nitric acid of sp. gr. 1.35 and 30°, so as first to immerse in the acid the oxidized end; the fork will, of course, not be affected. If now a common iron wire be put into the acid, and one of the ends of the fork touched by it, this end will immediately be acted upon, whilst the other end remains passive; but as soon as the iron wire with the oxidized end is put out of contact with the bend of the fork, its second end is also turned active. If the parts of the fork rising above the level of the acid be touched by an iron wire, part of which is immersed and active in the acid, no communication of chemical activity will take place, and both ends of the fork remain passive; but by the removal of the iron wire (with the oxidized end) from the bend of the fork this will be thrown into chemical action.

As all the phaenomena spoken of in the preceding lines are, no doubt, in some way or other dependent upon a peculiar electrical state of the wires, I was very curious to see in what manner iron would be acted upon by nitric acid when used as an electrode. For this purpose I made use of that form of the pile called the *couronne des tasses,* consisting of fifteen pairs of zinc and copper. A platina wire was connected with (what we call) the negative pole of the pile, an iron wire with the positive one. The free end of the platina wire was first plunged into nitric acid sp. gr. 1.35, and by the free end of the iron wire the circuit was closed. Under these circumstances the iron was not in the least affected by the acid; and it remained indifferent to the fluid not only as long as the current was passing through it, but even after it had ceased to perform the function of the positive electrode. The iron wire proved, in fact, to be possessed of all the properties of what we have called a passive one. If such a wire is made to touch the negative electrode, it instantaneously becomes an active one and a nitrate of iron is formed; whether it be separate from the positive pole or still connected with it, and the acid be strong or weak.

But another phaenomenon is dependent upon the passive state of iron, which phaenomenon is in direct contradiction with all the assertions hitherto made by philosophical experimenters. The oxygen at the anode arising from the decomposition of water contained in the acid, does not combine with the iron serving as the electrode, but is evolved at it, just in the same manner as if it were platina, and to such a volume as to bear the ratio of 1 : 2 to the quantity of hydrogen evolved at the cathode. To obtain this result I made use of an acid containing 20 times its volume of water; I found, however, that an acid containing 400 times its volume of water still shows the phaenomenon in a very obvious manner. But I must repeat it, the indispensable condition for causing the evolution of the oxygen at the iron wire is to close the circuit exactly in the same manner as above mentioned. For if, *exempli gratiâ,* the circuit be closed with the negative platina wire, not one single bubble of oxygen gas makes its appearance at the positive iron; neither is oxygen given out at it, when the circuit is closed, by plunging first one end of the iron wire into the nitric acid, and by afterwards putting its other end in connexion with the positive pole of the pile. In both cases a nitrate of iron is formed, even in an acid containing 400 times its volume of water; which salt may be easily observed descending from the iron wire in the shape of brownish-yellow-coloured streaks.

I have still to state the remarkable fact, that if the evolution of oxygen at the anode be ever so rapidly going on, and the iron wire made to touch the negative electrode within the acid, the disengagement of oxygen is discontinued, not only during the time of contact of the wires, but after the electrodes have been separated from each other. A few moments holding the iron wire out of the acid is, however, sufficient to recommunicate to it the property of letting oxygen gas evolve at its surface. By the same method the wire acquires its evoluting power again, whatever may have been the cause of its loss. The evolution of oxygen also takes place in dilute sulphuric and phosphoric acids, provided, however the circuit be closed in the manner above described. It is worthy of remark, that the disengagement of oxygen at the iron in the last-named acids is much easier stopt, and much more difficult to be caused again, than is the case in nitric acid. In an aqueous solution of caustic potash, oxygen is evolved at the positive iron, in whatever manner the circuit may be closed, but no such disengagement takes place in aqueous solutions of hydracids, chlorides, bromides, iodides, fluorides. The oxygen, resulting in these cases from the decomposition of water, and the anion (chlorine, bromine etc.) of the other electrolyte decomposed combine at the same time with the iron.

To generalize these facts, it may be said, that independently of the manner of closing the circuit, oxygen is always disengaged at the positive iron, provided the aqueous fluids in which it is immersed do not (in a sensible manner) chemically act upon it; and that no evolution of oxygen at the anode in contact with iron under any circumstances takes place, if besides oxygen another anion is set free possessed of a strong affinity for iron. This metal having once had oxygen evolved at itself, proves always to be indifferent to nitric acid of a certain strength, whatever may be the chemical nature of the fluid in which the phaenomenon has taken place.

I have made a series of experiments upon silver, copper, tin, lead, cadmium, bismuth, zinc, mercury, but none showed any resemblance to iron, for all of them were oxidized when serving as positive electrodes. Having at this present moment neither cobalt nor nickel at my command, I could not try these magnetic metals, which I strongly suspect to act in the same manner as iron does.

It appears from what I have just stated that the anomalous bearing of the iron has nothing to do with its degree of affinity for oxygen, but must be founded upon something else. Your sagacity, which has already penetrated into so many mysteries of nature, will easily put away the veil which as yet covers the phaenomenon stated in my letter, in case you should think it worth while to make it the object of your researches.

Before I finish I must beg of you the favour of overlooking with indulgence the many faults I have, no doubt, committed in my letter. Formerly I was tolerably well acquainted with your native tongue, but now, having been out of practice in writing or speaking it, it is rather hard work to me to express myself in English.

It is hardly necessary to say that you may privately or publicly make any use of the contents of this letter.

I am, Sir, your most obedient servant

C. T.(?) Schoenbein,
Prof. of Chem. in the University of Bâle.

Bâle, May 17, 1836.

Schœnbein to Faraday.

SIR

I feel much obliged to you for the kind manner in which you mentioned my late researches on iron in the philosophical Magazine.[1] It is this kindness which encourages me to address to you a second letter on the same subject. First allow me to make some observations regarding the explanation, you give about the cause of the peculiar voltaic condition of iron. If I have not misunderstood it, you account for the inactivity of this metal by two suppositions; one of which is, that a film of oxide is formed round the iron similar to that produced by heating the metall; the second, that this oxide has the property of not being dissolved by nitric acid of a certain strength. Now the formation of such an oxide takes place perhaps, when iron is in voltaic association for instance with platina; in this case water may be decomposed and the oxygen resulting from the decomposition combine with iron to form the supposed oxide. But, how is it, when iron is made inactive by plunging it into strong nitric acid? I should not think, that in this case either nitric acid or water is decomposed; that is to say, that an oxide is formed. There is another fact of a similar kind, which likewise makes me doubt of the existence of the film in question. This fact is, that iron wire turns inactive even in common nitric acid by repeated immersions, that is to say, after this metall has been acted upon in the usual way, after deutoxide of iron and a nitrate has been formed. Now I think, we may ask why, in this instance, the common chemical action is, at once, s[t]opt and how it happens, that, on a sudden an oxide is formed of a description quite different from what the first

---

[1] Phil. Mag. S. 3. vol. 9. 1836. p. 57, a letter communicated to Mr. Phillips, a joint editor of the Phil. Mag. In it Mr. Faraday points out that these experiments afford an additional proof that "voltaic electricity is due to chemical action. and not to contact." cf. Phil. Mag. vol. 6. p. 36.

one (deutoxide) was. I confess, I have not the slightest idea about the cause of such a change of action. There is another fact, which clearly shows, that under some circumstances at least, the inactive state of iron has nothing to do with a peculiar strength of nitric acid. In my last letter I had the honour to state to you, that iron serving as the positive electrode of a pile proves to be inactive in nitric acid, whatever its degree of aqueous dilution may be, whilst a wire made inactive either by immersion in strong nitric acid or by association with oxide of iron (produced by heating) is acted upon in the common way by nitric acid containing water beyond a certain quantity. Now if one of the circumstances determining the peculiar condition of iron were a peculiar strength of nitric acid, there should be common chemical action in one case as well as there is in the other, but the contrary being the fact, we are entitled to draw the conclusion, that the inactivity of iron is not always dependent upon a peculiar strength of the acid. As we must evidently give up one part of the explanation in one case, I am afraid, there is sufficient reason to make us doubtful of its holding good in other ones. As to the film of oxide, which you think to be formed round the iron in all cases, where this metall shows its peculiar condition, I have also observed, that a coating of a blackish substance is produced round an iron wire, when, being connected with the anode of the pile, it was plunged into common nitric acid, closing at the same time the circuit; but I could never remark the least change in the metallic state of the surface of the wire, in case it was immersed in dilute acid (containing about 10 times its volume of water) under the circumstances mentioned. In the very moment, when I brought the iron wire into the fluid, the evolution of oxigen began at the metall. The same experiment made in solution of potash, showed the same phenomenon. If for instance in the latter case a film were produced, I should think the wire provided with it and put into common nitric acid was to prove as inactive, as a wire, whose end had previously been oxidized by heating; such, however, is not the case. According to your experiments, there always dissolves some iron in nitric acid, even whilst this metall renders the function of the positive electrode. I found the same, but only when I made use of common nitric acid, never when it was considerably dilute. I, therefore, strongly suspect, that the nitrate to be met with in the first case, is not produced within the acid. I ascribe its formation to the vapours rising out of the acid, which corrode the iron laid bare to them. The salt thus produced and first deposited on the superior part of the iron wire is afterwards carried down into the fluid by capillary action. As it appeared to me a point of importance to know, whether iron, under the circumstances mentioned, is or is not dissolved in nitric acid, I took particular care of ascertaining the fact. For this purpose I made in one instance use of an acid containing 10 times its volume of water, left in it the wire (being connected with the pile) for fully six hours and afterwards saturated the acid with ammonia. Not the smallest quantity of oxide was precipitated, though the volume of oxygen evolved at the iron during the time had comparatively been considerable. From a second experiment I obtained the same result. I put a solution of potash into a tumbler, and dilute nitric acid upon it in such a manner, as to prevent the fluids from mixing with one another. An iron wire serving as the positive electrode and reaching down to the bottom of the tumbler, was left in it for three hours. Not the slightest bit of oxide made its appearance; as soon however, as the circuit was broken, greenish flakes of oxide of iron were precipitated; and the same substance was seen forming, in case the circuit had not been closed in the manner required for causing the evolution of oxigen. From these facts I think it may safely be inferred, that nitric acid does not dissolve iron, whilst this metall is placed under the influence of a current moving through it in a certain direction. As the existence of such a relation of a current to chemical action would be of the greatest importance to science, I lively hope, you will pay a particular attention of this subject and enter into a close investigation of it. I pass now to another subject. During my researches on iron, I often made the observation, that nitric acid, remaining the same with regard to its strength and temperature acts with a different degree of intensity upon the metall mentioned. If for instance iron wire, being in the same state, as it is sold, be plunged into nitric acid spec. grav. 1.35 and 12° the metall is violently acted upon and continues to be so, as long as there is any particle of iron left. But if the wire be taken out of the acid after a few moments' action, held for a second or two in the air, and replunged into the acid, the degree of intensity of action will already be a little diminished; and having four, at most, five times repeated the same operation, the metall will cease altogether to be affected by the acid, in fact it will then be in its well-known peculiar voltaic condition. Between the greatest violence of action and complete inactivity, there are certainly an infinite number of intermediate degrees of intensity of action. But we may distinguish two principal ones; one which is superior and another which is inferior to the degree of that influence of platina, which tends to stop chemical action. Indeed, if a platina wire is made to touch an uncleaned iron wire after having for the first time been immersed in nitric acid of the strength above mentioned, it cannot interrupt chemical action, but it will stop it, after the second or third immersion of the iron. Another fact worthy of remark is, that the degree of stability of the inactive state of iron called forth by immersing this metall several times in nitric acid spec. grav. 1.35, is much greater than that produced by voltaic association or by immersion in strong nitric acid. For if an iron wire made inactive by one of the latter means is turned again into the active state, it will be much more violently affected by the acid, than a wire brought into its peculiar condition by the way of immersions in common nitric acid. That the latter wire is more strongly inactive than one brought into this peculiar state by any other method is still more obviously indicated by the fact, that in most cases it turns by touching within the acid another wire, (which has been made slowly active in this acid) into an inactive one; whilst a common wire made inactive by immersion in strong nitric acid, or by transference or by a direct voltaic association is always thrown into a violent action by being touched by a slowly active wire. I must not omit to mention, that an iron wire having once been made inactive by repeated immersions, will under no circumstances whatever be so lively acted upon by nitric acid, as a common one, and the action commenced at it can always be stopt by platina, provided the acid be not too dilute or too hot. The peculiar lustre, the white colour and the soft touch of the surface of a wire turned inactive by immersions in common nitric acid likewise deserve to my opinion to engage attention of scientific men. Such a wire is, indeed, as to its appearance so like platina, that it can hardly be distinguished from this metall. Even after the file had several times passed over its surface, I thought the colour of the metall to be still whiter, than that of a common wire's surface (likewise produced by filing). Several persons to whom I showed such wires, were of the same opinion. If my observations should happen to be correct, it would prove, that the action of the acid upon the iron spoken of occasions a very remarkable change of aggregation of its particles; and it is, perhaps by such a change, that we may account for some of the anomalous bearings of iron. Before I conclude I must mention a fact I find already alluded to in a paper [1] of Herschel's,[2] a paper which by the bye I saw but a little while ago in looking over in periodicals, the articles treating on nitric acid. This fact consists

[1] Annales de Chimie et de Physique, 1833. T. 54. p. 87.
[2] Sir John Herschel was born in 1792 at Slough near Windsor and died in 1871 in London.

in a sort of action of nitric acid upon iron, which for its extraordinary character highly merits farther scientific inquiry. The best way of calling forth the phenomenon is the following one. A common iron wire having been made inactive by simple immersions in nitric acid sp. gr. 1.35 is touched within this fluid by a piece of copper; the wire will by this means be thrown into action which action, however, is not continuous, but takes place, as it were, by pulsations, in other words the wire will alternately be active and inactive. Sometimes it happens that the wire relapsed into its inactive state after the first touch of the copper; in such a case, it must repeatedly be retouched by this metall in order to obtain the effect desired. Temperature and the degree of dilution of the acid, within which the action occurs, remaining the same, the number of pulsations performed in equal spaces of time remain likewise the same. By augmenting the temperature and the quantity of water of the acid the intervals of action and inaction are made shorter and at last these two states follow each other in such quick succession as to pass into a continuous action. Different wires separate from one another, being in the same acid and exhibiting the phenomenon in question, do not pulsate together; but as soon as they are put in contact with each other either within or without the acid, the whole set of wires pulsate at the same time, a fact, which is worthy of remark. Herschel's assertion according to which only an acid, having already been made use of for inducing in iron wires the inactive state, is capable of exhibiting the phenomenon spoken of, does not agree with what I have observed; for I found, that quite pure nitric acid renders the service, when an iron wire made inactive by immersions is plunged into it and turned active again by the way described. This fact, I think, proves, that the cause of the pulsation-like action lies rather in the state of the wire than in that of the acid.

As the "Bibliothèque universelle" will before long publish some papers of mine, written on the same subjects, with which

I have taken the liberty to entertain you in the preceding lines, you will, perhaps, think it worth your while to have a look at them, and excuse me, when I do at present not enter into further details.

Recommending my humble individual to your kind indulgence I am, Sir, your most obedient Servant

Prof. SCHOENBEIN.

Bale Septb. 12th 1836.

Schœnbein to Faraday.

SIR

The Philosophical Society of Bale in one of their last meetings[1] elected you their honorary member and I am charged by our President to forward the diploma and ask you the favour to accept of the latter as a weak expression of the high esteem, which our Society entertain for you, on account of the eminent services, you have rendered to natural Science.

I take at the same time the liberty of sending you the paper enclosed and to beg you to lay it before the Royal Society, in case you should think it worthy of being submitted to this distinguished body. If not, there is, perhaps, something or other in it, which deserves to be published in the Philosophical Magazine.

You have, no doubt, taken notice of the hypothesis published in the number of Septbr. of the Bibliothèque universelle,[2] by which Mr. Mousson[3] tries to account for the peculiar condition of iron and all the phenomena connected with this subject. Though it may be ingenious in some respects it is overthrown

[1] Held on Nov. 23, 1836.
[2] A. Mousson Bibl. Univ. T. 5. 1836. p. 165.
[3] Joseph R. A. Mousson Ph. D. was born in 1805 at Solothurn and died in 1890 at Zürich. He was professor of Physics at the Grammar School and later at the Technical High School at Zürich.

by the single fact, that by a current the inactive state of iron may be called forth in fluids which do not contain nitric acid and which consequently do not allow of the formation of nitrous acid, the protecting substance of Mr. Mousson. But there are many other reasons besides, which put the fallacy of the theory in question beyond doubt. I have circumstantially stated them in a paper, sent the other day to the Editors of the "Bibliothèque" for being published. I cannot but take a second time the liberty to draw your attention upon the transference of the inactive state of iron from wire to wire, a fact which, to my opinion, is yet very far from being satisfactorily accounted for. Supposing the peculiar condition of iron being due to a film of oxide covering the metal, your hypothesis accounts, indeed, very well for an inactive wire's being thrown into action by another metal, which, itself active, touches the former. In this case, there is a current produced, by which hydrogen is set free at the inactive wire, which hydrogen reduces the film to the metallic state, renders consequently the wire active. Now if an inactive wire is associated with an ordinary one, and one end of the former immersed in common nitric acid previous to the one end of the latter, this wire will also become inactive. The galvanometer shows, that in the moment, where the end of the second wire is plunged into the nitric acid, a current is produced, passing, as in the first case, from the wire last immersed through the acid into the inactive one. Now in one case the current throws the inactive wire into action, and in the other it renders an ordinary wire inactive; that is to say, the same cause produces two effects exactly opposite to one another. It is obvious, that the current in the latter case should decompose water, evolve hydrogen at the inactive wire and render the latter active in the same way, as in the first case. Now I ask, why does hydrogen in one case decompose the film of oxide covering the inactive wire and not in the other? The two cases present no difference, except in the manner, in which the circuit is closed. It might, perhaps, be said, that in the second case, the current is so soon stopt, that it cannot separate hydrogen enough, as to reduce entirely the film to the metallic state. But this will not do, because the same current, which is supposed to be too weak, to set free that quantity of hydrogen necessary for the complete decomposition of the film of oxide round the inactive wire, is considered to be sufficiently strong to separate so much of oxigen, as is required for forming a protecting film round the ordinary wire. Now from the fact that the quantity of oxigen evolved at the positive electrode is exactly the chemical equivalent to the quantity of hydrogen set free at the negative electrode, we are obliged to draw the conclusion, that the quantity of hydrogen developed during the act of transfering the inactive state from the inactive wire to the ordinary one, is sufficient to decompose the film of the first wire. Insufficiency of the current can, therefore, not be the reason, why the inactive wire remains in its peculiar state under the circumstances mentioned.

I think the preceding observations are such, as to justify my former assertion, that we are still very far from knowing any thing about the way, in which the inactive state of iron is transfered from one wire to another. Before leaving this subject I cannot help recalling to you a circumstance, which bears strongly upon the point in question; it is the fact, that an iron wire performing the function of the positive electrode is rendered inactive in nitric acid, when by its being plunged into this fluid the circuit is closed; whilst the same wire is acted upon by the acid when the circuit is closed by the negative electrode. Now we remark the same difference of effect with a single voltaic pair consisting of ordinary iron and platina or any other negative metal, for when we close the circuit by its positive element ordinary iron, the peculiar condition will be called forth in this metal, when closed by the negative element, the same iron will be active, though, as already stated, there is in both cases a current produced, moving in the same direction. Now why do the different effects depend upon the manner of closing the circuit? This question once satisfactorily answered, we shall be much wiser, than we are now about the subject; but I suspect, it will be a difficult task to get up such an answer. It is not beyond possibility, that our phenomenon is independent of an electric current, though one is always accompanied by the other; and it is, perhaps this very circumstance that renders the tracing of its cause so very difficult. If it should be found to be impossible to explain the excitation of the peculiar state of iron and the destruction of it by the action of a current, then I am afraid, we shall be obliged to look out for another hypothesis, which may, perhaps, postulate a new agency different from Electricity for explaining the facts in question. But may heaven preserve us from more agencies, we have still enough of them.

Up to this present moment, I have not yet received the papers, which you were so kind to dispatch for me some time ago. Shall I, perhaps, apply to the british ambassador at Bern, to whom they have most likely been sent?

Before closing this letter, I take the liberty to ask you a favo[u]r. Our Establishment wants to get a good magnetic-electrical Machine, by means of which the principal experiments on Magneto-electricity may easily be made in classes. Now if it be not too much asked, the Committee of our Museum should feel themselves laid under great obligations to you, would you be so kind as to order such an apparatus to be sent to us by a Londoner instrument-maker.

Excuse my long letter and accept kindly the assurance of my being

Yours
very truly

Bale Nov. 26th 1836.   C. F. SCHOENBEIN.

Schœnbein to Faraday.[1]

DEAR SIR

Some weeks ago I had an opportunity to send you a paper "On a peculiar action of Iron upon some salts",[2] which, I hope, will by this time have reached you. Having since observed some new facts, regarding the transference of the active and inactive state of Iron from wire to wire, facts which I think to be of some importance to electro-chemical science, I take the liberty to communicate them to you by writing.

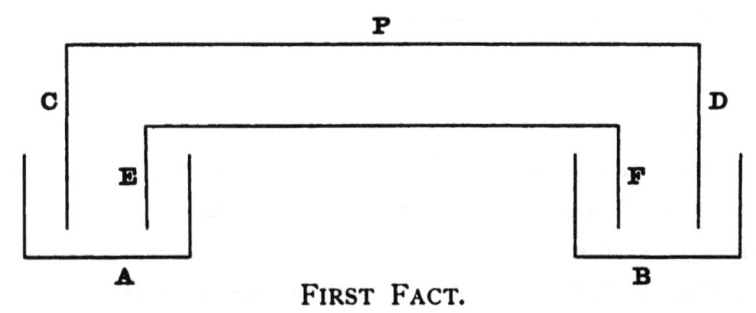

FIRST FACT.

A and B represent vessels containing nitric acid sp. gr. 1.35 and CPD a platina wire connecting them. If the oxidized end E of an iron wire EF be put into A, and F afterwards into B, F turns active, though a current passes from F through the acid into D. (Usual condition for calling forth the peculiar state.)

SECOND FACT.

If CPD be a wire of a metal, which is acted upon by the acid in A and B, for instance silver, copper, iron, brass etc.; the end F of the iron wire will turn inactive on its being plunged into B, after the immersion of the oxidized end E in A. (The same takes place, if the middle part of the connecting wire P consists of Platina; and the ends C and D of Silver, Copper etc.)

[1] This letter was inserted in the Phil. Mag. S. 3. vol. 10. 1836. p. 133 under the following heading: "Further experiments on a peculiar voltaic condition of iron.

[2] Phil. Mag. S. 3. vol. 10. 1836. p. 267.

Third Fact.

If C P D be an iron wire, its end D inactive, C active, and the end E (not oxidized) first plunged into A and F afterwards into B, F turns inactive, that is to say assumes the state of D. (The inactive iron end D may be replaced by platina and the active one C by any metal, which is acted upon by the acid in A, without causing a change of result by so doing.)

Fourth Fact.

If every thing be precisely so, as in the forgoing case, but E oxidized and first put into A, F turns likewise inactive on its being afterwards immersed into B.

Fifth Fact.

If CPD be again an iron wire the end D inactive (made so not by heating but by immersing it into strong nitric acid) and the end F put into B and E afterwards into A, not only E but also D turns active, whatever the number of wires may be similar to CPD, all their inactive ends in B turn active under the circumstances mentioned; though these wires do not touch each other at any point.

Sixth Fact.

If the four electrodes of two piles (each consisting of about half a dozen of pairs of Zinc and Copper) be introduced into two vessels containing common nitric acid in such a manner, that the positive electrode of one pile and the negative one of the other dip into the same vessel and the oxidized end of an iron wire be plunged into any of the vessels and its ordinary end afterwards into the other one, the latter turns inactive, just in the same way, as if the two vessels were connected by a copper-wire. But to obtain this result it is required to bend up the second, that is to say the ordinary end, thus ⊓, previous to immersion.

Now why does F in the first case not become inactive by the current produced by its being plunged into B? It seems to be an indispensable condition for calling forth the inactive state in iron, that in the moment of its being immersed into the acid a current of a certain energy is passing through it. The current produced by the part of the metal immersed is of sufficient strength, when both ends of the iron wire plunge into the acid contained in only one (small) vessel; but when this same current has to pass through the acid of two vessels and besides to enter and issue into and from the connecting platina wire, its strength is diminished below the degree necessary for producing the effect in question. But if this way of accounting for the fact be correct, it is to [be] asked, how it comes, that with a connecting wire, whose ends are attacked by the acid of the vessels different results are obtained. It is obvious, that in the second case, two currents moving in opposite directions and originating in C and D are established, as soon as the iron wire EF has connected the vessels A and B. Besides these currents a third one is produced by the immersion of F in B. But this current having to make the same way, which the current in the first case must pass, why is its effect different from what that of the latter is? Now it seems to me, that if two currents of opposite direction circulate through our circuit of the second case, they remove in some way or other the obstacles, which the third current (in itself of weak power) would have to overcome, if it was moving alone through the circuit; or in other terms if two opposite currents cross the nitric acid, its conducting power for a third current is increased. In the third case, there are likewise two opposite currents established, as soon as F dips in B; one produced by C the other by E; and there is again a current excited by F, which must be considered as the cause of the peculiar state of this end. It is only to be wondered at, why D when having been made inactive by immersion in strong nitric acid or by the help of platina, is not rendered active by the current produced by F; for from the same reasons, why F turns inactive, D should be thrown into action. But from many facts it appears, that a much stronger current is required to change the inactive state into the active one, than that current is, by which an ordinary wire can be rendered inactive. The fourth fact will be accountable, if we consider, that in this case, there comes a current from C to F, which added to that produced by F itself, becomes strong enough, as to call forth the inactive state in F, though it is still too weak, to render D active and probably only so on account of the absence of two other opposite currents. As to the fifth case, E turns active, because in the moment of its immersing there are no two opposite currents put into circulation; the current produced by E is therefore too weak, to excite in E the peculiar state and there are besides the two currents of C and F, which would more than neutralize the current of E. Now the current originated by F being continuous and besides powerful compared to that excited by an iron wire's turning inactive, would for itself throw D into action, but its energy is still increased by the two opposite currents produced at C and E. About the sixth fact, I say nothing, as its connexion with the foregoing ones is sufficiently clear. I allow the inference, I have drawn from the facts stated, is rather hazardous and in apparent contradiction to the generally established principle, that two equal but opposite currents annihilate each other and that the circuit, through which such currents move is exactly in the same state, as if no currents were passing through it. But I think that without adopting my view of the subject the facts spoken of remain quite unaccountable. Whatever cause however, they depend upon, to my opinion they deserve to be closely searched into, as their minute investigation will no doubt, lead to some interesting result.

The last number of the "Bibliothèque universelle"[1] contained a paper of mine "on the bearing of iron to oxigen", which happens

[1] Bibl. Univ. T. 5. 1836 p. 397.

to be full of most unhappy misprints. They will, no doubt, be corrected in the forthcoming number. I am very anxious to know your opinion about the contents of the said paper.

Begging your pardon for having repeatedly intruded upon you a badly written letter, I take the liberty of calling myself

Yours
very truly
DR. SCHOENBEIN.

Bale Dec. 26th 1836.

Faraday to Schœnbein.

Royal Institution 28 Jan. 1837

MY DEAR SIR

About a fortnight ago I received your letter of the 26 December last by Post and was so much interested by the facts that I took it to the Editor of the Philosophical Magazine for insertion in his periodical: it is now printed and on Monday, the day after tomorrow will be published. I have not added a word to it for I think with you that at present we do not understand the subject. The Editor showed me a translation of your paper from Poggendorff[1] on my explication or imaginary explication, which I was glad to see he was going to print, and to that I added a note in my own name namely saying that I was not at any time satisfied with my own idea and that neither you nor Mousson hat expressed it in the same manner that I had ventured to put it forth.[2] Whether this will be in the next N^o of the Philosophical Magazine or not I do not know. But you will see them in due time.

Only yesterday I received the packet which you referred to in your last letter though your letter in the packet is dated 26 November so it has been a long time on the Road.

[1] Poggend. Annal. Bd. 39. 1836. p. 137.
[2] Phil. Mag. S. 3. vol. 10. 1836. p. 172.

Will you do me the favour to express my sincere and humble thanks to the Society of Basle for the great honor it has done me. I only hope I may prove worthy of it but will trust on the kindness of the members to think I will try to deserve it.

With regard to your paper for the Royal Society. I do not want to read it, being anxious to acknowledge your letters by to nights post and the time is almost gone

I am My dear Sir
Your obliged and faithful Servant
M. FARADAY.

Faraday to Schœnbein.

London Royal Institution 6. Feby 1837

MY DEAR SIR

I now write to you upon the result of my inquiries. In the first place with regard to your Paper. I did not wish to present it unless I thought it would in all probability be printed in the Transactions of the Royal Society; and I found that that might not be the case because the Council seldom if ever print papers in the Transactions upon subjects which have recently been dealt upon and are matter of communication to other societies or Transactions or Journals; unless the paper sent to them has not some decisive news or some new discovery on the subject. But that I might be quite right, I showed your paper to some who would have been consulted and finding them to be of opinion that it would not come within the rules which regulate the Council I have kept it back.

If you approve therefore I will alter the wording of those parts which require it (or perhaps you will send me the alterations) and then I will send it to the Philosophical Magazine. If printed there and *you wish it* I could have 100 copies or less of the paper itself printed off separately by paying the expense of the paper or work but I do not know how I should send them to you. The copies of the papers I sent to you went from the Royal Society through the Ambassadors hands and very probably are lying at Bern. But I cannot tell.

With respect to the Magneto electric machine I inquired at Newmans the price of them: I found those of full size were 12 Guineas by themselves and 14 Guineas with the different apparatus required to heat a wire, shock the system, decompose water etc. If you approve the price I will order one; but send me word how it shall be addressed.

I am (in haste) my dear Sir
Very truly Yours obliged
M. FARADAY.

Schœnbein to Faraday.[1]

DEAR SIR

I take once more the liberty to address to you by writing a short account of the results of my latest researches on the peculiar condition of iron. To my opinion, these results, though they do not yet solve the riddle of the subject, are such as to excite scientific curiosity, at least, as much, as the facts did, a description of which I had the hono[u]r to communicate to you last year.[2] The space allotted to a letter being so small, I am obliged to be as concise as possible in discribing the phenomena, recently observed by me; but if you should be interested with the details of the subject, I take the liberty of referring you to a paper of mine, which in some time will be published in

[1] Faraday inserted this letter in Phil. Mag. S. 3. vol. 10. 1837. p. 425 under the following title: "Experiments on the peculiar voltaic condition of iron as excited by peroxide of lead.

[2] Phil. Mag. S. 3. vol. 9. 1836. p. 53; vol. 10. 1836. p. 133 and 267.

"Poggendorff's Annalen".[1] In the first place I must tell you, that the most powerful voltaic association, into which iron can be brought, in order to excite its peculiar condition, is that with peroxide of lead.[2] A common iron wire, one of the ends of which is covered with this substance proves to be inactvie not only towards nitric acid of a given strength, but towards nitric acid containing any quantity of water; whilst as you know, my oxidized iron wire, or one associated with platina etc. is acted upon by this acid if much diluted just in the same manner as unprotected iron. But the superiority of the association mentioned to any other at present known is exhibited in a still more striking manner by putting the two ends of an iron wire, (one of which is covered by peroxide of lead) into an aqueous solution of the common sulphate of copper in the same way, as the two ends of the oxidized wire etc. are plunged into common nitric acid. Under these circumstances not the smallest particle of copper will be precipitated on any part of the wire immersing into the said solution; this peculiar state of the wire, however, lasts only so long, as both ends of it are plunging in the solution; for no sooner the protected one is removed from the liquid, than the other one left immersing turns active, that is to say throws down copper. In this respect, therefore, there is a great difference between the action of the wire in question upon the solution of blue vitriol, and that of the oxidized one upon common nitric acid. This difference of action implies another, namely the impossibility of transferring within the copper solution the peculiar state from wire to wire, which to do is so easy within nitric acid. I must not omit here to state the remarkable fact, that by mixing the solution of the sulphate

[1] Poggend. Annal. Bd. 43. 1837. p. 89.
[2] In a letter addressed to Mr. Taylor (vide Phil. Mag S. 3. vol. 10. 1837. p. 175) Faraday, after reading Nobili's paper on his new chromatic scale, directs Schœnbeins attention to the condition of the iron plates in Nobili's experiment; his impression is that the colours of the thin plates are due to peroxide of lead formed at the positive electrode in the solution of acetate of lead used.

with a comparatively small quantity of chloride of sodium (common salt) the calling forth of the peculiar condition is prevented, not only in the foregoing case, but in all that will be mentioned afterwards. This fact is by no means an insulated one and depends upon the same cause, which prevents the disengagement of oxigen at the iron (whilst constituting the positive electrode of the pile) out of a solution of haloid salts etc. Presuming, that by rendering iron inactive towards sulphate of copper in the way discribed, a current would be excited as to its direction equal to that, produced by calling forth the peculiar state of this metal within nitric acid, and having had recourse to the galvanometer, I was very much struck on finding that the needle was not in the least affected. The instrument I made use of in my experiments, though indicating rather weak currents, does certainly not possess the highest degree of sensibility possible; (it contains about 100 coils) but as in a scientific point of view it is of very great importance to know, whether the peculiar condition of iron can in any way be called forth without exciting at the same time a current, I beg you to decide this question by means of your most delicate galvanometer. If your experiments should happen to place beyond doubt the absence of any current under the before mentioned circumstance, why such a result would allow of drawing very curious inferences from it, and prove, in the first place, that the inactivity of iron has as to its origin nothing to do with what we call a current. A series of phenomena, regarding the action of iron wire (associated with peroxide of lead) upon a solution of sulphate of copper may be called forth, which exhibits a beautiful analogy to that set of facts, communicated to you in my letter, you had the kindness to have inserted in the Phil. Magazine No. 59.[1] To obtain with iron in the said solution results similar to those mentioned in my letter, with regard to the action of this metal upon nitric acid, the following conditions

[1] Phil. Mag. S. 3. vol. 10. 1837. p. 133.

must be fulfilled.[1] In the first and second case the oxidized iron wire EF is to be replaced by a wire, whose end E is covered with peroxide of lead, every other thing remains the same as stated in my letter. As to the third fact, CPD is to be an iron wire having its end D associated with peroxide of lead; EF is to be a common iron wire. With respect to the fourth case, E instead of being oxidized must be covered with peroxide of lead. To obtain a result analogous to the fifth fact, the iron wire CPD its end D being associated with the mentioned substance, must first be put into the vessels. Supposing D to be within B, the end E of an iron wire EF is to be plunged into A and F afterwards into B. As the third case shows it, F will turn under these circumstances inactive. Things being in this state, put the one end of a third common iron wire into B and afterwards its other end into A, and F will cease to be in its peculiar condition. Now, whatever the number of wires similar to that of EF may be, all their inactive ends being within B turn active under the circumstances mentioned, though they do not touch each other anywhere. Concerning the sixth case, it is obtained exactly in the same manner as stated in my letter, provided the oxidized end be replaced by one covered with peroxide of lead. Bending up the common end of the experimental wire, is, hower, not required. The best way of associating an iron wire with peroxide of lead is, to make it the positive electrode of a crown of cups (containing about a dozen of pairs of copper and zi[nk]) and to put the free end of this wire into a solution of the common acetate of lead (Saccharum Saturni) for about 8—10 minutes. By the action of the pile the peroxide is deposited on the positive iron wire. En passant I must tell you, that many reasons lead me to believe, that iron associated with this substance will form the most powerful voltaic element known, and I am just about to construct out of such couples a pile. As to the chemical nature

[1] vide fig. in letter to Mr. Faraday. 26th of Dec. 1836. p. 17.

of the matter producing the colours of Nobili's[1] chromatic scale[2] a notice of mine will shortly be published in Poggendorff's Annals,[3] from which you will see, that your idea about the subject is entirely correct[4] and consequently the view of the italian Philosopher wrong. Some of the facts regarding the peculiar condition of iron and observed by Mr. Noad[5] are, as you will easily perceive, quite the same which were already stated in my letter above mentioned. In publishing them as new ones,[6] the gentleman was most likely not aware of my observations. I cannot close these lines without expressing you my sincere thanks for the service, which you so kindly rendered me by forwarding my last paper to the editors of the Phil. Magazine.[7]

I am, my dear Sir very truly your's

Bâle April 27th 37 C. F. SCHOENBEIN.

Faraday to Schœnbein.

Royal Institution 2nd May. 1837.

MY DEAR SIR

At last I have pressed on Mr. Newman our instrument maker to the point of having a Magneto-electric Machine

[1] Leopoldo Nobili formerly captain of artillery was professor of Physics at the Grand-ducal Museum at Florence. He was born in 1784 at Trassilico in Modena and died in August 1835 at Florence.

[2] Taylor, Scientific memoirs prt. I, 1837. p. 108. "A memoir on colours in general, and particularly on a new chromatic scale deduced from metallochromy for scientific and practical purposes," from Bibl. Univ. T. 44. 1830. p. 337.

[3] Poggend. Annal. Bd. 40. 1837. p. 621.

[4] Phil. Mag. S. 3. vol. 10. 1837. p. 175.

[5] Henry Minchin Noad Ph. D. (Giessen) was born in 1815 at Stawford in Somerset as the son of a cloth manufacturer upon whose death in 1845 he devoted himself wholly to scientific research, working under A. W. Hofmann in London. He was Professor of Chemistry at St. Georges Hospital, consulting chemist to several iron works and an F. R. S. He died in 1877 in London.

[6] Phil. Mag. S. 3. vol. 10. 1837. p. 276.

[7] Phil. Mag. S. 3. vol. 10. 1837. p. 133.

ready for you; until that was effected I delayed writing to you. He tells me that before the week is out the apparatus will be shipped and I shall go to his shop to-morrow to see it all complete before packing. He will write to you sending a bill of lading etc. so as to inform you of the conveyance and the time etc. etc.

In the packet there will be also the copies of your last paper in the Philosophical Magazine [1] about which you wrote to me. They are only just now printed. I was very much interested in the reading of the experiments but am as much puzzled as ever as to the direct cause of the condition into which the iron comes. I have no doubt however that your perseverance will in time meet with its due reward; and when we do learn what it is that so balances things, we may well expect that a great many other things will at the same time come into view, and new light be thrown on many matters now dark and obscure.

I have been doing nothing lately i. e. I have been labouring in the ordinary things of my vocation. Much business and little health have left me no time for research: but I hope in the autumn to follow your active example and then perhaps add a few things more to the magnificent accumulation of facts which has been brought together of late years by the conjoined efforts of the labourers in Electrical Science.

Wishing you all health and strength and happiness.

    I am
     My dear Sir
      Your very faithful servant
        M. FARADAY.

[1] Experimental researches on a peculiar action of iron upon solutions of some metallic salts. Phil. Mag. S. 3. vol. 10. 1837. p. 267.

Faraday to Schœnbein.

R. Instituion 4 May 1837.

MY DEAR SIR

I have just received your letter of the 27th of April[1] and rejoice at your continued progress. I have made one or two of the experiments but they want more care and attention than I can give them at present for I am exceedingly occupied. I shall send it to the Phil Mag for the Editor to print if he pleases.[2]

Ever. Truly Yours
M. FARADAY.

Schœnbein to Faraday.

MY DEAR SIR

I have just now published a little work in german containing a detailed account of my researches on the peculiar condition of Iron, which I was so presumptuous as to dedicate to You.[3] As my motive for doing so was no other than the desire of publicly expressing my feelings of respect and regards towards you, I entertain the flattering hopes, you will be indulgent enough, as to grant me a pardon for the great liberty, I have taken and accept in kindness of the feeble tribute offered by my humble individual to a Man, whose name stands so high in the scientific world. Should the British Association for the advancement of Science happen to receive scientific works as

---
[1] vide 23.

[2] Experiments on the peculiar voltaic condition of iron as excited by peroxide of lead. Phil. Mag. S. 3. vol. 10. 1837. p. 425.

[3] Das Verhalten des Eisens zum Sauerstoff. Ein Beitrag zur Erweiterung electro-chemischer Kenntnisse. Von Dr. L.(sic.) F. Schœnbein, Professor der Chemie in Basel. Basel 1837.

presents, you would oblige me very much by sending one of the copies laid by to the president of that society for being produced at their next meeting in Liverpool. Though it has been a favo[u]rite plan of mine, these last five or six years, once to attend the meetings of this learned body and to visit Old England once more, a country which I love as much as I do my own native land, up to this time I have not yet been able to satisfy my wishes in this respect. I hope, however, to see them one day fulfilled.

The other day I got a letter from Mr. Berzelius,[1] the contents of which relate to my observations on the peculiar state of Iron. This distinguished Chemist, though he does not yet give a decided opinion upon the subject, is inclined to think, that in one notice of yours, published some time ago in the Phil. Mag.,[2] which alludes to the observations of Ritter[3] and de la Rive[4] regarding the secondary piles and the electrical state of polar Platina-wires, the true cause of the inactivity of Iron is hinted at. According to the view of Berzelius, Iron performing the function of the positive Electrode undergoes a change, with regard to its primitive electrical condition in such a manner, as to be turned from a positive electrical body into a negative one. As my views with respect to electro-chemical subjects essentially differ from those of Berzelius', I cannot, on this account, think the idea of that Philosopher correct; but it appears to me that it is not in accordance even with one of the principles of the electro-chemical system, such as laid down by Mr. B. himself. For the suggested Idea implies the assertion, that Iron whilst performing the function of the anode, or to speak the old language, whilst acting the part of the positive pole, is

[1] May 4th 1837. vide Kahlbaum Briefwechsel Berzelius-Schoenbein, Basel 1898. p. 20.
[2] Phil. Mag. S. 3. vol. 9. 1836. p. 57 and 122.
[3] Journ. de Phys. T. 57. 1803. p. 401.
[4] Bibl. Univ. T. 3. 1836. p. 375.

capable of being, at the same time, in a negative electrical state; in other terms, that Iron, under the circumstances mentioned, exhibits two opposite electrical states and consequently attracts and repels Oxigen at the same time. But such a kind of action is, to my opinion, a thing quite impossible and must be held as such even by those, who agree with the views of B. I have reason to believe, that Mr. B. will treat this question more circumstancially in his next annual Report, and then we shall see, whether the obscure subject will be more cleared up, than it is now. Some of our continental papers, particularly german ones, have still much to do with Mr. Crosse's[1] insects, said to be manufactured out of siliceous matter by the agency of a current. As these Journals frequently make use of your Name to prove the truth of the pretended discovery and enter in this respect into particulars, such for instance, as to assert, those insects had been exhibited by you at the meetings of the Royal Institution I should be very much obliged to you, if you would have the kindness to tell me, what to think of such reports. You may easily imagine, that our scientific men strongly doubt of the correctness of these extraordinary tales or rather do no believe in them at all.

The magneto-electrical Machine, which you were so kind to procure for our institution, arrived here some weeks ago. During its passage through "la belle France" it was so roughly handled, most likely by the custom house-people and waggoners there that some parts of it were broken. Now it is arranged again and works exceedingly well.

I was very sorry indeed, to learn from one of your former letters, that you did not enjoy of full health. On account of Yourself and the scientific world at large I confidently hope and ardently desire it will and may, by this time, be entirely reestablished. A trip to the Continent and into our beautiful Alp[e]s would, perhaps do a great deal of good to you. Should

[1] cf. the following letter.

you ever cross the channel and happen to touch Bâle, I would feel myself highly honoured, if you had the kindness to visit me. Accept, my dear Sir, the assurance of my being.

Yours very truly

Bâle July 9. 1837. C. F. SCHOENBEIN.

Faraday to Schœnbein.

Royal Institution 21. September 1837

MY DEAR SIR

Your very pleasant and acceptable letter of the 9th of July with the accompanying books I received only last week, whilst at Liverpool, at the very meeting you refer to and I heartily wish that you had been there yourself. It is now five years since I have been able to attend any of these meetings but I was very much pleased with the one to which I now refer. — As to your book[1] and its dedication I thank you for both. With respect to the latter all the value it has in my eyes is due to the kindly and hearty feeling which it proves you have towards me for in that I feel honour far beyond the public expression of it: and in that respect your letter is equally valuable with the dedication and even more so. As the Association forms no collection of books or apparatus I gave the said copy of your work to Professor Henry[2] of Philadelphia in the United States with a view of extending what you have done as far and as fast as possible and wherever the English language is found. He was exceedingly obliged to me for it and I only wish that you and he had met at Liverpool.

[1] Das Verhalten des Eisens zum Sauerstoff. Ein Beitrag zur Erweiterung electro-chemischer Kenntnisse. Bâle. 1837.

[2] Prof. Joseph Henry was born in 1797 at Albany, N. Y. and died in 1878 at Washington, where he was professor of Physics.

Respecting Berzelius' opinion of the state of the Iron etc. etc. it enters into the general mass of uncertainty regarding this very strange yet beautiful subject and must wait until we see the true light before it can have its right place assigned it. My mind is I think as yours is; waiting until something appears before it with conviction and then let us hope that not merely the opinions but the facts themselves will all start into a perfect order not again to be disturbed.

With regard to Mr. Crosse's[1] insects[2] etc. I do not think anybody believes in them here except perhaps himself and the mass of wonder-lovers. — I was said in the English papers to have proved the truth of his statement, but I immediately contradicted the matter publicly and should have thought that nobody who could judge in the matter would have suspected me of giving evidence to the thing for a moment. Contradict it in my name as fully as you please. It is but just of me to say that in conversation with Mr. Crosse I was very much pleased with him and with the readiness with which he received my critical remarks. As regards the cristallization supposed as real he was lugged into view and must not be charged with having pressed himself forward. He is in fact a very modest man but has been dragged into an unkind situation.

I am glad to find the Magneto-electric machine pleases you now that it has been restored to a proper condition. What a nuisance it is that we cannot have philosophical things conveyed to and fro from one country to another without the risk of great injury or even destruction to them.

And now my dear Sir good-bye for the present. You cannot think how much each letter of yours tantalizes me

[1] Andrew Crosse who was born at Broomfield near Taunton in Somerset died in July 1855 at Bridgewater.

[2] A description of some experiments made with the voltaic battery for the purpose of producing crystals in the process of which experiments certain insects constantly appeared. Trans. Elect. Soc. of London 1837. p. 10. Vide also Sillim. Journ. vol. 35. p. 125.

for they all make me wish I had known you a little sooner. It is now just about two years since I and my wife were at Bâle for a day or two on our return home from Switzerland to England. Whether I shall ever see the continent again or not I cannot say

      I am My dear Sir
       Yours most sincerely
         M. FARADAY.

Schœnbein to Faraday.
      Bâle 5 Novemb. 1837.

MY DEAR SIR

  I am exceedingly obliged to you for your very kind letter of last month. It made me deeply regret not to have been present at the late meeting of the British Association, but as I told you before, my absence from Liverpool was rather a forced than a voluntary one. If possible I shall cross the channel next year to remain in dear Old England as long as circumstances will allow it; for I will not conceal it from you, that I am strongly attached to your native country, so much so that I should consider one of the most ardent wishes I am entertaining as fulfilled, if I could for ever live in that happy and interesting Island. Your langage, history, literature and science have been favo[u]rite objects of my study and leisure-occupation these last fifteen years and at this present moment everything regarding Great Britain has a peculiar interest with me.

  I do not know, whether I mentioned it to you in one of my former letters, that about a dozen of years ago, when I was in London a gentleman from there introduced me into the Royal Institution at the same day you delivered a lecture on the then new discovery of Arago,[1] respecting the action of rotating metallic plates on suspended magnets etc. I still recollect the great pleasure with which I witnessed your experiments on that subject, but being then rather a shy and bashful young man I did not venture to enter into a conversation with you in spite of my inclination to do so and though I had, after the lecture was over, a favo[u]rable opportunity to speak to you. I mention these trifling occurrences to show you that my acquaintance with you has already been of rather a long standing. You can easily imagine, how sorry I must be for having lost the favo[u]rable opportunity of seeing you at Bâle during your stay there; it is only the hope of meeting you soon on your side of the water, that mitigates a little my vexation. Mr. de la Rive[2] on his return from England to Geneva passed through Bâle about a fortnight ago and paying me a visit, I learned from him some particulars regarding the state of your health, after which I was very anxious to enquire, having been told by yourself, you were rather suffering. I wish from all my heart and as ardently as any of your friends can do, the speedy and complete reestablishment of your health. Mr. de la Rive seemed to be quite satisfied with the meeting at Liverpool.

The short notice contained in the last number of the Biblioth. univers.[3] respecting Dr. Andrew's[4] researches on the action of nitric acid upon Bismuth, has induced me to make some experiments on the same subject and I now take the

[1] Dominique François Jean Arago astronomer at Paris was born in 1786 and died at Paris in 1853.

[2] Auguste Arthur de la Rive, born in 1801 was originally a law student until he met Ampère and Faraday. He was appointed professor at the Academy of Geneva in 1823 as successor to Prevost and in 1825 as successor to Pictet. He was an F.R.S. and died at Marseilles in 1837.

[3] Bibl. Univ. 1837.

[4] Thomas Andrews M. D., professor of Chemistry in the Royal Belfast Institution was born in 1813 at Belfast and died in 1885.

liberty to give you a short account of the results obtained from them. It certainly cannot be denied, that there exists some analogy between the peculiar condition of Iron and that of Bismuth but my impression at present is, that there is only a similarity and not an identity of cases. This opinion is founded upon the following facts. The chemical action of Iron upon nitric acid can, as it is now well known, be entirely stopped by a variety of ways, whilst according to my experiments it is impossible to obtain such a result with Bismuth. I voltaically associated this metal with all the substances known to be capable of rendering Iron completely inactive but by so doing I could never succeed so far as to prevent Bismuth from being chemically acted upon by nitric acid. It is true, by putting in contact the metallic body in question with Platinum the chemical action of nitric acid spec. gr. 1.4 may be reduced to such a low degree of intensity, that no visible disengagement of binoxide of nitrogen takes place and the piece of Bismuth (immersed in nitric acid) assumes a bright appearance. But the oxidable metal being in this state is nevertheless uninterruptedly attacked by the acid fluid, as it can be easily shown by having recourse to the galvanometer. There are besides some other facts, which put the continuance of chemical action in the circumstances mentioned beyond any doubts. I think I have first ascertained the remarkable fact, that Iron can be rendered thoroughly inactive not only towards the oxigen of nitric acid (of any degree of dilution) but also to the oxigen disengaged (by the action of a voltaic current) out of aqueous solutions of any oxidized body or any oxyelectrolyte. You know, that such a state of Iron is called forth by making this metal act the part of the positive electrode of a pile and closing the circuit in a certain manner. Now if Bismuth be placed in these very same circumstances, it does not seem to undergo any change whatever, for it is violently acted upon by nitric acid (of spec. gr. 1.4) and unites with the oxigen resulting from the electro-chemical decomposition of water or any other oxyelectrolyte. It is particularly the last mentioned difference of bearing between the two metals, which makes me suspect, that the peculiar condition of Iron is not produced by the same cause which occasions the inactivity of Bismuth, that is to say that the latter effect is not brought about by a current passing in a certain direction through Bismuth. There is another fact which seems to speak in favo[u]r of this opinion. According to my experiments peroxide of Lead proves to be the most powerful of all substances, which are capable of turning common Iron into its peculiar state. Peroxide of Lead, in whatever manner I tried to combine it with Bismuth did not appear to have any action upon the metal, for this substance was dissolved by nitric acid just in the same way, as it was, when put into the said fluid without any voltaic association. Now it is to be asked in what manner does Platinum weaken the chemical action of nitric acid upon Bismuth? Are we to believe that in the case in question the former acts in a quite peculiar way, that it puts into play on agency of a nature as yet unknown and entirely different from current electricity? I am certainly not much inclined to draw any such inference from the fact alluded to but at the same time I must confess, that for the present at least, I am not able at all of accounting for the anomaly spoken of. Before passing from the subject of the peculiar condition of Bismuth to another one, allow me to mention to you some more phenomena, which bear upon the same matter and which have, perhaps, not yet been observed by Mr. Andrews. After (by the agency of Platinum) the violent action of nitric acid (spec. gr. 1.4) upon Bismuth has been changed into a slow one and both metals brought out of contact, Bismuth loses its metallic lustre and assumes a blackish appearance; after a short time, however, the metal turns bright again by itself and remains so, until it is touched a second time by platinum. As long as the contact between both metals is maintained, there is certainly no change of the surface of Bismuth to be observed, but no sooner have they ceased to touch each other, than the Bismuth begins to blacken again, it reassumes however after some lapse of time its former lustre. This change of surface can be effected as often, as you like. I have ascertained, that Bismuth covered with the said blackish coating is more energetically acted upon by nitric acid, than it is, when its surface appears to be bright. Now as Platinum by means of its contact with Bismuth causes a very considerable diminution of the energy of chemical action of the acid upon the latter metal and makes always and intantaneously disappear the black film from it, the reproduction of this coating under the circumstances before-mentioned is a fact very strange, indeed, and altogether anomalous. Another fact also worthy of being stated is that the black film can be produced either by moving the bright Bismuth about within the acid or by causing the acid to be moved about the metal. I do not yet know what the black substance consists of, but whatever it may be its production in the last-mentioned way is no doubt due to the removal of some stratum surrounding the bright metal and protecting the Bismuth against the violent action of nitric acid. This supposed stratum consists perhaps of a solution of nitrate of Bismuth mixt with some nitrous acid.

If Bismuth being in its peculiar state or covered with the blackish film be sightly touched with a platinum wire within nitric acid of spec. gr. 1.4 a gazeous substance will be disengaged at the wire all the while contact is maintained between the metals. Having not yet made the experiment on a scale large enough as to allow the collection of the gas, I do not know its nature. I have stated however the fact to you, because the development of a gazeous body under the circumstances alluded to must appear very odd, if we consider, that no gas whatsoever is disengaged at the negative electrode when nitric acid of some strength for instance one of spec. gr. 1.4, will be subject to the action of the current of a pile. Now in the case spoken of the platinum wire does certainly act the part of the negative electrode. As every circumstance connected with the peculiar condition of readily oxidable metals appears to me to be of some importance I will not omit to mention the fact, that inactive Iron cannot be brought into contact with inactive Bismuth, without being thrown into chemical action. Iron, however, voltaically associated with Platinum is proof to the exciting influence of the passive Bismuth and capable of destroying the often mentioned black substance just in the same manner, as Platinum. Some few words more on the peculiar state of Bismuth and I have done with this subject of which I am afraid I have already entertained you too long. By immersing that metal for a few seconds into nitrous acid it is turned inactive, so that it can be put into nitric acid of spec. gr. 1.4 without being sensibly attacked by the latter.

The Biblioth. univers.[1] also alludes to a paper read at Liverpool by Mr. Hartley on the preservation of Iron against the action of Sea water.[2] The fact stated by that gentleman is on account of its anomaly highly interesting and seems to enter into that class of electro-chemical phenomena, which have been the subject of my researches these last two years. If you recollect a statement of mine made in a paper "on a peculiar action of Iron"[3] etc. you will be aware that the result obtained from Mr. Hartley's experiments[4] does not quite agree with what I have found and to be a general fact.[5] The statement alluded

[1] Bibl. Univ. 1837.
[2] At the meeting of the British Association held at Liverpool in 1837. vide Brit. Ass. Rep. 1837 (pt. 2), p. 56.: On preventing the corrosion of cast and wrought iron immersed in sea-water.
[3] Experimental researches on a peculiar action of iron upon solutions of some metallic salts. Phil. Mag. S. 3. vol. 10. 1836. p. 267. cf. also Über das Verhalten des Eisens zum Sauerstoff. Poggend. Annal. Bd. 38. 1836. p. 493.
[4] Phil. Mag. S. 3. vol. 10. 1837. p. 554.
[5] A discussion of Hartleys work by Schœnbein is to be found in Poggend. Annal. Bd. 43. 1838. p. 13: Einige Bemerkungen über die Erfahrung Hartleys in Betreff des Eisens.

to runs as follows: In solutions, containing, besides oxyelectrolytes, others of a different nature, for instance hydracids, haloid salts etc., no evolution of oxigen takes place (at the Iron, being the positive electrode of the pile) in whatever manner the circuit may be closed. Now if in Mr. Hartley's voltaic arrangement Brass is to Iron (in an electrical point of view) what Platinum is to the latter or any other readily oxidable metal according to my experiments we should suppose that Iron, being voltaically associated with Brass, would be chemically acted upon by Seawater, that is to say be oxidized and chloridized. You may easily ascertain the correctness of my statement by plunging an Iron wire which is connected with the positive pole of a pile into an aqueous solution of chloride of sodium closing thereby the circuit. You will observe that Iron is not turned inactive, but corroded and effects are produced quite consonant to the well known electro-chemical laws. I made a couple of days ago some experiments with seawater itself and I found that Iron was attacked when a current passed from the metal into the fluid. As you can easily imagine the disagreement of Mr. Hartley's observations with mine makes me exceedingly desirous of getting as soon as possible acquainted with the particulars of that gentleman's researches. I hope the next number of the Philosophical Magazine will satisfy my curiosity on this point.

Last Summer during a short stay at Stuttgart I made in the laboratory of Professor Degen[1] there and in company with this able Chemist some experiments upon Cobalt and Nickel to ascertain, whether these metallic bodies are capable of being rendered inactive.[2] Having but a very small quantity of those metals at our disposal, we were obliged to limit the number

[1] August F. E. Degen, Professor of Physics and Chemistry at the Technical High School at Stuttgart, was born in 1802 at Ludwigsburg and died in 1850 at Stuttgart.
[2] Berzelius in a letter to Schœnbein dated May 4th 1837 had suggested repeating similar experiments to those which iron had been subjected to, on nickel and cobalt. Kahlbaum. Briefwechsel Berzelius-Schœnbein. Basel. 1898. p. 22.

of our experiments to very few ones and to execute them on a very small scale. The results obtained from them were, however, such as to convince us, that the peculiar condition cannot be excited either in Cobalt or in Nickel, at least not in the same way as it is done in Iron. This fact seems to indicate, that the peculiar voltaic state of the latter metal has nothing to do with its magnetic properties.

The french papers have been talking for some time about a discovery (said to have been made by a certain Mr. Sorel[1] a Frenchman) which if it should turn out to be something more than a mere news-papers' invention, would be indeed a most wonderful thing. By dint of god knows what sort of substance, the news-papers call it voltaic-powder, Mr. Sorel is said to be able of changing Iron and any other readily oxidable metal such, as to give them (with regard to their chemical bearings to oxigen) the properties of the precious ones. Such a discovery, of course, cannot be made in our days without being turned to practical advantage and so, indeed, the papers tell us, that Mr. Sorel is going to enter into partnership with the well known Mr. Cockerill in order to make use of his discovery in the large establishments of the latter gentleman. By the manner in which some German papers took notice of the results of my late researches[2] on the peculiar condition of Iron, I too have already

---

[1] In his pamphlet: Verhalten des Eisens zum Sauerstoff. Basel 1837, which he dedicated to Faraday and which is dated June 4th 1837, Schœnbein on p. 90 says that by means of passivity iron should be convertible into precious metals. Since we failed to come across Sorels paper — it is not even mentioned in the Catalogue of the Royal Society — or to discover anything about his history, we are unable fully to appreciate Schœnbeins reasons for taking such a lively interest in Sorels results.

[2] In a letter to Poggendorff Schœnbein however complains that on the continent so little attention is paid to his work on the passivity of iron. Poggendorff in his answer (Jan. 19th 1838) puts it down to the fact that such a subject is of too chemical a nature for philosophers, whereas chemists despise anything that requires more thought than is necessary to prepare and decompose chemical compounds.

gained the reputation of being a little bit of an Alchymist. Nay offers of money even have been made to me, in order to get the secret of changing Iron into Platinum or some such thing out of me.

You will oblige me very much by forwarding in a way most convenient to you the inclosed parcel to its place of destination.

Believe me ever to be
Yours very truly
C. F. SCHOENBEIN.

Schœnbein to Faraday.[1]

MY DEAR SIR

From a series of experiments lately made by me with the view of ascertaining the voltaic relations of some peroxides, platina and inactive iron to one another I have obtained some results, which, to my opinion, are such as to throw some additional light upon the cause of voltaic electricity and modify, to a certain degree at least, the notions we have, hitherto, entertained about that interesting subject. You will recollect that the voltaic relation of peroxide of lead to Iron engaged my attention some time ago and you are, perhaps also aware of the fact stated by me in "Poggendorff's Annalen"[2] that the peroxide in question if voltaically associated with iron disappears by degrees when plunged into nitric acid of any strength. Now, as we know, that no chemical action whatever takes place in the circumstances mentioned, iron being in its peculiar condition and having, in a voltaic point of view, all the properties of

[1] This letter is printed in Phil. Mag. S. 3. vol. 10. 1837. p. 225. the heading under which it was inserted reading as follows: "On the peculiar voltaic relations of certain peroxides, platina and inactive iron.

[2] Poggend. Annal. Bd. 41. 1837. p. 55.

platina, I could not but be very much surprised at the disappearance of the peroxide of lead. Although I was not able of tracing at the time any voltaic current and of accounting for any disturbance of the electric equilibrium of the arrangement alluded to, I nevertheless suspected, that the dissolution of the mentioned substance was effected under the influence of current electricity. Having now at my disposal a galvanometer, which is provided with 2000 coils and made in other respects very delicate, I have taken up that subject again and attempted first to ascertain, whether there is any voltaic relation of platina to inactive iron. In contradiction to the results which You and I obtained some time ago, I have found out by means of my galvanometer, that iron being in its peculiar condition and associated with platina gives rise to a sensible current if put into nitric acid, be the latter ever so strong or somewhat diluted with water. Making use of an acid of sp. gr. 1.4 the deviation of the needle (on putting the iron and platina wires in connection with the galvanometer), amounted to about 90^0. I must not omit to state, that the current excited in the circumstances mentioned is not a momentary but a continuous one and at the same time quite independent of any oxidation of the iron. The direction of the current in question is such as it would be, if the latter metal was attacked by the acid, that is to say, inactive iron is positive to platina. Another fact as curious and interesting as that just stated is the following one. Two platina wires being connected by one set of their ends with the galvanometer and by the other set with nitric acid or an aquous solution of sulfate of copper, excite a current, provided one of the ends (immersing in the fluid) of one of the platina wires be covered with a film of peroxide of lead. The current passes from the platina through the fluid to the peroxide. When the said film is so thin as to produce, what is called "Nobili's colours",[1] it disappears within a very few seconds after having been immersed

[1] Bibl. Univ. T. 44. 1830. p. 331.

into nitric acid and the whole arrangement connected with the wire of the galvanometer. From the facts stated, it appears that platina is positive with regard to peroxide of lead, and that the disappearance of that compound is caused by a current, which eliminates hydrogen at the negative peroxide, by which means the latter is reduced to protoxide of lead and rendered soluble in nitric acid. In a similar manner I have ascertained that the voltaic relation of inactive iron to peroxide of lead is exactly the same, as that of platina to the said peroxide. In using peroxide of silver instead of that of lead voltaic effects are produced quite the same as those which were just spoken of; that is to say, a continuous current is excited to which the peroxide acts the part of the cathode and either of the metals in question that of the anode. As to the voltaic relation, which one of the mentioned peroxides bears to the other my experiments have shown, that peroxide of silver is always negative with regard to the peroxide of lead, be the fluid made use of nitric acid or a solution of blue vitriol. Now from all the facts above stated, I think, we are allowed to draw two important inferences: 1. that peroxide of silver, peroxide of lead, platina and inactive iron represent a series of substances, in which the preceding one is always negative with regard to that which follows in the list 2. that any two of the four substances mentioned being voltaically associated with one another and put either into nitric acid or a solution of sulfate of copper excite a continuous current, which is not due to oxidation or any chemical change. It is hardly necessary to add that the currents produced in the said circumstances are extremely feeble, being only indicated by most delicate galvanometers. You will agree with me, that the facts spoken of are highly important in a scientific point of view, as they do produce evidence in favo[u]r of that theory, which asserts, that by the mere contact of heterogeneous substances their electrical equilibrium can be disturbed, quite independent of any chemical action taking place between them. All chemists certainly maintain, that pure nitric acid for instance, does not chemically affect at all either platina or peroxide of lead; and inactive iron too, as we now well know, is not the least attacked by the said acid. Now I ask, whence does the current originate, which is produced, when we combine the substances in question in such a manner, as to form with them a voltaic arrangement. I have attempted to answer that puzzling question in a paper, which, before long, will be published in Poggendorff's Annales[1] as well as in the Biblioth. univ.[2] and in which you will besides find a detailed account of all the experiments made by me upon the subject spoken of. If my time was not so much taken up with a variety of business I would have drawn up a memoir in English and sent it to the Editors of your excellent philosophical Magazine for insertion; but those gentlemen will, perhaps, give a translation of the paper. Before closing my letter allow me to communicate to you in a general manner the view, which I have taken of the subject in question. In the first place, I must tell you, that I am by no means inclined to consider mere contact in any case as the cause of excitement of even the most feeble current. I maintain, on the contrary, in accordance with the principles of the chemical theory, that any current produced in a hydroelectric voltaic circle is always due to some chemical action. But as to the idea, which I attach to the term "chemical action" I go farther, than You and Mr. de la Rive seem to go; for I maintain, that any tendency of two different substances to unite chemically with one another must be considered as a chemical action, be that tendency followed up by the actual combination of those substances or be it not and that such a tendency is capable of putting electricity into circulation. I will try to render this idea of mine somewhat clearer by applying it to some particular cases. Supposing a voltaic circle be composed of platina, peroxide of lead and nitric acid, I say, that

[1] Poggend. Annal. Bd. 43. 1838. p. 229.
[2] Bibl. Univ. T. 14. 1838. p. 395.

the current excited in such an arrangement is due first to the tendency of the acid to unite with the protoxide of lead or, what is the same, to the tendency of one proportion of the oxigen to separate from the peroxide; secondly to the tendency of water to combine with the same protoxide to form a hydrate and thirdly to the tendency of water to withdraw a proportion of oxigen from the peroxide to produce peroxide of hydrogen, wh(ich) tendency, from very well known chemical reasons, is yet increased by the presence of the acid. It is true, none of the said tendencies do lead to any chemical results; for no nitrate of lead, no hydrate, no peroxide of hydrogen is actually produced; but are we allowed to infer from the want of a practical result, that no chemical action whatever takes place, when nitric acid and peroxide of lead are put in contact with one another? I ask, are we to suppose, that the chemical affinities alluded to are entirely dormant and incapable of any exertion? The results from my late experiments induce me to answer the question in the negative. Being quite of your opinion, that chemical affinity and current electricity are but different forms of the same thing, I cannot help thinking that any sort of chemical action or tendency must be capable of being transformed into the shape of a current. For that current, which is produced by inactive iron (being voltaically associated with platina) I likewise account by a chemical tendency on the part of the former metal. Though inactive iron be not in the least attacked by nitric acid, its affinity for the oxygen of the latter is, on that account, by no means, entirely destroyed; the metal, whilst surrounded by the acid is continually tending to oxidize itself and the current excited in such a case is nothing else but as it were the electrical translation of a chemical exertion.

All the cases above stated, where currents are observed, independent of any chemical change, can easily be explained by applying to them the same principle, by means of which we have accounted for the current produced by nitric acid and peroxide of lead etc. Having already passed the usual limits of a letter, I add only one more observation to my former, and I have done. According to my experiments peroxide of silver proves to be the most powerful means for exciting in iron its peculiar voltaic condition. It surpassed in this respect even the peroxide of lead. An iron wire, for instance, one end of which is covered with only a small particle of the first-mentioned substance will not be attacked either by nitric acid of any degree of dilution or by a solution of blue vitriol. The voltaic association of one substance with the other is easily effected by connecting one end of an iron wire with the positive electrode of a pile and by plunging for a few minutes the other end of the wire into a solution of nitrate of silver. I am just about to write a paper on that interesting subject.

I am my dear Sir
Your's very truly
C. F. SCHOENBEIN.

Bâle Dec 31. 1837.

Faraday to Schœnbein.

Royal Institution 22 Jany 1838

MY DEAR SIR

I have received two kind letters from you since I wrote last and must reply although I shall be able to write only a very short letter for now my severe duties for the Season have commenced and I get little rest and not the time I require for experiments and papers. The greater part of the former and the whole of the last of yours I have sent to the Philosophical Magazine.[1] Your results are of the highest interest and must encourage you to work on in the mind which is your possession. The consequences which you produce with the

---

[1] Phil. Mag. S. 3. vol. 12. 1837. p. 225: On the mutual voltaic relations of certain peroxides, platina, and inactive iron.

peroxide of lead are in perfect accordance with my views of voltaic action and I go with you to the extent of labour in actions which are of a chemical nature in their origin though not producing i. e. not proceeding to the extent of causing combination or decomposition. See paragraphs 623. 624. etc. of the sixth series of my experimental researches.[1] I am not yet prepared to go the length of admitting that such an attraction can cause a *continuous* current of electricity i. e. that an action or force can produce an effect and not itself be lowered or equivalently affected at the same time. But I have not your letter at present and perhaps that is not what you mean.

In the peroxide of lead action I suppose you have a body which originates the current by its attraction for hydrogen, acts at the opposite side of the arrangement to what the zinc or other oxygen attracting body does. But the cause of the anions and cations with respect to the current produced is the same as in all other cases. Is it not so? I am half afraid of writing this chit chat not having your letter by me.

I have been working very hard lately on Induction. I have sent two papers to the Royal Society and am experimenting and writing for the third and fourth. You shall have them printed soon and I must not stop to tell you my views for to tell them piecemeal would give you no information. Since my unlucky letter to my late friend M. Hachette[2] hurried Nobili[3]

[1] Experimental researches in Electricity. Phil. Trans. 1834. p. 55.

[2] Jean N. P. Hachette was born in 1769 at Mézières. He was professor at the Academy of Science at Paris up to his death which took place in 1834.

[3] Bence Jones in his Life of Faraday describes the circumstances here alluded to as follows (vol 2. p. 17). The contents of a short and hasty letter written to M. Hachette by Faraday three weeks after his first paper was read at the Royal Society (Nov. 24. 1831) were printed in "Le Temps" Dec. 18. 1831. M. Nobili immediately considered the subject given to the philosophical world for general pursuit and wrote two memoirs both of which accuse Faraday of errors of experiments and theory, and, beyond that, of good faith. In the Phil. Mag. for June 1832 Faraday published a translation of Nobili's paper with notes and later in the year wrote a long letter to M. Gay-Lussac for the purpose of rectifying the misinterpretation given to his words.

into such mistakes I have been rather averse to giving short or premature accounts of my views.

Again I must have yours. For the present in haste
I am My dear Sir
Your obliged and faithful friend
M. FARADAY.

Schœnbein to Faraday.

MY DEAR SIR

Dr. Brabant whose agreeable and interesting acquaintance I made at Bâle is the kind bearer of these lines. Enclosed you will find a paper containing some hypothetical views on the peculiar condition of iron, which was first intended for the Phil. Magazine, but which I think, after having read it over again altogether unfit for publication on account of its being too much conjectural.[1] Nevertheless I take the liberty of sending the paper to you, hoping you will peruse it with kind indulgence.

You are, no doubt, now aware of the attacks[2] recently made by Mr. Fechner[3] upon your theory of the pile. I have abready tried to answer some of his objections in Poggendorff's Annalen[4] and have also written a paper for the Phil. Magazine[5] which is

[1] Conjectures on the cause of the peculiar condition of iron. Phil. Mag. S. 3. vol. 13. 1838. p. 256.

[2] Poggend. Annal. Bd. 42. 1837. p. 481; for a translation of this paper see Phil. Mag. S. 3. vol. 13. 1838. p. 205: Justification of the contact theory of galvanism, by G. T. Fechner.

[3] Gustav Theodor Fechner was professor of Physics at Leipzig from 1834—1839, subsequently also of Anthropology. He was born in 1801 at Gross-Särchen (Lusatia) and died in 1887 at Leipzig.

[4] Poggend. Annal. Bd. 44. 1838 p. 59: Einige Bemerkungen über Fechners Rechtfertigung der Kontakttheorie des Galvanismus.

[5] Phil. Mag. S. 3. vol. 13. 1838. p. 161: Discussion of Mr. Fechners views of the theory of galvanism, with reference, particularly, to a circuit including two electrolytes and the relations of inactive iron.

in the parcel addressed to Mr. Taylor.[1] I am confident, however, that you yourself will, before long, appreciate the facts which have been brought forward by Mr. F. and declared by him to be irreconcilable to the very first principles of the chemical theory of galvanism[2] and I must not conceal from you, that the scientific public in Switzerland and Germany are rather impatiently waiting for a refutation of Fechner's assertions on your part. Believe me to be

Yours
very truly

Bâle, June 14th 1838.   C. F. SCHOENBEIN.

Faraday to Schœnbein.

Royal Institution 30. July 1838.

MY DEAR SIR

You know how I value your letters and may conclude that the last was very pleasant to me; though there is always a feeling of deep regret that the treasures which accompany your communications being in the German language are sealed up to me. I was out of town when your letter arrived and have not had the fortune to see Dr. Brabant but I hope he enjoyed himself in England.

[1] Richard Taylor, owner of a large printing firm, from which he retired in 1803, was born in 1781 at Norwich and died in 1858 in London. He was, nominally, one of the editors of the Phil. Mag.

[2] Through Fechners arguments Poggendorff actually deserted from the chemical theorists. This change of opinion he relates in three letters to Schœnbein dated respectively Jan. 19, April 14 and May 31. 1838. According to the first, after weighing the arguments brought forward by either party, he is almost an the point of being convinced; in the second he confesses himself to have become a follower of Volta's theory and in the last he points out that Schœnbeins arguments in favour of the chemical theory are unavailing. "Ich bin durch sie nicht bekehrt" he writes "und glaube schwerlich dass Fechner es wird".

Your paper on the possible condition of Iron in its peculiar state I have taken to Mr. Taylor (as well as the parcel). Your theory is just now in that state as respects the facts of the case that one may very well be allowed the be *not too sure* either for or against it but you can hardly think I should consider any opinion of yours as unworthy of publication. I have far too much respect for the judgment you have shown in these very delicate and difficult enquiries.

You mention Fechner's objections to my theory and I am exceedingly anxious to see and consider them but do not know whether they are all acceptable to me or not. Would you mind referring me in your next to Poggendorff or other Journals in which they are; mentioning the pages in which the path of the objection or the positive experiments are and then I will have them translated. I am rather in hopes that the paper you say you have sent to Mr. Taylor will in fact refer to and perhaps state them. I am very anxious to know of all important objections but I do not mind about slight ones. Many have been made to me which been left to themselves have disappeared in a few months from the minds of the objecters themselves; but good and valid objections are of great importance and often I think prove the key to new discoveries.

Dr. Poggendorff[1] who was here lately told me of Fechners objections but when he learnt from me that I by no means go the length of De la Rive and that I admit *many other modes of electrical excitement* besides chemical action, I thought he seemed to think that Fechners objections were rather against De la Rive than me. Perhaps what I am saying has not reference to Fechners objections but what I believe is that the Electricity which characterises the Voltaic pile (binding [?] *the phenomenon*

---

[1] Johann Christian Poggendorff Ph. D. M. D. formerly an apothecary, was born in 1796 at Hamburg He was professor at the University and member of the Academy of Science at Berlin where he died in 1877. He edited 160 volumes of the Annalen which bear his name.

to that instrument) is of chemical origin; is another form of chemical affinity and I think the notes to paragraphs 856. 921. 928 indicate that to be my meaning, besides the general tenor of the papers and descriptions contained in it.

I have been writing on Induction and have three new papers (series 11. 12. und 13),[1] and shall soon have a fourth for you. I am rather uncertain whether you receive those I send you by our Royal Society. If you do not let me know: and if you know any channel which [is] fitter for the purpose and will tell me I will send them to you by it at once. —

I am very heavy in experiment just now and have some results with crystals which I think you will approve of. — I must now conclude in haste but not the less

Sincerely Yours
M. FARADAY.

Schœnbein to Faraday.

Bâle 12. Aug. 1838.

MY DEAR SIR

Your kind letter of the 30th ult lays me under the agreeable obligation to renew my correspondence with you and to thank you for the indulgence with which you received my communications.

As to the objections brought forward by Mr. Fechner against the chemical theory of galvanism, you will find the principal ones in Poggendorff's Annalen number 12. p. 508—510. 1837 and number 3. p. 433—440. 1838. I think Dr. Poggendorff was mistaken in believing Mr. Fechner's arguments not to be referable to your theory for as much as I understand the assertions of that philosopher they go so far as broadly to deny chemical action to be an electromotive force and to

---

[1] Phil. Trans. 1838. p. 1 and 79. p. 83 and p. 125.

make the current produced by a hydro-electric pile entirely independent of any chemical change taking place within the said voltaic arrangement. Now I should suppose such a doctrine disagrees not only with de la Rives' views, but also with yours. Mr. Fechner being esteemed as one of the ablest electricians in Germany, I think it is worth your while to appreciate the facts on which he has founded his opposition to the chemical theory. As for me I am not yet prepared to yield the point to Fechner and to osider his experiments as conclusive evidence against your views.

Last year a little work was published by Mr. Pfaff[1] in Kiel bearing the title: Revision der Lehre vom Galvanismus (Review of the doctrines regarding Galvanism). You are no doubt aware of Pfaff's having been these last forty years one of the staunchest supporters of Volta's theory in Germany. The work alluded to was written with the view of putting the correctness of his favo[u]rite hypothesis beyond doubt and to prove the entire fallacy of the chemical theory of the pile and contains at the same time an account of many voltaic experiments made by Pfaff for the purpose of supporting his views. A large portion of the book has reference to your researches.[2]

I think the publication of a short review of the work mentioned by the means of the Phil. Magazine would prove acceptable to the british scientific public.

The different branches of natural science being rather much cultivated at this present moment in the North of Europe and

[1] Christian Heinrich Pfaff M. D. Ph. D. professor of Medicine, Physics and Chemistry at Kiel was born in 1773 at Stuttgart and died in 1852 at Kiel.

[2] A passage from a letter from de la Rive to Schœnbein should not be omitted here, as it expresses very characteristically his view on the value of Pfaff's book. He writes on Oct. 20. 1838: "Vous pouvez compter que je ne parlerai de lui que pour dire que je n'en parlerai pas, car son ouvrage est aussi mauvais dans le fond que détestable dans la forme." These words illustrate the way in which at that time followers of either side would assail their adversaries; it does not however give a true estimate of Pfaffs importance as a philosopher or of the value of his contributions to the history of voltaic theories.

most papers of the philosophers there published in the german language the editors and reviewers of the british scientific journals will do well in paying some attention to german publications. The french are woefully neglectful in that respect. As you take so lively an interest in everything that relates to electrical science I must not omit to draw your attention upon the recent researches of Mr. Munk af Rosenschöld[1] on the voltaic pile. It seems to me that the swedish(!) philosopher has obtained some results which are novel and rather of importance. Pogg. Ann. number 2 & 3 1838 contain the papers on the subject.[2]

Having just now returned from a trip into the Alps ta[ken] during our holidays I am rather busy in experiments. They refer to transitory chemical changes (which certain compounds undergo by being heated) as connected both with a modification of colo[u]r and voltaic currents.[3] I think I shall be able to demonstrate or to render probable at least, that chemical decompositions and recompositions take place under circumstances, where such changes have not been suspected as yet.

You will lay me under many obligations by sending me your late papers on induction. Having got once a communication of yours by the means of the Royal Society I think this channel will be sure enough.

    Believe me to be

                      sincerely Yours

                       C. F. SCHOENBEIN.

My right hand having been a little injured lately by some accidental cause, you will be kind enough to excuse my bad writing.

[1] Peter Samuel Munk af Rosenschöld lecture assistant in Chemistry at the University of Lund, was born at Lund in 1804 and died in 1860.

[2] Untersuchungen über Electrizität. Poggend. Annal. Bd. 43. 1838. p. 193 und 440.

[3] These results he sums up in a paper in Poggend. Annal. Bd. 45. 1838. p. 263: Über die Ursache der Farbenveränderung welche manche Körper unter der Wärme erleiden.

Schœnbein to Faraday.

MY DEAR SIR

As an acquaintance of mine is on the point of leaving Bâle to go to London, I make use of the favo[u]rable opportunity to tell you in a few words, that some weeks ago I observed some voltaic phenomena which I think to be entirely novel and rather of great importance to our favo[u]rite science. Being just now occupied with drawing up for you a paper in English which is to contain a detailed account of my results,[1] I will not enter at present into particulars and confine myself to stating the general fact, that fluid compound bodies being at the same time electrolytes are capable of assuming a peculiar state, which I term their electrical polarisation; because such a fluid being in that condition possesses the power to produce a voltaic current quite by itself i. e. without the assistance of any chemical action going on between the fluid and a metallic body. The inferences which a fact of such an extraordinary nature allows to draw with respect to Chemistry in particular are very, as you will easily conceive, very interesting.

I have only yet time to call myself
Yours
very truly
Bâle 15. Septbr. 1838.   C. F. SCHOENBEIN.

Schœnbein to Faraday.

Bâle, Oct. 20. 1838.

MY DEAR SIR

I take the liberty to make you acquainted with some results which I have lately obtained from my researches and which I think are such, as to merit some attention on the part of philosophers.

[1] Phil. Mag. S. 3. vol. 14. 1838. p. 43.

Plausible and ingenious as the views of Mr. Becquerel on the cause of the currents of Ritter's [1] secondary piles and of the electro-motive power acquired by polar wires are, some facts led me the other day to doubt of the correctness of the theory of the celebrated french philosopher and induced me to investigate once more the circumstances under which what they call secondary currents are excited. I found that platina-wires acting as electrodes within aqueous solutions of chemically pure acids or alcalies acquire the property of exciting secondary currents just as well as they do within solutions of salts. As in those circumstances the decomposition and recomposition of a salt is quite out of the question, I think we must infer from such a fact, that the hypothesis of Mr. B. is erroneous. But is it not possible, that some portions of the constituent parts of the body electrolysed stick to the polar wires and produce by their reunion the secundary current? By the result of the following experiment, we are, to my opinion entitled to answer that question in the negative. Platina-wires plunging into chemically pure muriatic acid and being connected with the poles of a pile the current of which was so feeble as not to be capable of decomposing even jodide of potassium, I say wires, thus circumstanced, acquired in a few seconds an electro-motive power, which produced a deviation of the needle of my delicate galvanometer of 160^0. As under these circumstances, neither muriatic acid nor water could have been electrolysed, the secondary current obtained is consequently not due to the reunion of Chlorine and Hydrogen, or Oxigen and Hydrogen.

But there is another fact, to which I take the liberty of drawing your attention, a fact which on account of its novelty and peculiarity cannot fail exciting a good deal of scientific curiosity.

[1] Johann Wilhelm Ritter was born in 1776 in Samitz in Silesia and died 1810 in Munich. At first he was an apothecary's assistant, later he practiced as a physician in Gotha and Weimar and was a Member of the Academy in Munich.

When the branches of a tube bent in the shape of a U are filled with chemically pure muriatic acid and by the means of two platina-wires connected with the poles of a pile, whose current is not able of causing the electrolysation of the fluid mentioned, the two columns of acid (contained in the branches), after the current having for a few seconds passed through them, appear to be voltaically polarized.[1] For if the electrodes are removed from the branches and replaced by another pair of platina-wires a delicate galvanometer (of about 2000 coils) on being placed between the latter, indicates a current passing from the acid column, which had been connected with the negative polar wire to that column, which had been in communication with the positive wire; that is to say one column of acid is to the other like zinc to platina.

Having drawn up a paper, in which all my observations regarding the voltaic polarisation of fluid and solid bodies are stated and which, I hope will soon be published by the Bibliothèque universelle[2] as well as by Poggendorff's Annalen,[3] I do no enter now into any more details on that subject; but I cannot help communicating to you my views on the cause of the strange phenomenon in question.

You have shown, that weak currents can pass through electrolytes, without decomposing them; but are we to infer from such a fact, that a current incapable of electrolysing acts in no way whatever upon the electrolytic body? Is it not probable, that the current in question has so much power as to turn all the hydrogen-sides of the molecules of muriatic acid towards the negative electrode and the Chlorine sides towards the positive one, and is it not allowed to suppose, that the current weakens at the same time the affinity of the constituent parts of the

[1] cf. Schœnbeins letter to Berzelius Oct. 14th 1838. Kahlbaum. Briefwechsel p. 25.

[2] Bibl. Univ. T. 18. 1838. p. 166.

[3] Poggend. Annal. Bd. 46. 1838. p. 109.

electrolyte for each other? Now if we admit such a state of things and if it be further supposed that the effect does not immediately cease with its cause, we can, I think, rather easily conceive the way in which the secondary current is produced by the polarized muriatic acid. The particles of Chlorine and Hydrogen composing a molecule of acid will as soon as the current of the pile ceases circulating through the fluid, begin to act upon each other, i. e. enter again into their primitive state of intimate combination. Now such an action being of a chemical nature, a current must be produced by it, as to its direction precisely of the kind as observed. Though I must allow, that my hypothesis is rather bold, yet I cannot conceive another and I am inclined to think that neither the chemical theory of Galvanism nor that of Volta can easily account for the enigmatical phenomenon. Will you be so kind and let me have your views about the strange fact? Before passing to another subject I must not omit to tell you, that it is not only muriatic acid, which is capable of being voltaically polarized, other electrolytic fluids for instance the hydrate of sulphuric acid have the some property. — The controversy about the source of current electricity produced by the common voltaic arrangement is still continued in Germany and there is in that country an obvious leaning towards the views of Volta. The arguments, however, brought forward in favo[u]r of that Theory are, to my opinion at least, by no means such as to be called decisive ones. Mr. Pfaff, for instance thinks the fact, that a current is excited by muriatic acid acting upon chloride of sodium or by a pile charged with an aqueous solution of sulphate of zinc chemically pure, as quite irreconcilable with the principles of the chemical theory.[1] I must confess, that it is beyond my power to conceive, how objections of such a kind can be raised in earnest by such a distinguished philosopher, as Mr. Pfaff is. Will you not come forward and take part in the contest?

[1] Poggend. Annal. Bd. 41. 1840. p. 10.

We must indeed, stick closely together, if we are not to be overpowered, and considered as beaten by our antagonists. At the meeting of the german association at Fribourg I had an opportunity of reconnoitering the field.

I am my very dear Sir
Yours most truly
C. F. SCHOENBEIN.

Schœnbein to Faraday.

My dear Sir

As Mr. Iselin an acquaintance of mine is going to London I cannot let pass this favo[u]rable opportunity without presenting to you my best compliments.

Since I had the hono[u]r to write you my last letter I have been working rather hard in making voltaic researches and I think I may be allowed to say that my endeavours have not proved altogether fruitless. Amongst other facts hitherto not yet well understood I have been trying to clear up by experiment those which refer to the voltaic polarisation of polar wires, the polarisation of electrolytic fluids, the apparent change of the electro-motive power of metals and the secondary piles of Ritter. As far as I am able to judge the results of my researches are such as to throw a strong light upon the cause of the phenomena alluded to and to prove that the latter are only due to ordinary chemical action and that there is no such thing as any change of the electro-chemical nature of any metal or a true voltaic polarisation. The forthcoming number of the Bibliothèque universelle [1] will publish a memoir in which I have given an account of some of my investigations. In the same paper I have pointed out to the attention of

---

[1] Bibl. Univ. T. 23. 1839. p. 189.

philosophers the very remarkable and close analogy that exists between the voltaic action of Chlorine and Bromine and that of the peroxides of Manganese, Lead and Silver. I am almost sure that the way in which I explain the voltaic effects produced by the named substances will very nearly coincide with your views upon the subject. As to the peculiar condition of iron I think I have at last discovered its true cause. Having still some experiments to perform in order to put my theory beyond doubt I will not entertain you with the details of it, I can, however not omit to say that I have reason to consider the peroxide of hydrogen as the immediate cause of the anomalous bearings of inactive iron.

I hope to be able of publishing before long a satisfactory account of all the voltaic phenomena which that metal gives rise to; at the same time I shall communicate a series of new facts regarding the voltaic action of peroxide of hydrogen which by the bye is a most interesting substance in a galvanic point of view.

I am just writing a little work, in which (what the French call) the "galvanisation" of metals[1] is treated of according to the present state of electrical Science and proved by matter-of-fact arguments that the tensile electrical state of bodies does not in the least interfere with the chemical bearings natural to them. You know much better than I do that in a scientific point of view the principle laid down by Sir H. Davy with regard to the subject in question is erroneous and that nevertheless a great many scientific and practical men continue to consider it as true. You will therefore agree with me that it is rather a seasonable undertaking to remove false notions by establishing a true theory of galvanisation.

Do you think it likely that an english bookseller would be inclined to publish a little work (of about 4 sheets) of that

[1] Nouvelle théorie de la galvanisation des métaux. Communicated to the British Association at their meeting held at Birmingham in 1839. Bibl. Univ. T. 23. 1839. p. 189.

description and pay something for its copyright? You will oblige me very much by letting me know your opinion about this matter and give your kind council upon it.

I take the liberty to send you some papers of mine which I published in German last year;[1] that on voltaic polarisation will perhaps be known to you by the Bibl. univ. If you should happen to see Mr. Daniell[2] and Dr. Buckland[3] pray be so kind to deliver to them the parcels inclosed.

These last four or five months I have not seen any number of the Philosophical Magazine (the only scientific journal published in English I have access to at Bâle). I know consequently not the least of what is going on in the philosophical world on the other side of the water.

As to your recent researches on electric induction I am also almost completely unacquainted with their results.

Before closing my letter I take the liberty to recommend to you its bearer Mr. Iselin, he is an excellent young man and belonging to a highly respectable family of Bâle.

       I am my dear Sir
        Yours most truly
Bâle Febr. 18 1839.   C. F. SCHOENBEIN.

Faraday to Schœnbein.

      Royal Institution 8. April 1839.
MY DEAR FRIEND
   I should think that I might be teasing you with a letter unnecessarily by the post were it not that your last contains an enquiry that I think you would wish me to answer.

---

[1] Poggend. Annal. vol. 43. 1838. p. 229 and ibid. vol. 46. 1838. p 109.

[2] John Frederic Daniell F. R. S. professor of Chemistry at Kings College in London from its foundation in 1831, was born in 1790 and died in London in 1845.

[3] William Buckland F. R. S., canon of Christ Church and professor of Mineralogy and Geology at Oxford. He was a Trustee of the British Museum, was born in 1784 at Axminster and died in 1856 at Clapham.

I had not the pleasure to meet your friend Mr. Iselin and now I am writing from the country to which I have gone for the sake of general health. At the time however that it does me good in that respect it cuts me off from access to the Journals so that I hope when I return to see something of what you have been doing.

The points you write about in your letters are of the greatest consequence or at least they appear so to me and the general tenor of my thoughts and conclusions is such as to make me expect that you are in the right. I shall beg to know particularly the conclusions which you establish and the phenomena caused by the peroxide of hydrogen and especially too the full turn and particular history of the Iron actions. That has been a very provoking and stimulating subject; but I was quite sure your perseverance would have at last its full reward and I can say most honestly that I have been as it were merely waiting until you should tell us what it was.

About the proposed work I do not know what to say or advise as to its publication here. What I could wish is one thing and what I ought to urge you to is another. I think you are aware that books are very expensive here, I mean in the getting up and that therefore few if any booksellers will speculate except upon such as may be sure to have a sale. Now science has no such security in England and more is the shame for the country. Do you remember the pamphlet by *Moll*[1] on the *Alleged decline of science in England?*[2] That MS. he sent to me and I tried to get it published. At last I printed it, hoping the sale would defray a part at least of the printers bill which I settled. But strange to say I never received one shilling back towards

---

[1] Gerrit Moll, professor of Mathematics and Physics at Utrecht was born at Amsterdam in 1838 and died in 1875.

[2] Faraday in a letter to R. Phillips dated Sept. 23. 1831 writes: "I understand the new taken by Moll is not at all agreeable to some." S. P. Thompson in his Life of Faraday believes Faraday even had a large share in the production of Moll's paper.

the expences. I tell you this merely to account for my small hopes in your case for I confess I was much damped by the results of my confidence and experience. I have however made some enquiries but have not got farther than this that some booksellers would print and publish the work for you *at your risk* but I intend to go a little farther before I close this letter.

I have been working on electrical induction for some time past and hope by this that you will have received Nrs. XI. XII. XIII & XIV[1] of the experimental researches and that the argument will obtain your consideration and approval. You may think that I am anxious for the judgment which able man may pronounce on my view of the action of the particles of matter in this important electrical function — I am also reprinting the whole series of researches in one volume so as to place them within the reach of some who have inquired after them. That indeed has been the sole object for I expect no return.

These things nearly done I am now thinking of looking at the contact question again in reference to the paper with which Marianini[2] has honoured the VIII[3] series of my researches.[4] I feel in no hurry to do this for I think the point is already determined and that the progress of this part of Electrical knowledge will soon come in as tests and decide the true origin of the electricity in the pile. Nevertheless I mean to experiment and if any thing good arises publish. Adieu for the present my dear Sir

Yours faithfully
M. FARADAY.

[1] Phil. Mag. S. 3. vol. 12. 1838. p. 206. viz 11th series p. 206; 12th p. 426; 13th p. 430.
[2] Stefano Giovanni Marianini L. L. D. professor of Physics at Pavia, Venice and Modena, was born in 1790 at Zeme, Piemont and died in 1866 at Modena.
[3] Phil. Trans. S. 3. 1834. p. 425.
[4] Examination of a fourth experiment adduced by Prof. Faraday in support of M. de la Rive's Theory, and regarded by Dr. Fusinieri to be demonstrative. Mem. di Fis. sperimenti. Modena vol. 2. 1838. p. 1. cf. also Phil. Mag. S 3. vol. 18. 1841. p. 193

29th. April. — Ever since the former date of this letter have I been waiting for answers from booksellers and have only now received one which is of the nature I expected unfavourable. I will delay this letter no longer

Yours most truly
M. FARADAY.

Schœnbein to Faraday.

MY DEAR SIR

Presuming an account of the proceedings of the swiss association for the advancement of Science of last year will not prove disagreeable to you I take the liberty of sending you two copies of it one of which you will perhaps be so kind as to present to the Royal Society. The Gentleman who will deliver them to you is a former pupil of mine M. Burckhardt M. D. of Bâle. He is going to make a stay in London with the intention of getting acquainted with the principal hospitals and scientific establishments of your great metropolis. By furthering in any way you think fit the views of Dr. Burckhardt you will lay me under many obligations and I can assure you that by so doing your kindness will be bestowed upon a young man whose character is excellent and whose family connexions at Bâle are highly respectable.

My leisure time is continually devoted to making voltaic researches and in the course of these two last months I have been lucky enough as to ascertain a series of facts which, to my opinion, will sooner or later become of some importance to organic Chemistry. If possible I shall before long send a paper to the Editors of the Phil. Mag. which will contain a detailed account of my results.

Another subject intimately connected with the chemical theory of Galvanism has taken up much of my time lately. I have made out many cases, where currents are excited apparently quite independent of chemical action. According to the chemical theory of the pile no current ought to be produced by an arrangement consisting for instance of spungy platina, compact platina or gold and strong acetic acid, there coming no chemical action into play in the case. But the fact is that under the circumstances mentioned a current makes its appearance and what is still more strange, that the current during circuits being closed changes its direction in such a manner, that s[p]ungy platina is in the beginning negative and afterwards positive.

Another circumstance also ill agreeing with the theoretical views of the present day is the fact, that Silver and even Copper being placed within acetic acid bear to spungy platina the same voltaic relations as Gold or compact Platina does. All the currents spoken of disappear after having lasted for some time but by introducing bubbles of air into the acid fluid near the metals immersed new currents can be excited. Being convinced of the correctness of the chemical theory of Galvanism I cannot but suspect that the currents in question are due to some (as yet hidden) chemical action proceeding from spungy platina. I shall not spare either pains or time to trace out the true cause of the strange phenomena alluded to.

Flattering myself with the hopes of being soon fav[o]ured with a letter from you I am my dear Sir

                                      Yours most truly

Bâle April 21. 1839.   C. F. SCHŒNBEIN.

Schœnbein to Faraday.

Bâle July 3. 1839.

MY DEAR SIR

I am very much obliged to you for your very kind letter of the 28th[1] of April and I offer you my most sincere

---

[1] cf. postscript to Faradays letter of the 8th of April p. 81.

thanks for your friendly endeavours to get for my manuscript a publisher. What you had the kindness to communicate to me regarding that affair induced me to abandon the idea of having my little work[1] published in English, I should like however very much to lay its principal contents before the association in Birmingham[2] and to submit the results of my late researches to the consideration of the british philosophers and most particularly to yours.

As I think to be able to prove by facts that the electrical state of bodies has no influence whatsoever upon their chemical bearings i. e. that the very first principle of the electro-chemical theory of Berzelius is erroneous; as I am also prepared to show that the protection of metals for instance of copper or iron against the chemical action of seawater being apparently effected by voltaic means has directly nothing to do with the play of electrical forces and as I am pretty sure to have found out the true theory of what is called the galvanization of metals and so have accurately determined the circumstances under which an (apparent) change of the chemical relations of the metallic bodies is effected I should suppose that communications of such a kind would prove rather acceptable to the association and be received with some interest by them. Desirous, however, as I am of attending the meeting at Birmingham I am afraid I shall not be able of crossing the water on account of the great expense which such a journey would occasion to me. Certainly if there were a chance of the association's granting some money for the purpose of continuing the researches on the subjects alluded to I should not hesitate to undertake the journey. Now if it would not be too importunate on my part I should venture to ask you the favo[u]r of letting me know your opinion upon that point.

[1] Nouvelle théorie de la galvanisation des métaux. Bibl. Univ. T. 23. 1839. p. 189.

[2] Communicated to the British Association at their meeting held at Birmingham in 1839.

By the same mail I send you this letter a paper of mine is forwarded to the Editors of the Phil. Mag. which treats of a peculiar voltaic arrangement[1] being in some respects the very reverse from what our ordinary hydro-electric circles are. The memoir contains at the same time the statement of some curious facts which seem to refute the principle laid down by de la Rive[2] and Becquerel[3] according to which any sort of chemical action is capable of producing a current. These gentlemen laboured to my humble opinion under a great mistake in making such an assertion and I am inclined to think that the views the philosopher of Geneva takes of Galvanism at large and of the pile in particular are very far from being correct and founded upon facts.

Within a short time I shall publish the details of the results of my researches regarding that interesting question and I imagine that it will be no very difficult task to me, to demonstrate that the oxidation of any metal caused by nitric acid etc. does not throw the least quantity of electricity into circulation and that it is only to the chemical action of electrolytic bodies that we must ascribe the power of exciting currents.

Your important discoveries regarding the intimate connexion which exists between electrolysation and current-electricity have, as far as I understand the subject, not yet been duly appreciated by the philosophers of the the Continent and least so by de la Rive and Becquerel.

I hope your stay in the country will have entirely reestablished your health and enabled you to resume your wonted scientific occupations. I am now left alone in Bâle, my family having gone into the mountains of the Jura to spend the summer

---

[1] Notice on some peculiar voltaic arrangements. Phil. Mag. S. 3. vol. 15. 1839. S. 136.

[2] Phil. Mag. S. 3 vol. 11. 1837. p. 274. vide also Annal. de Chem. et Phys. vol. 37. 1828. p. 225 and vol. 39. p. 297.

[3] Annal. de Chimie T. 23. 1323. p. 135.

there; as soon, however, as the vacations will have begun, I shall join them. A six week's living on the heights of the Jura and breathing the pure air of the hills would, perhaps, do you a great deal of good; can you not manage it to come over to us? I should be exceedingly happy, if I could ramble about with you in our valleys und wander in your company from one crag to another.

Entertaining the pleasing hopes of seeing you sooner or later I am my dear Sir
Your's most sincerely
C. F. SCHOENBEIN.

Faraday to Schœnbein.

Royal institution 17. August 1839.

MY DEAR SIR

I ought to have written to you sooner but I have hitherto been unable to say whether I could go to the Meeting at Birmingham or not. I find now that *I cannot*. As regards any opinion that I can form respecting their appropriation of funds; not having been at any of the Commitees I do not know on what principles they proceed but I am told they have not as yet granted money except for expts. in England or by Englishmen but I cannot suppose that is a rule. At the same time I should be afraid to give you any impression which might lead to error.

I shall be most anxious for your researches especially those bearing upon the necessity of electrolytes in the current and the inutility of bodies not acting as electrolytes yet poss[ess]ing oxidizing powers etc. I suppose that your explications will include Becquerels pile of acid and alkali about which much is now said and I presume properly also. But folks are so apt to neglect the **amount** of action that I cannot trust all I hear of it; I hear it is very energetic and very effective etc. but I do not hear how much current force is produced for a certain amount of acid and alcaline force used.

I hope you are now in excellent health and all your family. I never think of the time when I was in Bâle a few years ago without regret since being there I did *not* see you.

I am My dear Sir
Your faithful Snt.
M. FARADAY.

Faraday to Schœnbein.

Royal Institution 24. Septbr. 1839.

MY DEAR SCHOENBEIN

I leave town this afternoon for a week or ten days to join my wife at Hastings and least I should not see you again write this note as a remembrance. I have been pulled about a good deal or I should have looked after you but I expect you have been out of town until to day.

You left a number of the Bibliotheque Universelle here which I join with this note least any mistake should arise respecting it. I have read your paper carefully and the effects are certainly very remarkable.

If I do not see you again I wish you a most happy return to your family and the delight of finding them all in excellent health.

I shall send this note etc. to Blackfriars road where I hope it will find you.

Remember me to Cooper.[1]

I am, dear Sir, Yours faithfully Snt.
M. FARADAY.

[1] He was staying with John Thomas Cooper, teacher of Chemistry at the Russel Institute and subsequently at the Aldersgate School of Medicine in London. He was born in 1790 at Greenwich and died in 1854 in London.

Schœnbein to Faraday.

My dear Sir

I was very sorry indeed, I could not have the pleasure of bidding personally farewell to you before my leaving England and of expressing viva voce my thanks for the many proofs of kindness and friendship which I received from you during my late stay at London. Several times I called at the Royal Institution with the view of seeing you but to my infinite regret I invariably received the disappointing answer: Mr. Faraday is not at home, he is still in the country. I will not conceal it from you that I intended to take up much more of your precious time than I actually did and that my principal view in visiting England was to enjoy as often as possible the society of that philosopher to whom I feel myself attached by a sort of intellectual affinity and by feelings of congeniality more than to any other man. I ardently wish and confidently hope it will fall to my lot to see you once more in this world and to have an opportunity of making good again what accidental circumstances made me lose. I am just now reading the accounts of your late researches on electrical induction [1] and I cannot help telling you that some of your results appear to me to be of the utmost importance and such as to throw a strong light upon a series of highly interesting phenomena and particularly upon that of electrolysation. The fact that electrical induction is an action of contiguous particles seems to me to vie in interest with any other discovery ever made in electrical science and what I am only surprized at is the circumstance, that amongst our continental philosophers that fact has not yet met with that attention which it so eminently deserves. I am however confident that before long the subject will be taken up and excite general interest.

[1] Experimental researches in Electricity 11, 12 and 13 series. On induction, Phil. Trans. 1838. p. 1. p. 83. p. 125. Poggend. Annal. Bd. 44. 1839. S. 1 u. 537; Bd. 47. 1839. S. 33, 271 u. 529; Bd. 48. 1839. S. 269, 424 u. 513.

A most extraordinary circumstance at first sight is, that magneto-electrical and voltaic induction do apparently not depend upon such a molecular action. What are we to conclude from that difference? Though I am not fond of making conjectures on dark subjects, still I cannot help starting some hypothetical ideas regarding the point in question. It appears to me that what we call static electricity is only a state of tendency of something to move in certain direction and that current-electricity is the actual motion of that something. That motion must not be considered as one of weighty particles but as a motion of something that is not affected by gravity; as a peculiar motion of ether if you like. According to these hypothetical views we can easily conceive, how a vibratory motion might be propagated through a space or medium empty of weighty particles but filled up with some imponderable matter which is capable of being brought into a moving state. The only thing difficult to conceive is the relation of that imponderable agency to the weighty particles in their natural and excited condition that is to say the way in which both are acting upon each other. It is possible that a state of tendency to motion may be brought about in ether only by a peculiar action of ponderable particles upon that fluid and that consequently such a state cannot exist in it without the presence or agency of matter, whilst moving ether of itself has the power to impart motion to ether being at rest. The fact that currents of perceptible energy can make their appearance only in matter is perhaps dependent upon a considerable condensation of the ethereal fluid round the ponderable particles and it may be that the degree of the conducting and inducteous power of a substance is proportionate to the density of ether contained in it, as for instance the degree of density of the air is proportionate to its conducting power of sound. Vague and venturous as all these views may appear they are perhaps at the present state of electrical science the only ones which we are able to conceive.

In the last number of Poggendorff's Annalen there is a very interesting paper of Jacobi[1] to which I take the liberty to direct your attention. The german philosopher proves in it by a matter of fact argument that the amount of magnetic power produced by any voltaic arrangement is always proportionate to the chemical effects of the latter or that what is called the intensity of a current is not independent of its quantity.[2]

Bearer of these lines Mr. Bachofen[3] Juris Doctor of Bâle a friend of mine and an excellent young man is making a stay in England with the view of getting acquainted with your laws and administration of justice, he is therefore very much desirous of being introduced to some eminent english lawyers and judges. As you have perhaps some means to procure to my friend such a sort of acquaintance I should be very much obliged to you if you would be kind enough to render to Mr. Bachofen that favour.

Pray remember me most friendly to Mrs. Faraday and believe me to be
        Yours
       most sincerely
Bâle Dec. 17th 1839.   C. F. SCHOENBEIN.

Schœnbein to Faraday.[4]

MY DEAR FARADAY

Having of late been much taken up with researches of a peculiar sort and obtained results from them which I am vain enough to think not entirely unworthy of your notice I

---

[1] Moritz Hermann von Jacobi, originally an architect in Prussia, was a Member of the Academy of Science at St. Petersburg. Born in 1801, died in 1874.

[2] Poggend. Annal. Bd. 48. 1839. p. 26.

[3] Johann Jacob Bachofen was born in 1815 at Bâle. In 1842 he became professor of Roman Law at Bâle, but resigned in 1848.

[4] This letter was read at the meeting of the Royal Society held on May 7. 1840 and a short abstract appeared Phil. Mag. S. 3. vol. 17. 1840. p. 293 under the

take the liberty to give you a short account of my doings. The phosphorous smell which is developped when electricity (to speak the profane language) is passing from the points of a conductor into air or when lightn'ng happens to fall upon some terrestrial object, or when water is electrolysed, has been engaging my attention the last couple of years and induced me to make many attempts at clearing up that mysterious phenomenon. Though baffled for a long time, at last I think I have have succeeded so far as to have got the clue which will lead to the discovery of the true cause of the smell in question. The facts which refer to that subject are as follows:

1. The phosphorous smell given off during the electrolysation of water is only disengaged at the positive electrode and no trace of it at the negative one.

2. The odoriferous principle can be preserved in well closed glass bottles for any length of time.

3. The disengagement of that smell depends

   a) upon the nature of the metal constituting the positive electrode

   b) upon the chemical constitution of the (electrolytic) fluid being placed between the electrodes

   c) upon the temperature of that fluid. With reference to

   α) I have to state that of all metals examined by me it is only gold and platina which do yield the smell. The more readily oxidable metals as well as charcoal will not allow the disengagement of that principle, not even iron though this substance when acting the part of the positive electrode resembles so very much the precious metals. As to

---

following heading: "On the odour accompanying electricity and on the probability of its dependencé on the presence of a new substance." Copious corrections (presumably in the handwriting of the Secretary, Mr. S. H. Christie) have been omitted; the letter is here given just as Schoenbein wrote it.

β) I have found out that the smell is disengaged out of dilute (chemically pure) sulphuric, phosphoric, nitric acid, of aqueous solutions of many salts, and that it is never obtained from common or strong nitric acid, from solutions of protosulphate of iron or any substance having a great affinity for oxigen, from aqueous solutions of chlorides, bromides, jodides, muriatic acid, hydrobromic acid etc. If only a small quantity of nitrous acid, protosulphate of iron, protochloride of iron or of tin be added to dilute sulphuric, phosphoric, nitric acid, the disengagement of the odoriferous principle will not take place. With reference to an aqueous solution of potash I have made the curious observation that sometimes it yields the smell and sometimes it does not; even dilute sulphuric acid exhibits that anomaly but very rarely. .I have not yet been able to ascertain the cause of that phenomenon. With reference to

δ) I have made out that any electrolytic fluid which is capable of disengaging the phosphorous smell at a moderate temperature will not yield it when heated near its boiling point.

4. If a comparatively small quantity of powdered charcoal, iron, zinc, tin, lead, antimony, bismuth, arsenic or some drops of mercury are thrown into a bottle containing the odorous principle (received at the positive electrode) the smell will be very quickly, almost instantaneously destroyed. Charcoal powder and iron filings act the most rapidly. The same effect is produced by pouring a small portion of nitrous or common fuming nitric acid or solutions of protosulphate of iron, protochloride of iron or of tin into such a bottle. If platina or gold be brought in a red-hot state into the vessel, the smell will also be annihilated.

5. If platina or gold plate be plunged only for a few seconds into an atmosphere of oxigen gas having been disengaged at the positive electrode and exhibiting the peculiar smell the metals mentioned will be powerfully polarized in the negative way, just in the same manner as if they had been plunged into the vapours of bromine or chlorine. But to obtain that effect it is necessary that the metals be not covered with moisture. The thinnest film of water surrounding their surface will prevent them from assuming the electro-negative condition. To a very slight degree copper acts like gold or platina. I was not able to polarize zinc, brass, iron.

6. Gold and platina being heated are incapable of assuming the polar state.

7. If a piece of platina be polarized in the way before mentioned and afterwards brought for a few moments into an atmosphere of hydrogen the electro-motive power of the metal will be destroyed (if not too long kept in the latter gas). The some effect is obtained by heating the polarized plate.

8. A polarized stripe of gold or platina plate preserves its voltaic condition for some time in the open air.

9. The current produced by polarized gold or platina is of a short duration.

10. Oxigen having been deprived of its odoriferous principle by the means indicated at 4 for instance by charcoal has altogether lost its polarizing power and you may keep platina as long you like within such oxigen, the metal will never acquire any perceptible degree of voltaic polarity.

11. If a stripe of clean platina or gold plate be held opposite to a blunt point of a metallic rod (which is attached to the first conductor of a well working common electrical machine) at a distance of about an inch or so, few turns of the glass-plate will be sufficient to polarize to a sensible degree the metallic stripe. The voltaic state excited in the metal

under these circumstance is the electro-negative one. I made my experiments with a platina plate 1½ inch long and ⅓ of an inch wide; after having alternately exposed the two sides of my plate to the action of the electrical brush (produced at blunt point of the rod) for about 25 seconds I obtained a deviation of 170°. The fluid into which I plunged the plate was water containing ⅑ of sulphuric acid and my galvanometer made use of is provided with 2000 and some hundreds coils. Gold acts in the same way as platina does, copper is very slightly polarized under these circumstances but not so zinc, iron and brass; at least I could not succeed to excite in the latter metals that voltaic condition.

12. Gold or platina is negatively polarized whether being held in the hand or insulated.

13. The same metals do not assume the polar state if they are attached to the first conductor i. e. if the electricity is made to pass from those metals into the surrounding air.

14. Gold and platina are negatively polarized be the first conductor charged with positive or negative electricity.

15. If those metals are covered with the thinnest film of moisture they are incapable of being polarized by the electrical brush, neither is the peculiar voltaic condition called forth in them when they are exposed to the action in a heated state.

16. When the point from which the brush issues is heated or wetted cold or dry gold and platina will also not be polarized by the latter (brush).

17. That point being heated or moistened* does not disengage the phosphorous smell.

18. The brush having been deprived by any means of its peculiar smell has entirely lost its polarizing power.

* The best way to destroy the electrical smell or rather to piece its appearance is to envelop the blunt point with a peace of linen impregnated with distilled water.

19. Platina being negatively polarized by common electricity loses its electro-motive power when plunged into an atmosphere of hydrogen for a few seconds and the same effect is obtained by heating the metal.

20. In common air the polarized gold or platina preserves its peculiar voltaic state for some hours.

21. The current produced by these (polarized) metals are of so short a duration, that they may be considered as instantaneous

It seems to me that the above mentioned facts allow some important conclusions to be drawn from and a series of conjectures to be founded upon. Allow me to mention some of them.

- a) The peculiar smell produced by lightning, common electricity and the voltaic current is due to some particular gazeous body
- b) The voltaic and chemical bearings of that body are very similar to those of chlorine and bromine.
- c) Water, atmospheric air and perhaps all sorts of matter do contain an electrolyte whose anion is the odoriferous principle in question and whose cation is most likely hydrogen.
- d) That electrolyte is decomposed by lightning, common electricity and the voltaic current and its odoriferous anion liberated.
- e) The polarizing or electromotive power of that anion is resulting from its great tendency to unite with the hydrogen of water etc. It acts in that respect like chlorine or bromine.
- f) The chemical affinity of the odoriferous substance for other bodies is such as to surpass with respect to intensity that of most, perhaps of all what they call electronegative elements.
- g) The electrolyte spoken of being present in water and atmospheric air it is probable that that compound acts

an important part in the house-hold of nature and it is not unlikely that its workings are closely connected with the more general electrical phenomena of our globe.

My first Idea was that the smell in question might be due to a compound being produced at the positive elektrode by some secondary action, but the whole body of facts above-mentioned are to my opinion not favorable to such a view. To raise my conclusions and conjectures to undoubtful certainty, the supposed elementary substance must be obtained pure and in an insulated state. The beautiful voltaic arrangement of our friend Mr. Grove can alone make us arrive at that end and I shall write to him in order to engage his attention to that subject. What I have communicated to you, is as you will easily perceive a very rough and imperfect sketch of the results of my late researches. The subject is far from being exhausted and requires a good deal more of experimental investigation. I hardly want to tell you that I am working night and day to get deeper into the mine and nearer to its hidden treasures. In the report I have to lay before the british association next autumn a detailed account of my investigations will be given and I hope it will be such as to be considered as not being quite void of scientific interest.

If you should think the contents of my letter important enough as to merit the attention of the royal Society or the royal institution you are entirely at liberty to communicate them to those learned bodies. I have not yet made them known in any continental journal or to any society except to our philosophical society at Bâle.

The other day I saw in Galignani's Sunday Observer a very imperfect account of your last paper read before the Royal Society on the source of current-electricity.[1] Some of

[1] Read in part on March 19th and concluded at the meeting of March 26th 1840. The paper was entitled: Researches in Electricity, 17th series. On the source of power in the Voltaic Pile.

your proofs for the truth of the chemical theory of Galvanism were mentioned and to my opinion they are such as to leave no doubt about the subject. But I am afraid the philosophers of the north will hear no reason, and find out some new piece of sophistry in order to keep up their favorite hypothesis.

Our friend Grove wrote me the other day[1] communicating to me some very interesting results of his late researches with which you are no doubt acquainted. What do you think about the fact that the transfer or oxidation of particles in the voltaic arc is definite for a definite current?[2] Important as such a fact is I cannot yet understand it, that is to say, I cannot conceive that by the simple oxidation of the positive electrode the current can be conducted in the same way as by electrolysis, both actions being so very different from each other.

From Mr. Grove's letter I also learned to my infinite regret that you are not yet enjoying perfect health.[3]

My dear Faraday allow me to repeat my former request and permit me to readvise you not to overwork yourself and to manage a little your mental and physical forces, for your health and life are most precious to your friends in particular and to the scientific world at large. We cannot yet spare you and you must continue to be our leader for many years

[1] March 7. 1840.
[2] With a battery of 36 zinc and platina pairs he found that the spark taken between platina points in pure oxygen diminishes the volume of the gas; consequently platina is slightly oxidable by the voltaic heat. In pure Hydrogen not the slightest difference is observable between the two electrodes, wheter the zinc be positive and platina negative or vice versa. "I endeavoured" he continues "and not without some success to prove that the transfer or detachment of particles in the voltaic arc is definite for a definite current" By taking the discharges in a graduated vessel of atmospheric air to which a little oxygen had been added, between a positive point of zinc and a negative point of platina, he found that the quantity of oxygen absorbed by the deflagration bore to the oxygen evolved a ratio of $1 \cdot 00$ to $1 \cdot 17$.
[3] "I saw Dr. Faraday yesterday" he writes "he is far from well I regret to say."

to come. But to have our wishes accomplished and our hopes realized you ought to listen a little to the entreaties of your friends and to grant to your mind and body some rest. I am sure Mrs Faraday will be of my opinion and confident she will not cease reminding you of it.

Pray remember me most friendly to your Lady and let me have before long good tidings from you.

     Believe me, my dear Faraday
         yours faithfully
Bâle April 4th 1840.   C. F. SCHOENBEIN.

Faraday to Schœnbein. [1]

Brighton 24 April 1840.

MY DEAR SCHOENBEIN

Here I am in the country again, to which I often run for a short period each time for the good of my health. It refreshes me and makes me able to get on with the duties of the season. Your last letter I received just before I left town and though I have it not here and cannot pretend to remember it yet shall give you a sort of an acknowledgment. It is certainly very important and you seem to me to have got a good hold of the subject so that I feel sure you will pull it entirely out of its hole and before you have done will let us know *all* about it. The many facts you bring to bear on the matter and the way in which you make their relations evident is most striking. I am waiting most anxiously for the full development of the partially known anion. If you do succeed in establishing its independent existence and obtaining it in sensible

---

[1] The deciphering of this letter of Faraday's was attended with anusual difficulties.

quantities (by weight) it will be really a wonderful thing. But what cannot electricity do and what deeper and more refined searcher-out is there in experimental philosophy than it.

The smell at the positive pole or electrode I had often observed and I will tell you what happened to me respecting it as I was working on the *Voltameter*.[1] In trying the definite inductions of that instrument I had made the same platina plate positive many times in succession and observed in consequence that the peculiar smell of the evolved gas diminished (the fluid was dilute Sulphuric acid). Knowing at that time that the Pos. pole gave the smell, the observation led me to go in rendering the same plate positive, and at last I obtained mixed gases from the instrument which *had not* the smell in question and when afterwards I obtained more gas, making the contacts in the *same way,* still there was no smell. There was a darkish deposit upon the platina plate which had been so often rendered positive, which gradually appeared, as the uniform application of the voltaic battery to the plates went on, but having attained this state of the instrument, I now made that plate negative, which had been so long positive and that Pos. which had been Neg. and now the gas evolved had its full smell as before. I made contact in that direction till smell was exhausted and then reversing contact it again appeared. Other things then took me off from this *scent.*

As to your letter and its matter I did not know what to do with it, for as you said the expts. would be printed in your Report for the association, so they could not according to their rules print them in the Phil. Transactions, if they had agreed as to the matter; I then thought of sending it to the Philosophical Magazine but at last gave it to the Secretary of the Royal Society, Mr. Christie, to read[2] and if Council thought fit to notice in the proceedings and in the mean time thought I would tell

[1] Sept. 1832.
[2] Phil. Mag. S. 3. vol. 17. 1840. p. 293.

you. After the reading I can withdraw it and then send it to the Phil. Magazine at once. It ought to be published somewhere and *directly*. You probably know the Royal Society will read a paper but however good its character they do not print it in the Transactions if it is intended to go anywhere else first.

Your doubts of Groves[1] announcement of a definite transfer of matter accross air etc. coincide with my own. I cannot deny it but it is a thing so peculiar that it requires the most convincing proofs. Many thanks for your encouragement about induction. Hare[2] has written me a letter in Silliman's Journal[3] which I have just been answering here.[4] His criticismus have not yet driven me from my ground. As to dynamic induction I wont attack that again. I perceive you have had since notice of my papers on the origin of electricity in the voltaic pile. As soon as printed you shall have the papers. I experimented very carefully for my own conviction and have come to De la Rive's view exactly as regards the origin. I say nothing of his theory of the pile as an instrument consisting of many voltaic elements. There I do not go with him.

I am most grateful for your very kind expressions. They encourage and cheer me when I feel low. Understand me, I mean your kind expressions as a friend and after my health which in the whole is pretty well. But the memory goes. Your friend Mr. Bachofen has been here and I hope enjoyed himself you know that I should not make company for him, for my retiring habits are likely to increase rather than diminish and

[1] Phil. Mag. S. 3 vol. 16. 1840. p. 338.
[2] Robert Hare M. D. Professor of Chemistry at Philadelphia, was born in 1781 and died in 1858 at Philadelphia.
[3] A letter to Prof. Faraday, on certain theoretical opinions. Silliman. Journ. Vol. 38. 1840. N° 1. vide also Phil. Mag. S. 3 vol. 17. 1840. p 44.
[4] An answer to Dr. Hare's letter on certain theoretical opinions. Phil. Mag. S. 3 vol. 17. 1840. p. 54.

it is for those I already know, amongst which you are a principal one, that I wish to keep my thoughts. I am ever

My dear Schœnbein
Your obliged and faithful friend
M. FARADAY.

Schœnbein to Faraday.

MY DEAR FARADAY.

Only to show you that I am still alive and have not entirely forgotten my dear friend in the Royal Institution I am taking up my pen to write a few lines. — Having these last six months been obliged to lecture a good deal I could not find much leisuretime for carrying on my investigations on "ozone" and for that reason I am unable to communicate to you any scientific news from me. After Christmas I shall however set to work again and renew my attempts at insulating the principle which produces the electrical smell.

Berzelius[1] wrote me the other day and invited me to continue my researches on the subject alluded to in so flattering and encouraging a manner that I cannot help complying with the wishes expressed by such an authority. The swedish philosopher is much inclined to adopt the views I have taken of the subject and thinks it highly probable that there exists an electrolytic body being composed of ozone and hydrogen and invariably associated with water just in the same way as, according to the most recent results of Mr. B., chloride of sodium is always found to be accompanied by small traces of bromide and Jodide of Sodium. Berzelius says in his letter that if I should happen to succeed in insulating ozone such a result

[1] Nov. 3. 1840. Kahlbaum. Briefwechsel. p. 40.

would constitute one of the most brilliant discoveries ever made in chemical science. My object now is to get at my disposal a pile of great electrolysing power, a pile, of course, being constructed after Grove's principle. My pecuniary means being of rather a limited nature I do not know yet how to arrive at my end, a pile, being such as I think it ought to be in order to enable me of working out my subject, would perhaps cost £ 80—100. Do you think it likely that some institution or some private individual in London or England would be inclined to lend me for some time an apparatus of the description desired?

I have not yet seen abstracts from your late paper on the source of voltaic electricity in the german scientific periodicals. Is it perhaps not yet published? The germans and Poggendorff at the head of them are getting daily deeper involved into the meshes of the contact-theory. I am rather anxious to see your recent results made known in my country as soon as possible. If you could send me a copy of it I would myself translate the memoir and make some proper comments upon its contents.

Pray pay my best respects to Mrs. Faraday and believe me
Yours
most sincerely
Bâle Dec. 20th 1840. C. F. SCHOENBEIN.

Faraday to Schœnbein.

Royal Institution 27. March 1841

MY DEAR SCHOENBEIN

I write, not because I have any thing to say, but because I should be glad to attach a link to memory's chain that you may not forget me, as well also as to rejoice with you in your activity, though it reminds me that I have very little at present of my own.

My medical friends have required me to lie bye for a twelvemonth and give me hopes that memory (without it is very hard work to go on) may perhaps come on. They want to persuade me that I am mentally fatigued and I have no objection to think so. My own notion is, I am permanently worse: we shall see. Now for the principle the ozone, have you proceeded further with it yet? As to the battery, I have mentioned the matter of your last letter to some persons but have not much to say to you in consequence. Grove has had a powerful battery of his own construction but you know him as well as I do would I conclude if you thought fit apply to him.

You letter though dated 20th Dec. 1841, speaks as if you had not received my last papers, those on the chemical action of the voltaic element etc. I trust you have had them long since; for me I have been laid bye so long as almost to have forgotten them.

Neither have I read much lately so that I seem quite out of the knowledge of things. But nothing can make me forget *your kind feelings* and it is to ..... them[1] and to preserve them I now write, for there value seems to grow upon me whilst that of mere philosophy seems to decrease.

But I must conclude. My wife desires to be friendly remembered to you and hopes that all yours are well. We both desire your happiness.

Ever my dear Schœnbein
Yours faithfull
M. FARADAY.

[1] The verb between to and them is missing in the original.

Schœnbein to Faraday.

My dear Faraday

It was indeed with heartfelt joy and no small degree of pleasure that I received the other day your kind letter, though its contents are not quite such as I had wished them to be. I am however confident that the predictions of your medical friends will be fully realized and a temporary relaxation and abstinence from mental exertions go a great way in restoring the primitive elasticity of your mind and all the powers of your memory. To a certain degree I can speak from my own experience for after having worked rather too hard and overstrained a little too much my intellectual faculties I felt more than once a sort of mental drowsiness coming upon me and an ebbing of spirits which made me almost entirely unfit for any thing requiring a certain degree of moral force but the healing powers of time and quietness gave me always quickly back the freshness of my mind and why should this not be the case with you?

A temporary change of air and social relations would according to my humble opinion do a great deal of good to you for I cannot help thinking that the thick and heavy atmosphere of London in connexion with its neverceasing noise and bustle must be very far from proving congenial and beneficial to your constitution. On the other hand I am almost sure that inhaling for a couple of months the light and ethereal air of our mountainous regions would produce wonderful effects upon your frame and be the true panacea for your complaint. You have, my dear Faraday, no idea of the delicious sensations which alpine nature never fails exciting and you cannot imagine how refreshing, bracing and invigorating a montain life of some weeks duration only proves to be. I have often seen men mentally and bodily fatigued going to the heights of the Rigi or other spots of a similar kind and returning replete with health and good spirits, after having spent no more than a month there.

Can you not make up your mind for carrying such a plan into execution and coming over to Switzerland in the course of next summer, say July or August, the best season for making a stay in the higher parts of our country? I know a certain place in the Canton of Vaud being not very far from the lake of Geneva and delightfully situated near the entrance of the valley of Valais which I am almost sure you would like very much. They call it Bex and it is the residence of my friend Mr. Charpentier[1] director of the salt-works there, an eminent geologist and what is still more valuable the most amiable and good-natured man you can possibly meet with, who would do any thing in his power to make your temporary stay at Bex as agreeable as possible. There you could live quite to your taste, move about entirely at your ease and remain thoroughly unmolested from unwished-for visitors and other inconveniences of town life. And if you had no objections to it, I should feel most happy to act as your cicerone for a week or two. Pray think seriously of my proposals and do not reject them at once for they have proceeded not from any selfish views, that is to say from the wish of enjoying your personal presence in my country, though I openly confess that your visit would make me a most happy man no! they have originated in the purest and most disinterested motives of friendship. I hope Mrs. Faraday will be a warm supporter of my idea and readily enter into my views.

In case you should feel inclined to spend part of the summer in Switzerland, pray let me know your mind as soon as you can in order to enable me of taking the preliminary steps with Mr. Charpentier.

[1] Johann G F. Charpentier, manager of saltworks at Bex was born in 1786 (or 1787) at Freiberg in Saxony. He was Honorary Professor of Geology at the Academy of Lausanne and died at Bex in 1855.

How I would glory if my counsels should be followed up and lead to those results which I am now anticipating from them.

Though I have not been altogether idle this winter I have done very little in the way of scientific research, lectures and other sorts of unphilosophical occup[ations] having taken up all my leisure time. With the beginning of May I trust I shall be able to commence working again and that the ozone will be the very first subject I shall take into my hands is hardly necessary to say. But my small battery, from which I can get only 15 cubic inches of mixt gases per minute will, I am afraid, not furnish a sufficient quantity of the subtle principle; I shall however try to make the best of it.

I am very sorry to tell you, that your last papers have not yet reached Bâle which makes me fear that they are lost. Pray remember me kindly to Mrs. Faraday and believe me

Your's
most faithfully

Bâle April 8th 1841.   C. F. SCHOENBEIN.

Faraday to Schœnbein.

Royal Institution 4 June 1841

MY DEAR SCHOENBEIN

I must write you but a short note for I feel the need of doing all to procure rest, but I could not longer let your most kind letter pass unnoticed. Such feeling is too valuable to allow me to run any risk of letting you suppose I do not estimate it and more, feel greatly cheered by it. I think we shall be in Switzerland this year but the advice to me is to avoid all towns, all friends and all scientific thought or occupation. We shall be lead in part by the progress of things and though I may not see you do not think it will be whithout some sorrow if I found that must be the case. If we are at or near Basel you will see me. Whether we shall see Bex or not is doubtful but I shall take your letter with me and if there, shall go to M. Charpentier with it.

As to science I know nothing of its progress at present; hereafter perhaps. In the mean time I feel the good affect of rest and am, when resting, well in health and happy in thought.

Ever My dear Schœnbein
Yours affectionately
M. FARADAY.

I am ashamed to make you pay any postage for this but cannot help it. M. F.

Faraday to Schœnbein.

Zug 7. Septr. 1841

MY DEAR SCHOENBEIN

I write from this place to say that we expect to be at Bâle in our very rapid passage homewards on Monday or Tuesday next, but are not sure. If you will have your papers ready I will call on you as soon as we arrive. I hope we shall find you, Madame Schœnbein and the family quite well and hope you will make our best respects. We have been pretty well on or Journey, but just now some of us are suffering from bad colds. I think however they are leaving us. We have been round to Bienne, Berne, Thun, Brientz, Interlaken, Grindelwald, Hospenthal, Lucerne etc. including the Wengernalps, the Gemmi, the Grimsel etc. and now must go home. Trusting to find you happy, active and well I am

My dear friend
Yours Ever
M. FARADAY.

Schœnbein to Faraday.

MY DEAR FRIEND.

Mr. Forbes passing on his journey to Scotland through London I send through him a few lines to you with the view of letting you know that your kind letters arrived here when I was absent from Bâle. I could therefore not answer them nor charge you with the papers, I intended to forward through your kindness to England. Nevertheless I thank you very much for your goodness. I was very glad indeed to learn that you were doing pretty well when you left Switzerland and must ardently hope, that you will feel for a long time the beneficial effects of your stay at Zug. You will lay me under great obligations by favouring me with a few lines and letting know your friend, how you are now and how you performed your way home. May the answer be such as true friendship and heartfelt sympathy must wish it to be. My wife and children are quite well and the former was indeed very sorry for not having seen you once more before your departure; for you must know that she is a great admirer of you and that you are standing very high in her graces since your visit. Pray remember me kindly to Mrs. Faraday and accept the assurance of my being

Yours most truly

Bâle Sept. 27th 1841. C. F. SCHOENBEIN.

I was in the greatest hurry when I wrote these lines and you will therefore be kind enough to excuse my bad writing.

Faraday to Schœnbein.

Royal Institution 14. Octr. 1841.

MY DEAR SCHOENBEIN

I write a very hasty note in reply to your kind letter by Mr. Forbes to say we are here safe and well and happy to be at home again. I feel myself exceedingly well in health. Memory is where it was, but if I do not make too many or too early calls upon it perhaps it may improve. I regretted much that I could not see you or Madame Schœnbein again, but was obliged to give up the thought. Give my most respectful and earnest remembrances to her. I rejoice that you have that greatest source of earthly happiness, the source of happiness at home.

I know nothing of scientific matters and have not looked at a Journal yet. I have nothing to write you and am ashamed to send you this letter and would not do it, *making you pay double postage*, but that you have desired it

Ever My dear friend
Truly yours
M. FARADAY.

Schœnbein to Faraday.

MY DEAR FARADAY

You can hardly imagine how gratified I felt at the contents of your last letter short as it was. You are well again and by that I understand that you have become the Faraday of former days, that your health is entirely reestablished, that your spirits have regained their wonted elasticity and that you are allowed to resume your favo[u]rite studies. I did certainly not learn quite so much from your own note; an article however which I saw in some english paper contained statements going that length. I congratulate you upon that happy state of things from all my heart and do confidently hope that you will enjoy for many years to come that degree of health without which life is hardly a desirable gift. "Modus est in rebus" do the classics say, and pray, my dear friend, mind that maxim, i. e. do not any more overwork yourself and manage both your mental and physical powers. You have already done enough for Science and if there is any man being entitled to the enjoyment of "otium cum dignitate" it is you, my dear Faraday.

I wonder whether you will guess at the author of the work[1] of which I am charged to forward you a copy. I should think you know him well enough.

These last three months I have been rather busy in my laboratory. My investigations turned upon the electrolysing power of simple voltaic circles and to the peculiar condition of iron.

As to both the subjects I was fortunate enough to ascertain a series of novel facts which, I trust, will render some little service to the chemical theory of voltaic electricity. I intend to publish my results in one of the next numbers of de la Rive's "Archives".[2]

Mrs. Schœnbein is quite well and charges me with her best compliments to you and Mrs. Faraday

Believe me
Yours
most sincerely

Bâle, April 9 1842.   C. F. Schoenbein.

Pray be so kind to forward the parcels inclosed to their respective destinations, by such an act of kindness you will very much oblige

Your
friend S.

[1] Mitteilungen aus dem Reisetagebuche eines deutschen Naturforschers. Basel 1842. An anonymous pamphlet by Schœnbein, extracts of which appeared in the Athenæum. See letter to Schœnbein Sept. 6. 1843.
[2] Arch. de l'Électr. T. 2. 1842. p. 241 and ibid p. 267.

Schœnbein to Faraday.

My dear Faraday

As an acquaintance of mine is going to London I cannot let pass such an excellent opportunity without writing a few lines to you.

Some weeks ago I was myself on the point to cross the water with the view of attending the meeting of the british Association at Manchester, when some unlooked for circumstances occurred which prevented me from putting that plan into execution. I was very sorry for this failure and am the more so now that I know you were there, but we must patiently submit to what we cannot alter. About a week previous to the opening of the meetings of the said association I sent a paper to one of its secretaries and asked him the favo[u]r to put it into the hands of the president of chemical Section. I trust the memoir has reached Manchester and been read; in that case its contents will be known to you and as they bear upon some important points regarding the theory of Galvanism I am rather anxious to know what you will think about the views I have taken of the case. I am inclined to believe that some of the facts stated in my paper do offer additional evidence in favo[u]r of that theory according to which hydro-electric currents are due to chemical action. The phenomena being exhibited by iron when acting the part of the cathode within an aqueous oxy-acid appear to me to be rather of an interesting nature though very difficult to be accounted for. The longer I am examining the peculiar condition of iron the more does that state become enigmatical to me so that at this present moment I cannot conceive the least idea about the cause of that extraordinary phenomenon.

Having of late worked a good deal again on that subject I have ascertained some novel facts which are very curious indeed and of which I take the liberty to mention one. Under certain circumstances iron is capable of maintaining its peculiar condition within common nitric acid though acting as the negative electrode of a voltaic arrangement. Supposing that condition to be due to a superficial oxidation of iron or a film of oxigen covering that metal, should the hydrogen, being eliminated at the iron electrode, not unite with that oxygen and throw the metal into chemical action? Before long I shall publish a memoir on the subject in de la Rive's "Archives".[1] In the next number of that periodical you will see a notice of mine regarding a voltaic pile I have constructed out of mere cast iron.[2] The power which that arrangement exhibits is really wonderful and beats that of any other if we take into consideration the cheapness of the materials being employed for its construction.

Some time ago I took the liberty to send you by an acquaintance of mine five copies of a work on England[3] asking you at the same time the favo[u]r to forward them to their respective places of destination. I entertain the flattering hopes that the remarks which the author of the said book has ventured to make on your account will not have proved in any way unpleasant to your feelings. You will easily recognize in the publication alluded to the pen of a friend of yours and of a friend who feels most warmly for you. Mrs. Schœnbein unites with me in her best regards to you and Mrs. Faraday and begs me to remember her friendly to her friends in Albemarl[e]-Street

For ever
Yours
most faithfully

Bâle July 8th 1842.   C. F. Schoenbein.

[1] Arch. de l'Élect. T. 2. 1842. p. 267.
[2] Arch. de l'Élect. T. 2. 1842. p. 286.
[3] vide p. 92, note 1.

If you should happen to have anything to be sent to me, Mr. Worringer, bearer of these lines, who will communicate you his address, will be kind enough to take charge of it.

S.

Faraday to Schœnbein.

Tynemouth 10 August 1842.

MY DEAR SCHOENBEIN

I have received both your letters i. e. those of the dates of April 9th and July 8th; the last just now at Tynemouth so that if your friend went to the Institution, I lost the pleasure of seeing him and in any little attention to him the pleasure of doing anything as thanks to you for your continual and unvarying kindness which is to me a great value, for though I now feel pretty nearly excluded as a workman in science it would grieve me much to think that I was forgotten by the few friends which similarity of pursuit has accidentally, as it were, made for me. I rather hope and am persuaded of it in your case that whilst they vigorously run their successful career they will let me look on and rejoice in their progress.

We have been here (Northumberland) for 5 or 6 weeks and must soon return home again. Although I am ashamed to write about myself yet I am sure you will wish to know that I am well in bodily health and in good spirits; as long as I do not exert my memory it remains just as it was.

You appear to have heard that I was at Manchester and so I was, in a manner, but if you had been there I should not have seen you and did not have the pleasure of hearing your papers which however I think were read, but I have no access to any report here and cannot from memory tell you whether I did or did not read a report of it in the papers sent me. The facts are these: I did not mean to go, but the Society of

Sciences at Modena wrote to Herschel[1] and myself saying they had appointed us to represent them at the Association and as he at first said he could not go and wrote to me on the matter I went to Manchester and made my appearance at the Committee meeting on the day previous to the opening of the General Meeting and reported the credentials of the society which I represented; having done that I left Manchester early in the morning in which the great body met und so escaped London.

The volumes you sent[2] and of which I think I know the author I immediately conveyed to their destination. You know I do not read German but just before I came here I was looking at some of the words which caught my attention and guessing at the meaning suspect the book was written by a very partial friend of mine. The volume is now in the hands of a friend who when I go back is to tell me something of what it says.

I shall look for your paper in the "archives" with some impatience I see that in No. 4 De la Rive says he was obliged to postpone it to the next number[3] where I suppose I shall find the account of the Iron battery also.[4] That Iron is a very various matter and evidently must be of great importance to the theory of Electrical action because it is a case of one substance assuming such different conditions of electrical action. I hope you will ultimately find the key to all the phenomena which no doubt are simple and [I] am fully persuaded great discoveries (now unexpected) [will] be the reward.

Pray give my kindest remembrances to Mrs. Schœnbein and try to raise up a recollection of me in the minds of the children. I wonder whether they would know me if they saw

---

[1] Sir John Herschel, was born in 1792 at Slough near Windsor and died in 1871 in London. He was very wealthy and spent many years in South Africa for the purpose of making astronomical observations.

[2] vide note 1, p. 92.

[3] Arch. de l'Élect. 1842. p. 267.

[4] ibid. p 286.

me again. My wife unites in best wishes and thought to yourself and your wife. May you both enjoy together all the health and happiness that a contented mind can desire.

Ever Most Truly Yours
M. FARADAY.

Schœnbein to Faraday.

MY DEAR FARADAY

An opportunity offering itself to me for sending letters to England, I cannot help making use of it and expressing you my thanks for the kind lines you had the goodness to address to me from Tynemouth the other day. I am very happy indeed to learn from your letter, that you are enjoying health and what is still more valuable that you are in good spirits. I am strongly inclined to consider such a state of body and mind as a sure indication that your memory will also be entirely restored to its primitive power and that you will soon be enabled to reenter into your scientific career. Should however our expectations not be quite fulfilled and should you be obliged to be a little careful with yourself, as to undertaking philosophical researches, you must bear in mind that you are entitled to the "otium cum dignitate"; for you have contributed your full share to the general stock of science and already done more in that line, than it falls to the lot of the great majority of philosophers to be able of doing during their whole life. You know as well as I do that we are not to measure the length of our earthly existence by the number of years to which it extends; the true magnitude of life is determined only by the intrinsic value of our doings and in that respect, it may be said that some men do and live in one single year more and longer than many others do in fifty.

My papers on the electrolysing power of simple voltaic circles[1] and the peculiar condition of Iron[2] will he published in the forthcoming number of the "Archives" and I am really very curious to know what you will say about the subject. As to the cause of the inactive state which that metal assumes under certain circumstances I am still in the dark and must say that the longer I am investigating the subject the more inexplicable and enigmatical it becomes to me. I have now succeeded to make Iron the negative electrode within common nitric acid, without destroying, by so doing, its peculiar condition, into which state that metal is brought previous to its performing the function mentioned. Such a fact seems to exclude altogether the Idea of a film of oxygen being the cause of the inactivity of Iron. In spite of the difficulties I have hitherto met in my endeavours to solve the problem in question I shall not give up the hope to succeed at last. My letter and paper sent to the British Association to Manchester have not yet been acknowledged, an ommission of formality which I rather wonder at. Or is it perhaps the custom not to acknowledge such communications? I dare say you have heard of Moser's[3] discoveries.[4] If true, they are really wonderful, and to my opinion the most important ones made in our days. What interesting conclusions may be drawn from the simple fact that in utter darkness the image of a medal is impressed upon a common plate of silver etc. this effect being produced at a sensible distance. In the last number of Poggendorff's

[1] Arch. de l'électr. T. 2. 1842. p. 241.

[2] ibid. p. 267.

[3] Ludwig Ferdinand Moser was born in 1805 at Berlin. From 1839 he was professor of Physics at Königsberg where he died in 1880.

[4] Schœnbein is alluding to the so called breath-images which he adopted as a support of his theory of contact action. It is well known however that Mosers explication no longer holds good, but has been replaced by a more rational one by Waidele, whereby the importance of his discovery was greatly minimized.

Annals[1] you will find all the particulars about the subject alluded to. Though the little work,[2] I took the liberty of sending you some months ago, is hardly worth your notice still I should not be sorry if you were made acquainted with the contents of some of its chapters. They contain in some respects the articles of faith of the author and would give you some insight into the views he takes of nature, mankind etc. Though some of those views will most likely not quite agree with your way of thinking, I trust and am confident that such a difference of opinion will on your part not loosen the bonds of friendship by which the author feels himself so intimately attached to you. The germans are a very queer set of beings and you are well aware, that the author of the said publication belongs to that nation and has not altogether divested himself of the peculiarities of his country men. These are said to be born metaphysicians, very fond of the subtilities of philosophy and prone to mysteries. Though I believe to have taken my stand on rather a solid ground and being very averse to obscure and misty speculations, still there is a german bias left in my mind which looks in the midst of the material world for something immaterial, and which is strongly inclined to see even in the most common phenomenon, exhibited to our senses, the immediate and direct manifestation of something spiritual, of that power in and by which every thing lives and exists and which is the foundation and the source of the most minute being, as well as of the infinity of the universe. The way in which the majority of philosophers consider Nature is to me, I openly confess it to you, *too crude, too material, too narrow, too onesided.* It is true, they declare nature to be an admirable machinery constructed with consummate skill, arranged with infinite wisdom; but for all that it is to them a machinery only, and that is too little for me. I must look upon the visible and material

---

[1] Poggend. Annal. Bd. 56. 1842. p. 177 u. 569 Bd. 57, 1842. p 1.
[2] vide note 1. p. 92.

world with very different eyes in order to satisfy the demands of my mind. But enough of a subject which is too delicate and extensive to be spoken of in a letter.

A few days ago I returned from a trip which I took into the south of Germany during our Midsummer-holidays and which carried me through some parts of the Black Forest. Most of the valleys of that chain of mountains are really delightful, and such as I am sure you would like; fresh air, picturesque hills, dark woods, limpid streams etc. are to be found there in abundance. Could you not manage it, to spend next summer some weeks with Mrs. Faraday in some retired corner there? Mrs. Schœnbein and myself would be exceedingly happy to join you.

My wife and Children are quite well with the exception of my eldest daughter who fell ill of nervous fever two or three weeks ago. We have however reason to hope that she will recover. The good Child recollects you perfectly well, even in her illness, and Mrs. Schœnbein continues to think you the most amiable of all philosophers she ever met with in her life, which opinion I do, of course, not combat at all. I flatter myself that Mrs. Faraday has not forgotten Mrs. Schœnbein and does still reckon her amongst the number of her friends. Pray remember me most friendly to her and be so kind to tell her that Mrs. Schœnbein is very anxious to make her personal acquaintance. We must therefore go with our wives to the Black Forest.

In concluding my letter, I beg you to believe me

Yours
most faithfully

Bâle Aug. 22. 1842.	C. F. SCHOENBEIN.

Faraday to Schœnbein.

Royal Institution 18 Feby 1843

MY DEAR FRIEND

I was about to write to you the other day and was stopped by a reason, which you will perhaps think very odd and insufficient unless indeed you bring a little German subtlety of thought to bear upon it. I had put *the book,* which to me is a sealed book, into the hands of Grove and just as I was about writing he sent me two pages of writing, a translation of part which his wife has made: — it was the authors opinion of myself[1] and was a character so beautiful and of which I felt myself so utterly unworthy, even if it had come from my loving wifes thought, that I was quelled under it and constrained to be pen-dumb. I do not doubt your sincerity in the least, but knowing a little of my own heart I cannot help thinking of the hypocrisy, which must have contributed to such an impression. You see I have my fancies as well as you; you will perhaps count amongst them this, that I think but poorly of human nature, but certainly in my own heart I find nothing to raise my estimate of it; at the same time, I must allow that I find a great deal which does do so amongst my friends. The upshot is, that though I cannot appropriate your good opinion, I thank you most earnestly for it and will try to become in some degree what you describe. I wish your book was translated here. I heard very highly of it from Kohl the Russian traveller who spoke of its character also in Germany.[2]

[1] The passage here referred to by Faraday is in Schœnbeins Reisetagebuch (Bâle, 1842) p. 277. "It is my conviction" he says "that, so far as scientific merit is concerned, Faradays discoveries surpass those of Davy, his teacher; though we may call the work of the latter more brilliant, more striking. However, even if we merely owed to Faraday the discovery of magneto-electricity, that alone would suffice to entitle him to immortal fame."

[2] Johann Georg Kohl was born in 1808 at Bremen, lived for many years in Russia, and died in 1878 at Bremen.

I have now your paper in the "Archives" and purpose taking it on Monday to Brighton to read, but I must not delay my letter for that, for I do not know what else may come over me to stop my writing — a small thing is to me a great obstacle at times and I fear to trust the future. I think I saw in some paper of Herschels[1] lately a notion that the peculiar Iron was Iron in another state and yet iron[2] — like the existence of two states of carbon or sulphur or other bodies that show at times and under certain circumstances these or such differences.

I am surprised at what you say of the British Association not acknowledging your paper. If I can *remember* I will take the first opportunity of asking the reason.

Moser's papers[3] I am now reading in the translation in Taylors Scientific Memoirs.[4] So many persons were putting forth accounts of effects, that I ventured in a short note in the Literary Gazette to suggest, that all such experiments and statements should now be accompanied by some fundamental experiments made in Vacuo and others made with rock salt. Many of the effects I have heard described, I have no doubt are due to mere vapours. Such effects may be separated from those of radiation in a certain degree by making them in vacuo —

---

[1] Phil. Mag. S. 3. vol. 14. 1839. p. 32. which deals with meteoric iron from South Africa. In dissolving a specimen of it in nitric acid for the purpose of analysis, Herschel found that towards the end of the solution the iron assumed the peculiar state of resistance to the action of the acid, observed by Schœnbein.

[2] A similar suggestion was made by Berzelius in Stockholm Akad. Handl. 1843. p. 1. Schœnbeins reply to this is contained in a letter to Berzelius dated Feb. 23. 1844 in which he says: "The only remarkable thing about it is, that the allotropy should be confined to the surface, and not extend in any degree to the interior of the iron; for the current which determines the passivity of the iron goes through every part of the iron, which serves as positive electrode." Kahlbaum, Briefwechsel. p. 42.

[3] vide note 4. p. 98.

[4] Scientific Memoirs (Taylor) Prt. 3. 1843 p. 422. The treatises giving an account of his discoveries are: On the action of light on bodies; On invisible light; and On the power which light possesses of becoming latent.

and also again by interposing rock salt — for there seems no reason to doubt that Moser's experiments of *true radiation* would succeed, though a thin plate of rock salt were interposed.[1]

During the last 8 or 9 months I have worked a little on the Electricity of high pressure steam and sent a paper to the Royal Society[2]; perhaps they may print it and then I shall again have the pleasure of sending you a paper of mine. The electricity is not due to evaporation — nor to the steam itself — but solely (I believe) to the friction of the particles of water which the steam carries with it and I can make it Positive or Negative on either side at pleasure. Water standing above . . . . .[3] and all other bodies yet tried on, become Positive when rubbed against other bodies.

Peltier's[4] expts and views of the relation of the earth and space rather startle me. What do you think? I do not think I shall be able to assent to the properties which he gives to space.

You really hold out very tempting pictures of the Black forest etc. etc. etc. but none more tempting than the hearty pleasure of seeing you and Mrs. Schœnbein and the children — to *all* remember us very kindly. But this year will not see us out of Britain, and Scotland will be the farthest place we shall go to. There, family friends have looked for years for us

---

[1] Robert Hunt F.R.S. (of the Mining School, at Chelsea) comes to the conclusion that the effect in question is dependent on a chemico-mechanical action, or what Berzelius has called catalytic action. Prater on the other hand, replying to Hunt in the Athenaeum (1843, p. 598) reminds him, that Mosers images cannot be taken at any distance from the plate when polishing, boiling or screens are used. The effect in question seems therefore, according to Prater, to be mere chemical action, produced by direct contact.

[2] An abstract of it is to be found. Phil. Mag. S. 3 vol. 22. 1843. p. 570. vide also 18th ser. Researches on Electricity. Phil. Trans. 1843. p. 17.

[3] The word after above is, in the original, illegible.

[4] Jean Charles Athanase Peltier was born at Ham in 1785. He was a watchmaker and dealer in clocks till 1815, after which he lived on his own means in Paris, where he died in 1845.

and I doubt whether even they will see us this year after all. Again with heartiest feelings of remembrances to you and Mrs. Schœnbein from *us both*.

I am My dear friend
Gratefully Yours
M. FARADAY.

Schœnbein to Faraday.

MY DEAR FARADAY

Having for a great length of time neither seen nor learned anything from you I felt, as you may easily imagine, no small degree of satisfaction and pleasure at the receipt of the letter you had the kindness to write to me some months ago. The mere sight of lines written by your hand, independent of their contents, does call forth in my mind feelings very similar to those which we experience in looking at the portrait of a beloved absent friend.

As to that part of the "German Philosopher's Work" which refers to the amiable philosophical inhabitant of the Royal Institution, I must beg to be allowed to differ widely from you and am bold enough, as to say that to my opinion the german writer knows, in some respects at least, the british philosopher much better, nay infinitely better, than you do. Having to write about some other things I cannot give you the reasons which make me hold such an opinion; one of them I shall however mention. As you are a Philosopher yourself, you must be well aware that objects being placed too near to the eye cannot be distincly seen by that organ. It is your case, my dear friend, you have seen the man of whom I am speaking at a distance which is too small, as to allow you to see him well, and so distinctly, as our german did, who was more favo[u]rably placed than you are. If you think that the book in question would be relished by british readers we could perhaps manage here a translation of it, as some english persons capable of doing such a work are living at Bâle.

Knowing a little of the language myself, and the author too, I could perhaps also render some service to make the translation as correct as possible. Pray be so kind and let me know your opinion about that subject in your next letter.

I have read with much interest the notice in which you gave an account of some experiments made on electrical induction.[1] As far as I am able to judge, I think that the results you have obtained are conclusive in favour of the views you developed some years ago in your papers "on the phenomena of induction." I only wonder that our continental philosophers have as yet not paid that degree of attention to the subject, which it so fully deserves and which will ultimately not fail being excited. It is perhaps a certain laziness, inherent to human nature, that makes even men of science unwilling to shift out of old-beaten tracks and enter into paths newly opened, though these should happen to be ever so well laid out.

The fact that the electricity developed in steam of high pressure[2] is due to friction appears to me rather a surprizing one.[3] Is it not possible that the dispersion or disaggregation of the fluid water, caused by the expansion of steam, has something to do with the phenomenon alluded to? If I am not mistaken it has been observed that the atmosphere near a cataract, i. e. the small particles of water flying about at such a place, are in an excited state. I am indeed very curious to see the paper in which your results are discribed.

[1] Speculation touching electric induction. Phil. Mag. S. 3. vol. 24. 1844. p. 136.
[2] Phil. Trans. S. 3. vol. 22. 1843. p. 570.
[3] Davy says on p. 138 of his Chemical Philosophy: "All cases of vaporization produce negatve electricity in the bodies in contact with the vapour". In 1843 Peltier contributed the following paper to the Acad. Sci. Bull. at Brussels T. 10. p. 318: Sur le développement de l'électricité par un jet de vapeur.

In a small way I am continually occupied with voltaic researches and think I shall be able to send you some memoirs within a short time. One of these papers will treat on the frequency of chemical effects produced by mere contact[1] and another on the phenomena of electrolysis.[2] I am afraid you will think some of my conjectures rather too bold. — What do you say about Grove's gaseous Battery?[3] You will perceive that I published a paper on that subject in the last number of de la Rive's Archives.[4] It seems our friend thinks the combination of isolated oxigen with isolated hydrogen to be a source of voltaic electricity. I cannot yet make up my mind to believe such a thing; my experiments at least do not lead to such an inference. De la Rive read the other day in the french Academy a memoir on the chemical action of a simple pile which as far as I know its contents, offers a good deal of scientific interest. The philosopher of Geneva has made use of a voltaic combination pointed out by me some years ago and arranged it so, that it yields a considerable power. Peroxide of lead is the electronegative and zinc the electropositive element of de la Rive's arrangement. Peltier's statements are to me as yet no more than mere assertions and highly improbable conjectures. Although I dislike the very shadow of a controversy I could not help addressing a few words[5] to Mr. Martens[6] who has been writing very

[1] Über die Häufigkeit der Berührungswirkungen auf dem Gebiete der Chemie. Basel 1843.
[2] Über die Ursache der Erhöhung des Leitungsvermögens des Wassers durch Säuren, Alkalien und Salze.
[3] Phil. Mag. S. 3. vol. 21. 1842. p. 417. Ibid. vol. 22. 1843. p. 376. See also ibid. vol. 23. p. 165: On the theory of the gaseous voltaic battery, by Schœnbein.
[4] Arch de l'Électr. T. 3. 1842. p. 69.
[5] Einige Bemerkungen in Betreff der Arbeit des Herrn Martens über die Passivität des Eisens. Poggend. Annal. Bd. 59. 1843. p. 149.
[6] Martin Martens was born in 1797 at Mastricht. Originally physician, he became professor of Chemistry and Botany first in Mastricht, then in Loewen, where he died in 1863.

strange memoirs on voltaic subjects these last two or three years.[1]

I regret very much indeed that your last letter cuts off my hopes, of seeing you on the continent in the course of this summer. If you won't come to me, you are running the risk of having your privacy broken in upon by my humble Individual, but do not be afraid that such a thing will happen in the year 1843.

Mrs. Schœnbein and my children are doing well, the latter were during the whole winter suffering a good deal by a violent hooping-cough.

I confidently hope that the state of your health will be daily improving and the whole strength both of your body and mind entirely reestablished. Mrs. Schœnbein unites with me in her kindest regards to Mrs. Faraday and to yourself.

Ever Your's most truly

Bâle April 26. 1843.   C. F. SCHOENBEIN.

Schœnbein to Faraday.

MY DEAR FARADAY

As a friend of mine is going to England, I take the liberty to send you through him some papers in the contents of which you will perhaps take some interest. I am rather sorry that one of the memoirs is written in german, I trust however that before long a french version of it will be published in the "Bibliothèque universelle" and in that case I ask you the favo[u]r to let me know, what you are thinking about the views I have taken of the chemical effects which are produced by contact.[2]

---

[1] Martens published the results of his investigations, which he commenced in 1841 in the Acad. Sci. Bull. at Brussels. Sur la théorie de la pile voltaique, ibid. T. 9. 1842. p. 192.

[2] vide note 1. p. 106.

A circumstance that appears to me to offer a good deal of scientific interest and to which I have paid a particular attention in my paper, is the fact, that the chemical affinity of some elementary bodies, for certain substances, is, in many instances, very much enhanced by bringing those bodies into such a state, as ought, according to our present notions, to make them less inclined to enter into a chemical combination, than they are when not so conditioned. Chlorine for instance does not chemically unite with isolated hydrogen at the common temperature and in darkness, whilst chlorine being placed under the same circumstances readily combines with hydrogen, if the latter body happens to be chemically associated with Sulphur, Selenium, Phosphorus, Nitrogen, Arsenic, Antimony, Tellurium etc. Oxigen does not unite with hydrogen without being heated or put in contact with Platinum, if both elements happen to exist in an isolated state; but oxigen being associated with sulphur, and hydrogen being combined with the same substance, do readily form water even at very low degrees of temperature. Chemistry teems as it were, with facts of a similar description. As far as I know very little or no attention has as yet been paid to the influence exerted by one ingredient part of a binary compound upon the chemical bearings of the other constituent part. This influence, however, is to my opinion well worthy of being closely studied and very far from being explained by the principles of what they call the electro-chemical theory. As to the latter, do you not think it high time to subject it to a most severe and scrutinizing review? To my humble opinion it rests upon a very doubtful and unsatisfactory matter of fact foundation.

If Mr. Ryhiner[1] the bearer of these lines should happen to deliver them in person to you, pray receive him kindly and let

---

[1] A very well known name at Bâle. Perhaps he was a son of Prof. J. H. Ryhiner of Bâle. A Madame Ryhiner is mentioned in letters to Schœnbein from Grove (Nov. 14th 1843), who speaks of Mr. Ryhiner as her son, and from de la Rive (Jan. 11th 1847).

him see the Royal Institution. He was once a pupil of mine and is in every respect a most excellent and amiable young man.

In offering to you and Mrs. Faraday my most hearty salutations

I am my dear Faraday
Yours
most truly

Bâle May 11. 1843. C. F. SCHOENBEIN.

Faraday to Schœnbein.

Royal Institution 16 May 1843

MY DEAR FRIEND

I must begin to write you a letter, though feeling, as I do, in the midst of one of my low, nervous attacks, with memory so treacherous, that I cannot remember the beginning of a sentence to the end — hand disobedient to the will, that I cannot form the letters, bent with a certain crampness, so I hardly know whether I shall bring it to a close with consistency or not. But that most valued thing, your kindness, moves me to write, when to another I would not reveal my weakness by a halting letter. As to your opinion and power of judgment etc. of a certain person[1] I have no doubt the advantages you possess which, I admit, have shown you blemishes as well as beauties; but I will not put your candour to the tets by asking for them. The glass of a kind heart through which you look has something to do with the matter.

Now as to the book in English I am afraid to say any thing on the matter, not because of my opinion of it, for how

[1] p. 277 of his 'Mitteilungen aus dem Reisetagebuch eines deutschen Naturforschers."

can that be anything but favourable; but because of the woeful mistakes which I have made in judgments of this kind before. I will tell you a case. A dear friend, a foreigner, now dead, sent me a M. S. on English scientific matters, which I thought good, and booksellers of character told me they thought good and attractive. In one way or another it led to the printing and publishing of the work. I paid for the printing and did not receive one farthing back from the sale. I could not tell my friend this; he never asked for or had an account, and the thought often comes back to my mind that up to the day of his death, he might perhaps imagine I had made a profit by his work and never rendered him an account. — So much for my judgment in these matters. In fact I find the Booksellers prospects are nothing but words, words, words. — I wish Murray would take your work in his own hands, for then I know he would use a sound discretion, but I do not know how to get him to do so.

As to the steam paper,[1] it is now printing and when you have it I hope you will think the reasoning satisfactory. The point that the water must be pure is a very strong one as a ground for conclusions — As to Grove I do not recollect that he says isolated oxygen and hydrogen can by combining produce a current of electricity[2] — but I have no confidence in my memory in such matters. — I have been reading with great pleasure some of your papers lately, but am so confused I cannot just now remember which; but I have not yet touched No. 7 of the "Archives" where I see your name — it now lies before me, but fear to read because of the giddiness.

[1] On the electricity evolved by the friction of water and steam against other bodies. Phil. Trans. vol. 6. 1843 p. 17.

[2] Phil. Mag. S. 3. vol. 14. 1839 p 130. Grove says at the conclusion of an account of an experiment in which a galvanometer was deflected when connected with two strips of platina covered by tubes containing oxygen and hydrogen: "I hope, by repeating this experiment in series, to effect decomposition of water by means of its composition".

De la Rive is here and I have seen his experiment on the increase of the decomposing power of a single pair of plates by adding in the inductive power brought into play at the moment of interrupting the current.[1] Grove brought the account over from Paris and tells me that he found all there, that he spoke to, apparently aware of the effect. I imagine this was only because they recognized in it an action due to the principle I had examined in Exp. Researcs series IX.[2], especially as illustrated at 1084. For myself I thank De la Rive for a very beautiful form of the application, though it is the same principle, and I do not see why a thermo-current should not be exalted in the same manner until it could effect chemical action and now indeed I have a faint recollection that Watkins or somebody has done that also.

I grieve to hear of Mrs. Schœnbein's illness and cares with the children, I wish there were nothing but happy pleasure in her way. But all these cares have their reward in a mothers bosom, and though we dislike them at the moment, it is better they should be than *not*. Nevertheless I am very glad to find that all are improving. The kindest thoughts from us both to you both.

Ever My dear Schœnbein

Your faithful friend
M. FARADAY.

Faraday to Schœnbein.

London Royal Institution 8 Aug 1843

MY DEAR FRIEND

I have the opportunity, though in haste, of sending you a copy of my last paper, probably the last. I know you

---

[1] Grove relates in a letter to Schœnbein (Nov. 14. 1843) that he has been working on what he calls voltaic reaction, a method of increasing the force of a voltaic combination by adding to it a reaction occasioned by itself. vide Phil. Mag. S. 3. vol. 13. 1843. p. 443.

[2] Phil. Trans. S. 3. vol. 18. 1835. p. 41.

will accept it kindly. — I have had and still feel part of a strong attack of giddiness, so must not write much. If Dr. Yates[1] sees you do me the favour to receive him as my friend; if he should not be able to see you, still he has promised to send on this letter and the paper. — You remember a little word that pased about a translation of a certain book.[2] Now a young man of my acquaintance who is a corrector of the press and acquainted with many languages, more or less, has had some thoughts of translating it if he could find a bookseller to publish it — *but he has not found that yet.* — I told him you were connected with the author of the book and that from what *I knew* he ought to write to you first. — I believe he has done so. — I saw him the other day and found that he had no knowledge of any publisher as yet; indeed that he had not inquired among his connections in the trade or intended to do so till he heard from you. — I wish the book more published in our language — and I wish the translation were made at Bâle. — But it is the undertaking publisher we want and I am afraid that in that respect both plans will fall through. — However I do not know Mr. Vincents resources or connexions; — all that I know is he is in a printing house and can manage that part of the affair and its expences in a very different way to what I could.

I received your letter by a friend not long ago and conclude you had one from me by post about the same time.

With kindest remembrances to Mrs Schœnbein and the family I am as ever

Your faithful friend
M. FARADAY.

My wife is not with me just now or she would desire to join me in every good wish to you   M. F.

---

[1] James Yates F.R.S. at first a clergymen, retired into private life in 1848; he was born in 1789 at Toxteth Park and died in 1871 at Highgate.

[2] vide note 1. p. 92.

Faraday to Schœnbein.

R. Institution 6 Septr. 1843

MY DEAR FRIEND

I wrote to you 5 or 6 weeks ago by Dr. Yates, but do not feel sure you will have seen him yet. Now I find your friend Mr. Ryhiner is on the point of returning to Basle and so spoil half a sheet of paper for a word with you. — I hope all are well and happy. My kindest remembrances to Mrs. Schœnbein — — interrupted — — now I return. I called at the Royal Society to day and found my paper on steam for you was gone. — I have not another copy or I would send it. — Mr. Armstrong[1] has constructed a magnificent steam electric apparatus,[2] which I should think produces about 8 or 10 times as much electricity as our large machine in a given time. — I have seen nothing of your book yet except some extracts in the Athenaeum. — Several are longing for it.

I must conclude, for both head and hand are very unsteady.

Ever Dear Schönbein
Your faithful friend
M. FARADAY.

Schœnbein to Faraday.

Bâle Febr 17. 1844.

MY DEAR FARADAY

An acquaintance of mine going to London I avail, myself of the opportunity for sending you a little work[3] in

[1] Sir W. G. Armstrong L, L. D. born 1810 at Newcastle-on-Tyne, was brought up to the bar and practiced as a barrister at Newcastle. He then founded the well known engine-factory, became military-engineer, but in 1863 again took charge of his factory.

[2] Phil. Mag. S. 3. vol. 23. 1843. p. 194. see also ibid. vol. 22. 1843. p. 1. Grove writes to Schœnbein (Aug. 20. 1842): "When I left London Faraday was at work upon the electricity of steam. I lent him an apparatus by means of which I had obtained the spark at the London Institution."

[3] This little book is doubtless Schœnbeins pamphlet on contributions to physical chemistry, dated Dec. 1844, which he devides into three sections: 1. Über

which I have tried to develop some theoretical views regarding the source of voltaic electricity and some electrolytical phenomena. There is also a paper in the book treating of chemical effects produced by contact, on which I should like very much to have your opinion. Having these many years entertained strong doubts about the correctness of the atomic theory and been inclined to consider what is called a "molecule" of a body as a centre of physical forces, I have tried to make that view bear upon the chemical actions being produced by contact (See page 22—25). Mr. Grove writes me in his last letter,[1] that the other day you had broken a lance against the atomic theory in the Royal Institution.[2] As our mutual friend does not tell me any particulars about the view you have taken of the subject, I am indeed very curious to see the next number of the Phil. Magazine[3] which I understand will give the substance of your lecture. Having had no less than 19 hours to lecture a week in the course of this winter, you may easily imagine that I had no time for making researches: I grow indeed impatient of that everlasting schoolmastering and am longing for being placed under circumstances more favorable to scientific pursuits.

It is possible that I shall have the pleasure of seeing you in England about the mid-summer holidays, the execution of this bold plan of mine does however depend upon circumstances over which I have got very little control. Once being sure of the possibility of the journey I shall take the liberty to acquaint you with the probable date of my arrival at London.

die Häufigkeit der Berührungswirkungen in der Chemie. 2. Über die Ursache der Erhöhung des Leitungsvermögens des Wassers durch Säuren, Alkalien und Salze. 3. Über die Ursache der hydroelektrischen Ströme.

[1] Jan. 30. 1844.

[2] "I saw Faraday a few days ago" he writes "he has been giving a lecture at the Royal Inst. on some speculations on the nature of matter in which he has run a tilt against the Atomic Theorists".

[3] A speculation touching electric conduction and the nature of matter; Phil. Mag. S. 3. vol. 24. 1844. p. 136.

Mrs. Schœnbein and the Children are doing quite well; the two eldest girls are now going to school and promise to become very blue; I shall however take good care that that coloring does not grow too intense, for that sort of blue is not much to my liking.

My wife desires to be most particularly remembered to you and Mrs Faraday and reckons upon the great pleasure of seeing you both once more at Bâle.

Pray present my humble respects to your lady and believe me

Your's
most faithfully
C. F. SCHOENBEIN.

NB. The Philosophical Faculty of our University has conferred its degree upon our Friend Grove.[1]

Be kind enough as to forward the inclosed parcels to their respective places of destination. S.

Schœnbein to Faraday.

Bale, March 30. 1844.[2]

MY DEAR FARADAY

Some weeks ago I took the liberty to send you, through an acquaintance of mine a little work containing some memoirs on voltaic and other philosophical subjects. I should like very much indeed that you were made acquainted with the substance of those papers, as they relate to some interesting questions of voltaic and chemical Science.

---

[1] "Will you convey my most grateful thanks to the Philosophical Faculty of your University and say that I feel most highly honoured by the degree conferred upon me and that I shall study to deserve the good opinion which has induced them to grant it." (Letter from Grove to Schœnbein, Jan 30. 1844.)

[2] The date has been added later and is in Faradays hand.

In case I should happen to succeed in isolating the principle of ozone, as I hope I shall before long, I have a good mind to go to York with the view of performing my philosophical miracle before the British association. What do you think of that plan? Its execution would perhaps give some zest to the proceedings of the chemical section there. From having lately worked a little too much I am rather knocked up and want some relaxation. A trip to England would no doubt do me a great deal of good, but Mrs. Sch. will hear of no such thing and declares such a locomotion as downright wantonness.[1] But after all she would not throw any great obstacle in my way, if I insisted upon the visit. She charges me to present to you and Mrs Faraday her humble respects, in which I of course join

Your's

S.

Schœnbein to Faraday.[2]

MY DEAR FARADAY

Having of late made a series of experiments with the view of producing by chemical means that odoriferous principle which I have called "Ozone" and which is, as you are well aware, disengaged at the positive electrode during the electrolysis of water, as well as near the points, out of which common Electricity is passing into the atmospheric air, and believing that I have succeeded in the attempt, I think you will

---

[1] Schœnbein's frequent journeys, in fact, never seem to have been much to Mrs. Schœnbeins liking. Thus he wrote to his wife from London, Sept. 1. 1839: "Du siehst also, meine liebe Frau, dass man den Mann doch in manchen Dingen machen lassen muss".

[2] Faraday on receipt of this letter sent it to Mr. Christie, by whom it was received on April 9th, to read at the Royal Society. With the exception of some slight alterations, it was read unchanged under the following title: "On the production of Ozone by chemical means. By Professor Schœnbein." The Phil. Mag. (vol. 24. 1844. p. 466) and the Proceedings of the Royal Society (vol. 5. 1844. p. 507) both contain short abstracts of it.

read with some interest a summary account of my proceedings and results. *(The details regarding these researches will be described in a paper which is to be published in one of the forthcoming numbers of the "Archives" and "Poggendorff's Annals".)*[1]

If at the common temperature, a piece of phosphorus be put into a bottle filled with ordinary air, an atmosphere is very rapidly formed in it, which possesses the property of polarizing positively a plate of Gold or Platinum *which is*[2] plunged into the said atmosphere for a few moments. In one instance, the needle of my galvanometer was deflected 90° by a gold plate, which had remained for twenty seconds within a bottle, whose air had previously been in contact with phosphorus for *only*[3] one minute.

The positively polarizing power of that atmosphere arrives at its maximum of intensity, sometimes, within the space of a few minutes, sometimes *in*[4] that of as many days, according to circumstances, into the description of which I cannot enter at this present moment.

That maximum being once reached the intensity of the polarizing power decreases, and within more or less time sinks down to zero, but not to remain in that state. The atmosphere, after having assumed a neutral, or inactive voltaic condition, passes into an opposite state i. e. acquires the power of polarizing negatively a plate of Gold or Platinum *which is*[5] put into it (the atmosphere) for a few seconds. This newly acquired power is, according to circumstances, either slowly or rapidly gaining in intensity until it reaches also its maximum. Having arrived at that point the atmosphere does not undergo any other change of state, if left to itself. *I am able*[6] to bring

---

[1] The italics are our own and signify that the passages in question were omitted at the reading of the paper, or otherwise amended; whereas the notes will in each case give the original reading of Schœnbeins letter.

[2] being. [3] but one. [4] within. [5] being. [6] I have got it under my control.

about the described variations of the voltaic condition of our atmosphere, either in a slow or sudden manner, and with respect to that point of my experiments I will only say that the rapidity of the changes alluded to, essentially depends upon the degree of temperature at which phosphorus is acting upon the atmospheric air. Supposing our atmosphere *to have*[1] assumed its neutral condition, remove the phosphorus from the bottle and put into the latter any readily oxidable metal, being in the *form*[2] of filings or powder, e. g. iron, tin, zinc etc. or any other substance being eager to unite with oxygen, for instance the protochloride of tin or of iron, or the common iron vitriol, shake the atmosphere with one of the bodies named and it (the atmosphere) will almost instantaneously be brought again to a positive condition of consi[de]rable intensity, which state does not seem to be liable to change any more. If on the other hand our atmosphere, after having acquired its highest degree of negatively polarizing power, be treated in the manner described, for instance with iron filings, this power is not only entirely and suddenly destroyed, but the atmosphere changes altogether its voltaic nature and assumes a highly electropositive condition. It is a matter of course that by the quantity of oxidable matter put into the negative atmosphere, we may regulate at pleasure its voltaic condition. *(The intensity of its negatively polarizing power may be only diminished, or the atmosphere may be rendered neutral, or more or less positive from the slightest degree of that state to its maximum.)* Before farther proceeding in the account of my researches, I must not omit to mention the fact that by putting a solution of chloride of Gold into an atmosphere, whose positive condition has been restored by means of readily oxidable substances, that condition is suddenly and irrecoverably destroyed.

From the facts stated, it appears that by the slow action of phosphorus upon atmospheric air two gazeous princibles

[1] having. [2] shape.

are simultaneously produced, which are opposite to each other with regard to their voltaic properties; one of them is an eminently electropositive body, the other a still more powerfully electro-negative one. Under ordinary circumstances the generation of the first principle prevails at the beginning of the said action over that of the second one, but in the more advanced stages of that chemical process the contrary takes place. The production of the electro-negative principle becomes more copious than that of the positive one and hence it comes, that our atmosphere, whilst remaining in contact with phosphorus passes through different stages of voltaic condition until it arrives at the maximum of its negatively polarizing power.[1] But what is the nature of the two principles? As to the electropositive one, I am inclined to think it to be vaporous phosphorus mixt up with particles of what is called "phosphatic acid". *(Et voici mes raisons for making such a supposition. If you pass very slightly a piece of phosphorus over a plate of gold or platinum, the latter deflects very perceptibly the needle, if it be voltaically combined with a similar metallic stripe being in its ordinary state. The said deflection is such as to indicate a current passing from the phosphorated plate to the common one. I have also ascertained the fact that a plate of platinum or gold being surrounded with a solution of phosphorous acid, as well as of phosphatic acid, is positive to a similar plate being plunged either into acidulated (by muriatic acid for instance) or chemically pure water. That phosphorus is capable of assuming the vaporous state at the common temperature, no Chemist I think doubts of and that by the slow action of phosphorus upon atmospheric air phosphatic acid is produced*

---

[1] Grove writes in a letter to Schœnbein (Jan. 5. 1845): "Some of your results are very curious; particularly that of the two different sorts of polarisation by phosphorus. I have been making some expts. with Phosphorus but had not observed or indeed sought for such an effect."

belongs to the class of well-known facts.) It is *however* possible, and I think it even likely, that besides the two positive substances mentioned a third one of the same voltaic kind is generated in my experiment, but I do not think it reasonable yet to state the reasons for my holding such an opinion. I must however not omit to mention that the electropositive principle or principles, if shaken with a solution of chloride of gold throw down a perceptible quantity of that metal a fact that merits to be taken into consideration.

·But what is the chemical nature of the electro-negative substance generated during the slow action of phosphorus upon the atmospheric air? Do not be startled at my telling you at once that it is my "Ozone", for I have got my good reasons for making such a bold assertion. The princible ones are as follows:

1. As long as our atmosphere exhibits a notably strong polarizing power of the positive kind, its smell is similar to that of garlick i. e. *to*[1] the smell which we ascribe to phosphorus; as soon however as that atmosphere is approaching to its neutral voltaic state, an easily perceptible change in its odor takes place also. It now begins to resemble that of Ozone. That smell grows stronger and stronger, the more exalted becomes the electro-negative condition of our atmosphere, and before having arrived at the maximum of its negative intensity, it is utterly impossible to the most delicate nose to perceive the slightest difference as to smell, between the odoriferous principle disengaged at the positive electrode during the electrolysis of water, and that being generated by the slow action of phosphorus upon the atmospheric air.

2. All the substances being possessed of the power to annihilate almost instantaneously the odor of ozone are without any exception capable also of destroying suddenly the same smell of our atmosphere.

[1] is.

3. All the substances having the property of destroying the negatively polarizing power of the odoriferous oxigen *being* eliminated at the positive electrode during the electrolysis of water, do also destroy the same power possessed by our ozone-like smelling atmosphere. To the facts mentioned I might yet add some others which you could hardly help considering as sufficient to prove, I think, beyond any shade of doubt the identity of the two principles in question.

The alleged matter-of-fact reasons are however, to my opinion at least, such as will fully bear out the correctness of my assertion, according to which "Ozone" is formed during the slow action of phosphorus upon the atmospheric air. The question "what is ozone itself?" I am not yet prepared to answer, I hope however to be able *to send*[1] you very soon some scientific news *upon*[2] that subject, being at *this* present *moment* very busy with isolating that curious principle. But whatever ozone may be, it appears to me to be a most remarkable fact, a phenomenon highly worthy of all the attention of philosophers, that the odoriferous principle spoken of is generated under circumstances, being, apparently at least, so essentially different from each other. For I ask what similarity *exists*[3] between the passing of common electricity from a charged conductor into the atmosphere, the electrolysis of acidulated water and the slow action of phosphorus upon atmospheric air? Different as these circumstances appear to be, it will and must ultimately turn out that, with regard to the possibility of the generation of "Ozone" offered by them, they are alike. At any rate, you will agree with me in the opinion that a great number of accurate experiments must yet be made before we shall be enabled to clear up the mystery which still hangs about the subject.

I think however that the path is now opened which will lead us to the solution of our problem and it is not necessary

---

[1] of sending. [2] about. [3] does exist.

to assure you that I shall endeavour to the utmost of my powers to arrive at that end.

Should you think the contents of this letter interesting enough to be communicated to the Royal Society I have no objection to your doing so or to your making any use of them you think fit.

I remain
My dear Faraday
Your's
most faithfully

Bâle March 30 1844   C. F. SCHOENBEIN.

P. S. To obtain the results such as they are described in the preceding lines it is indispensably necessary to depolarize the electrodes after each experiment made with them and the galvanometer. Heating them red hot is the easiest method to effect that depolarization.

Faraday to Schœnbein.

Royal Institution 12. April 1844

MY DEAR FRIEND

I received your letter three or four days ago and was very greatly interested by it. I have given it to Mr Christie[1] to read at the Royal Society. — I do most earnestly hope that you will make out and establish this *Ozone*; it is a very fine thing to do and as you say, though the means of proving it seem to be anomalous and strange when composed together, yet most great discoveries in science have appeared equally strange and confused to us in the first instance. — I have not yet repeated the experiments for certain private troubles

---

[1] Samuel Hunter Christie, F. R. S. Professor of Mathematics at Woolwich, was born in 1784 in London and died 1865 at Twickenham.

have brought me low in health and spirits and my dear wife and I are now at Brighton (tho' I date by habit us above, from the Royal Institution). But I hope we shall soon be better and this what you say leads me to think, we may have the pleasure of seeing you here i. e. in London and also at York, for I believe I must go there myself this year if I possibly can. — I do not know that we have any scientific news here, but I am a very bad indicator, for my bad memory both loses recent things and sometimes suggests old things as new, making all appear misty and doubtful to me. — Our communications through the Royal Society are quite closed or else I should have sent you a short paper, being a speculation about matter[1] — perhaps you may have seen it in one shape or another, at all events when you come, you will put the few pages into your portmanteau.

One hundert remembrances to Mrs. Schœnbein and all the little (? big) ones. It would be pleasant to see your fauns (?) in Switzerland amongst (?) the rock and hills etc. but that is a fancy only. I doubt whether I shall ever leave England again. — I hope that the next news of you will be news of still further advance in the ozone discovery but any will be pleasant to my thoughts.

Ever Very Affectionately Yours
M. FARADAY.

Schœnbein to Faraday.[2]

My dear Faraday

Since I wrote you last I have continued my researches on "ozone" and obtained from them results which seem

---

[1] vide sopra Schœnbeins letter of Febr. 17th 1844. p. 113. and Phil. Mag. S. 3. vol. 24. 1844. p. 136.

[2] This letter also Faraday sent to the Royal Society. The Phil. Mag. printed an abstract of it in vol. 24. S. 3. 1844. p. 467 under the following heading: "On the production of Ozone by chemical means". An abstract is also to be found in the Proceedings of the Royal Society vol. 5. 1844. p. 508.

to be important enough, as to justify my addressing to you another letter on the subject. I have succeeded *in putting it*[1] beyond even a shade of doubt that the odoriferous principles *which are*[2] disengaged during electrical discharges in the common air, the electrolysis of water and the slow action of phosphorus upon the atmosphere are absolutely indentical to one another, as to their chemical nature and that my ozone, as I originally suspected it be, is really a halogenous body very closely resembling to Chlorine.[3] The named principle has the power 1) of destroying vegetable colors, 2) of decomposing a variety of compounds which are decomposed by Chlorine, for instance sulphuretted hydrogen, Ammonia, Jodide of potassium. Water also is decomposed by Ozone in similar circumstances under which Chlorine produces that effect, ex. gr. when sulphurous acid or a number of readily oxidable matters are simultaneously acting upon water. 3) of changing the yellow ferro-cyanide of potassium into the red one. I could add many other facts more, showing the chlorine-like nature of ozone, but the stated ones are sufficient to prove the correctness of my assertion. Ozone, if inhaled, proves very deleterious to the constitution and produces effects similar to those called forth by Chlorine. A mouse *has*[4] already fallen victim to my discovery and I myself have strongly felt the powerful action of ozone upon the system. Having drawn up a paper in which I have given a detailed account of the results obtained from my researches and which I hope will soon be published, I take the liberty to refer you for the sake of particular information to that memoir.[5] I cannot however help adding, that

[1] to put it.   [2] being.
[3] Grove in 1840 in a letter to Schœnbein dated Oct. 13, suggested a new name for ozone, for the purpose of giving expression to this close resemblance: "By the bye, why not call it ozine," he writes, "as you consider it an analogue of chlorine, iodine etc., and not of boron."
[4] is.
[5] Über die Erzeugung des Ozons auf chemischem Wege. Basel 1844.

the whole body of facts which I have been lucky enough to ascertain, render it highly probable, if not certain, that ozone is derived from azote, that is to say that the latter body is a compound consisting of ozone and hydrogen. Starting from that conclusion or if you like supposition the disengagement of Ozone taking place under circumstances apparent[l]y so widely differing from each other, is very easily accounted for. 1) The disengagement of Ozone in atmospheric air by means of common electricity. If an electrical discharge takes place in the common air, the oxigen of the latter unites with the hydrogen of azote and sets Ozone at liberty. Should hydrochloric acid happen to be a constituent part of our atmosphere instead of Azote, a series of phenomena would take place at the points of emission of an electrical machine closely resembling those which we observe now at those points. A smell of Chlorine would make its appearance there, a stripe of gold held into the electrical brush would become negatively polarized, starch mixt up with jodide of potassium would turn blue, the yellow ferro-cyanide be changed into the red one, organic coloring matter be bleached, etc and the whole series of the phenomena mentioned, rendered impossible to take place, if the points of emission were surrounded by an atmosp[h]ere holding some sulphuretted hydrogen, sulphurous acid, vaporous phosphorus, etc dissolved. Indeed the disengagement of ozone at those points is entirely stopt by mixing up the atmosphere with very small quantities of the gazeous substances last mentioned, as you will learn from my memoir.

2) The disengagement of ozone by the slow action of Phosphorus upon the atmospheric air. Phosphorus being simultaneously in contact with Azote and Oxigen causes the latter to unite with the hydrogen of azote, whilst another portion of oxigen combines with phosphorus to form phosphorus acid. Ozone is set at liberty, part of which reacts however upon phosphorus, forming ozonide of phosphorus, whilst another part

is thrown into the air, being placed above the phosphorus. That compound being in contact with water is changed into phosphoric acid and ozonide of hydrogen i. e. Azote. The transformation of phosphorus into phosphatic acid, whilst that elementary body is acted upon by atmospheric air essentially depends upon the action mentioned. I must not omit to mention that all vaporous or gazeous substances which, when mixt up with atmospheric air prevent phosphorus from emitting light (for instance vapo[u]r of ether, alcohol, carburetted hydrogen etc.) do also stop the disengagement of ozone, as well as the oxidation of phosphorus.

3) The disengagement of Ozone by voltaic electricity. Azote being an electrolyte, like hydrochloric acid, is decomposed into its constituent parts by a current, if dissolved in water i. e. rendered liquid by that agency. According to the results of my recent researches water, being deprived of atmospheric air, i. e. Azote, does not yield the smallest quantity of Ozone at the positive electrode and acquires that property again by shaking that sort of water with atmospheric air. I may as well mention here, that water containing only very small quantities of sulphurous acid, sulphuretted hydrogen, in short those substances which have the power to prevent the disengagement of Ozone near electrical points, does not yield the slightest trace of ozone. From the preceding remarks you will perceive that the disengagement of Ozone brought about by electrical, voltaic and chemical means is easily and simply accounted for by supposing azote to be ozonide of hydrogen. Conclusive however as my results appear to me to be as to the compound nature of azote, I readily allow that many more experiments must be made and in particular that of isolating Ozone, before my conclusion or supposition can or will be considered as decisive. On treating my ozone with a solution of potash I obtain nitrate of potash, which fact goes rather far to prove the identity of nitric and ozonic acid. You have made

the same experiment in causing the electrical brush to act upon a piece of paper being impregnated with a solution of potash. You got salpeter by the electrical ozone, I by ozone being produced in the chemical way. In your experiment, as well as in mine, the formation of nitric acid, is due to a secundary chemical action and not to the immediate or direct union of Azote and Oxygen. I think it likely that during the action of Ozone upon the alkaline solution, not only ozonate of potash is formed, but also ozonide of potassium, just in the same manner as out of Chlorine and potash, chlorate of potash and Chloride of potassium are produced. It is however a chemical possibility also that ozone and potash generate nothing but Ozonate of potash. If you wish to repeat my principal experiments I strongly recommend to you the use of paper being impregnated with starch and jodide of potassium. It is a test for ozone being far superior even to the most delicate galvanometer. By that means you will easily ascertain the disengagement of ozone near a piece of phosphorus if that body is put into the open air after, having been a little rubbed and dried by filtering paper. Provided the slow oxidation of phosphorus be rather rapid, your test-paper will not fail being turned blue in a few instants. At a low temperature no such result will be obtained. To give you a matter-of-fact proof of the bleaching power of ozone I lay by three stripes of litmus paper[1] of which No. 1 was bleached by the electrical brush (produced by a four hours working of the machine), Nr. 2 by voltaic ozone and Nr. 3 by chemical ozone. As the latter one is in a more condensed state it bleaches more rapidly than the two other sorts of ozone do.

[1] These strips are however missing. Attached to a letter to Berzelius, dated April 14th 1844 are three strips shewing clearly the similarity of the bleaching actions of voltaic, chemical and electrical ozone. In fact one of them is the identical strip with which he for the first time proved the bleaching power of the electrical smell. Kahlbaum, Briefwechsel Berzelius-Schœnbein Basel 1898. p. 48.

To produce a fair quantity of ozone, put a piece of phosphorus into a bottle being filled with common air and expose the whole to a temperature of 15—25 ° C. Within a few minutes you will find your air charged with ozone already sufficient to turn your test paper into blue, and after an hours action the bleaching power of our atmosphere is such as to render (within a short time) a piece of litmus paper, not strongly colo[u]red, entirely white.

As the matter which I have now got into my hands promises to become rather a rich mine for scientific research, I flatter myself that you will not think me intrusive if I take the liberty to acquaint you from time to time with my results. I trust however, that before the year will be much older, I shall have the pleasure of paying you a visit and work with you in the Royal Institution; for I have a strong mind to cross the water in the month of July. Pray let me soon hear from you and excuse my hastily and badly written letter. As you may easily imagine I am now in rather a feverish state, working from morning to night in my laboratory and sleeping very little at night. *(Mrs. Schœnbein is quite surprized at my taciturnity and prolonged absences from home. She unites with me in kind regards to you and Mrs. Faraday and begs to be kindly remembered by you)*

Your's very faithfully

Bâle April 19th 1844.   C. F. SCHOENBEIN.

(Do you think a paper on Ozone would prove acceptable to the Royal Society?)   S.

Faraday to Schœnbein.

Royal Institution April 29. 1844.

MY DEAR FRIEND

Though I wrote you only a few days ago yet having received two other letters from you I think it will be better to trouble you with a line, though I hope with no postage. — Your Swiss postage always embarrassed me, for I was told I could pay and yet found, there was always something of a double postage in one direction.

But to reply. I have received a few days ago your letter of Feby 17. with the books and the diploma for Grove[1] — I thank you heartily for the share for me and only regret that I cannot read it — and have sent the other things to their destination. Your friend I did not see, I believe I was at Brighton at the time. —

Your last letter I have also had and it really is one to surprize and delight your friends, among whom I count myself one, and not the least warm in his feelings. I have read it but once and it is now out of my possession for I sent it at once to the Royal Society. — You will have seen by my answer to your first letter that, as you told me to use them as I thought fit, I had sent it there, wishing it at all events to be read there and communicated to the Fellows, and therefore on receipt of your second I sent it also to Mr Christie, the Secretary, without loss of time. As my health will not allow me to go to the meetings I do not know as yet whether they have been read. One of your letters says something about the question whether a paper for the R. S. would be acceptable. — Now here I must explain or else you will perhaps think I have not done rightly with your letters. I have the impression that the Royal Society prints no papers that are not original and do not appear first in *their own Transactions,* but that they would be glad to hear such valuable letters as yours and print them

[1] Grove had received an honorary degree of the University of Bâle. In a letter to Schœnbein dated June 1. 1844 Grove acknowledges the safe arrival of the diploma. The degree was conferred on Feb. 12. 1844, when Schœnbein was Vice-chancellor, or Rector as he is termed at Bâle. Grove is described as a "vir doctissimus, acer et diligens rerum, quae ad physicam pertinent, investigator, ... columnarum voltaicarum conditor nec non pneumaticæ columnæ, cuius in rerum naturae cognitione maxima vis est, inventor etc.

in their proceedings which, as they are reported and indeed given at full length in the Philosophical Magazine, would produce an early publication and show that the letters and the matter had been at the Royal Society. All your letters gave me to understand that your papers would appear immediately in the "Archives" and also probably in some other form, so I could not promise Mr Christie an original memoir from you. You must correct me if I have been in error.

From your letters I conclude we shalll have the pleasure of seeing you this summer either at York or here or both. Speaking of York reminds me that a communication from you on your subject of ozone and your last discoveries would be of great value to the Association and sure to be warmly received. With the best wishes and remembrances from my wife and myself to Madam Schœnbein and family I am ever

Yours

M. FARADAY.

Schœnbein to Faraday.

MY DEAR FARADAY

I have at last succeeded in isolating my Ozone and think you will be rather curious to know how that result has been obtained. I made use of twelve bottles, each holding about 30 litres, put in each of them a piece of phosphorus of about an inch long and suffered that body to act upon the atmospheric air, being contained in the bottles, at a temperature of 12—16° R. for 24 hours. After that time the atmosphere of the vessels was rather richly charged with ozone. I then carefully removed the phosphatic acid, having been formed during the process, by rinsing the bottles with distilled water and treated their remaining gazeous contents with a solution of jodide of potassium. In shaking the bottles with that liquid

Ozone is instantly taken up and Jodine eliminated. I had of course to repeat the same operation many a time before the solution of jodide of potassium was completely decomposed and changed to what I consider to be ozonide of potassium.[1]

As far as I have examined the latter compound it appears to be a white substance, not very soluble in water, feeble taste, is decomposed by a variety of acids, notably by sulphuric and muriatic acid, yielding at the same time ozone in its free state. Ozonide of potassium when newly prepared is completely neutral i. e. does not change in the least either blue or reddened litmus paper, but during evaporation it becomes alcaline and bleaches by degrees a piece of litmus paper, if the latter be alternately plunged into the solution of ozonide of potassium and taken out to let it dry in the atmosphere.

That solution being mixt up with some jodide of potassium throws down jodine, if acidulated by a variety of acids. And hence it follows that the presence of ozonide of pot. may easily be detected by starch containing some jodide of pot. and acidulating the substance to be examined with muriatic or sulphuric acid. The presence of the smallest traces of the ozonide is indicated by the blue colo[u]ring of the mixture. If the purest potash is heated and kept in fusion at the open air for some time, the remaining part, if dissolved in distilled water and acidulated with dilute sulphuric acid turns deeply blue starch mixt up with some jodide of pot. That fused potash acts exactly, as an artificially made mixture of ozonide of potassium and pure potash would do. I am inclined to think that under the circumstances mentioned part of the potash is really changed into ozonide of potassium. By heating strongly nitrate of potash, or any other nitrate containing an alkaline base, a substance is produced which being dissolved in water and acidulated exhibits the same properties as potash acquires by being strongly heated.

---

[1] vide p. 134, where he writes to Faraday, May 31th, informing him that this salt is not pure, but contains appreciable quantities of an iodate.

It is hardly possible, that peroxide of potassium is the cause of the elimination of jodine, that substance being instantly decomposed when brought in contact with water or acids. If moist starch containing jodide of potassium be exposed to the open air, by degrees it turns blue; if a piece of linen be drenched with an aqueous solution of jodide of potassium and suspended in the open air for a couple of days, it yields a feeble yellow solution if treated with distilled water. That yellow liquid colors pure moist starch into blue which indicates the presence of free jodine. And if the said yellow solution be heated to drive off the free jodine the remaining part being acidulated causes a blue coloring in liquid starch. You obtain the same results, only to a slighter degree, in making use of asbestum fibres instead of linen or paper. Heat jodide of potassium in the open air and hold a piece of paper being drenched either with pure starch or with starch containing jodide of potassium and you will find that for a great length of time the test paper is perceptibly colored. If you dissolve the remaining part of the fused jodide in water and put some muriatic acid to it, the solution assumes a yellowish tint and turns pure starch bluish. It seems therefore that under the circumstances indicated ozonide of potassium is formed, for I cannot account for the reactions observed in another manner. By burning potassium on a foil of platinum you obtain a substance which, if dissolved in dilute muriatic acid colours deeply blue starch containing jodide of potassium and that reaction takes place even after having heated for a short time the said acid solution. It seems to be a fact also connected with the ozone business. If dilute and chemically pure sulphuric acid, holding however some air dissolved, be heated to the boiling point with pure peroxide of manganese or peroxide of lead, a gazeous substance makes its appearance which has the property of turning my test-paper blue. Having entertained the boiling of the said mixture for some minutes the reaction ceases to take place.

Let the open vessel cool down again and be exposed for some time to the air, the starch paper will be colored afresh, if you heat the mixture again to its boiling point. As often as you repeat the same operation you will invariably obtain the same result. It seems to me that there cannot be the question of Chlorine as being the cause of the elimination of jodide, it must be something else. Now if azote happens to consist of Ozone and Hydrogen and if nascent Oxigen be capable of taking up the Hydrogen of azote in the same way, as it unites with that element being contained in hydroch[l]oric acid, all the reactions stated may easily be accounted for, if we take at the same time into consideration the slight degree of solubility of azote in water. Indeed, if we suppose the azote of the atmospheric air to be replaced by hydro-chloric acid and if we farther suppose the latter compound to be as slightly soluble in water as azote is, the very same phenomena would take place. I have ascertained many other facts not yet mentione[d] to you, all of them are such as to speak in favour of my notion, that azote is an electrolytic compound and consists of Ozone and Hydrogen.

I finished yesterday a little work [1] which contains a detailed account of all my researches on ozone; it consists of about 10 printed sheets and de la Rive cau[sed] a french translation [2] to be made in Geneva. As the subject is rather original and important, don't you think that an english version of the book would be favo[u]rably received in England. I wrote Grove about it, but have not yet got any answer from him.[3]

[1] He refers to his pamphlet: "Über die Erzeugung des Ozons auf chemischen Wege". Basel 1844.

[2] De la production de l'ozône par voie chimique. Extrait des Archives de l'Électricité No. 15, Genève 1844.

[3] Grove writes to him on Jan. 5th 1845 "I do not think many would purchase it in England; the few Electricians and Chemists who read French have already seen it at the Institutions in the Archives; but if you have several volumes to spare, there can be no harm in your sending them to Watkins to sell on commission."

In confidently hoping that you will enjoy perfect health I am
my dear friend
Your's
most faithfully

Bâle Mai 29. 1844.   C. F. SCHOENBEIN.

Dont forget to present Mrs. S. and my humble respects to Mrs. Faraday and excuse my bad writing.

Schœnbein to Faraday.

MY DEAR FRIEND

I write you a few lines to tell you that after having more closely examined the salt of which I spoke in my last letter as of pure ozonide of potassium, I found it to contain appreciable quantities of a jodate. I must therefore ask you the favo[u]r not to communicate my letter to the Royal Society at least not that part of it which regards the isolation of Ozone. It seems that in treating my ozoniferous atmosphere with jodide of potassium a good portion of ozone is taken up and does occasion the formation of the jodate mentioned. But even this action appears to be an additional proof of the analogy which exists between Chlorine and Ozone. Berzelius, to whom I communicated my results about six weeks ago,[1] takes a very lively interest in the ozone affair and encourages me to sift the matter to the bottom.[2]

Your's
very faithfully

Bâle 31. Mai 1844.   C. F. SCHOENBEIN.

[1] April 14th 1844.
[2] In a letter dated May 16th 1844 which he concludes as follows: "You must devote all your time to this so important investigation, you must follow it

Faraday to Schœnbein.

R. Instution 19 June 1844.

MY DEAR SCHOENBEIN

I have received yours and written again so closely lately as to have little to say upon the present occasion other than that I wait to hear in due time more of Ozone — and to introduce my good friend Dr. Holland[1] to you. I only wish I could have brought him to your house myself and so astonish you and Madam Schœnbein and my playmates. Any kindness you can show him will be very acceptable to your

sincere friend

M. FARADAY.

Schœnbein to Faraday.

MY DEAR FARADAY

Having made a journey into Germany with Mrs. Schœnbein and the children during our mid-summer holidays I could not have the pleasure of seeing your friend Dr. Holland who had favo[u]red Bâle with a visit whilst we were absent. I was indeed very sorry for it.

My first series of researches "on ozon"[2] was finished about eight weeks ago and I take the liberty to send you a copy of the little work in which You will find my results fully described. Had the french translation been out I should have offered you a copy of it, instead of the german original, I

---

up with the true perseverance of a Bunsen, and if possible not abandon it until we are perfectly clear about it". Kahlbaum Briefwechsel Berzelius-Schœnbein Basel 1898. p. 60.

[1] Most likely Sir Henry Holland M. D. F. R. S. physician-in-ordinary to Prince Albert who was born in 1788 at Knutsford and died in 1873 in London.

[2] He is evidently again alluding to his pamphlet: "Über die Erzeugung des Ozons auf chemischem Wege".

hope, however to find before long an opportunity for sending you the french book.

The subject in question is far from being exhausted and I think I shall be obliged to work hard next winter to get at the bottom of the matter. I am afraid I shall not be able to carry my plan into execution and attend the meeting at York; but you know perhaps some person who will undertake making some abstracts from my work with the view of communicating them to the association.

In that case you will perhaps have the kindness to read them there, provided you think them interesting enough for such a purpose.

If the committee of the british association, of which you are no doubt a member, should consider the subject of ozon as worthy of its attention and wish me to make a report on the farther researches I am about to institute on that matter, I shall undertake the task with the greatest pleasure and attend in person their next meeting for that purpose.

I am quite sure that a good deal of interesting facts will yet be brought to light with regard to the subject of ozon.

Should I be able to cross the water, next autumn, I shall not fail sending you word in time and try to arrive at London about a week previous to the opening of the meeting.

Mrs. Schœnbein and the Children are quite well and I am charged to remember them to their constant friend in Albemarle Street. Pray present my best compliments to your Lady and believe me

Your's
most truly

Bâle Aug. 27. 1844. C. F. Schoenbein.

P. S. Suppose the french translation of my work on ozon to be finished early enough as to arrive in England at the time of the meetings of the Association, do you think it advisable to send a certain number of copies there for sale? The work will cost about two shillings.[1]

Faraday to Schœnbein.

Dover 14. Septr. 1844

MY DEAR SCHOENBEIN

I received your letter etc here where I had come with my wife for a week or ten days, for a little revival of general health and where we are kept at present by a sad accident which happened to my only brother, who was also here with is wife. In bathing from a machine the sea shook the machine, he lost his footing, fell and broke *two ribs*. After that he dressed and walked to his lodgings and whether in so doing or at the time of the accident we cannot say, but the broken ends of the ribs had injured the lungs in some degree, so that air escaped. This happened last monday and though he is going on favourably at present, yet it makes us very anxious. — I had engaged and intended to go to the meeting at *York* and may still go, if he goes on well next week; but it is, as you will see, very possible that I may not be there. However we hope for the best in his case.

As to Ozone you know now that my bad memory and weak head cuts me off from many things and amongst others from that as to working, for I am not able to preserve anything

---

[1] Schœnbein not only wished the results of his researches to become known, he also hoped to gain some pecuniary advantage by them, such was his inexperience in such matters. Thus de la Rive, in whose "Archives" the French translation of his memoir appeared writes to him (June 30. 1844): "Mais, mon cher et illustre professeur, vous êtes bien innocent de croire qu'on en vendra... Croyez moi, n'espérez jamais tirer un parti quelconque financier de mémoires scientifiques."

constantly, as I used to do, and only by great management contrive to follow up piecemeal some views and pursuits of my own — my inability to bring them to a quick and distinct conclusion is to me evidence, I cannot work as I have done. But I read your letters with great interest and though the subject is very difficult, still am satisfied you will not leave it till you have settled it. — I sent them to the Royal Society with the restriction you made and also shewed them to Grove, Daniell and others. Now we have your accounts also in the Archives. — When I return home, which will be for *one day* if not more next week, I will send Your German book to Grove who reads german, I believe, and ask him about it and extracts from it for York.

It is so many years since I was at any of the meetings of the Association (except a few hours only at Birmingham or Manchester I forget which) that I really know nothing of their nature and whether a book like yours, if ready, would sell there or not. Judging by my own feelings I should think it would. Rich[d] Taylor of the Phil Mag whose brother is the treasurer would be very like to know, but the time is so near that it does not allow me to enquire and communicate his opionion, so as to enable any arrangements — and I am tied up here.

I will take care that either by myself or by your letter your kind offer to report at the next meeting on the state of the Ozone subject shall be laid before the proper body.

My wife is with me and desires her kind remembrances; she had not forgotten your intention of being here this year. Remember us both to Mrs. Schœnbein and to the growing up flock. I suppose I should see a difference now to what I saw when at Basle

Ever My dear Schœnbein
Yours
M. FARADAY.

Faraday to Schœnbein.

Royal Institution 25. Octr. 1844.

MY DEAR SCHOENBEIN

I write a brief note now that the York meeting is over (and I have returned from Durham, whither I was sent immediately after by our Government to be present at an inquest on the death of 95 men who were killed by explosion in a coal mine) to say that I stated at the meeting your propositions or willingness to report to them next year on Ozone and I found that there was *already* a resolution on the books in which they had agreed to ask you to do so. I conclude therefore that you will hear to that purport in due course and I earnestly hope that you will then have a specimen to show us. If it be possible, I have no doubt you will, for I know your energy and I never yet knew such energy to fail, unless nature were against it. — The next years meeting is to be at Cambridge — and the time is settled, which I intended to have told you but I cannot remember it and cannot remember where to look for it — my old infirmity — but you very likely have seen the date and know far more about it than I do. —

I am working but I cannot get on. — Work is now closed with me and one thing or another is continually occurring to prevent progress — I think I must at last entirely shut out this world for now my progress is slow and like that of the tortoise — a trifle to others stops me altogether.

Remember us both most kindly to all with you. I should like to see [. . . . .] Basle again.

Ever Your faithful

M. FARADAY.

Schœnbein to Faraday.

Bâle November 25th 1844.

My dear Faraday.

I think it is full time to acknowledge the last two letters you have been kind enough to address to me.

The official invitation to prepare a report about my researches on ozon for the british association I received the other day and certainly I shall not fail complying with the wishes expressed to me. If possible I shall read that report myself at Cambridge and perform the necessary experiments. You know perhaps that I attended the meeting of the italian association at Milan[1] to make there a communication on my recent investigations; unfortunately however the chemical section was not such as I could have wished it to be, only a few chymists being there who really deserved that denomination. Amongst them was Piria[2] who suggested the idea, that all the effects I ascribe to a peculiar principle, "to my ozon", might be due to nitrous acid. Though the smell of the two substances be as different as possible and other properties of ozon stated in my last memoir be not those of nitrous acid, the italian Chymist stuck rather tenaciously to his opinion. Immediately after my return from Milan I took up the subject again and made a series of experiments with the view of getting the most decisive matter of fact evidence for proving the peculiarity of my principle and I think I have perfectly succeeded in putting even beyond the shade of a doubt that Ozon and nitrous acid have nothing to do with one another.

My principal proofs are as follows:[3]

---

[1] Discussion sur l'ozone. Compt. rend. d. séances du congrès scient. de Milan. 1844. Sulla produzione dell' ozono per via chimica. Milano. 1845.

[2] Rafaello Piria was born in 1815 at Sevilla in Calabria. He was professor of chemistry at Turin where died in 1865.

[3] Vide Poggend. Annal. Bd. 63. 1844. p. 520.

1. Two stripes of platinum after having been plunged equally long, one into atmospheric air mixt up with vapour of nitrous acid the other into air containing ozon, produce a current the direction of which is such as to indicate the ozonized stripe to be the negative part of the circuit. Ozon is therefore a body more electro-negative than nitrous acid.

2. A stripe of platinum having been negatively polarized by Ozon looses its voltaic condition and becomes neutral when plunged for a short time into an atmosphere containing nitrous acid.

3. Air being ever so much charged with Ozon looses its peculiar smell, its electro-motive power, its property of destroying vegetable colours etc. when mixt up with the proper quantity of the vapour of nitrous acid. The smell of the latter acid also disappears under the circumstances mentioned.

4. An ozonized atmosphere may be shaken for a great length of time with peroxide of lead being suspended in some water without loosing its characteristic properties, whilst air charged with vapours of nitrous acid and treated in the same manner becomes inodorous and looses its properties which are due to nitrous acid.

5. A solution of sulfate of protoxide of iron turns brownish when shaken with an atmosphere containing only traces of nitrous acid, whilst the same solution being treated with air, which happens to be ever so much charged with Ozon remains, as to its colour, unchanged and yields a whitish precipitate.

6. Blue and humid litmus-paper placed within a strongly ozonized atmosphere is completely bleached within about 10—15 minutes without assuming the slightest reddish tint, whilst paper of the same description being suspended in vapours of nitrous acid first turns red and requires hours or even days to become entirely bleached. And in that case the paper is very strongly acid i. e. impregnated with nitric acid, whilst the paper bleached by Ozon is always quite free from any trace of acid.

7. Phosphorus being (in darkness) introduced into atmospheric air which is only slightly charged with vapours of nitrous acid, ceases to give out any light and becomes and continues to be completely dark, whilst phosphorus put into strongly ozonized air happens to shine even more lively than it does in common air.

The facts above mentioned clearly show that Ozon is no acid principle and not to be confounded with nitrous acid.[1]

I must not omit to mention that the voltaic bearings of Chlorine and Bromine to nitrous acid are strikingly similar to those in which Ozon and the last-named acid are standing to each other. A stripe of platinum ever so powerfully polarized either by Chlorine or Bromine looses its negative polarity when plunged into an atmosphere containing vapours of nitrous acid.

The electro-motive power enjoyed by a chlorine or Bromine atmosphere is also destroyed if mixt up with a proper quantity of the vapour of nitrous acid. Such a close analogy as does exist between Chlorine, Bromine and Ozone appears to me to be an important fact and to speak in favour of the view I have taken of the nature of Ozon. Indeed the more I compare experimentally the properties of Chlorine and Bromine with those of Ozon the more I get struck with the similarity of the three [principles]. But whatever Ozon may be, it is at any rate a very interesting substance and just the thing made to excite the curiousity both of Chymists and natural philosophers. As to me, I shall do what I can to clear up the subject.

You may easily imagine that I feel very anxious to hear soon about the results of your present philosophical doings and I am quite sure that they will be highly interesting to science, for allow me to tell you, you cannot take any subject into

---

[1] See Poggend. Annal. Bd. 63. 1844. p. 520: "Ozone ist nicht salpetrige Säure".

your hands without getting something excellent out of it, be it sooner or later.

Mrs. Schœnbein and the Children are quite well and all of them charge me with their best salutations both to you and your lady. Pray remember me also very kindly to Mrs. Faraday and believe me

Yours
most truly
C. F. SCHOENBEIN.

I ardently wish and earnestly hope that your brother will by this time have entirely recovered from his serious accident.

Faraday to Schœnbein.

Royal Institution 20. Feby. 1845.

MY DEAR FRIEND

I cannot call to mind whether I wrote to you last, or whether yours to me still remains unanswered, in which things my memory becomes more and more treacherous. My impression is, that I heard from you not very long ago — but now I cannot find the letter — as I write it comes to my mind that I have sent it to Mr. Christie for the Royal Society — but the order of these events or the order of the matter contained in your letters and papers on Ozone I cannot remember. I have lately been reading the account you give in the Archives de l'Électricité[1] and am astonished as I read at the mass of concurrent evidence: it is so great. Surely you must some day succeed in getting Ozone in quantity — it seems whilst reading, as if you were every moment on the point of doing so. — Yet when I want to recall and arrange the

---

[1] Archives de l'Electr. T. 5. 1845. p. 11.

many facts and arguments I become altogether confused; my memory will not serve me and I really become dull sometimes, to find how in this way I am left behind in the use and appreciation of what others have done. Unless there be some visible body before my eyes, or some large fact approaching with force to the external senses, and easy to be produced, to sustain, by a sort of material evidence the existence of a thought, the thought fades away and however much I may have endeavoured to measure out and fix my judgment at the time of receiving and considering the thought, afterwards I fear to trust to the conclusion I have come to, because the thought and the considerations in which it was founded have left me. It is only in this way, I can account for the hesitation I have in making up my mind on many points of chemical philosophy which are now before the scientific world.

I have been at work these last 6 or 8 months on the condensation of gases — a very tangible subject, giving very strong impressions of its nature and effects every now and then by an explosion, though I have met with very few, only two indeed, and these rather expected and in some degree prepared for. — You will have seen the general result in the Annales de Chimie[1] but I hope soon to send you the paper from the Philosophical Transactions,[2] that is, if I can find a way to send it. I have been waiting to write to you, that I might send you at the instant of doing so an account of the condensation of *oxygen*, but as yet he will not yield, though I have given him a pressure of 60 atmospheres, at a temperature of 140° F. below 0°;[3] and now I must lay by the experiments for a while — for, first I am not well, having been confined almost entirely,

[1] Annales de Chimie, T. 15. 1845. p. 257.
[2] On the liquefaction and solidifaction of bodies generally existing as gases, Phil. Trans. 1845. p. 155.
[3] Cailletet of Paris and Pictet of Geneva, it will be remembered, succeeded in liquifying oxygen, but not till 1877, at a pressure of 320 atm. and a temperature of —140° C.

to my rooms for the last three weeks — next my head is becoming giddy with the continuance of the investigation — and finally I must prepare to lecture after Easter. — Yet I could not lay down all these things and amongst them my intention of writing to you, without carrying the latter into effect, though as you will see in a very imperfect manner. But that does not stop me. I do not expect to make my letters scientific communications, for from the reasons I have given you, they must ever be unsteady and doubtful in that respect, my memory of the things thus to be spoken of being so — but I write them and especially to you, my dear friend, as kindly remembrances of good feeling and grateful expressions for encouragement and happiness, communicated to me from minds having feelings akin to my own. — With kindest remembrances to Mrs. Schœnbein and the growing flock

I am as Ever
Your faithful
M. FARADAY.

Schœnbein to Faraday.

MY DEAR FARADAY

I have made up my mind to read my report on Ozone myself and illustrate the subject by a series of experiments to be exhibited before the chemical section. Intending to leave Bâle the 12th instant I hope to arrive in town Monday the 16th and I need not say you, how delighted I would be to see you on that or the following day. As I shall pass the shop of Mr. Watkins (Charing cross), pray send me a few lines there to acquaint me whether I can have the pleasure of meeting you at the Royal Institution.

K

In entertaining the pleasing hopes of shaking very soon hands with you and paying my humble respects in person to your Lady I am, my dear Faraday

Your's
most faithfully

Bâle June 4th 1845.   C. F. SCHOENBEIN.

Faraday to Schœnbein.

R Institution 14 June 1845

DEAR SCHOENBEIN

We are in town. I do not know, when you will be here, but I hope to be at home when you call. I shall be engaged from 4 o'clock on Monday, but I expect my wife will be at liberty then, as well as before.

Ever Yours
M. FARADAY.

Schœnbein to Faraday.

MY DEAR FARADAY

Ever since my return from England I have been rather busy, and tried to make out the relations which Ozone bears to nitrogen and its oxycompounds. I think I have succeeded in ascertaining some facts, being calculated to throw some light upon the cause of what is called spontaneous nitrification, and I am inclined to believe, that I have extended a little the limits of our knowledge regarding the oxycompounds of azote. As you will learn from some papers[1] sent to the chemical

---

[1] vide Chem. Soc. Mem. vol. 3. 1845—1848. p. 2. cf. also Poggend. Annal. Bd. 67. 1845. p. 127 and Bibl. Univ. T. 1. 1845. pag. 31.

society, my strong opinion is that there exist only three primitive degrees of oxidation of nitrogen, NO, NO_2 and NO_4. As to the hydrate of nitric acid, it is to me $NO_4 + HO_2$ and agreeably to that view, I must consider a normal nitrate as $NO_4 + RO_2$. It appears to me highly probable that nitrous acid $= NO_6$, is nothing but a loose compound of $NO_4 + NO_2$, and a normal nitrite $NO_2 + RO_2$, instead of $NO_3 + RO$. The reasons for admitting the existence of a compound $= NO_2 + HO_2$ seem to me very strong and some facts stated in the papers before mentioned, can, to my opinion, only be accounted for by that admission.

If you think the notice laid by of sufficient importance, as to interest the Royal Society, you will oblige me by laying it before that body. If not, you have full liberty, either to insert it (perhaps in the shape of a letter addressed to you) in the philosophical Magazine, or read it before the chemical Society. At any rate, I should be very glad indeed if you would favour me with your opinion about the subjects alluded to in this letter.

Mrs. Schœnbein and the children are quite well and charge me to offer both to you and Mrs. Faraday their kindest regards. In the pleasing hopes of hearing soon good news from you, I am my dear Faraday

Yours most truly

Bâle Oct. 20th 1845. C. F. SCHOENBEIN.

P. S. I had nearly forgotten telling you, that I have made a good many experiments on the bleaching powers of atmospheric air, ozonized by the means of phosphorus.

The results obtained with linnen are such as to make me believe it possible to bleach œconomically into ozon and establish a process upon that principle, being superior to any hitherto employed. One of the bits of linnen laid by was bleached with the only means of ozone within a fortnight, the other is a pattern of the raw linen.[1] Do you not think that something might be made out of that affair? I am told that a german Chymist, who has got some knowledge of my process, is about to take out a patent upon it in England. He ought to be prevented from doing so, as he has no right for it.

Faraday to Schœnbein.

Brighton 13 Nov. 1845

MY DEAR SCHOENBEIN

I received yours of the 20th Ultimo and have sent off the paper to the Royal Society[2] with my humble opinion, that it is good. You know I am not (and have no time to be) in the Councils. Your bleaching is very remarkable and good.

At present I have scarcely a moment to spare for any thing, but work. I happen to have discovered a direct relation between magnetism and light, also electricity and light, and the field it opens is so large and I think rich, that I naturally wish to look at it first. — I have sent one paper to the Royal[3] and am about another. — I actually have not time to tell you what the thing is, — for I now see no one and do nothing but just work.

My head became giddy and I have therefore come to this place, but still I bring my work with me. When I can catch

[1] The strips of linen are no longer attached to the letter.
[2] Phil. Trans. 1846. p. 137.
[3] For fully forty years he searched after the relation of electricity and magnetism to light. In 1845 it was that while experimenting with heavy glass through which he passed lines of magnetic force and, at the same time, a polarized ray of light he proved that magnetic force and light have relations to each other. As a result he sent his 19th series of researches in electricity to the Royal Society (Phil. Trans. 1846. p 1): "On the magnetic affection of light and the illumination of the lines of magnetic force" (see Bence Jones vol. 2. p. 195.).

time I will tell you more. But in the midst of all this philosophy, do not forget to remember both my wife and myself to Mrs. Schœnbein. The thought of being quietly with you in the mountains, or on the river forms a strange contrast with my present most active state.

Ever, Dear Schœnbein
Your grateful friend
M. FARADAY.

You can hardly imagine how I am struggling to exert my poetical ideas just now for the discovery of analogies and remote figures respecting the earth, sun, and all sorts of things — for I think that is the true way (corrected by judgment) to work out a discovery.

M. F.

Schœnbein to Faraday.

MY DEAR FARADAY

I am much obliged to you for the very kind letter you favoured me with some weeks ago and you may easily imagine that its contents, vague and general as they were, proved highly interesting to me and set my curiousity on tiptoe. As far as I can judge, your last discovery will eclipse all your former ones, brilliant as they are.

The other day I had a letter from de la Rive [1], who I see entertains as yet the opinion, that the action excited by magnetism upon polarized light is not directly due to that force but to a change brought about in the molecular arrangement of your glass by magnetism.[2] It seems, that the same view

---

[1] Oct. 12th 1845.

[2] "Elle est d'une grande importance," he writes, though he does not agree with Faradays interpretation of its cause, for he continues "Je crois que l'aimant ou les courants électriques exercent leur action non sur la lumière, mais sur les

of the case is taken by the parisian philosophers. I am as yet too little acquainted with the particulars of your discovery, as to be capable of forming a correct notion about it, but the little I know of it makes me strongly believe, that de la Rive and the french are wrong and you in the right. It appears to me that the prime focus of the case is such, as to lead every impartial philosopher to the conclusion you have drawn from the fundamental phenomenon ascertained by you. How the molecular arrangement of a bit of amorphous glass can be changed by magnetical action in such a way, as to make that medium act upon a beam of polarized light in the manner you have observed, is a thing, which, I openly confess it, goes beyond my conception. I am however confident that you will not be long in bringing forward such an overwhelming mass of the strongest matter of fact evidence in favour of the view you have taken of the subject, that all those little objections, which I am afraid do not entirely originate in the love of truth, will be easily reduced to what they really are. I hail in your discovery, the beginning of a new era in the history of philosophy, and am at any rate sure that it will ultimately lead to great things.

As to my little self I have of late turned entirely Chymist, being almost exclusively occupied with researches on nitric acid and the other oxy-compounds of nitrogen, subjects which appear to be closely connected with my Ozone business. As to nitric acid, I am now almost quite sure that it does not exist and that what Chymists call the first hydrate of that imaginary compound is $NO_4 + HO_2$ and not $NO_5 + HO$, much less $NO_6 + H$. The normal nitrates exempl. gr. nitrate of baryte,

molécules du cristal et que c'est un phénomène du même genre que les phenomènes moléculaires de vibration qui resultent sur les corps non magnetiques de l'action des currants discontinués."

Grove in a letter dated Nov. 16. 1845 writes to Schœnbein: "Faraday has made a great dicovery.... I am anxious to know what the point is that has enabled him to succeed. I tried last year for several weeks and failed."

nitrate of lead, are to me $NO_4 + BaO_2$, $NO_4 + PbO_2$ etc. Our poor late friend Daniell[1] would be very sorry to hear such heretical doctrine.

Before long I hope to be able to reassume some voltaic researches regarding electrolysis, having a notion, that much is to be done yet in that branch of science, in spite of your beautiful doings in that line. — Whether I shall succeed in establishing what I think at present to be true, I can of course not say; I am however confident that my endeavours will not prove entirely fruitless.

They say that Dr. Neef[2] of Francfort has made a discovery establishing also a connection between light and electricity,[3] but I dont know the particulars about it. I confess however that I doubt as yet of the correctness of the fact.

Pray present my best compliments and Mrs. Schœnbein's also your Lady and believe me

Yours
most faithfully

Bâle Dec. 30. 1845.   C. F. SCHOENBEIN.

Schœnbein to Faraday.

MY DEAR FARADAY.

Amid the glories of your really grand and admirable discovery I venture to trouble you with a comparatively insignificant and prosaic subject. I have of late also made a little chemical discovery which enables me to change *very suddenly*,

---

[1] J. F. Daniell it will be remembered died on March 13. 1845.

[2] Christian Ernst Neef Ph. D. physician in Frankfort on the Main where he was born in 1781 and died in 1849.

[3] Schœnbein is alluding to his paper bearing the following title "Üher das Verhältnis der elektrischen Polarität zu Licht und Wärme" which is printed in Poggend. Annal Bd. 64. 1845. p. 414.

very easily and *very cheaply* common paper in such a way, as to render that substance exceedingly strong and entirely water proof.[1] Inclosed you will find a specimen of paper of the said description and a sample of common paper, out of which the former has been prepared. In throwing the prepared paper into water you will easily convince yourself that it stands the action of that fluid for any length of time, without loosing in the least its leather-like toughness. Paper which has been lying in water for many days is still as tenacious as it was in the beginning.[2] The same sort of paper being written allows to be laid up in water, strongly acidulated with muriatic acid and freed in that way from its ink, without receiving the slightest injury, or leaving the least trace of the letters. The most brittle and thinnest paper, after having for a few seconds only, been exposed to the action of my agent, becomes very tough, substancial and water proof.[3] Hence it follows that in employing my process, out of the same quantity of rags, a much larger number of sheets of paper can be manufactured than it is possible to do in following up the present way of making paper,[4] without diminishing the strength of the production. Another essential advantage connected with my method of preparing paper is, that the injurious effects produced by chloride of lime are entirely

---

[1] On March 5th 1846 Schœnbein writes to Berzelius acquainting him at some length with the properties and mode of preparation of his paper, and encloses specimens of it to illustrate his communication. Kahlbaum, Briefwechsel Berzelius-Schœnbein. p. 80. By citing a few parallel passages from his letter to Berzelius we have endeavoured to illustrate the similarity of the terms in which he has in each case put his ideas into words.

[2] However long it is exposed to the action of water it retains its coherence. ibid. p. 81.

[3] Thin and extremely brittle paper acquires by my process a firmness and toughness equal to that of much thicker ordinary paper of the toughest texture. ibid. p. 81.

[4] ...and moreover my process has the advantage, that it allows of a much larger number of sheets being made from the same quantity of rags, than in the ordinary method of paper making. ibid. p. 81.

paralysed by it. My prepared paper can be easily written and printed upon. Paper enjoying the properties mentioned is, to my opinion, a valuable substance and in many respects very superior to common paper, it ought therefore to be manufactured on a large scale. My process of giving common paper those properties being of a very easy application and very cheap too, I do not see any reason why, it should not be made use of at once. I am of course desirous of turning, if possible, the discovery alluded to to some account in favour of a certain poor schoolmaster of Bâle, who in the interest of science is rather anxious to get a little more independent, than he is now. To obtain that end, I ask you the favour to grant me your kind advice regarding that affair. You are perhaps connected with some first-rate british paper manufacturer or it lies in your power to put me in communication with one or some of them.[1]

Before long you will hear of some other little chemical exploits I have of late performed; they consist principally in remarkable transformations of the most common vegetable substances. These and other things I found out in making researches on my favorite subject, ozone.

Pray present Mrs. Schœnbein's compliments and my own to your Lady. Favo[u]r me soon with an answer to this letter and believe me

Your's
most sincerely

Bâle Febr. 27. 1846.　　　　　　　　C. F. Schœnbein.

[1] Concerning his offer to give the Swedish Government instructions concerning this new method of his in the interest of the paper industry of that country Schœnbein does not seem to have received an answer on the part of Berzelius.

The only encouragement Grove could give him, after enquiring in several quarters, was that it might be worked into something, if it could be applied very cheaply to brown paper, for outer wrappers. Letter to Schœnbein, Aug. 16. 1846.

Faraday to Schœnbein.

R. Institute 5 March 1846.

MY DEAR SCHOENBEIN

Excuse my sending you a very short letter, but I am just now burdened with business and thought and my head often aches. — I received your letter the day before yesterday and sent it at once with the specimens to Mr. Dickenson one of our largest paper makers (whom I slightly know) and desired him, if the result interested him, to communicate at once with you. Of course I have not as yet had time to hear any thing, [even] if he should think of writing to me.

I did not examine your paper[1] but sent it off at once. It reminded me of some that I had seen some years ago, in which the paper had been passed through a clean infusion of tannin and so had its gelatine size converted into leather. That process at one time looked very promising, and I do not know, why it was not pursued, except it was because, soon after, gelatine was to a great extent dismissed as the sizing material, and resin and oil in the form of soap, decomposed by alum, substituted for it.

I should be glad to send you a copy of my last papers but our Royal Society is very slow and I see many descriptions of results obtained in France, Italy and elsewhere — all of which are in my papers of *last year* — but which have been reobtained by those who have worked on the notices.

I am also puzzled about the best way of sending them to you with certainty.

Our best thanks and remembrances to Mrs. Schœnbein and her flock

Ever Yours

M. FARADAY.

[1] Schœnbein also sent specimens of his paper to Poggendorff who suggests employing it for making window panes, and writes as follows (May 1, 1846) "Das

Schœnbein to Faraday.

MY DEAR FARADAY

Don't take it ill if I venture to trouble you once more with my little affair, I flatter myself however that the interest which seems to be connected with the subject will excuse my intenseness. To give you an idea of what may be made out of vegetable fibre, I send you a specimen of a transparent substance which I have prepared out of common paper. This matter is capable of being shaped out into all sorts of things and forms and I have made from it a number of beautiful vessels. The first perfect one I obtained is destined to be sent to the Mistress of the Royal Institution, as soon as a convenient opportunity will offer itself for doing so and I shall ask the Lady mentioned to preserve it as a sort of scientific keepsake. In taking the liberty to forward to you a little piece of my transparent paper, I must beg you to keep it entirely to yourself and consider it as a stric[t]ly confidential communication, and I ask you this piece of favour because my secret with regard to my water proof paper is connected with that substance. I shall however be obliged to you if you will have the kindness to exhibit it before a Friday Meeting of the Royal Institution.

There is another point about which I take the liberty to ask your kind advice. I am enabled to prepare in any quantity a matter which, next gunpowder, must be regarded as the most combustible substance known. So inflammable is that matter, that on being brought in contact with the slightest spark, it will instantly be set on fire, leaving hardly any trace of

glasartige Papier ist in der That sehr schön, und ich möchte wünschen, dass Sie ein solches dick darstellen könnten, um es als Fensterscheiben anzuwenden." In the same letter he advises him to apply to the directors of the Prussian Bank as his paper might with advantage be employed for the manufacture of bank notes.

ashes and if the combustion be caused within closed vessels a violent explosion takes place. That combustible substance is, as I will confidently tell you, raw cotton, prepared in a simple manner, which I shall describe you hereafter. I must not omit to mention that water has not the least action upon my matter, i. e. that it may be immersed ever so long in that fluid, without loosing its inflammability, after having been dried again. A substance of that description seems to be applicable to many purposes of daily life and I should think that it might advantageously be used as a powerful means of defense and attack. Indeed the congrevian rockets [1] can hardly be more combustible than my prepared cotton is. What shall I do with that matter? Shall I offer it to your government? I have inclosed a little bit of that really frightful body and you may easily convince yourself of the correctness of my statements regarding its properties.[2]

As to my prepared paper you will be interested in learning that it proves to be a highly electrical substance as will appear from the following facts.[3]

1. In putting half a dozen of sheets one above another and passing once or twice the hand over the uppermost one, all the sheets will stick together so, as if they had been joined by the means of a glutinous matter.

2. The experiment being made in the dark, a prepared sheet rubbed becomes luminous, and on separating two excited

---

[1] The Congreve rocket was invented for use in war by Sir William Congreve (born 1772 in Staffordshire, died 1828 at Toulouse). When used for bombardment it was armed with a combustible material, inclosed in a metallic case, which is inextinguishable when kindled, and scatters its fire on every side.

[2] Berzelius writing on Nov. 18th 1846 congratulates him on his discovery in the following terms: "Allow me to convey to you my sincerest compliments on this interesting and significant discovery, the practical nature of which you promptly understood how to appreciate". Kahlbaum, Briefwechsel Berzelius-Schœnbein. p. 87.

[3] See also: "Über elektrisches Papier". Poggend. Annal. Bd. 68. 1846. p. 159.

sheets from each other a great number of beautiful sparks are seen breaking out between the paper.

3. An excited sheet held over the head makes the hair stand on end.

4. The disc of the common electrophor placed upon an excited sheet, lying upon the naked table, yields sparks of some inches in length.

5. A couple of sheets being lively rubbed develop a strong odour of ozone.

6. The electricity developed by my paper is the negative one.

The facts stated render it almost certain that out of my paper powerful electrical machines may be constructed, which will perhaps replace the plate arrangements. I shall soon have a paper machine. I need hard[l]y say that the transparent substance is still more electrical than the prepared paper.

Before I conclude I must offer you my grateful thanks for the kindness with which you put me in communication with Mr. Dickenson. Before entering into any negociation with him, I will wait a little longer for other offers, for it seems to me that he has not quite fully appreciated the qualities of my paper.

Don't you think the Bank would like to have their notes made of that paper? From the specimens of what we call silkpaper laid by, you will see how much the prepared bit surpasses in strength and impermeability the common one. I inclose also a specimen of paper having been very slightly prepared and being distinguished by its beautiful play of colour. Perhaps some use may be made of it.

I am overcurious to learn more particulars regarding your investigations and it is indeed a great pity that the regulations of the Royal Society cause such a delay in publishing scientific results communicated to that body.

Mrs. Schœnbein and the girls are doing well and beg me to present to you and Mr. Faraday the kindest regards.

Believe me my dear Faraday

Your's most faithfully

Bâle March 18. 1846. C. F. SCHOENBEIN.

NB. To shelter the transparent matter from injury I have put it between some bits of prepared paper glued together by wafers at their four corners. — In drying a little the prepared stripes Nr. I and II you will easily recognise their electrical condition by rubbing them with the hand over a common bit of paper.

Schœnbein to Faraday.

MY DEAR FARADAY

A favo[u]rable opportunity is just now offering itself for sending you some larger bits of my prepared paper. They will enable you to try its electrical power and other qualities. The degree to which it can be excited will perhaps astonish you and I should think that on this account it will prove an acceptable substance to electricians.

Ever Your's most truly

Bâle March 23. 1846. C. F. SCHOENBEIN.

NB. My prep. paper being in a completely raw state it of course cannot look well. The thin one seems to be very fit for bank notes.

I open the letter to tell you that I have just now made some preliminary experiments about the explosive power of my prepared cotton and found that it is rather considerable. A common soldier's gun charged with the eighth part of an ounce only, caused a pretty strong explosion.[1]   S.

[1] cf. letter to Berzelius June 10th 1846. Kahlbaum, Briefwechsel Berzelius-Schœnbein, p. 85.

It was most likely the first time that a gun had been fired by the means of cotton. That substance so advantageous to brother Jonathan might one day prove dangerous to him, particularly as an easy means to cause wholesale conflagrations.

Schœnbein to Faraday.

MY DEAR FARADAY

Mr. Prevost[1] is kind enough to charge himself with the little box containing a liliputian bell made out of my transparent paper. It is however not that mentioned in my last letter to you and destined for Mrs. Faraday. This little piece of chemical workmanship must find its way to Albemarle Street through another channel and at another time.

Your's
very truly

Bâle, March 24 1846.   C. F. SCHOENBEIN.

Schœnbein to Faraday.[2]

(Aug 22. 1846)

MY DEAR FARADAY

Having learned from Grove[3] the great loss you had to suffer some days ago[4] I hardly dare to ask you whether

---

[1] J. L. Prevost, a genevese emigré who settled in London and became partner of the firm Maurice Prevost & Co.

[2] The letter bears no date; the postmark is Aug. 22nd 1846.

[3] In a letter dated Aug. 16. 1846. He merely writes: "Faraday's brother was killed last week, being thrown from his gig."

[4] Faraday writes to Mrs. Faraday: "It is supposed the horse must have been frightened, or run against a post, but the cart was overturned, my poor brother cast out, and so injured on the head as not to recover his consciousness again." He died Aug. 13. 1846. Bence Jones vol. 2. p. 226.

one of these days I could see you, and communicate with you on some important subject. Pray remind me kindly to Mrs. Faraday and believe me
Yours
very truly
6 Golden Square
Regent Street.
C. F. SCHOENBEIN.

Faraday to Schœnbein.

Tunbridge Wells. 24 Aug 1846.

MY DEAR SCHOENBEIN

I received your letter here and though sad events make me unable to profit at once by your presence in London, yet I should like to see you if it can be. Now I shall be in town *next Monday* morning (alone) and if you should be in town and would perhaps like to see an experiment or two on the Magnetic action of bodies, I would undertake to show them to you. In that case I would stop in town an hour or two and devote the morning to you and we would experiment and talk from any hour you please, beginning at 9 o'clock A. M. — Besides I want to talk with you about *the paper etc*.

Write me a note to the Institution saying what you will do and the hour and send it to the Royal Institution and it will be forwarded to me wherever I am.

Mrs. Faraday unites in kind wishes to you

Yours affect.
M. FARADAY.

Schœnbein to Faraday.

MY DEAR FARADAY

I have just recived your kind note and am glad to learn from it that there is a chance of seeing you here. I shall not fail being at the Royal Institution Monday morning and most happy to witness some experiments and have some talk with you. The affair which has brought me over to England refers to my explosive cotton, which I have so much improved that it has all the appearance of becoming a dangerous rival to gunpowder. As to its explosive powers "gun cotton", as I call it, is very superior to powder; in given cases one part of it does the work of four parts of gun-powder and under the most unfavo[u]rable circumstances the force of gun-cotton is as 2:1 to that of gun powder. In the course of the two last months I have made many experiments with cannons, mortars, rifles etc. and obtained results which I am allowed to call highly satisfactory. The same way be said with regard to blasting rocks.[1]

The residuum left by gun cotton amounts to nothing; it does not heat perceptibly the fire arms, nor produce any smoke, if prepared to its maximum. The way of preparing it is simple, cheap, and without any danger of explosion. I myself and many friends who have seen the effects of the matter are inclined to believe, that gun cotton will be made use of in many cases, where gun powder is at present employed.

Now the object of my journey to England is to see, whether something might be done with that explosive matter[2] and I

[1] On June 20. 1846. He writes to Berzelius: "I have several times used my gun cotton for blasting in a tunnel which is being made through shell-limestone in our neighbourhood and in the opinion of the workmen it was as effective as three times the quantity of powder." Kahlbaum, Briefwechsel. p. 85.

[2] The results of his application for patents are mentioned (at a later date) by Grove at different occasions. Thus on Febr. 1. 1847 he writes: "I have drawn up an agreement by which you are to have one fourth part of the profits of the working of your invention within the States of Mexico. Col. Colquhoun says he thinks you will make more by your Mexican, than by your English patent. I hope you may realize a good fortune by both." In a letter of an earlier date (Nov. 13. 1846) he writes: "I have a letter from M. Louyet Professor of Chemistry Brussels; he is anxious to patent your gun cotton there. He says he is informed that the government will not grant anything and therefore if you are inclined to patent it, he will get the patent taken out and worked, and arrange with you for your share of the profits, as you may agree."

shall take the liberty to take some quantity with me to the Institution to show you the effects. It is not unlikely that some experiments will be made at Woolwich to prove the power of my production. Hershel has already taken some steps to that effect,[1] and you will perhaps be able to give me some hints respecting the affair.

In hoping to see you monday next, I beg you to present my humble compliments to Mrs. Faraday and believe me

Your's
very truly

6 Golden Square   C. F. SCHOENBEIN.
25. Aug. 1846.

Faraday to Schœnbein.

Royal Institution 18. Decr. 1846.

MY DEAR SCHOENBEIN

I really feel as if I wished to know whether you are yet in the flesh or whether you have gone off altogether like a piece of your own cotton.[2] I can never hear of your name now, except from some one who has a commercial value attached to it, either one way or the other; and nobody suggests you to my mind as that dear, quiet, lively, philosopher, and yet somewhat sentimental friend that I so much like to think of. Your name is now a name of power: — it always has

---

[1] In October 1846 the British Government voted a grant of £1500 for the purpose of experiments with gun cotton; these took place on Oct. 9 1846, in the presence of Schœnbein himself and, among others, of Sir James Hogg, President of the East India Company, and were very successful.

[2] This reminds one of an éxpression employed by Grove in a letter to Schœnbein (Aug. 31. 1848). After giving want to his great disappointment at Schœnbeins not attending the british Association at Swansea, Groves native place, he says: "All chemists were there, but no Schœnbein. You ought to be "hoist with your own petard" i. e. blown up with gun-cotton."

been a name of mental power; — but now it is powerful in the gross things of this world: — and it often makes me smile when I hear people talking of Schœnbein — I mean of the Gun-cotton Schœnbein, to think how little they know of his true spirit and pleasant ways. Each sticks something on to the name like that he would have himself desired to have it, had he been the Gun-cotton man. But joking apart I am glad to think, that, now there is some, and I suppose a great, chance that a portion of the good things of this life will fall to your share, who have so well deserved them; and in causing them, have done so, not for their own sakes merely but in the true and correct pursuit and love of science. Long may *you* and *yours* live to enjoy, first a contented and happy mind, and with it those temporal goods which God may think fit to give you.

I suppose you heard of Mr. Lancaster's accident with some Gun-cotton prepared by a Mr. Taylor. His gun burst and it is well he was not more than slightly wounded in the arm.[1] It was the time of his going out next after you and I and he were together. — I hear talking all round me and see advertisements, from the parties representing you, continually in the papers; but as you know I do not meddle with any thing commercial, so I know little or nothing of what has been done or is likely to be done. — I hope we shall some day have a simple and philosophical account of the substance; — its analysis, and above all the philosophical views and reasonings you connect with it; for I know, by a few words which you dropped that you have such. — Mr. Brande[2] is going to give

---

[1] Berzelius in a letter to Schœnbein (March 12. 1847) mentions that at a meeting of the Royal Academy of Stockholm serious disasters were reported to have occurred at Brunswick, caused by the bursting of rifles through too powerful a charge of gun cotton. Kahlbaum, Briefwechsel, p. 91.

[2] William Thomas Brande, professor of Chemistry at the Royal Institute was born in 1788 in London. He succeeded Sir Humphry Davy in 1813; from 1854 he held the post simultaneously with Faraday. He died in 1866 at Tunbridge Wells.

an account of Gun-cotton on the first Friday Evening here, and thus I expect to get a summary of that which is known.[1]

I have worked since you were here, but have nothing particular as yet: — and now I cannot work, for I am laid on the shelf for a while. — My health generally is very good; but an affection has come on in the knee, like that I had in the other leg ten years ago (too much fluid in the joint;) and so I am obliged to bandage it, and incline it, and lay it up in a stool or couch: — and in fact nurse it, and consequently the body and head and hands belonging to it. I am obliged to write now over a table; and that to one who has heretofore written and done all things standing, is troublesome, because it brings on oppression of the lungs and head. So I think I will even cut short this rambling letter, which is just intended to come as a little chat, and to produce, as I hope it will soon, some account of your whereabouts; that I may know where my old friend is, and what he is about. Do not forget in the midst of your other thoughts to speak of me with all kind feelings to Mrs. Schœnbein and the family. If things run upon velvet I should not wonder if you brought somebody with you next time.

Ever Dear Schœnbein Yours Truly
M. FARADAY.

Schœnbein to Faraday.

MY DEAR FARADAY

I am very much obliged to you for the really kind and friendly lines you favoured me with the other day and I won't be long in acknowledging them. As to the late doings of your humble friend they have been of very little

[1] Grove at the meeting of the British Association at Southampton, Sept. 1846 read a paper on Schœnbeins gun-cotton with experiments some of which were most effective; for example when he exploded guncotton while in contact with powder, without igniting the latter.

consequence ever since my return from England and Mrs. Schœnbein's having been delivered of a girl six weeks ago has interfered with my usual occupations and kept me out of my laboratory. And to tell you the truth my scientific zeal has been checked by a variety of annoying occurrences connected with the gun cotton affair. True it is, my knowledge of the World has been vastly increased these last four or five months, but I am afraid that my esteem for mankind has not grown in the same ratio. I could tell you a great many things of an incredible description, but I will not trouble you with datailing facts which I should like never to have become acquainted with myself. So much however I must say that by the occurrences alluded to my temper which is usually not much liable to be ruffled and the placidity of my mind have been suffering these many months. I hope however that time, the powerful physician, will remedy what has been spoiled. As you take some interest in the substance I had the fortune, or misfortune, to find out and to which I have given the name "guncotton", you will allow me to communicate to you some facts I ascertained previously to having made the noisy discovery. You are perhaps aware that my researches on Ozone led me to think NO_5 a chemical non-entity and consider what they call monohydrate of nitric acid not as $NO_5 + HO$ but $NO_4 + HO_2$, the normal nitrates as $NO_4 + RO_2$, $SO_3 + HO$ as $SO_2 + HO_2$ and Rose's Compound $2 SO_3 + NO_2$ as $SO_2 + NO_4$. Those views and some other considerations made me conjecture that on mixing together $2 (SO_2 + HO_2)$ with $NO_4 + HO_2$, $2 SO_2 + NO_4$ would be formed and $3 HO_2$ either eliminated or brought into a loose state of combination with Rose's bisulphate of binoxide of Nitrogen. Supposing such a reaction to take place, I of course inferred farther that the acid mixture mentioned would act as a highly oxidizing agent, as a sort of aqua regia in which HO_2 replaces Chlorine; I likewise conjectured that in taking away by the means of oxidable substances HO_2, supposed to exist in the said acid mixture, the latter would exhibit the properties of Rose's Compounds.[1] It may be that those hypothetical views are as wrong as they militate against the notions Chymists of the present day are entertaining regarding the nature of nitric acid etc., but in putting myself under their guidance I succeeded in ascertaining a number of facts which appear to me to be entirely novel and not void of scientific interest, facts too which seem to speak rather in favour of my hypothesis. The statements I am going to make will show how far I am entitled to say so. If some flores sulphuris are stirred up with a mixture of nitric acid of 1.5 and common oil of vitriol or chemically pure sulphuric acid of 1.85, a lively disengagement of sulphurous acid gas will issue, the temperature rise, the sulphur disappear and a colourless liquid be left, out of which binoxide of nitrogen is abundantly disengaged, when mixed up with water. That fluid exhibits in other terms all the chemical bearings of a solution of Rose's $2\,SO_3 + NO_2$ in the monohydrate of sulphuric acid. The action described, i. e. the formation of sulphurous acid, takes place even at a temperature of 32^0 F. (For farther particulars I take the liberty to refer you to a paper which will soon be published in Poggendorff's Annalen on the subject.[2]) I have found out that if one drop only of nitric acid of 1.5 be mixed up with four ounces of oil of vitriol, flores sulphuris, being added to that mixture, will cause a still perceptible formation of sulphurous

---

[1] H. Rose, professor of Chemistry at Berlin, in 1839 contributed to Poggend. Annal. (Bd. 47. p. 605) a paper entitled: "Über eine Verbindung der wasserfreien Schwefelsäure mit dem Stickstoffoxyd," in which he describes a compound which we to day call nitrosyl sulphuric acid $= SO_2 {NO_2 \atop OH}$ or $SO_2 {ONO \atop OH}$. On leading a current of nitric oxide, carefully dried by means of calcium chloride, into anhydrous sulphuric acid, the oxide is absorbed and a compound produced in the form of white crystals, which when thrown into water decompose readily, giving off dark red fumes. From the results of his analyses Rose gives it a formula "made up of one atom of sulphuric acid and one atom of nitric acid," i. e. $\ddot{S} + \dot{N}$.

[2] Über die Salpeter-Schwefelsäure und deren Verhalten zum Schwefel, Selen, Phosphor und Jod, Poggend. Annal. Bd. 70. 1847. p. 87.

acid gas, which may be easily shown by holding, some paste of starch mixed with jodide of potassium and rendered blue by Chlorine over the vessel, which holds the acid mixture. The blue colour of the paste will be discharged under the circumstances mentioned. Phosphorus and Selenium are likewise readily oxidized in our mixture at very low temperatures changing the latter such as to render it capable of disengaging binoxide of nitrogen on being mixed with water. Even Jodine, exhibiting so little tendency to unite with oxigen, is at low temperatures readily oxidized in our acid mixture, being partly transformed into jodic acid, partly into a lower degree of oxidation (most likely into the jodic oxide of Millon[1]) which unites with sulphuric acid and remains dissolved in the acid mixture. A good deal of jodic acid contaminated with some sulphuric acid is precipitated. To obtain the reaction described it is required to shake powdered jodine with the nitro-sulphuric acid without applying any heat. (For farther particulars see the paper alluded to.)

After having made many-experiments with inorganic substances and the acid mixture and recollecting the curious bearings of olefiant gas[2] to Ozone I tried a number of organic matters and began with common sugar. That substance being in a powdered state at a temperature of about 36° F was stirred up with a mixture of one volume of nitric acid of 1.5 and two volumes of oil of vitriol. The sugar first assumes a semi-transparent appearance but after a few minutes stirring gathers up into a lump of a very tough paste which sticks to the stirring rod and can easily be removed from the acid mixture. On kneading that paste with warm water all the adhering acid particles are taken away and a substance is left, enjoying all

---

[1] Nicolas Auguste Eugène Millon, professor of Chemistry at the Military Hospital of Val-de-Grace at Paris. He was born in 1812 at Chalons sur Marne and died at St. Seine-l'Abbaye (Côte d'Or) in 1867. See Memoire sur de nouvelles combinaisons oxygenées de l'iode. Annal. de Chimie, T. 12. 1844. p. 353.

[2] Basl. Ber. Bd. 7. 1845. p. 7.

the essential properties of resinous matters. It is nearly tasteless, yellowish white, insoluble or nearly so in water, solid and brittle at low temperatures, easily fusible; at the common temperature it can be malaxated, assuming a most beautiful but transient silvery hue, easily soluble in essential oils, ether etc. and going off like gunpowder when heated to a certain degree. Some more statements regarding that curious matter will soon be published in Poggendorff's Annales.[1] After having gone so far, the discovery of those substances of which I took the liberty to send you specimens last March and of which they talk now so much in Paris, was a matter of course. Guncotton, transparent paper, fulminating paper etc. made rapidly their appearance one after the other and I must not omit to state that all those results were obtained in the months of December (1845), January and February (1846). As to gun cotton I send you an account of an analysis made by Mr. Böttger in Frankfurt who used acetic ether as a solvent to obtain that fulminating matter in a chemically pure state from common gun cotton. Hundred parts of pure guncotton contain [2]

	found	calculated
Carbon	27.43	28.1
Hydrogen	3.54	3.1
Nitrogen	14.26	14.5
Oxigen	54.77	54.3

After Ballot's Analysis Xyloidin contains

	found	calculated
Carbon	37.29	37.31
Hydrogen	4.99	4.84
Nitrogen	5.17	5.76
Oxigen	52.55	52.09

[1] Über eine eigentümliche Veränderung des Zuckers, durch Salpeter-Schwefelsäure bewerkstelligt. Poggend. Annal. Bd. 70. 1847. p. 100.

[2] Dr. Pettenkofer's numbers differ somewhat from these. He finds for C 26.26 H 2.75 N 4.52 O 66.47, from which he calculates the following formula for gun-cotton $C_{12}H_7NO_{18}$. (Augsburger Allg. Zeitg. Dec. 12. 1846.)

Hence it appears that the chemical composition of gun cotton differs essentially from that of Braconnot's[1] xyloidin, which latter substance besides, as you well know, easily dissolves in strong acetic acid and muriatic acid and is thrown down by water from such solutions whilst gun cotton is not acted upon by those acids. Nitric acid of 1.38 readily takes up Xyloidine not to be thrown down again by water, whilst the same acid has no action upon gun cotton.[2]

It is perhaps not unknown to you that the french philosophers took no notice of gun cotton sooner than after the meeting at Southampton[3] and were in the beginning rather incredulous as to the reality of that substance. But when there could exist no longer any doubt about the matter it was declared by more than one Chymist to be Braconnot's Xyloidine and consequently the invention of the poudre-coton claimed as a french one.[4] Silently I smiled at the assertion, knowing it to be unfounded and so very easy to find out the mistake. Indeed in the middle of last month the french academy was informed that as to properties and composition, gun cotton essentially differs from Braconnet's Xyloidine and the former is made up of what the have called Pyroxyloidine. Though the existence of such a substance had even not in the slightest

---

[1] Henri Braconnot was born at Commercy in 1781 and died at Nancy in 1855. cf. Annal. d. Chimie I. 52. 1833. p. 290. De la transformation de plusieurs substances végétales en un principe nouveau (Xyloidine).

[2] The difference between gun cotton and Xyloidine forms the substance of a letter to Mr. Louyet (Nov. 17. 1846) an abridgment of which appeared in Compt. Rend. T. 23. 1846. p. 983.

[3] Grove, it will be remembered, read a paper on Schœnbeins gun-cotton at the British Association meeting at Southampton 1846. vide p. 164. note 1.

[4] J. Pelonze also, at a meeting of the French Academy in 1846, said he had 10 years ago found, that in a solution of amidon, wood fibres, paper, rags etc. in conc. nitric acid, xyloidine is formed when water is added. Comp. Rend. T. 7. 1838. p. 713: "Note sur les produits de l'acide nitriqué sur l'amidon et sur le ligneux." cf. also: "Observations sur la pyroxyline, considerée principalement comme base des amorces fulminantes." Ibid. T. 23. 1846. p. 1020.

manner been hinted at before the middle of November last, and though it be well known that I have been experimenting upon guncotton the whole year round, I am, after an opinion expressed before the french academy and echoed by many french papers, entitled only to the hono[u]r of having first applied to the purposes of gunpowder what had been discovered by another. I openly confess that I cannot conceive with what right such an assertion could have been made, if it have been ever made and I must leave it to the judgment of impartial scientific men to decide who is to be considered as the first discoverer or inventor of gun cotton. I must beg you a thousand pardons for having spoken so much of my little affairs, but as you have yourself expressed a wish to be informed about them you will, I am sure of it, be indulgent.

Up to this present moment I have not yet derived any pecuniary advantage from my discovery, I hope however to get something out of it. I was very sorry to learn your being laid up and fervently wish you will soon be able to make use of your limb. Mrs. Schœnbein and the Children are well and beg to be kindly remembered to you and Mrs. Faraday.

Should you think some of the facts mentioned in this letter interesting enough to be communicated in one of your Friday Meetings or elsewhere I don't think I can have any objection to their being made known. Wishing you and your Lady a very happy new year I am

    My dear Faraday
      Your's
       most truly

Bâle Dec. 26. 1846.   C. F. SCHOENBEIN.

Schœnbein to Faraday.[1]

MY DEAR FARADAY

Having a good opportunity for sending you a few lines, I will make use of it to tell you something about my little doings. You are no doubt struck with the peculiarity of the ink in with this letter is written, and I am afraid you will think it a very bad production; but in spite of its queer colour, you will like it when I tell you what it is, and when I assure you that as long as the art of writing has been practised, no letter has ever been written with such an ink. Dealing now again in my ozone business, I found out the other day that all manganese salts, be they dissolved or solid, are decomposed by ozone, hydrate of peroxide of manganese being produced and the acid set at liberty. Now to come round again to my sulphate of manganese. The writing being dry, the paper is suspended within a large bottle, the air of which is strongly ozonized by means of phosphorus. After a few minutes the writing becomes visible, and the longer you leave it exposed to the action of ozone the darker it will become. Sulphurous acid gas uniting readily with the peroxide of manganese to form a colourless sulphate, the writing will come out again when again exposed to ozonized air. Now all this is certainly mere playing; but the matter is interesting in a scientific point of view, in as much as dry strips of white filtering paper drenched with a weak solution of sulphute of manganese furnish us with rather a delicate and specific test for ozone, by means of which we may easily prove the identity of chemical, voltaic and electrical ozone, and establish with facility and certainty the continual presence of ozone in the open air. I have turned brown my test-paper within the electrical brush, the

---

[1] This letter is reprinted here from Phil. Mag. S. 3. vol. 21. 1847. p. 176. to which Faraday communicated it under the following title: "On a new test for ozone." See also Erdm. Journ. Bd. 42. 1847. p. 383.

ozonized oxigen obtained from electrolysed water and the atmospheric air ozonized by phosphorus. The quantity of ozone produced by the electrical brush being so very small, it requires of course some time to turn the test-paper brown.

As it is inconvenient to write with an invisible ink, I will stop here; not however before having asked your kind indulgence for the many blunders and faults which my ozone bottle will no doubt bring to light before long.

Bâle July, 1. 1847.
Yours very truly
C. F. SCHOENBEIN.

Faraday to Schœnbein.[1]

Royal Institution 23 Octr. 1847.

MY DEAR SCHOENBEIN

With absolutely nothing to say I still feel a lingering desire to write to you and though I have waited days and weeks in hopes that my thoughts would brighten I will wait no longer, but just make a return to your very characteristic letter by one which will be distinguished only by its contrast with it. You would perhaps see by the Philosophical Magazine[2] that I had received yours for the whole was printed there except three or four lines at the end. The novelty and beauty of your new test for ozone is very remarkable and not less its application to the detection of Ozone from such different sources as Phosphorus, the Electrical brush and Electrolysis· I shame to say that I have not yet repeated the experiments, but my head has been so giddy that my Doctors have absolutely forbidden me the privilege and pleasure of working or

---

[1] Bence Jones in his Life of Faraday (vol. 2. p. 231) prints this letter, except a few lines at the end.

[2] "On a new test for ozone" Letter to Mr. Faraday 1. July 1847. Phil. Mag. S. 3. vol. 31. 1847. p. 176. vide p. 171.

thinking for a while and so I am constrained to go out of town be a hermit, and take absolute rest. In thinking of my own case it makes me rejoice to know of your health and strength and to look on whilst you labour with a constancy so unintermitting[1] and so successful. Long may it be so to the joy and happiness of yourself, wife and family. My wife desires to be remembered to you most earnestly and is always glad when your name turns up either in reading and conversation. Remember me in the same manner to Mrs. Schœnbein and those of yours that I have seen and believe me to be

Ever My dear Schœnbein
Yours Most Truly
M. FARADAY.

I do not talk about Gun cotton: because I think you will let me know when anything philosophical or important turns up respecting it which would give you pleasure to tell me. But you may suppose that I do not hope the less in respect of it.   M. F.

Schœnbein to Faraday.

MY DEAR FARADAY

I am very sorry indeed to learn from your kind letter that the state of your health is not such as your friends so ardently wish it to be. I think turning your back to noisy smoky London and living in some retired quiet corner blessed with a pure atmosphere is by far the best you can do. And the winter past I should in your place quit England for a time and take up a temporary abode at some spot on the beautiful lake of Como, or at Meran or somewhere there about. Placing yourself in the midst of a serene, grand scenery will afford

---

[1] Faraday certainly wrote unintermitting; Bence Jones has changed it into unremitting.

your mind a beneficial excitement and inhaling a pure balmy air will strengthen your frame and recall the elasticity of your spirits. Beautiful as England is in many respects, nature there is too tame and uniform, the sky too pale, the air too thick to suit your present condition. Excuse my acting the part of a medical adviser but as my council comes from the conviction that it is the best which can be given to you, I am sure you will not take it ill.

You know my heterodoxical [1] notions regarding the nature of Chlorine which after the old creed I hold to be an oxy-compound similar in constitution to the peroxides of hydrogen, manganese etc. Now those notions are the source of all the experiments I have made these many years and if I have been fortunate enough to ascertain some interesting facts, I owe it entirely to my strange hypothetical views and to reasonings founded upon them. You are also aware that Ozone bears in many respects a very close resemblance to Chlorine, Bromine and Jodine and the strongest atmosphere of ozone being almost instantaneously destroyed by powder of Charcoal, I was curious to see how Chlorine Bromine etc are acted upon by powdered charcoal and my experiments have led to results of which I shall give you a summary account.[2]

[1] This habit of Schœnbeins to apply to his new ideas the term "heterodoxical" is often wet with in letters to and from his friends. Pettenkofer, for example writes, March 6. 1866: "I am eagerly awaiting news from you and anxious to know what satanic trick you heretic have again been up to." Henri St. Claire Deville in a similer strain, in December 1859 addresses him as a consummate master of chemical sorcery. Vide note 1. p. 40. Kahlbaum und Thon, Briefwechsel, Liebig-Schœnbein. Leipzig 1899.

[2] See also his paper: Das Verhalten der Kohle zu Chlor, Brom, Jod, Chlorkalk und Untersalpetersäure. Poggend. Annal. Bd. 73. 1847. p. 326. That this resemblance is closely associated with the naming of ozone is rendered evident by a passage from a letter from Schœnbein to Arago, reprinted in the Comptes Rend. of April 27. 1840. p. 709, where he says, that being all but convinced that his odoriferous principle must be grouped together with chlorine and bromine, he proposes giving it the name of ozone. This passage is interesting from the fact that it is the first time the name "ozone" appeared in print.

1. The strongest atmosphere of Chlorine on being shaken with powder of common charcoal is almost instantaneously destroyed at the common temperature as well as at 212⁰.

2. A current of Chlorine passing through a tube filled with powder of charcoal is readily taken up, much heat being disengaged from the latter. The charcoal thus treated does not exhibit the odour of Chlorine, even if considerably heated, but emits fumes of muriatic acid and yields the same acid to water. The freshly prepared chlorified charcoal has however like Chlorine the power of discharging the colour of an Indigo solution and decomposing jodide of potassium, but in leaving it for some time in contact with water or atmospheric air it looses that property.

3. The strongest aqueous solution of Chlorine, if shaken with a sufficient quantity of charcoal powder quickly looses its yellow colour, smell, bleaching power etc., muriatic acid being produced. Powder of charcoal is also capable of completely destroying the bleaching power of aqueous solutions of hypochlorites, for instance that of the common Chloride of lime. The same effect is produced by Charcoal upon what Berzelius considers as deutochloride of manganese and which is obtained by treating peroxide of manganese with muriatic acid at the common temperature. Charcoal transforms the solution of that compound into that of the common protochloride of manganese.

4. The densest atmosphere of Bromine Vapour most rapidly and completely disappears even at a temperature of 212⁰ when brought in contact with powder of Charcoal, and liquid Bromine on being mixt up with the same powder is rendered so latent, that the mixture may be heated to 212⁰ without yielding a trace of bromine; at a higher temperature however some Bromine is given off. The brominiferous charcoal has the power of discharging the colour of Indigo solution and decomposing jodide of potassium. The strongest aqueous solution of Bromine on being shaken with powder of charcoal becomes colourless, looses, its smell, bleaching power etc.

5. Charcoal powder causes rapidly the disappearence of the densest vapour of Jodine even at a temperature of $212°$ and an intimate mixture of 9 parts of Charcoal and one part of jodine exhibits not the slightest smell and does not yield a trace of vapour of jodine even at the boiling point of water, at a considerably higher temperature however some Jodine vapour is disengaged. The colour of an acqueous solution of Jodine is quickly discharged by powder of charcoal.

6. A colourless mixture of one part of hyponitric acid and 9 parts of water on being mixt up with charcoal powder gives rise to a most lively and abundant disengagement of deutoxide of azote, no carbonic acid being produced under these circumstances. Monohydrate of nitric acid on being put in contact with charcoal powder even at a temperature of $0°F$ is partly decomposed, hyponitric acid being eliminated but no carbonic acid produced. You know that I consider that monohydrate as $NO_4 + HO_2$ and hold the opinion that on mixing hyponitric acid and water together two compounds are formed: $NO_4 + HO_2$ and $NO_2 + HO_2$. Now as to the decomposition of what they call monohydrate of nitric acid effected by Charcoal, I am inclined to ascribe it to the well known power of that substance of composing the peroxide of hydrogen and agreeably to the same hypothesis, I account for the disengagement of deutoxide of azote out of the mixture before mentioned. HO_2 united to NO_2 is decomposed by Charcoal into water and oxygen, the latter being thrown upon some $NO_2 + HO_2$, to form $NO_4 + HO_2$ and the NO_2, being freed from HO_2, set free. —

It seems to me that the facts above mentioned are not due to the well known power of charcoal of absorbing gazeous bodies, but to something else, of which we have not yet got a clear notion and I am inclined to think that the cause which makes charcoal act upon Chlorine, Bromine, Jodine in the manner described is the same that gives to charcoal the power of destroying Ozone, Thenard's peroxide of hydrogen, permanganic acid, monohydrate of nitric acid, what they call aqueous hyponitric acid, solutions of the hypochlorites etc, without producing carbonic acid. But what that cause is, I am far from being prepared to say. At any rate it is a fact worthy of consideration, that all the substances that are so peculiarly acted upon by charcoal bear the same electromotive character; they are electro-negative bodies.

Before I conclude, allow me to mention to you another fact which I ascertained some time ago and will interest you. If paste of starch being mixt up with so much jodide of lead, as to give the former a lively yellow colour, be spread over a band of white paper and exposed to the action of direct solar rays, it suddenly turns its colour, becoming green in the first instance and dark blue within a very few seconds. This change of colour effected by direct solar light is almost as instantaneous as that brought about by a strong atmosphere of chlorine or ozone and of course due to an elimination of jodine from the jodide of lead.[1]

I am not aware of any other substance being so suddenly and perceptibly affected by solar light as the said paste proves to be, and on that account I think it might be used as a means for examining more closely the relative chemical powers of the different species of rays of which white solar light is made up.

Living at this present moment amidst the clamour of civil war and writing under the impression of extraordinary events, I am sure you will be indulgent to me as to the great imperfection of this letter. Pray present my best compliments to Mrs. Faraday and believe me, my dear Faraday,

Your's most truly

Bâle November 19. 1847.   C. F. SCHOENBEIN.

[1] This subject is dealt with in Poggend. Annal. Bd. 73. 1847. p. 136. Über die Einwirkung des Lichts auf Jodbleistärke. See also Erdmann Journ. Bd. 46. 1847. p. 442.

Faraday to Schœnbein.

Brighton 17 March 1848

MY DEAR SCHOENBEIN

I find my letters begin to take a character which cannot be wondered at, considering all things, but which recurs oftener than I could wish; however it shall not prevent me writing to you. I find a difficulty in answering or even acknowledging properly a scientific letter, for I cannot now hold it at once in my mind, so as to make the expression of my thoughts consistent and applicable. The memory of the parts fail me. Therefore I am not about to reply to your last (Nov. 1847) but just to write a word or two of affectionate remembrance and nothing else. Indeed I cannot altogether make up my mind that, as my scientific occupation passes away, the many kind remembrances of friends, thoughts and acts, should pass away with it, so you must just bear with me and whilst you write me letters full of energy and interest, be content to receive almost incoherent scraps in return. When I received yours, if I remember my feelings aright, I think I felt doubtful whether you did or did not wish me to send it to the Phil. Mag. and I think I did not send it. Will you by a single word let me know your mind on these occasions. — I wrote a paper in the P. M. on the diamagnetism of gases and flame[1] and sent you a copy by some channel. If you have seen it I hope you approve. I feel as if every paper I write must be my last — but no one knows. Things may revive again — and if not, what great cause I have to be thankful for the health and strength and blessings that have been and are at this moment granted me. — With our kindest remembrances to Madame Schœnbein and the children I am, my dear friend,

Ever most truly yours

M. FARADAY.

[1] On the diamagnetic conditions of flame and gases. Phil. Mag. S. 3. vol. 31. 1847. p. 401.

You will be sorry to see the tone of this short note, but my dearest husband is not quite so well as usual, but I hope he will improve. May I add my kind remembrances to his and sign myself

Yours very truly

S. FARADAY.

Schœnbein to Faraday.

MY DEAR FARADAY

To give you a sign of life I send you some lines through a former pupil of mine, Mr. Burckhardt of Bâle. In spite of all the revolutions and commotions which have taken place around us these last eight months I have not given up my favorite researches and been rather industrious in my laboratory. Amongst other things I have made many experiments on the action exerted by Ozone upon metals at the common temperature and obtained pretty results. I have found out that with a few exceptions all metallic bodies are oxidized by Ozone to the highest degree they are capable of, Silver and Lead for instance being transformed at once into the peroxide of those metals, arsenic and antimony into arsenic and antimonic acid, without passing through their intermediate degrees of oxidation. Though Silver be reputed to be much less oxidable than Copper, Zinc, Tin etc., it is more rapidly oxidized by Ozone, than the metals mentioned. Polished plates of Silver Copper, Tin, Zinc being suspended within a strongly ozonized atmosphere are very differently acted upon. After half an hour's suspension the silverplate will have lost its metallic lustre and be covered with a layer of peroxide of Silver, whilst the plates of the other metals may remain for 24 hour's within our atmosphere without losing sensibly of there brilliancy. It may therefore be said that with regard to Ozone Silver is one of the most readily oxidable metals, provided silver and the other metals be exposed to the action of our oxidizing agent in the shape of compact and polished plates. Being in a state of minute mechanical division all the common metals, silver of course included, appear to take up the oxigen of ozone, equally rapidly. The specimen laid by is a layer of peroxide of silver having been produced within 24 hours round a plate of very pure and highly polished silver. Arsenic and Antimony in the shape of brilliant metallic spots produced upon glass tubes or porcellain according to Marsh's method exhibit interesting bearings to Ozone. The arsenious spots are rapidly acted upon by Ozone and transformed into arsenic acid. 10—15 minutes are sufficient to make entirely disappear an arsenious spot, when placed in air richly charged with ozone, whilst a similar spot of antimony, put under the same circumstances requires many days, to loose its metallic lustre and be turned into the white hydrate of antimonic acid. I must not omit to state that Ozone produced by common electricity acts exactly upon the two kinds of spots like voltaic or chemical Ozone. With my rather poor electrical machine I succeeded in making entirely disappear a strong arsenious spot within 10—12 minutes, whilst a similar antimonious spot placed aside the former one and exposed at the same time to the action of the electrical brush was not yet sensibly affected, and had retained all its metallic brilliancy. Ozone is therefore one of the means by which arsenic may be easily distinguished from antimony.[1]

I think I have also succeeded in tracing out the cause of phosphorus being not able to produce ozone or (what is most intimately connected with it) undergo slow combustion in pure oxygen of the usual density and common temperature. The slow combustion of phosphorus being caused by Ozone, it follows that all the circumstances which prevent or favor the generation of that oxidizing agent must also prevent or favor that slow combustion. Now a most essential condition

[1] Poggend. Annal. Bd. 75. 1848 p. 361: Das Ozon als Mittel zur Unterscheidung der Arsen- von den Antimonflecken.

of the production of ozone is a certain degree of rapidity of the evaporation of phosphorus; (only vaporous but not the solid phosphorus determines the formation of ozone); any physical circumstance facilitating the said evaporation favors therefore the generation of ozone, or enlivens the slow combustion of phosphorus. In oxigen, rarefied to a certain degree, ozone is produced and phosphorus becoming luminous at the common temperature, and in common oxigen the same phenomena take place, provided the temperature of the gas be raised by a certain number of degrees. Rarefaction or the heating of oxigen gas favors the evaporation of phosphorus and consequently the formation of ozone etc.

In Hydrogen and Nitrogen, having the same elasticity and temperature as oxigen, phosporus evaporates more rapidly than in the last named gas and hence it comes, that in a mixture of hydrogen and oxigen, nitrogen and oxigen of the usual elasticity and temperature, ozone is produced and phosphorus becoming luminous, whilst in pure oxigen of the same temperature and elasticity the phenomena mentioned do not take place. I have circumstancially described my results in Poggendorff's Annals and I hope they will soon be published.[1]

During the summer I made with my family a stay at a beautiful spot near the lake of Lucerne on the "Rotzberg" in the Canton of Unterwalden. We were very happy there and often said that our hill would be a place for our friend Faraday and his Lady. We led a truly dolce far niente life and my girls were jumping about in the hills like chamois. Confidently hoping you and Mrs. Faraday will enjoy at least tolerable health, I am, my dear friend,

Your's most truly

About Oct. 1848 perhaps.[2]   C. F. SCHOENBEIN.

[1] Über die Erzeugung des Ozons durch Phosphor in reinem Sauerstoffgas. Poggend. Annal. Bd. 75. 1848 p 377.

[2] This date was added by Faraday at a much later period. On the same sheet of paper on which Schœnbein wrote a sketch for an obituary notice on

Faraday to Schœnbein.

Royal Institution 15. Decr. 1848.

MY DEAR SCHOENBEIN

What a delight it is to think that you are quietly and philosophically at work in the pursuit of science; — or else are enjoying yourself with Madame Schœnbein and the children amongst the pure and harmonious beauties of nature — rather than fighting amongst the crowd of black passions and motives that seem now a days to urge men every where into action. What incredible scenes every where, what unworthy motives ruled for the moment, under high sounding phrases, and at the last what disgusting revolutions. Happy are we here who have thus far been kept from these things and hope to be so preserved in the future.

You last letter was quite a treat. I cannot tell when it came for my memory is worse than ever and it happens to have no date. The condition of Silver is indeed very curious — indeed the longer you work at this subject the more unexpected your results are and I cannot doubt that you will some day soon have them all opening out and taking their respective places in one consistent, bright and beautiful whole.

I have been working also a little and have sent two papers to the Royal Society on the Crystalline Polarity of bismuth and other bodies and its relation to the Magnetic force.[1] — A cristal of bismuth is subject to the action of the Magnet, for there is one direction through it which always tends to place itself in the Magnetic axis. This direction I have called the

Berzelius (see Kahlbaum, Briefwechsel p. 96) we have discovered a draft of this letter. Now Berzelius died on Aug. 7. 1848; the letter must therefore have been begun about the middle of August at Rotzberg. Therefore, although some time must have elapsed before he completed it — for it was posted at Bâle — it seems very probable that it was written as early as September and not October.

[1] On the crystalline polarity of bismuth and other bodies and on its relation to the magnetic form of force. Phil. Trans. 1849. p. 1.

Magnecrystallic axis of the crystal. It makes the crystal point as a magnetic needle would point, yet is the result not an effect of attraction or repulsion or polarity, for the bismuth is repelled, as a diamagnetic body, as much and no more than if it had not this set. If it be fused and then resolidified, all this power is lost, because it belonged to a regular crystallization and that has now become irregular.

Antimony and Arsenic are also *magnecrystallic*, like bismuth — and crystalline plates of these metals taken from broken up masses point well, provided the whole of the fragment be uniformly crystallized.

Not only are diamagnetic bodies, like those mentioned, but also Magnetic bodies, *Magnecrystallic*. Thus a crystal of protosulphate of iron is so, having the *Magnecrystallic* axis perpendicular to two of the faces of the rhombic prism, in which that salt crystallizes.

I can by arrangement oppose the *Magnecrystallic* force either to the magnetic or the diamagnetic condition of bodies — so that I can make a crystal of Sulphate of iron receed from a magnetic pole, or a crystal of bismuth approach towards it, against what we should otherwise consider their natural tendency.

As I said just now this effect is not one of *attraction* or of *repulsion* but of *position only*, and is as far as I can see a new effect or an exertion of force new to us.

At first I thought the cause of these phenomena different to that which produced Pluckers[1] results described in his paper[2] on the "repulsion of the Optic axes of crystals by the Magnetic poles", but now I think it is the same, though my forces are

---

[1] Julius Plücker Ph. D. was born at Elberfeld in 1801. He was professor of Mathematics at Halle, and professor of Mathematics and Physics at Bonn where he died in 1868. He was recipient of the Copley medal.

[2] Über die Abstossung der optischen Axen der Krystalle durch die Pole der Magneten. Poggend. Annal. Bd. 72. 1847. p. 315.

axial and he refers his results to equatorial forces or to repulsion. I will however tease you no more with these matters, but send you the printed papers as soon as I can.

With our kindest remembrances to Madam Schœnbein

I am, My dear friend,
Most truly Yours
M. FARADAY.

Schœnbein to Faraday.

MY DEAR FARADAY

Our Chief Magistrate Burgomaster Sarasin, friend to your friend and a liberal patron to science, taking a trip to England will be kind enough to deliver these lines and the papers laid by into your hands and I am sure you will be glad to make the acquaintance of the highly worthy gentleman.

The paper in octavo[1] deals with the voltaic pile and that in quarto[2] contains an account of my recent researches on ozône[3] of which I talked in my last letter to you.[4] To give you a substantial proof of the correctness of my statement I send you a little bit of peroxide of silver and nitrate of potash

[1] Über die chemische Theorie der Volta'schen Säule. Poggend. Annal. Bd. 78. 1849. S. 289.
[2] Über das Ozon, Denkschrift zur Einweihung des neuen Museums in Basel, 1849.
[3] Schœnbeins spelling of ozone is anything but consistent. Sometimes he writes ozon, at other times ozone; in this letter he has even added a circumflex accent. Professor Vischer of Bâle, at Schœnbeins request, offered to devise a name for his new body and derived it from ὄζων, the present participle of ὄζειν, smelling We would therefore emphasize the fact that, for this reason, the correct pronunciation is ó/zōn, and not ozön/.
[4] Whether Schœnbein, in referring to his last letter, alludes to the one written in September 1848 is not quite evident; there seems in fact to be a gap here; we are however unable to determine by how many letters it was filled up.

both the substances having been prepared by the means of ozône.

Little being known of ozône in England, don't you think the subject fit for being once treated before one of the Friday meetings of the Royal Institution? It allows of a great number of striking experiments to be made. — Should you like the Idea I would give you a list of those I think to be the most interesting and instructive ones.[1]

As you know no doubt Mr. Henry, the Chymist who is Headbrewer in some great brewery of the City, pray let him have the enclosed.

My best compliments to Mrs. Faraday and my kindest regards to yourself

Yours
most truly

Bâle, March 27. 1850.   C. F. SCHOENBEIN.

Faraday to Schœnbein.

Royal Institution 11 May 1850

MY DEAR SCHOENBEIN

I have seen Burgomaster Sarasin who has very kindly brought me your papers and letter. I wish I could show him any useful attention, but you know what an out-of-the-world man I am. Your German papers are very tantalizing, I know the good there must be within and yet I cannot get at it. But now my thoughts are on Ozone. I like your idea of an Evening here, but it cannot be this season for the arrangements are full. Yet that in some degree suits me better, for though I should like to give it, I am a slow man (want of memory) and therefore require preparation. Now I shall lock up your

[1] Faraday delivered this lecture in June 1851.

letters and reread them and also the papers; but let me pray you to send me a list of the experiments which you know to suit a large audience, also, if you can, the references to the best French (or English) papers giving an account of its development and progress. Also your present view, — also the best and quickest methods of making ozonized air and such other information as I shall need. Probably other matter will arise before 1851 and I will get possession of it as we go along. If you come over here you shall give the subject yourself i. e. if you can arrange and keep to time etc. if not, I must do my best. But every year I need more cramming, even for my own particular subjects. — Now do not delay to send me the list of experiments, because you suppose there is plenty of time etc etc, but let me have them that I may think over them during the vacation. I should like to do the matter to my own satisfaction: there are however very few things in which I satisfy myself now. I hoped to have had a paper to send you ere this, but Taylor is slow in the printing. Give our kindest remembrances to Madame Schœnbein

Ever, My dear friend,
Yours truly
M. FARADAY.

Faraday to Schœnbein.[1]

Royal Institution 19. Novr. 1850

MY DEAR SCHOENBEIN

I wish I could talk with you instead of being obliged to use pen and paper. I have fifty matters to speak about, but either they are too trifling for writing, or too im-

---

[1] A portion of this letter is reprinted in Silvanus P. Thompson's Life and Work of Faraday, p. 206, a most excellent and fascinating book. Bence Jones. vol. 2. p 258 gives the whole of it.

portant; for what can one discuss or say in a letter? Where is the question and answer, and explication that brings out clear notions in a few minutes? whilst letters only make them more obscure, because one cannot speak freely one's notions, and yet guard them merely as notions. But I am fast losing my time and yours too. I received your complimentary kindness, and like it the better because I know it to be as real as complimentary. Thanks to you, my dear friend, for all your feelings of good will towards me. The bleachings by light and air are very excellent. I see a report of part of your paper in the account of the Swiss Association, but not of the latter part.[1] However, a friend has your paper in hand and I hope to have the part about atmospheric electricity soon sent to me. I should be very *glad indeed* to have from any one, and above all from you, a satisfactory suggestion on that point. I know of none as yet.

By the bye I have been working with the oxygen of the air also. You remember that three years ago I distinguished it as a Magnetic gas in my paper on the diamagnetism of flame and gases founded on Bancalari's[2] experiment. Now I find in it the cause of all the annual and diurnal, and many of the irregular, variations of the terrestrial magnetism. The observations made at Hobarton, Toronto, Greenwich, St. Petersburg, Washington, St. Helena, the Cape of Good Hope and Singapore all appear to me to accord with and support my hypothesis. I will not pretend to give you an account of it here, for it would require some detail and I really am weary of the subject. I have sent in three long papers to the Royal Society and you shall have copies of them in due time and reports probably much sooner in Taylors Magazine.

[1] Schweiz. Naturf. Gesellsch. Verh. 1850. p. 44. The meeting was held at Aarau. Aug. 5—7. 1850.

[2] Michele Alberto Bancalari, professor of Physics at Genua was born in 1805 at Chiavari. He was the discoverer of diamagnetism of the flame. Sull magnetismo dei gasi (Giornale di Roma. Vide also Poggend Annal. Bd. 73. 1848. p. 257 and 286).

I forwarded your packets immediately upon the receipt of them.

But now about ozone. I was in hopes you would let me have a list of points with reference to where I should find the accounts in either English or French Journals, and also a list of about 20 experiments fit for an audience of 500 or 600 persons, — telling me what sized bottles to make ozone by phosphorus in — the time, and necessary caution etc. etc. etc. — My bad memory would make it a terrible and almost impossible task, to search from the beginning and read up; whereas you, who keep all you read, or discover with the utmost facility, could easily jot me down the real points. — If you refer to any such notes in your last letter when you ask me whether I have received a memoir on Ozone and *some other things* then I have not received any such notes and I cannot, indeed I *cannot*, remember about the memoir.

I was expecting some such notes and I still think you mean to send me them and though I may perhaps not give Ozone as an Evening *before Easter*, still do not delay to let me have them, because I am slow, — and losing much that I read of, have to imbibe a matter two or three times over; and if I do *Ozone* I should like to do it well.

My dear wife wishes to be remembered to you and I wish most earnestly to be brought to Madame Schœnbein's mind. Though vaguely I cling to the remembrance of an hour or two out of Bâle at your house, and though I cannot recall the circumstances clearly to my mind, I still endeavour again and again to realise the idea.

     Ever My dear Schœnbein
       Yours most truly
         M. FARADAY.

Schœnbein to Faraday.

MY DEAR FARADAY

Will you be kind enough to forward the parcels inclosed to their places of destination. There is no hurry in it, you may deliver them quite beseemly. If you should happen to get the parcel with my sulphuret-papers, it is very possible that those of lead have turned brown again. I see that by degrees sulphate of lead is acted upon by paper in the dark, so as to become brown i. e. sulphuret of lead.

I at least cannot account in another way for the fact that sulpuret of lead paper often, having been completely bleached by ozonized or insolated oxigen, turns gradually brown again in the dark.

The silhouettes laid by, which, except the figures, were once quite white, will show you that action.

Bâle 25. Nov. 1850.

Yours
very truly
C. F. SCHOENBEIN.

Faraday to Schœnbein.[1]

Brighton 9 December 1850

MY DEAR SCHOENBEIN

I have just read your letter dated July 9. 1850[2] exactly *six months* after it was written. I received the parcel containing it just as I was leaving London and I do not doubt it was in consequence of your moving upon the receipt of my last to you a few weeks ago. Thanks, thanks, my dear friend, for all your kindness. I have the Ozonometer and the

---

[1] Reprinted in part in Bence Jones vol. 2. p. 261.
[2] This letter to Faraday of July 9. 1850 is missing.

summary and all the illustrative packages safe, and though I have read only the letter as yet, and that I may acknowledge your kindness, write before I have gone through the others; yet I see there is a great store of matter and pleasure for me. As to your theory of atmospheric electricity, I am very glad to see you put it forward; of course such a proposition has to dwell in one's mind, that the idea may be compared with other ideas and the judgment become gradually matured; for it is not like the idea of a new compound which the balance and qualitative experiments may rapidly establish; still as I study and think over your account of Ozone and insulated oxygen, so I shall gradually be able to comprehend and imbibe the idea. Even as it is I think it is as good as any and much better than the far greater number of hypotheses which have been sent forth, as to the physical cause of atmospheric electricity — and some very good men have in turns had a trial at the matter. — In fact the point is a very high and a very glorious one: — we ought to understand it and I shall rejoice if it is you that have hold of the end of the subject. You will soon pull it clearly into sight.[1]

The German account[2] you sent me of insolated oxygen and your theory of atmospheric electricity is in the hands of a young friend who is translating it. — Whilst it is going on and also in reading your letter a question arises in my mind about the *insolated oxygen* which perhaps I shall find answered when I come to read the paper. It is whether the oxygen

---

[1] Schœnbein derives electricity of clouds from a chemical process, or rather from a voltaic source, the essential conditions being the presence of atmospheric water, atmospheric oxygen and sun light. Ordinary oxygen, under the influence of solar rays, becomes more active, its behaviour being then somewhat like that of ozon. In this state it polarizes water, of which the clouds are made up, by means of its chemical affinity to hydrogen, and thus atmospheric electricity is produced.

[2] Über den Einfluss des Sonnenlichtes auf die chemische Thätigkeit des Sauerstoffs und den Ursprung der Wolkenelektrizität und des Gewitters. Basel 1850.

having been insolated is then for a time a different body out of the presence of light as well as in it. I think an American [1] (I forget who) says that Chlorine after being exposed to the sun is of brighter colour and acts far more readily than such as has been kept in the dark for a time. Suppose a little box blackened inside, with two little glass windows, that a ray of sun light could be passed through it, and the box filled with oxygen, and a proper test paper put up in the dark part of the box: would it show change or must the test paper be in the ray to be acted upon? Of course Ozone would act upon it in the dark place. Is insolated oxygen like ozone in that respect? — I do not doubt that I shall find the answer amongst the data that I am in possession of and so do not trouble yourself for a reply just now. As I told you in my last I must talk about atmospheric *Magnetism* in my Friday evenings before Easter and I am glad that Ozone will fall in the summer months, because I should like to produce some of the effects here. I think I told you in my last how that oxygen in the atmosphere, which I pointed out three years ago in my paper on flame and gases as so very magnetic compared to other gases,[2] is now to me the source of all the periodical variations of terrestrial magnetism; and so I rejoice to think and talk at the same time of your results which deal also with that same atmospheric oxygen. What a wonderful body it is.

Ever my dear Schœnbein
Yours faithfully
M. FARADAY.

[1] John William Draper, professor of Chemistry at New-York, made this observation. His chief paper on the subject, however, was not published till 1857. See Phil. Mag. S. 4. vol. 14. 1857. p. 3: "The influence of light upon chlorine etc."

[2] Phil. Mag. S. 3. vol. 31. 1847. p. 410. This paper was also published at full length in Poggend. Annal. Bd. 73. 1848. p. 256.

Faraday to Schœnbein.[1]

Brighton 13 Dec. 1850

MY DEAR SCHOENBEIN

It will be very strange if I do not make your subject interesting. I have gone twice through the M S. and the illustrations. Both are beautiful. — As soon as I reach home I shall begin to prepare for ozone, making and repeating your experiments. This morning I hung out at my window one of the Ozonometer slips. That was about two hours ago. — Now when I moisten it, a tint of blue comes out between Nos 4 and 5 of the scale. Though I face the sea and have the wind on shore, still I am not aware that the spray can do this or any thing that comes from the sea water; but before I send off this letter I shall go down and try the sea itself.

Well! I have been to the sea side and the sea water does nothing of the kind — nor the spray — but as I walk on the shore holding a piece of the test paper in my hand for a quarter of an hour, at the end of that time it, by moistening, shows a pale blue effect.

That which is up at my window has been out in the air four hours and it, when wetted, comes out a strong blue tint about as Nr. 6 of the scale. The day is dry but with no sun, the lower region pretty clear, but clouds above.

After reading your notes and examining the illustrations, I could not resist writing to you, though, as you see, I have nothing to say.

Ever truly yours

M. FARADAY.

[1] This letter is printed in full in Bence Jones. vol. 2. p. 262.

Faraday to Schœnbein.[1]

Royal Institution 5. March 1851.

MY DEAR FRIEND.

I had your hearty Christmas letter in due time [2] — and was waiting for the papers referred to in it when lo! they arrived about four days ago and your friend Professor Bolley [3] called and left them, and his address. I was ill and, I believe, in bed and could not see him. I have not been out of the house for a week or more, because of inflamed throat and influenza, being unable to speak and obliged to give up lecturing, but I am now improving and trust I shall see the Professor soon. The papers and the specimens of oil of turpentine are all quite safe and most valued treasures. I have read the papers through and I think you must now begin to rejoice in ozone, for though it has cost you a great deal of trouble and work, still it has surely made wonderful way and, what is more, is progressing and will progress. Though you may sometimes get tired of it, still I think you never take it up afresh without being rewarded. I have been consulting with a medical friend about the medical paper [4] and he (Dr. Bence Jones [5]) recommends that it be sent to the Medico chirurgical society — where it will be introduced *at once* into the minds of the Medical Profession and appear in the transactions. Tomorrow we shall

---

[1] Bence Jones gives this letter vol. 2. p. 281, but more or less abridged.

[2] This letter alluded to is, we regret to say, not among those in our possession.

[3] Alexander Pompeius Bolley Ph. D., Director of the Technical High School at Zürich from 1859 to 1865. He was born at Heidelberg in 1812 and died in 1878 at Zürich. Together with Eisenlohr, Bolley was one of Schœnbeins most intimate friends.

[4] "Über einige mittelbare physiologische Wirkungen der atmosphärischen Elektrizität." Med. Chir. Soc. Trans. Vol. 34. 1851. p. 205.

[5] Henry Bence Jones M. D. a pupil of Liebigs was born in 1813 at Thorington Hall in Suffolk and died in 1873 in London. He was physician to St. Georges Hospital, London and wrote the well known History of Faradays Life.

meet again when he will have read the paper and we shall decide. — The chemical paper I have sent off at once to the Chemical Society, it will appear there in time for me to have access to, and use of it, on my or rather your evening, which I expect will be 13th June or the middle of our Great Exhibition. When I drew out a sort of preliminary sketch of the subject, I was astonished at the quantity of matter — real matter — and its various ramifications; and it seems still to grow upon me. What you will make it before I begin to talk, I do not know.

I do not as yet see any relation between the magnetic condition of oxigen and the ozone condition, but who can say what may turn up? I think you make an inquiry or two as to the amount of magnetic force which oxigen carries into its compounds. This is indeed a wonderful part of the story, for magnetic as *gaseous oxygen* is, the substance seems to lose all such force in compounds. Thus water which is $8/9$ ths oxygen contains no sensible trace of it: and peroxide of iron which itself consists of two most magnetic constituents — is scarcely sensibly magnetic; so little have either of these bodies carried their forces into the resulting compound. Sometimes I think we may understand a little better such changes by thinking that magnetism is a physical rather than a chemical force, but after all, such a difference is a mere play upon words, and shows ignorance rather than understanding. But you know there are really a great many things we are as yet ignorant of — and amongst the rest the infinitesimal proportion of our knowledge to that which really is *to be known*. I have a copy of my last papers ready for you and if Professor Bolley can take charge of it, shall give it into his hands.

I read your theory of the pile[1] in the Geneva journal with great pleasure and go with you, I think, to the full extent. My mind was quite prepared for the view years ago. I do

---

[1] "Über die chemische Theorie der Volta'schen Säule." Poggend. Annal. Bd. 78. 1849. p. 289. cf. also Archives de Genève. T. 13. 1849. p. 192.

not suppose you ever see the back numbers of an old work, which s'ill drags its slow length along, or else you would see that at Paragraph 949. 950. and again 1164 and 1345, 1347, and elsewhere, that I was ready to agree with you 10 or 15 years back.

I have no doubt I answer your letters very badly — but, my dear friend, do *you remember* that *I forget*, and that I can no more help it than a sieve can help the water running out of it. Still you know me to be your old and obliged and affectionate friend, and all I can say is, the longer I know you the more I desire to cling to you

Ever My dear Schœnbein
Yours affectionately
M. FARADAY.

Faraday to Schœnbein.[1]

Hastings 19 April 1851.

MY DEAR SCHOENBEIN

Here we are at the seaside; and my mind so vacant (not willingly) that I cannot get an idea into it. You will wonder, therefore, why I write to you, since I have nothing to say, but the fact is I feel as if I owed you a letter and yet cannot remember clearly how that is. Still I would rather appear stupid to you than oblivious of your kindness, and yet very forgetful I am. In six or seven weeks I shall be talking of Ozone. I hope I shall not discredit you or fail in using well all the matter you have given me, abundant and beautiful as it is. But I feel that my memory does not hold things together in hand as it used to do. Formerly I did not care

[1] With the exception of a few lines towards the end Bence Jones' Life contains this letter in full, vol. 2. p. 282.

about the muliplicity of items, they all took their place and I picked out what I wanted at pleasure. Now I am conscious of but few at once and it often happens that a feeble point which has present possession of the mind obscures from recollection a stronger and better one, which is ready and waiting. But we must just do the best we can, — and you may be sure I will do as well for you as I could for myself.

I set about explaining the other evening my views of atmospheric magnetism[1] and found when I had done that I had left out the two or three chief points. I only hope that the printed papers contain them and that they will be found good by the men who are able to judge — The copy for you is either with your or on the way for the gentleman whom you introduced to me whose name I forget (from Aarau?)[2] kindly took charge of it.

And now, my dear Schœnbein, with kindest remembrances to Madame Schœnbein (and my wife joins all she can to you and yours)

I am as ever
Most truly yours
M. FARADAY.

Schœnbein to Faraday.

MY DEAR FARADAY

I think an excellent likeness of our illustrious countryman Euler[3] will prove acceptable to you. It was made at the expense of Basle and I am charged by the Council of

---

[1] See "Experimental researches in Electricity" 26. and 27. Series. Phil. Trans. 1851. p. 29 and 85. R. Inst. Proc. Vol. 1. p. 56.

[2] Professor Bolley.

[3] Leonhard Euler, professor of Physics at St. Petersburg, and for a time professor of Mathematics at Berlin. He was born in 1707 at Riehen near Bâle and died 1783 at St. Petersburg.

our Museum to send you a copy of it, as an humble homage they desire to render you. There are some other copies joined and intended for the Royal Society etc. and I beg you to be kind enough to forward them quite leisurely to their respective places of destination. From Mr. Burckhardt I learned that you are doing well, he was highly pleased with the Lion of the Royal Institution. I am continually riding my hobby horse and now and then pick up something new. I am very sorry I did not sooner ascertain some facts; they would have made a good figure in Ozone. You shall before long have details about them. By this time I think your lecture on that subject will be over; let me know something of the matter. In the beginning of August I intend to go to Glarus, where the meeting of our association will take place. Have you no mind to come over and ramble about a little with me?

Pray present my best compliments to Mrs. Faraday and believe me

Quite in a hurry. Your's

very truly

Bâle Aug. 25. 1851.[1] C. F. SCHOENBEIN.

P. S. Mr. Sarasin a young friend of mine has the kindness to take charge of the parcel; should he happen to deliver it in person pray receive kindly. S.

---

[1] This date is misleading and evidently incorrect. Faraday's answer to this note bears the date Aug. 1 and can be verified by the postmark. Moreover Schönbein himself speaks of his going to Glarus at the beginning of August. Hence we are justified in dating this letter July 25, in the place of August 25.

Faraday to Schœnbein.[1]

Tynemouth 1 August 1851

MY DEAR SCHOENBEIN

On running away from the bustle and weariness of London I brought your letter here intending to answer it long before now and lo! I have been attacked by inflammation of the throat, have had a quinsy and been held in much pain and debility until now. I will not longer delay, believing that a few words are better than none. I have not yet received the portrait of Euler but doubt not it is at home. Will you do me the favour to return my most sincere thanks to the Council of the Museum for the great [honour] they have done me in favouring me with a copy, which I shall ever look upon with great pleasure. The others I will deliver according to their addresses.

The Ozone Evening went off wonderfully well; our room overflowed and many went away unable to hear (my account at least) of this most interesting body. Through your kindness the matter was most abundant and instructive, and the experiments very successful. The subject has been sent into the world so much piecemeal, that many were astonished to see how great it became when it was presented as one whole, and yet my whole must have been a most imperfect sketch, for I found myself obliged to abridge my thoughts in every direction. — Many accounts were printed by different parties and some very inaccurately, since they had to catch up what they could. A notice of four pages appeared in the proceedings of the Royal Institution[2] and though I think that has appeared in the Athenaeum or the Philosophical Magazine, yet I shall send you copies of it when I can. The subject excited great

---

[1] This letter also Bence Jones prints (vol. 2. p. 283); the beginning and end are omitted.

[2] On Schönbein's ozone, R. Inst. Proc. Vol. 1. 1851. p. 94.

interest and from what the folks said I had no reason to be ashamed either for the subject or myself.

And now my dear Schœnbein I am very weary. Perhaps to day you are at Glarus — I was two days at Ipswich at our meeting, no more for want of strength. Queens balls — Paris fêtes — etc etc etc, I am obliged (and very willing) to leave all to others.

With kindest remembrances to Mad. Schœnbein and yourself in which my wife has full part.

I am ever yours

M. FARADAY.

Faraday to Schœnbein.

Royal Institution 16 Decr. 1851

MY DEAR SCHOENBEIN

If I do not write at once (and even though I may seem to have but little to write about, yet if I delay) all that I have to say passes from my remembrance and I involuntarily become remiss in my duty. Dr. Bence Jones has just called on me to say that the Society, having printed the paper you sent to me, in their Transactions, have sent 25 copies of it to (him), however for you. It occupies 16 pages. Can you help me in telling me how I shall send these to you? I will do whatever you may instruct me in. I have, besides, a formal letter of thanks to you from the British Museum for the Portrait of Euler which I will send at the same time.

I keep working away at Magnetism, whether well or not I will not say. It is at all events to my own satisfaction. Experiments are beautiful things and I quite revel in the making of them. Besides they give one such confidence and, as I suspect that a good many think me somewhat heretical in magnetics or perhaps rather fantastical, I am very glad to have them to fall back upon.

Remember me very kindly to Madam Schœnbein and believe me to be

Ever most truly yours
M. FARADAY.

Schœnbein to Faraday.

MY DEAR FARADAY

What may be the cause of the very long silence kept by your friend on the Rhine? This question has perhaps more than once been asked in the Royal Institution these last six months. First of all, let me assure you that that somewhat strange taciturnity has nothing to do with any thing being in the remotest degree akin to forgetfulness.

Why, I don't know, but the fact is, that Mr. Schœnbein has of late conceived an almost invincible dislike to pen and ink, so that nothing but the most cogent reasons can force him to make use of them. He therefore has become a most lazy correspondent to all his friends. Whether that antipathy be a symptom of advanced age or only one of those unaccountable fits and whims, which even the strongest minds are now and then liable to, I cannot say, but this I know, that he trusts your inexhaustible kindness will grant full pardon and indulgence to this piece of human frailty of his. Though strongly disinclined to handle the pen, he has not yet lost his relish for scientific pursuits and, as far as I know, was rather active last winter. It cannot be unknown to you that our mutual friend entertains very curious and even highly strange notions regarding oxigen, which he considers as the first-rate Deity, not only of the chemical but of the whole terrestrial world He is indeed a most enthusiastic devotee to that Deity, talking and thinking of nothing but of her, praising and exalting her glory, wherever he can. He pretends that our philosophers, much as they think to know of oxigen, are as yet blinded and ignorant of the omnipotence of that mighty ruler of the elementary world. Upon many agents, considered as equal to oxigen, he looks down as upon upstarts and usurpers, assuming powers and privileges to which they have no right and declares that an infinite number of glorious deeds ascribed to the agency of inferior deities, are in fact the work of what he calls the "Jove of the philosophical Olympos."

As a matter of course, our friend entertains feelings of peculiar love and esteem towards those, whom he considers as high-priests to his Jupiter and who tend to increase the authority and glory of the king of elements. He asserts that you are the leader of those chosen adepts; that you more than any other have unravelled the mysteries of the wonderful workings of oxigen in nature and that you are the man who first has brought to light, that the influence of our friends favorite deity reaches far beyond the limits of the chemical world. He goes even so far as to maintain that upon your discovery of the magnetical powers of oxigen a new philosophical era will be founded.

Having said so much about our queer and enthusiastic friend you will not be surprised when I tell you that he is continually worshipping his goddess in a little smoky room, which he calls "Jove's temple" and if I be not misinformed, there, upon a sort of "tripod", he asks all sorts of questions with the view of getting as deep as possible into the mysteries of his deity. The other day he hinted at very strange answers having received from his oracle. Oxigen, he says, is the lord and master even of the most subtle and all pervading beings in existence, destroying and creating light, making and unmaking colors at pleasure etc. Indeed, he showed me some very strange tangible substances exhibiting in a most extraordinary manner the nature of a chameleon, for within a few minutes I saw the very same thing assuming white, green, yellow, orange, light-red, dark-red and even black colors. Heaven knows how such a wonderful change was brought about; our friend says that his oxigen and nothing but his oxigen had been the Charmer; but being afraid that he is a little cracked, I am rather sceptical about his assertions. He also talks now and then of oxigen being closely allied to the great powers of Electricity and Magnetism and gives to understand that their apparent might and force are only borrowed from his sovereigns.

I wonder whether he will divulge his queer Ideas to the world; but I should like to see them kept back from the philosophers of our days, for these people are too sober and rational, as to relish the extravagant notions of our hot-headed friend.

Mrs. Schœnbein and the Children are well and have not forgotten their English friend to whom they beg to be kindly remembered. Mrs. Faraday, I hope, recollects still the writer of these lines and will be indulgent enough as to accept friendly his compliments.

Pray let me soon hear of your doings and believe me

Yours most truly

Bâle, Mai 7. 1852. C. F. S.

Faraday to Schœnbein.

Royal Institution 2 June 1852

MY DEAR FRIEND

Though very stupid and weary yet I write, chiefly for the purpose of thanking you for your last very kind letter — it was quite a refresher and it did me good. — I wish more had such power, then I should think I might be of some little use amongst my friends by cheering them up.

Your paper in the Chirurgical Transactions[1] — I think I asked you what I should do with some copies that were printed off. However I forget whether you told me any thing about them — and I find by enquiring that Dr. Bence Jones has sent them to you by a friend that hoped to see Basle, perhaps you have them already.

Presently you will have three papers[2] of mine all at once. Two from the Phil. Trans. and one from the Phil. Mag. — They all relate to one subject i. e. the lines of magnetic force.

Every now and then I stir up my audience by talking about your ozone — and then there are many enquiries. I wish we had a good general English account of it, both as to its preparation, actions, and history. An acquaintance of mine, the Rev^d Mr. Sidney, is busy putting slips from your ozonometer, which I have supplied him with, through the cleft stems of vegetable and says he procures many effects just like those of ozone. — In such cases however there is a great deal to eliminate, as due to other actions of the ozonometrical strip, and the juices, before he will have his subject clear. Still experimentation is always useful.

What are your mysterious results — or what the results of your mysterious friend? — Have you made gold or even rather...,[3] for it is a more useful metal, or have you condensed oxygen? — I wish you could tell me what liquid or solid

---

[1] vide sopra p. 193.

[2] "On the physical lines of magnetic force" Phil. Mag. Vol. 3. 1852. p. 401, "On lines of magnetic force; their definite character, and their distribution with a magnet and through space." Phil. Trans. 1852. p. 25 and "On the employment of the induced magneto-electric current as a test and measure of magnetic forces." Ibid. p. 137.

[3] This passage is unintelligible unless we assume that after "rather" Faraday forgot to name the metal he was thinking of. What it was, we are of course unable to say, but would suggest inserting, for example, "iron".

oxygen is like. I have often tried to coerce it and long to know. With kindest remembrances to Mrs Schœnbein

I am My dear Schœnbein
Your lazy friend
M. FARADAY.

Schœnbein to Faraday.

MY DEAR FARADAY

To give you a sign of life I write these lines quite in a hurry. They will be delivered to you by the kindness of our mutual friend Dr. Whewell.[1] Your last letter shall be answered at a more convenient time and so, as it merits, for your friend is in this present moment not in his writing-mood. He has continued to ride his hobby-horse and found out different little things. If you have got a friend knowing german, he will perhaps give you the substance of papers, I have published in Erdmanns' Journal for pratical Chemistry.[2]

Tuas litteras expectabo, quum ut, quid agas, tum, ubi sis sciam, cura, ut omnia sciam, sed maxime ut valeas. Tuae uxori carissima salutem

Bâle Aug. 29. 1852. C. F. S.

[1] William Whewell D. D. Master of Trinity College Cambridge was born in 1794 at Lancaster. He was professor of Mineralogy till 1832, and from 1838 to 1855 professor of Moral Philosophy at Cambridge, where he died in 1866.

[2] Erdmanns Journal for 1852 contains eleven papers by Schœnbein, dealing among other subjects with ozone (Bd. 51. p. 343 and 349), the relation of oxygen to electricity, magnetism and light (p. 135) and the active oxygen in nitrous acid (p. 129).

Schœnbein to Faraday.

MY DEAR FARADAY

I trust you received in due time the letter I sent you through Dr. Whewell some months ago. Now I avail myself of a friend going to London, to forward to you a paper of mine, which I hope will not remain a sealed book to you. If you should feel curious to decipher that whimsical letter I once wrote you about oxigen, get the memoir translated by some friend of your's and you will perhaps be interested in the matter, as it regards some of your most important discoveries.

Entertaining the notion that in many, if not in all cases, the color exhibited by oxycompounds is due to the oxigen contained in them, or to express myself more distinctly, to a peculiar chemical condition of that body, I have continued my researches on the subject and obtained a number of results which I do not hesitate to call highly curious and striking. Far be it from me to think, on that account, my hypothesis correct and proved; but the fact is that I owe the discovery of a number of remarkable phenomena solely and exclusively to the conjecture mentioned. I am nearly sure that you will be pleased to repeat the experiments, for either by mere physical means or by chemical ones you may make and unmake or change the color of a certain substance without altering the chemical constitution of those matters. To my opinion, that wonder is performed by changing the chemical condition of the oxigen of the oxycompound.

I cannot help thinking that the colors of substances, which up to this present moment have been very slightly treated (in a chemical point of view) will one day become highly important to chemical science and be rendered the means to discover the most delicate and interesting changes taking place in the chemical condition of bodies. In more than one respect the color of bodies may be considered the most obvious "signatura rerum", as the revealer of the most wonderful actions going on in the innermost recesses of substances, as the indicator of the most elementary functions of what we call ponderable matter. But alas! Whilst we are pleased with and wonder at that rich field of chromatic phenomena, which continually strike our eye, we know as yet little or nothing of the connexion which certainly exists between the chemical nature of bodies and the influence it exerts upon light. We must try to dissipate that thick darkness which still hangs about and obscures the most luminous phenomena. Clearing up but the smallest part of that vastly important subject would be of more scientific value, I think, than discovering thousand and thousand new organic compounds, things which I cannot help considering in the same light as I do the infinite number of figures which may be produced by the caleidoscope.[1]

What would the world say of a man, who should take the trouble to shake for whole years that plaything and de[s]cribe minutely all the shapes (pretty as they might be) he had obtained from his operation!

You know, I am no great admirer of the present state of Chemistry, and of the Ideas leading the researches, made upon that field. Atoms, weight, ratio of quantities, endless

[1] This metaphor, we are informed, is one to which Schœnbein was very partial, in writing as well as in conversation. Passages from two letters to Liebig will suffice to bear this out. On September 5. 1853 he writes, after agreeing with Liebig that many fundamental facts are still required, if the scope of chemistry as an exact science is to enjoy a material expansion of its limits, as follow; "Now a days" he says "the results achieved are only the growth of facts of inferior importance, and the value we attach to the information thus acquired is hardly greater than what we would attribute to the production of novel combinations in the kaleidoscope."

Then again, on September 22. 1867 he says: "The aim of modern chemistry appears hardly apt to increase our knowledge of such phenomena. An infinite number of kaleidoscopic images, which the perseverance of chemists brings to light, after all, contributes but little to a better comprehension of chemical affinity, and adds but feeble information to the leading questions of the day."

production, and formula of compounds, i. e. the "caput mortuum" of nature, are the principal if not only subjects with which the majority of our Chymists know to deal. Force, power, action, life in fact, are, as it were, phantoms to them, disliked if not hated. The world being a system of Ideas, its very essence, power and intellect, how can we expect great things from men who so much mistake the nature of nature? In perusing what is written above I find it is not worth of being sent over the water, but having no more time to write another letter, you must take it as it is and excuse my random talking. Mrs. Schœnbein and the Children are well and beg to be kindly remembered to you. My best compliments to Mrs. Faraday and to you the assurance that I shall for ever remain

Yours
most truly

Bâle Oct. 17. 1852.   C. F. SCHOENBEIN.

Faraday to Schœnbein.[1]

Brighton 9 Decr. 1852

MY DEAR FRIEND

If I do not write to you now I do not know when I shall — and if I write to you now I do not know what I shall say — for I am here sleeping, eating and lying fallow, that I may have sufficient energy to give half a dozen juvenile Christmas lectures. The fact is I have been working very hard — for a long time — to no satisfactory end; all the answers I have obtained from nature have been in the negative, and though they shew the truth of nature as much as affirmative answers, yet they are not so encouraging and so for the present I am quite worn out. I wish I possessed some of your points

[1] Bence Jones reproduces portions of this letter. in vol. 2. p. 292.

of character. — I will not say which, for I do not know where the list might end, and you might think me simply absurd and, besides that, ungrateful to Providence.

I had your letter by Dr. Whewell and I have received also your last of the 17th October and the paper and I hope when I return home to get the latter done into English. It is a very great shame to us that such papers do not appear at once in English but somehow we cannot manage it. Taylor appears to be much embarrassed in respect of the Scientific memoirs. I hope now that they have changed their shape and are to appear in two series, physical and chemical, that they will be more servicable to such as I am.

Your letter quite excites me and I trust you will establish undeniably your point. It would be a great thing to trace the state of combined oxigen by the colour of its compound, not only because it would show that the oxigen had a special state, which could in the compound produce a special result — but also because it would, as you say, make the optical effect come within the category of scientific appliances and serve the purpose of a philosophic induction and means of research, whereas it is now simply a thing to be looked at. Believing that there is nothing superfluous, or deficient, or accidental, or indifferent, in nature I agree with you in believing that colour is essentially connected with the physical condition and nature of the body possessing it, and you will be doing a very great service to philosophy if you give us a hint, however small it may seem at first, in the development, or as I may even say in the perception of this connexion.[1]

As I read your letter I wondered whether there was any connexion between your phenomena and those recently inves-

[1] That idea which continually governed Schœnbeins theoretical views was that the same matter, independently of its chemical character, is capable of acquiring diverse properties, under varying curcumstances. Proof of this is furnished by the change of colour at different temperatures; hence it is that he time and again reverted to questions of this nature.

tigated by Stokes.[1] I do not mean any immediate likeness, but distant connexion. He has been rendering the invisible, chemically acting rays, visible[2] — that is to say he has been converting them into visible rays. — You, by giving a given condition to a substance, make it, when in compounds, send one ray to the eye — and then by giving it another condition cause it to send other rays to the eye, the body being chemically the same. Both these are phenomena of radiation, and both are connected with chemical agencies or forces. If they could be connected, what a heap of harvests would spring up between the two. — I do not know enough yet of Stokes' phenomona to form any thing but a crude idea and I know nothing of yours yet, so that you will think me very absurd to write such stuff; but then it is only to a friend.

You are very amusing with your criticisms on Organic chemistry.[3] I hope that in due time the chemists will justify

[1] George Gabriel Stokes, professor of Mathematics at Cambridge was born in 1819 at Skreen, Co. Sligo, Ireland.

[2] "On the change of refrangibility of light," Roy. Soc. Proc. 1850—1854. p. 195 and 333. "On the change of refrangibility of light and the exhibition thereby of the chemical rays," Roy. Soc. Proc 1850—1854. p. 259.

[3] He seems to have expressed similar criticisms to Grove, for in a letter dated Jan. 5 1845 the latter writes: "I quite agree with the remarks at the close. I think chemistry is being frittered away by the hairsplitting of the organic chemists; we have new compounds discovered, which scarcely differ from the known ones and when discovered are valueless — very illustrations perhaps of their refinements in analysis, but very little aiding the progress of true science." On the other hand he writes, after commenting on Becquerels process for extracting metals by voltaic means: "Who would not have been laughed at if he had said in 1800 that metals could be extracted from their ores by electricity or that portraits could be drawn by chemistry." (Aug. 20. 1847.)

We might also quote Graham's views, which are contained in a letter to Schœnbein, dated Jan. 9. 1862: "Your very kind letter acknowledging receipt of my paper has afforded me much gratification; the more so, that the standpoint from which you have always surveyed chemistry, is high and philosophical.... The various modifications of oxygen (an element) which you have established, with the compounds into which they carry their properties are discoveries of a fundamental character, leading into new regions of science, quite aside from the routine chemistry of the day."

their proceedings by some large generalisations deduced from the infinity of results which they have collected. For me I am left hopelessly behind and I will acknowledge to you that through my bad memory organic chemistry is to me a sealed book. Some of those here, Hoffman [1] for instance, consider all this however as scaffolding, which will disappear when the structure is built. I hope the structure will be worthy of the labour. I should expect a better and a quicker result from the study of the *powers* of matter, but then I have a predilection that way and am probably prejudiced in judgment. My wife's kindest remembrances to you and yours. My earnest wishes for the happiness of you all

Ever my dear Schœnbein
Your Affectionate friend
M. FARADAY.

Schœnbein to Faraday.

MY DEAR FARADAY

I had already given up the hope of my paper having reached you, when I was most agreeably undeceived by your kind letter from Brighton. I am really curious to know what you will think about my notions on the relations of the different conditions of oxigen to the voltaic, magnetic and optical properties of that body. The conviction of their being correct has by no means been shaken by my recent experimental results, of which you shall hear before long. But however they may turn out, I trust, they will at any rate draw the attention of philosophers to a most important set of phenomena.

---

[1] August Wilhelm Hofmann Ph. D. was born at Giessen in 1818. In 1848 he was professor at the Royal College of Chemistry in London; in 1865 professor at Berlin, where he died in 1892.

I am not acquainted with the experiments of Stokes, but from what you say about them, I am inclined to believe that they are closely connected with my subject. I am just now working upon the optical action of nitrous gas (NO²)[1] upon the solutions of the protosalts of iron, which, as you are well aware, is so very striking. As I entertain the notion that the deep coloring[2] of those solutions produced by NO² is due to a change of the condition of the oxygen, being contained in the base of the ironsalt, i. e. to the transformation of the inactive state of that oxygen into the active one, I suspect that the paramagnetic force of the black liquid is smaller than the sum of the paramagnetic forces of its constituent parts. You know that by uniting 1000 equiv. of inactive i. e. paramagnetic oxigen to one equiv. of paramagnetic deutoxide of Nitrogen, a diamagnetic compound is produced and you are likewise aware, that the two eq. of oxygen united to NO² exist in hyponitric acid in the ozonic or excited condition. Again by associating 2 equiv. of the highly paramagnetic protoxide of iron to one equiv. of paramagnetic oxigen a compound is obtained being, according to your own experiments, magnetically indifferent. I have shown in my paper that $Fe^2 O^3$ is $= 2 Fe O + \overset{\circ}{O}$, that is to say that the third equiv. of the peroxide of Iron exists in the exalted condition. From these facts I infer, that in the first case the diamagnetism of 2 equiv. of ozonic Oxigen is stronger than the paramagnetism of the two equiv. of inactive oxigen contained in NO²; and that in the latter case the diamagnetism of one equiv. of ozonic Oxigen neutralizes the paramagnetism of 2 equiv. of. protoxide of Iron. Now I conjecture that by uniting the two paramagnetic compounds: a protoiron salt to NO², either a diamagnetic or

---

[1] Schœnbein has in this letter placed the indices above, whereas, it will be remembered, he usually writes them below.

[2] vide his papers on changes of colour. Sitz -Ber. der Wiener Akad. Bd. II. p. 464.

a less paramagnetic fluid will be obtained. I should it consider as a great favor, if you would settle that point by experiment.

I trust the bracing air of Brighton will refresh your body and mind so much as to enable you not only to resume your Lectures, but what is more important, your scientific labors. We cannot spare you, our present age being so woefully deficient of original thinkers and experimental Philosophers. There are indeed but a very few to whom I might say: You are the salt of the Earth, but if the salt have lost his savour, wherewith shall it be salted? Permit me to tell you that I count you amongst those few.

Mrs. Schœnbein and the Children are well. My eldest daughter is now rather a big Child i. e. a grown up Lady. They charge me with their best compliments to you and Mrs. Faraday, to whom you will remember me in particular and in the most friendly manner. Excuse my badly written letter, which I was obliged to scribble down in a great hurry and believe me, my dear Faraday

Yours
most truly
C. F. SCHOENBEIN.

Bâle Dec. 18th 1852.

Schœnbein to Faraday.

MY DEAR FARADAY

Many months ago I sent you a letter and some papers of mine without having received from you any answer since. Being afraid of my parcel having been miscarried I forward to you another by the kindness of Mr. Drew[1] of Southampton and hope you will get it in time.

---

[1] John Drew, a school teacher at Southampton, was born in 1809 at Bower Chalk, Wiltshire and died in 1857 at Surbiton in Surry.

The single paper treats of a subject of a general nature, and if you should feel curious to get acquainted with certain views of your friend Schœnbein, you will perhaps find somebody translating it for you.

The question of the nature of Ozone seems to have been settled in the laboratory of Mr. Bunsen[1] at Heidelberg and it appears that both views hitherto entertained about that subtle agent are correct[2]; there is one sort of Ozone containing nothing but Oxigen and another that contains some hydrogen. Common oxigen, being absolutely anhydrous, is transformed into the first one by electrical discharges, as de la Rive[3] and Berzelius[4] maintained some years ago. The odoriferous principle disengaged at the positive Electrode on electrolysing water is a compound consisting of two Eq. of pure Ozone or allotropic oxigen and one Eq. of water = HO^3.

How such a wonderful change of properties can be effected in oxigen without adding to or taking away any ponderable substance from that body is indeed very difficult to say; I at least know nothing about it, but suspect that something very fundamental is at the bottom of that fact. It is a riddle to be solved by you only.

Just preparing for a journey to Vienna and Munich, I am in a great hurry and you will therefore excuse the emptiness of this letter. I promise you to write a better one after my return, which will not be prolonged beyond four weeks. I intend to go down the Danube, the scenery of which is as yet entirely new to me.

---

[1] Robert Wilhelm Bunsen, professor of Chemistry at Marburg, Breslau (1851) and Heidelberg (1852). He was born in 1811 at Göttingen and died at Heidelberg on the 16th of August 1899.

[2] cf. Baumert: "Über eine neue Oxydationsstufe des Wasserstoffes und deren Verhältnis zum Ozon." Poggend. Annal. Bd. 89. 1853. p. 38.

[3] cf. Arch. de l'Élect. T. 5. 1845. p. 11.

[4] Berzelius, Jahresbericht. Bd. 26. 1847. p. 64.

Pray transmit leisurely the volume laid by to Mr. Grove, who I think now and then sees you in the Royal Institution.

In asking you the favor to present my best compliments to Mrs. Faraday I am

My dear Faraday
Your's
most truly

Bâle July 11. 1853. C. F. SCHOENBEIN.

Faraday to Schœnbein.

Royal Institution 25 July 1853

MY DEAR SCHOENBEIN

I believe it is a good while since I had your last letter i. e. the one previous to that I received by the hands of Mr. Drew. — But consider my age and weariness and the rapid manner in which I am becoming more and more inert — and forgive me. Even when I set about writing I am restrained by the consciousness that I have nothing worth communication. To be sure many letters are written having the same character; but then there is something in the manner which makes up the value: and which when I receive a letter from a kind friend, such as you, often raises it in my estimation far above what a mere reader would estimate it at. So you are going down the Danube, one point on which I once saw, and are about enjoying a holiday in the presence of pure nature. May it be a happy and a health giving one and may you return to your home loving it the better for the absence and finding there all the happiness which a man, sound both in mind and body, has a right to expect on this earth.

I have not been at work except in turning the tables upon table turners — nor should I have done that but that so many enquiries poured in upon me that I thought it better to stop the inpouring flood by letting all know at once what my views and thoughts were.[1] What a weak, credulous, incredulous, unbelieving, superstitious, bold, frightened, what a ridiculous world ours is, as far as concerns the mind of man. How full of inconsistencies, contradictions and absurdities it is. I declare that taking the average of many minds that have recently come before me (and apart from that spirit which God has placed in each) and accepting for a moment that average as a standard, I should far prefer the obedience, affections and instinct of a dog before it. Do not whisper this however to others. There is One above who worketh in all things and who governs even in the midst of that misrule to which the tendencies and powers of man are so easily perverted.[2]

The Ozone question appears indeed to have been considerably illuminated by the researches in Bunsen's laboratory. — But why do you think it wonderful that Oxygen should assume an allotropic condition? We are only beginning to enter upon the understanding of the philosophy of molecules and I think, by what you say in former letters, that you are feeling it to be so. Oxygen is of all bodies to me the most wonderful, as it is to you. And truly, the views and expectations of the philosopher in relation to it would be as wild as those of any table turner etc. etc. etc. were it not that the philosopher has respect to the *laws* under which the wonderful things that he acknowledges come to pass, and to the never failing recurrence of the *effect* when the *cause* of it is present. — At the close of our Friday Evenings I gave a little account

[1] Faraday after opening the question, which had taken so strong a hold of the public mind, in a letter to the "Times", in June, so Bence Jones tells us, wrote a long letter to the Athenæum for Juli 2 1853, of which he was a little ashamed for "I think it ought not to have been required". He does not hope to convince all who refer this purely physical subject to electricity, or to some unrecognised physical force, or even to some supernatural agency.

[2] This passage is given in Thompsons Life and Work of Faraday. p. 252.

to our members of Fremy and Becquerels[1] expts. in producing Ozone by Electricity — and I confess myself glad that, whilst, at Heidelberg, they have shewn an HO^3, they have also proved the existence of a trace of $\overset{\circ}{O}$.

My dear Schœnbein, I really do not know what I have been writing above and I doubt whether I shall reread this scrawl, least I should be tempted to destroy it altogether. So it shall go as a letter carrying with it our kindest remembrances to Madam Schœnbein and the sincerest affection and esteem of

Yours Ever Truly
M. FARADAY.

Schœnbein to Faraday.

MY DEAR FARADAY

Some weeks ago I returned from the journey I have undertaken to Bavaria, Austria etc. during our mid-summer-holidays; and I can assure you that it was a very plesant one. The first stay I made at Munich, where I remained no less than ten days, finding that town highly pleasing and interesting both for the men and the things, I chanced to meet and see there. I think you would relish it as much as I did and if you should have any mind to cross the water once more, I strongly recommend you taking a trip to the Capital of Bavaria. The number of exquisite objects of painting, sculpture, architecture etc. accumulated there, is very great indeed and placed so closely together that you may see and enjoy them with perfect ease and comfort. Of course I met Liebig[2] at Munich,

---

[1] Frémy et Becquerel, Recherches électrochimiques sur les propriétés des corps électrisés, Paris Comptes rendus. T. 34. 1852. p. 399.

[2] Justus von Liebig Ph. D. M. D. started life as an apothecary's assistant. Later he became professor of chemistry at Giessen and at Munich (from 1852). He was born at Darmstadt in 1803 and died at Munich in 1873.

whom I knew before little more than by sight, but within the first five minutes we had found out the footing upon which both of us could move comfortably enough.[1] You will laugh when I tell you that Liebig asked me to deliver a lecture before a very large audience in his stead and Mr. Schœnbein, though reluctantly, yielded to that strange demand. The subject treated was that queer thing called "Ozone" which ten or twelve years ago as you are perhaps aware, was declared by a countryman of your's and pupil of Liebig's to be a "nonens". Nothing was easier to me than proving its corporeal existence and our friend Liebig, in spite of the unfriendly feelings he formerly entertained towards my poor child, has now taken it into his favor and seems even to have fallen deeply in love with the creature. He has therefore repeatedly entreated me to write a sort of biography of my progeny and give an account of its education and the accomplishments it has acquired under my tuition during the last decennium. I do not know

---

[1] Schœnbein relates this meeting with Liebig in his "Menschen und Dinge" (published in 1855) which in fact is a record of his esperiences and adventures during this trip. We must however confine ourselves to quoting a few passages descriptive of this meeting with Liebig:

"It was about the year 1820, that two youths were wont to attend daily the lectures delivered by the professor of chemistry at Erlangen, sitting together on the same bench, knowing of each other their names only and nothing else. The one was slender and slim, his gait erect, boldly he faced the world; the other short and stout, and stooping somewhat; a physiognomist might have taken him for a theosophist or a fanciful philosopher.

Even as they lived at Erlangen, so they parted, neither having any knowledge of the aims the other had determined upon. Not many years elapsed before the fame of one spread over the world; whereas to the other fell a more humble lot.

Without avoiding, or seaking each other, a friend (Professor Pettenkofer of Munich) brought them together. Veni, vidi, victus sum, the one exclaimed and gladly was he vanquished. What two terms at college, what a period of thirty years were incapable of achieving, was now brought to pass by a few moments.

Notwithstanding the great dissimilarity of their characters, they were alike in one respect: "in their devotion to science and in their zealous aspirations and endeavours to reveal to mankind the operations and the functions of nature".

yet whether I shall comply with his wishes being not very fond of copying myself over and over again.

My trip on the Danube down from Ratisbonne to Vienna proved highly delightful to me, though I experienced the mishap of losing my pocket-book and along with it may passport, no joke to a travaller who was about to enter the austrian Empiry. No unpleasant results however issued from that adventure. The scenery down the river merits to be called beautiful; now and then the Danube is forced to make its way through very deep and narrow ravines, the top of the hills being covered with ruined castles, churches, convents, country seats etc. and their declivities richly woo ded; another time you enjoy a beautiful and extensive view on the Alps of the Tyrol, Salzburg, Styria etc. —

Vienna itself is a fine and a noble town, full of interesting objects of science and arts and its inhabitants have become proverbial for their good nature. There is therefore no wonder that I enjoyed there very agreeable days. - In going home I passed through Prag, Dresden, Leipzic, Frankfort etc seeing little more of those cities than their steeples and towers, for having stayed out so long, I was obliged to return to Bâle as quickly as possible. Mrs. Schœnbein and the girls have during my absence been living in the hills, according to our usual style of passing the midsummer holidays. My eldest daughter has been absent from home these last 5 months and lives very happy on the beautiful lake of Geneva, at a little place called Rolle. She hast almost grown up into womanhood, is very like her mother, only a little taller and upon the whole a goodnatured and dutiful child. I think you would like her. Our friend de la Rive was kind enough to invite her to pass the approaching season of the vintage at his country seat, near Geneva.

Now having talked so much about myself and my family, it is time to ask you how you and your amiable Lady are doing. I hope well, in spite of the oriental and other affairs of the world. I should feel over happy if it fell to my lot to see you once more and to accomplish my wishes I see no other means than your coming over to us.

Mrs. Schœnbein joins me in her kindest regards to Mrs. Faraday and I beg you to believe me for ever

Your's
most truly

Bâle Septbr. 24. 1853.   C. F. SCHOENBEIN,

Faraday to Schœnbein.

Royal Institution 27 January 1854

MY DEAR FRIEND

Your letter of Octr. last was well timed, for it found me somewhat tired and out of health and by its happy, affectionate feeling was quite a cheerer. I do not find that as my philosophical past wears out, I at all diminish in my desire for the kindly, sympathizing and brotherly feelings which have grown up with it. Your holiday trip must have been a delightful one, but such things are for quasi young men. I have become a mere looker on. Still I and my wife do get a few short trips, for instance to Wales, or Norfolk, or Brighton, but as to crossing the Channel again I doubt it. — I enjoy greatly the account of your meeting with Liebig, and the Ozone affair: — it was very excellent and came off well for you. I like such an end to a controversy, and I think you must feel that you have had a very refined revenge upon your too hasty and too positive opponents. Furthermore I think the chronology of Ozone, as you speak of it, would be a very desirable thing.

Your family account is very pleasant and I try to imagine Miss Schœnbein upon the model of what I remember of Madame Schœnbein when we were in Basle: — but I have no doubt my idea is a great mistake. — No matter, it is very pleasant, and you must give our kindest remembrances to Madame Schœnbein. I do not suppose there is any body else at home who remembers me. It would be a delightful thing to accept your invitation and pop in: — but unless I can go by the telegraph line I am afraid that will not happen.

By the bye I have lately been examining some very curious facts obtained with telegraph lines of which you will see a report in our proceedings[1] in due time for I gave an account of them last Friday to our Members. They cover copper wire with Gutta Percha here (for insulation in submarine and other cases) so perfectly, that it remains beautifully insulated. I worked with 100 miles in coils immersed in the water of a canal; yet with 360 pairs of plates the conduction through the gutta percha was able to deflect a delicate galvanometer only $5°$. The copper wire is $1/16$ of an inch in thickness and the thickness of the Gutta percha on it is about $1/10$ of an inch — so that 100 miles gives a Leyden jar, of which the inner coating (the copper wire) has a surface of 8272 square feet, and the outer coating (the water at the G. P.) four times that amount or 33 000 square feet. -- This wire took a charge from a Voltaic battery and could give back the electricity in a discharge having all the characters of a Voltaic current.

Furthermore such a wire when under ground or under water is so affected by the transition of dynamic into static electricity, as to require a hundredfold the amount of tension for the transmission of an electric pulse, as the same wire suspended in the air: an effect of this kind is the interpretation of the extraordinary diversity in the expression of electric

[1] "On subterraneous electrotelegraph wires." Phil. Mag. Vol. 7. 1854. p. 396 and "On electric conduction." Roy. Inst. Proc. Vol. 2. 1854—1858. p. 123.

velocity given by different experimenters. — But you will hear of all this in the report, when it comes out, which will be soon.

Our librarian Mr. Vincent tells me that the Berichte der Verhandlungen der Naturforschenden Gesellschaft Basel, *Band 1 to 8* are not in our Library and he cannot get them here. He thinks your University distributes them to different bodies. If so is it possible for us to have that privilege? I ask you in all ignorance. — But do not by any means let me be ignorantly intrusive.

Ever My dear Schœnbein
Yours
M. FARADAY.

Schœnbein to Faraday.

Bâle Febr. 10th 1854.

MY DEAR FARADAY

At last I have seen again some lines from the Master of the Royal Institution and I can assure you that the mere sight of his handwriting gave me infinite pleasure, as it yielded me a visible proof of his being still amongst the living, and able to handle the pen, for I will not conceal it from you, that the long silence he kept this time, had already begun to cause feelings of uneasiness about the well-being of the dearest of my friends.

What you tell me of your late electrical experiments makes me very curious to learn the details of them, which I hope will soon be the case. It seems to me that we are as yet very far from having arrived at a standstill in electrical researches.

As to my little scientific doings I have continued to study the influence exerted by temperature upon the colors of substances and obtained some pretty results. You are perhaps aware that some time ago I tried to prove that a great number of oxycompounds being more or less colored at the common temperature, would turn colorless on being sufficiently cooled down, each of such substances having its peculiar temperature at which its color entirely disappears. I think I have satisfactorily proved that even common Ink is in that case, and you may easily convince yourself of the correctness of the statement. Color a weak solution of gallic acid, by some drops of a dilute solution of perchloride of iron, darkblue, even to opaqueness; put the colored liquid into a frigorific mixture of muriatic acid and snow until frozen, and you will of course obtain a darkcolored ice; cool it then down to about 40^0 below zero, or somewhat less, and you will have a colorless ice, which on increasing its temperature again will reassume its color, before having arrived at its melting point. From some reasons, I was led to conjecture that there must exist a series of bodies that exhibit the reverse behaving i. e. grow colored on their temperature being sufficiently lowered, and my conjectures proved to be correct. The coloring matters of a great number of red and blue flowers such as Dahlias, Roses etc. being associated to sulphurous acid, are at the common temperature nearly or entirely colorless; now aqueous solutions of those matters, having been uncolored by aqueous sulphurous acid, become beautifully and intensely recolored on being sufficiently cooled down, to lose their color again on raising the temperature of the ice, and I must not omit to mention that the colorless state is reassumed before the melting of the ice.

I have particularly worked upon the coloring matter of a certain sort of darkbrown Dahlia, very common with us, which exhibits the change of color indicated in a most beautiful manner. On account of the easy mutability of that matter in its discolored state, I preserve it by the means of filtering paper, which I rub with the leaves of the flower and suffer it to dry; such paper, of which I send you a little specimen, yields very easily the coloring matter to water, coloring beautifully the latter. A fresh solution of that kind should always be employed on making the experiment and you will be successful, when you employ my paper for preparing the solution.

It is a fact worthy of remark that such a solution rendered colorless by SO^2 turns colored also by heating it to its boiling point.

In want of something better, you might perhaps give the substance of my late researches on colors and the connexion with the chemical constitution of the matters exhibiting them in a Friday Evening, for the effects are very striking. Part of the results are described in the X volume of the proceedings of the Phil. Society of Bâle, part in a memoir published in the proceedings of the Academy of Vienna which most likely will be republished in Liebigs Annals and some, notably those above mentioned, are not yet made known at all.

You are most likely aware that Dr. Baumert[1] has of late confirmed the results previously obtained by de la Rive, Marignac, Berzelius and myself as to the capability of the purest i. e. absolutely anhydrous Oxigen of being thrown into its ozonic state by the means of the electrical discharge and I am therefore inclined to think that we can no longer doubt of the important fact that oxigen may exist in two different states, in an active and inactive one, in the ozonic condition and in the ordinary state.

Now such a fact cannot fail bearing upon a great number of chemical phenomena and I am just now drawing up a sort of memoir in which I try to embody the Ideas and Views on Electrolysis, Thermolysis and Photolysis (sit venia verbis). I have been carrying about in my head, these many years,

[1] Friedrich Moritz Baumert was born in 1818 at Hirschberg in Silesia and died in 1865. He for many years practiced as a physician at Breslau and in 1855 was nominated Professor of Chemistry at Bonn. It is very probable that his paper on ozon was worked out at Breslau, when Bunsen was professor there in 1851 and 1852.

ideas so very strange and queer, that they will meet with but very little favour.

To give you some notion about their singularity and heterodoxical character allow me to state some of them, but in doing so I must ask you the favor to consider them as mere Ideas and Views.

1. There are no other electrolytes (taken that term in the limited sense, you attach to it) than oxycompounds.

2. There are no compound Ions such as acids, and it is only the basic oxide of salts upon which the electrolysing power of the current is exerted.

3. The theory of Davy on the nature of Chlorine, Bromine, Jodine, the acids and salts is unfounded.

4. Electrolysation depends, in the first place, upon the capability of common oxygen to assume the ozonic state, when put under the influence of electrical discharge, and in the second place, upon the power of the current to carry, under given circumstances, matters from the positive to the negative electrode i. e. in the direction of the current itself.

5. The transfer of the electrolytic fluid from the positive to the negative electrode, as observed by Wiedemann, and others, is closely connected with the travelling of the kation in the same direction.

6. The travelling of the anion, i. e. Oxigen, is only apparent or relative, being caused by the real travelling of the kation.

7. Chemical decomposition caused by electricity, heat, and light depends upon allotropic modifications of one or the other constituent part of the compounds decomposed.

8. Chemical synthesis caused by electricity, heat and light is closely connected with allotropic modifications of one or the other matter conserned in that chemical process.

9. The notions of chemical affinity such as they are entertained at present cannot be maintained any longer.

You see such assertions are bold enough, so bold indeed, that I am afraid even You, the boldest philosopher of our age, will shake your head; but I think there is no harm in going a little too far, truth will make its way in spite of it and if the feelings of our cook-like Chymists, who are brewing on and on their liquors and puddings, without paying much attention to the conditions of the primary matters they are continually mixing together, should be roused even to wrath, I would not only care very little about it, but even take some pleasure in it, for I cannot deny that now and then I grow very angry about the narrow, or little-mindedness of the generality of the tribe.[1] Being now in a confessing mood of mind, I will openly tell you that Davy's theoretical views are most particularly unpalatable to my scientific taste, and I cannot help thinking that they have retarded rather than accelerated the progress of sound chemical science. — As to some of his scientific doings they are certainly of a superior kind and nobody can value them more than I do. The heterodoxical memoir alluded to will not henceforth go forth to the world, for I shall try to work it out as well as I can.

In April next I think to fetch my eldest daughter back again from the "Welschland"[2] to put the second there. Your

---

[1] This harsh verdict was one frequently returned by the old school of chemistry — we have on several occasions given illustrations thereof — and perchance they were not far wrong. Notwithstanding its great practical value and importance, its extraordinary development, of so extreme consequence to political economy, organic chemistry remains — this should not be forgotten — the chemistry of one element only, of carbon. We have therefore no reason to be surprized, if such a system caused displeasure to those, who were as yet unacquainted with so one-sided a training.

Even Wöhler expresses himself dissatisfied with the position of organic chemistry, for he writes to Schœnbein, May 21. 1862, from Göttingen: "I am afraid I shall have to give up my trade; I am far too inert to keep up with organic chemistry, it is becoming too much for me, though I may boast of having contributed something to its development. The modern system of formulæ is to me quite repulsive."

[2] By "Welschland" is meant French Switzerland, whese children were sent to learn French.

P

imagination gives you a correct idea of Miss Schœnbein, for she is really in many respects a second edition of her Mother. Our phil. society will take great pleasure in sending you the whole series of their proceedings and in receiving, what your Institution is publishing. As the crossing of the channel and coming over to Switzerland is a matter of a couple of days, I will not give up the pleasing hopes of seeing you and Mrs. Faraday once more with us in Bâle, where you have more friends and admirers than you are aware of.

Pray present my most humble compliments to your Lady and believe me
Your most affectionate friend

C. F. SCHOENBEIN.

NB. Mrs. Schœnbein and the Children charge me to remember them kindly to you.

As I have something to send to Southampton you will receive my letter from that town.

P. S. In reading over the preceding lines I feel I have written a very bad english letter, but I will not write another for fear of making it still worse. Being entirely out of the habit of speaking, writing and I may say even reading in your native tongue, I must necessarily lose the knowledge of it. And that you must take for my excuse.   S.

Schœnbein to Faraday.

MY DEAR FARADAY

These lines will be delivered to you by Mr. Merian of Bâle a former pupil, and the son of a most intimate friend of mine, the well know swiss Geologist Peter Merian.[1] My young friend being an Engineer and going to England with the particular view of seeing your railways and establishments for manufactoring locomotives etc. you would render him a great service by getting him introduced to some superintending railway engineers and manufacturers of locomotives. Mr. Merian is a very excellent man, distinguished mathematician, well versed in engineering, and in every respect highly respectable. You may therefore strongly and confidently recommend him to any of your friends and I need not say that by doing so you will lay me under very great obligations.

You have no doubt received my last letter as well as a memoir of mine, which I sent you through Mr. Gould, the Ornithologist, and I have gratefully to acknowledge the receipt of your last paper on Electricity.

Its contents proved highly interesting to me and most particularly to that part of it which refers to the variations of the velocity of the current.[2]

Having repeatedly been called upon by Mr. Liebig to draw up for his annals a paper embodying all the leading facts relative to Ozone I have a last complied with the wishes of my new friend, and send you a copy of it.[3] From a note of Liebig's joined to my paper you will perceive that the celebrated Chymist of Munich has taken a lively interest in the matter[4] and in a letter, he wrote me a couple of days ago, he

[1] Peter Merian was from 1820—1828 professor of Chemistry at Bâle, where he was born in 1795 and where he died in 1883. From 1835 he was honorary professor of Geology.

[2] Benjamin Apthorp Gould, Director of the Albany Observatory N. Y. (born in 1824 at Boston) also contributed a paper on the velocity of galvanic currents. vide Sillim. Journ. (N. S.) vol. 11 and 17. 1851.

[3] It is a compilation of everything concerning Ozone and appeared in Liebigs. Annal. Bd. 89. 1854. p. 257 under the following heading: "Über verschiedene Zustände des Sauerstoffs"

[4] He writes to Schœnbein, Sept. 19. 1853: "Your visit to Munich was a momentous one for me, for through it I have become acquainted with the

expresses his conviction, that the discovery of the ozonic Condition of Oxigen, and the facts connected with that subject, will exert a great influence upon the future development of Chemical Science.[1] I have been of a similar opinion these many years.

My paper on the chemical effects produced by Electricity, Heat and Light, of which I talked to you in my last letter is going to be printed[2] and as soon as finished, you shall have it, but I am sorry for you to say that it is written in my native tongue; being however not very voluminous you may easily get it translated for you. I should like very much indeed that you would take notice of its contents.

Mrs. Schœnbein and the girls are doing well and charge me with their best compliments to their friend at the Royal Institution. I join my kindest regards to Mrs. Faraday and am for ever

Your's
most truly
C. F. SCHOENBEIN.

Bâle April 9. 1854.

Schœnbein to Faraday.

MY DEAR FARADAY

Mr. Stehlin, Juris utriusque Doctor, of Bâle will perhaps take the liberty to call upon you, to enquire after the interesting results of your investigations; I look upon them as of the greatest consequence to the development of natural philosophy." Vide Kahlbaum and Thon, Briefwechsel Liebig-Schœnbein, p. 18. Leipzig 1899.

[1] Liebig says: "Professor Schœnbein, at my request, has compiled his investigations on this subject. To me these phenomena and observations, which this renowned investigator describes, are of the highest importance and consequence to science, for the disclosure of new properties of matter has ever been the origin of new laws and the source of insight into phenomena hitherto not accounted for."

[2] Basl. Verh. Bd. 1. 1854. p. 18.

address of Mr. Grove and in that case I beg you to be friendly to my young friend, who is an excellent and uncommonly well informed man. Going to England with the intention of making himself acquainted with the law and courts of the country, you may perhaps be able to favor the views of Dr. Stehlin by giving him an introductory line to some of your friends, who happen to be a lawyer or otherwise connected with a court or a lawyer's inn.

I am back again from the journey I made the other day to the lake of Geneva, and thank God brought home my eldest daughter in perfect health. She has turned out a good girl, being highly affectionate to her parents and sisters. I think you would like her.

Pray let me soon hear from you and believe me

Your's
most truly

Bâle Mai 4th 1854. C. F. SCHOENBEIN.

Mrs. and Miss Schœnbein join me in their kindest regards to Mrs. Faraday and yourself.

Faraday to Schœnbein.

Royal Institution 15 May 1854.

My dear Schoenbein

Your letters stimulate me, by their energy and kindness, to write, but they also make me aware of my inability, for I never read yours, even for that purpose, without feeling barren of matter, and possessed of nothing, enabling me to answer you in kind: — and then on the other hand, I cannot take yours and think it over, and so generate a fund of philosophy, as you do, for I am now far too slow a man for that. What is obtained tardily by a mind, not so apt as it may have been, is soon dropped again by a failing power of retention, and so you must just accept the manifestation of old affection and feeling in any shape that it may take, however imperfect. — I received your paper: and though a sealed book to me at present, I have put it into thehands of Mr. Stokes whose researches on light I think I mentioned to you.[1]

I made the experiments on the Dahlia colours, which you sent me, and they are very beautiful. Since then I have also made the experiment with ink, and Carbonic acid (liquid), and succeeded there also to the extent you described. I had no reason to expect, from what you said, that dry ink would lose its colour, but I tried the experiment and could not find, that the carbonic acid bath had power to do that. Many years ago, I was engaged on the wonderful power, that water had, when it becomes ice, of excluding other matters. I could even break up compounds by cold; thus, if you prepare a thin glass test tube, about the size of the thumb, and a feather so much larger, that when in the tube, and twirled about, it shall rapidly brush the sides: if you prepare some dilute sulphuric acid, so weak that it will easily freeze at $0°$ Fhrt. — and putting that into the tube, with the feather, you put all into a good freezing mixture of salt and snow: — if finally, whilst the freezing goes on, you rotate the feather continually and quickly, so as to continually brush the interior surface of the ice formed, clearing off all bubbles and washing that surface with the central liquid; you may go on until a half, or two thirds, or more, of the liquid is frozen and then, pouring out the central liquid, you will find it a concentrated solution of the acid. After that, if you wash out the interior of the frozen mass, with two or three distilled waters, so as to remove all adhering acid, and then

[1] vide sopra p. 209.

warm the tube by hand, so as to bring out the piece of ice, it, upon melting, will give you pure water,

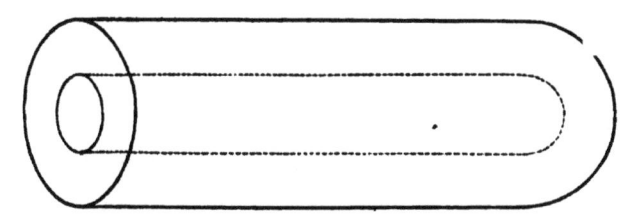

not a trace of sulphuric acid remaining in it. The same was the case with common salt solution, Sul. Soda, Alcohol, etc etc, and if I remember rightly, even with some solid compounds of water. I think I recollect the breaking up of crystals of Sulphate of Soda by cold, and I should like very much now to try the effect of a carbonic acid bath on crystals of Sulphate of copper. So it strikes me that in the effect of the cold on the colourless dahlia solution, the reappearance of the colour may depend upon the separation of the Sulphurous acid from the solidifying water.

Your nine conclusions in the letter you last sent me are very strong and will startle a good many, but if the truth is with them, I should not mind the amazement they will produce nor need you mind it either; but the chemist, of which body I do not count myself one now a days, will want strong proof and be slow to convince. — As to the electrical matters I referred to, I expect you have received by post a printed account of what I there referred to.

I think some of my letters must have missed; you scold me so hard. As I cannot remember what I have sent or said, I am obliged to enter in a remembrance the letters written or received and looking to it find the account thus:[1] 1852 Dec[r] 8. S. to F.[2] — Dec. 9. F. to S.[3] — Dec. 29. S. to F.[4] — 1853

---

[1] Faraday, in enumerating these letters apparently gives the dates on which he received them from Schœnbein, so that the dates at first sight do not seem to correspond with Schœnbeins.

[2] Missing: unless we assume that he received the October 17. letter as late as December. In his letter to Schœnbein of December 9 he at all events speaks of it as Schœnbeins last letter.   [3] vide p. 207.   [4] vide p. 210.

July 24. S. to F.[1] — July 25. F. to S.[2] — Oct' S. to F.[3] — 1854. Jany 27. F. to S.[4] — Feby 17. S. to F.[5] — May 15. F. to S[6]. and considering that I have little or nothing to say and you are a young man, in full vigour, that is not so very bad an account, so be gentle with your failing friend.

You say that in April you are to fetch a daughter from the "Welchland" etc. I had the foolish thought (perhaps), that you were coming to England and have been hoping to see you, but I suppose mine was all a mistake, for here is May. As for us, we do not expect to move far from home now; the imagination rambles and the desire also, but the body is too heavy and earthly. Our kindest remembrance to Madame Schœnbein and to all, who remember us. Young folks cannot be expected to retain much idea of old ones, after so long a while

Ever My dear friend
Affectionately Yours
M. FARADAY.

Schœnbein to Faraday.

MY DEAR FARADAY

Now a days people talk so much about the wonderful improvements of the ways of communication, and intercourse being established between the different parts of the civilized world and to us it is a most difficult matter to send a little parcel from Bâle to London. Without that deplorable deficiency, you had certainly received many weeks ago the

---

[1] probably Schœnbeins letter of July 11th. [2] vide p. 214. [3] perhaps Schœnbeins letter of September 24, p. 216. [4] vide p. 219. [5] vide p. 221 letter of February 10th. [6] vide p. 229. Between No. 5 and 6 are the two letters brought over by Mr. Merian and Dr. Stehlin respectively, which Faraday has forgotten to mention.

paper enjoined, but I was forced to wait until chance yielded me an opportunity to forward it to you. I should like very much, you would read the memoir for it contains my views on the proximate cause, not only of Electrolysis but also of what I have ventured to term Thermolysis, Photolysis, Electrosynthesis, Thermosynthesis and Photosynthesis, i. e. of chemical decompositions and compositions being effected by the agencies of electricity, light and heat. My leading idea is this, that the phenomena mentioned are due to allotropic modifications, which the elementary bodies, being concerned in those analytical and synthetical processes, undergo, when placed under the influence of the agencies named.

HO is decomposed, because its O, on being put under the influence of the current happens to be transformed into $\overset{o}{O}$ [1] (by which I mean ozonized Oxigen) which as such cannot form water with H. Oxide of Silver, which I hold to be Ag$\overset{o}{O}$ is decomposed by heat, because this agency transforms $\overset{o}{O}$ into O, which cannot combine with Ag etc. etc. etc. Perhaps a friend of your's will take the trouble to translate the paper, for without reading the whole chain of my reasoning and arguments, I am afraid, you will not well understand the neological views of your friend. As to the electrosynthesis of oxigen and oxidable matters, I think I have been entirely successful in proving that it is due to the ozonisation of oxygen being effected by electrical discharge.

[1] The history of the origin of these signs is to be found in a paper read by Schœnbein before the Scientific Club of Bâle, on April 21. 1847, an abstract of which appeared in the "Verhandl. der Naturf. Gesellsch. in Basel." Bd. 8. 1846—1848, p. 6. In it he proposes calling oxygen, capable of combining with other bodies at ordinary temperatures, *"oxylised oxygen"*, and giving expression to this difference, in their respective formulæ, by the addition of the letter o, for *oxylised oxygen*. Thus the peroxides of hydrogen and of manganese he writes, respectively, HO + $\overset{o}{O}$ and MnO + $\overset{o}{O}$ Since, according to his views, chlorine, bromine, and iodine are normal peroxides, their formulæ must be MuO + $\overset{o}{O}$, BrO + $\overset{o}{O}$ and IO + $\overset{o}{O}$.

At this present moment I am busily engaged in researches on the desozonising influence, being exerted by ponderable matters upon $\overset{\circ}{O}$, and the results already obtained leave, I think, no doubt, that a number of substances enjoy, conjointly with heat, the power of transforming both free and latent $\overset{\circ}{O}$ into O, a fact which is interesting enough, but by no means surprizing to me. Ozonized oxigen by whatever means, electrical or chemical, it may have been generated, on being put in contact with the peroxides of lead, manganese, silver, the oxides of mercury, the oxide of copper or silver and gold, the peroxide of iron etc., is immediately brought back to its inactive state and the simplest way of showing this desozonizing action is as follows: Charge bottles with air being strongly ozonized by phosphorus, introduce some finely powdered peroxide of Silver, Lead, Manganese, Iron etc. and shake the whole for half a minute, or less, and you will find that your Ozone is gone, no smell and action upon the test-paper being perceived any more. The substances just named, being saturated with oxigen cannot, as oxidable matters do, take up Ozone and hence it seems to follow that in one case the disappearance of ozonized oxigen is due to its having been transformed into O, in the same way as this change of state is effected by heat.

Thenard's [1] peroxide of Hydrogen [2] is to me HO + $\overset{\circ}{O}$ and you know well enough that the oxides, which, according to my late experiments, destroy the ozonized condition of oxigen, have also the power of decomposing HO + $\overset{\circ}{O}$ into HO and O.

Chlorate of potash is to my notion ozonized oxigen, associated to muriate of potash, now this $\overset{\circ}{O}$ may speedily be transformed into O by the aforesaid oxides and peroxides and I find that peroxide of iron enjoys that power to a very remark-

---

[1] Louis Jacques Thénard, professor of Chemistry at the Collège de France was born in 1777 at Louptière and died in 1857 at Paris.

[2] Paris Mém. Acad. Sci. T. 3. 1818. p. 385. cf. a Gilb. Annal. Bd. 64. 1820. p. 1.

able degree, for $^1/_{1000}$ part of it only, being mixt with the melted salt, will cause a lively disengagement of oxigen, even at a temperature, at which the pure chlorate does not yet yield a trace of that gas. $^1/_{100}$ part of the peroxide named gives rise to such a violent elimination of oxigen as nearly to approach an explosion and produce an incandescence of the salt.

A small portion only of a large and intimate mixture of one part of peroxide of iron and 50 parts of chlorate of potash being just heated to the point of fusion of the salt occasions such a rapid and complete decomposition of the latter, that the whole mass quickly and spontaneously becomes incandescent without having time to fuse. The higher the degree of mechanical division given to the oxide employed, the greater the desozonising or decomposing power of that matter. I entertain very little doubt that the same cause which acts in the peroxide of iron etc, and determines the transformation of free $\overset{\circ}{O}$ into O, also produces the same effect upon ozonized Oxigen, being contained in the peroxide of Hydrogen, Chlorate of potash etc; in other terms that the desozonisation of the oxigen of the oxy-compounds named and their decomposition are phenomena depending upon each other. It appears to me, to be a very singular fact, and therefore worthy of remark, that the oxigen of all the oxides or peroxides, which enjoy the power of desozonising free $\overset{\circ}{O}$ etc, exists either wholly or partly in the ozonized state itself. I hardly need add that what they call catalytic actions are to my opinion referable to allotropic phenomena. But of that more another time. From the preceding communications you will easily perceive, that I cannot get out of the charmed circle, drawn round me by that arch-conjurer called oxigen, and I am afraid, so long as I can walk, I shall move on that narrow ground.

I cannot conclude without expressing you my most grateful thanks for the kind letter, with which you favored me some weeks ago and I must tell it you over and over again, that the mere sight of your hand writing gives me infinite pleasure and always conjures up the image of its author, whom I revere and love more intensely than any other of my friends.

I read your remarks on the chemical effects produced by cold with the greatest interest; it is indeed a subject of research worth while to pay the greatest attention to and I very little doubt, that your conjecture on the proximate cause of the recoloring of the Dahlia pigmentum is correct.

I must not omit to tell you that we have kept in readiness the numbers of the proceedings of the Phil. Society of Bâle for the library of the Royal Institution, these many months; but up to this present moment we have not yet found a convenient opportunity for sending them off and beg therefore not to be charged with carelessness.

Next month I shall take a trip to the eastern Cantons of Switzerland, to attend a meeting of our Swiss Association and go perhaps for a week or so to Munich and Nuremberg. Mrs. Schœnbein intends to pass some time with her parents at Stuttgart, and the girls, who are at home, will be placed on the heights of the Jura to inhale its bracing air, jump about like chamois on rocks and in dales, in woods and on meadows. They charge me to offer to yourself and Mrs. Faraday their kindest regards, to which I join my own. Believe me my dear Faraday for ever

Your's

Bâle July 4. 1854.

C. F. SCHOENBEIN.

Faraday to Schœnbein.

Royal Institution 15 Septr. 1854

MY DEAR SCHOENBEIN

Just a few scattered words of kindness, not philosophy, for I have just been trying to think a little philosophy (magnetical) for a week or two, and it has made my head ache, turned me sleepy in the day-time as well as at nights, and, instead of being a pleasure has for the present nauseated me. Now you know that is not natural to me, for I believe nobody has found greater enjoyment in physical science than myself; but it is just weariness, which soon comes on, but I hope will soon go off, by a little rest. However, rest is not to be had yet, for as I have not been to the British Association for some years, I have promised to go next week to Liverpool, and I know from experience, that is not rest. I do not intend to stop more then three days. Though I date from the Institution, I may say that we are 12 or 14 miles out of town, getting some fresh air. We are often obliged to go out of town and that is the reason why I have not seen your friend Mr. Stehlin whose letter I had, I think, some time after that of the 4th July though dated before it.

The July letter was a great delight; both your kindness and your philosophy most acceptable and refreshing. I hope to get your paper translated, but there is a great deal of vis inertia in our way, and I cannot overcome it, as I would wish to do. It is the more difficult for me to criticize it, because I feel a good deal of it myself, and am known to withdraw from the labour and responsibilities of Scientific work, and this makes me very glad that you have got hold of Liebig, for I hope he will aid[1] in developing your Ozone views.

Much of your letter of the 4th of July I should like to have sent to the Philosophical Magazine; it was such a fine, free, brief comment on Ozone, in many of its positions, and I think might have helped to call the attention of chemists, where an elaborate memoir might fail; but I did not take the liberty. In fact I should not like to send all you write, for if I were to put in some of your former remarks about the errors of the theories and the nonsense of organic chemistry etc, we should both be extinguished, or at least sent to Coventry.

[1] Bence Jones, who gives this letter, reads "act in developing," vol. 2. p. 341.

I said we were in the country and I met lately here the Dr. Drew (that I believe is the name) who undertook to obtain Ozone observations for you in England. He spoke, as if his correspondents were discouraged by the uncertainty of their results, and indeed Airy[1] also wrote to me, to ask me if I was aware, that test papers which would give, after exposure, a certain degree of indication of ozone, lost much of the power in 2 or 3 hours after, and then gave a less degree. Dr. Drew talked about these points, but I said little and rather referred him to you, to whom he said he was about to send some communications.

You give a happy account of your family. You are a happy man to have such a family, and you are happy in the temperament which fits you for the enjoyment of it. May God bless every member of it and yourself with a cheerful and relying spirit and love to each other. Remember us to them all

Ever my dear friend,
affectionately yours
M. FARADAY.

Schœnbein to Faraday.

MY DEAR FARADAY

From the very long silence I have kept, you will draw all sorts of conclusions, but I am quite sure, that none of them proves to be correct, for the simple reason that even Mr. Schœnbein himself cannot account for his taciturnity. I have been neither unwell, nor low-spirited, nor overbusy, nor any thing else that could have prevented me from breaking

[1] George Biddel Airy, professor of Astronomy and Physics at Cambridge, and, from 1836 Director of the Greenwich Observatory. He was born in 1801 at Alnwick in Northumberland.

it sooner, and least of all, I have forgotten my dear and amiable friend at the Royal Institution.

But if I have not written *to,* I have written, at least, *about* you and in telling you so much, I have revealed to you an author's secret, which I beg you however to keep as yet to yourself. The matter stands thus: I have been composing a book these last six months, certainly not a scientific one, for doing such a thing suits, as you well know, neither the taste nor the powers of your friend; it is a sort of "quodlibet" or as the musical term runs a "potpourri" i. e. a most variegated motley of things. You recollect perhaps the trip I made to Munich and Vienna some time ago, and its having turned out so very pleasant, induced me to try my graphic powers with the view of making Mrs. Schœnbein and the girls, as it were, partners of my journey.

Wives and Children are very partial judges of the litterary productions of their husbands and fathers and you will therefore not be surprized, when I tell you that my excellent helpmate and young ladies made no exception so the rule. They found, indeed, every thing I had written and read to them so very excellent that they started one day the idea of having my scribbling published. However great my dislike to bookmaking is and how little I care for gaining laurels in the line of authorship, I at last yielded to the entreaties of my darlings, that is to say, promised to try what I could do in the matter. And, indeed, I have finished the work and a copy, legibly and nicely written out, lies in my desk, but when it will go to the printer and be published, that is a thing, which I cannot tell.

You will laugh, when I inform you that in spite of the embryonic state of my spiritual child, I have already baptized and given it the name "Glosses on Men and Things by an elderly Man".[1] This title has, as you see, elasticity enough,

[1] "Menschen und Dinge. Mitteilungen aus dem Reisetagebuch eines deutschen Naturforschers." Published anonymously in 1855.

and I will not conceal it from you that I have made full use of its vagueness, having thronged all sorts of reflections and queer ideas into the opusculum.

On account of its motley character I should like you could read that strange composition, but it being written in german, I am afraid its contents will never come to your knowledge.

It is, however, time to return to yourself and tell you in what manner I have written about you. In the above mentioned book there is a little chapter bearing the title "Fachmänner" gallicé "Spécialités" and anglicé perhaps — but I am unable to translate the word into your language — I mean to denote by that term Men devoting their whole life and mind to one object. By no means admiring what they call universal geniuses, and being convinced that it is the "spécialités" to whom we owe every real progress in science, arts etc., I have, with a view of proving the correctness of my opinion, drawn up four slight sketches of such "Fachmänner", of Berzelius, von Buch, Cuvier and of — of — but be it spoken out, of Faraday. I hope you will not tax me with indiscretion for having taken that liberty and believe that in doing so your friend has been actuated by the best motives.

As to science I have of late done nothing at all and do not recollect to have passed a winter so inactively and lazily as the last. When spring calls forth again the dormant powers of the earth, I hope I shall then feel too its congenial influence, and be stirred into action, for there is matter enough to work upon and of laborers there are not too many.

My collegue Professor Wiedeman[1] an excellent philosopher has (partly on my instigations) taken up Electrolysis again,

---

[1] Gustav Heinrich Wiedemann was born in 1829 at Berlin. He was professor of Physics at Bâle, at Braunschweig, Karlsruhe and from 1871 to his death, which took place in April 1899, at Leipzig. From 1877 he was the editor of the Annalen der Physik und Chemie, as successor to Poggendorff.

that fundamental phenomenon, I used to call the true copula of Chymistry and natural philosophy and obtained some results that seem to speak very much in favor of my heretic opinion, according to which in all the oxysalts the electrolysing power of the current is solely and exclusively exerted upon their basic oxides and that there is no such thing as an oxy-compound Jon.

I proposed Mr. Wiedemann to electrolize salts containing the same base and acid in different proportions and see whether, by the same current, different or equal quantities of metal be eliminated from such salts. If my notion should happen to be correct, it is manifest that under the circumstances mentioned, equal quantities ought to be eliminated. The salts as yet carefully electrolyzed are the mono-and tribasic acetates of lead and Mr. Wiedemann has ascertained, that on electrolysing them by the same current they yielded equal quantities of lead. I may add that in those experiments my collegue uses as a sort of voltameter a solution of nitrate of silver i. e. the weight of metal being eliminated from that salt as the .... measure of the amount of the electrolysing power of the current employed. Now upon one equivalent of silver Mr. W. obtained one equiv. of lead, both from the neutral and tribasic acetate. Hence it seems to follow, that the current has nothing to do with the acid; in other terms that the latter is no Anion. In my late paper "on the chemical effects of Electricity, Heat and Light" I have circumstancially developed my notions on the Electrolysis of the Oxy-salts and you have perhaps taken notice of them.

I entertain no doubt you have spent the winter in high scientific spirits and performed some exploits in spite of the warlike mood of the public mind, which by the bye, I do not relish at all and am inclined to consider as madness. I hardly need tell you how happy I should feel if you would favor me soon with your good news and not requite silence by silence. All my family are doing well and charge me with their best compliments to you and Mrs. Faraday, to which I join my own. Believe me my dear Faraday for ever

Your's
most truly

Bâle Febr. 27. 1855.   C. F. SCHOENBEIN.

Faraday to Schœnbein.[1]

Hastings 6 April 1855

MY DEAR FRIEND

I have brought your letter here, that I might answer its great kindness at some time when I could remember quietly all the pleasure I have had since the time I first knew you. — I say remember it *all*, but that I cannot do; for as a fresh incident creeps dimly into view, I lose sight of the old ones, and I cannot tell how many are forgotten altogether. But think kindly of your old friend; you know it is not willingly, but of natural necessity, that his impressions fade away. I cannot tell what sort of a portrait you have made of me; all I can say is, that whatever it may be I doubt whether I should be able to remember it, indeed I may say, I know I should not, for I have just been under the sculptor's hands, and I look at the clay and I look at the marble, and I look in the glass, and the more I look the less I know about the matter and the more uncertain I become. But it is of no great consequence; label the marble, and it will do just as well as if it were like. The imperishable marble of your book will surely flatter.[2]

[1] This letter is given in Bence Jones vol. 2. p. 355.

[2] We here give a translation of some of the passages devoted to Faraday: "The disciple came to the master, one worthy of the other; keen perception

You describe your state as a very happy one — healthy, idle, and comfortable. Is it indeed so? or are you laying up thoughts which are to spring out into a rich harvest of intellectual produce? I cannot imagine you *a do-nothing*, as I am; your very idleness must be activity. As for your book, it makes me mad to think I shall lose it. There was the other (which the "Athenaeum"[1] or some other periodical reviewed) in German, but we never saw it in English.[2] I often lent it to others, and heard expressions of their enjoyment, and sometimes had snatches out of it, but to me it was a shut book. How often have I desired to learn German, but headache and giddiness have stopped it.

I feel as if I had pretty well worked out my stock of original matter, and have power to do little more than reconsider the old thoughts. I sent you by post a notice of a Friday Evening here, and would have sent you a paper from the Philosophical Magazine; — but I am afraid of our post, i. e.,

and individual deeds soon developed under the teaching he here received. The wings of the young eagle quickly stretched out and qualified him to the highest flights; the scholar outdoing his teacher: and so he came to be the profoundest and most productive among discoverers. His refined spirit forced its way into the most hidden workings of the forces of nature and revealed them to the unenlightened mind; his prophetic eye enabled him to penetrate to undiscovered fields, which he made accessible to others . . . . Following the impulse of his mind he, in maturer years, limited his researches to a definite sphere. To comprehend the primary function of matter as manifested in its relation to the phenomena of electricity, magnetism, chemical affinity and gravity: that is the goal which the genius of Faraday is striving after, and which, as the highest reward for his astonishing energy, he will surely reach."

[1] vide Faradays letter to Schœnbein Sept. 6. 1843. p. 113

[2] Had it not been for the difficulty of finding a publisher, an English translation of his "Mittheilungen (vide p. 112) would most likely have appeared. For Mr. Benjamin Vincent writing to Schœnbein from London, Juli 3. 1843, after reading through Schœnbeins book, tells him that he found so much to interest and amuse him, that he felt very much inclined to present it to the British public. In fact he began a translation of it and to his letter subjoins specimens of his work, which show that he had quite entered into the spirit and individuality of Schœnbeins style.

I am afraid that unawares, I may put my friends to much expense. I receive almost daily newspapers and journals, which, coming by post, are charged to me two, three, and four shillings, until I absolutely cannot afford it; and fearing that with equal innocency I may be causing my friends inconvenience, I have abstained. However, I hope that a friend of mine, Mr. Twining, will, in the course of a month or two, put the paper I speak of in your way. You will therein perceive that I am as strong as ever in the matter of lines of magnetic force and a magnetic medium; and, what is more, I think that men are beginning to look more closely to the matter than they have done heretofore, and find it a more serious affair than they expected. My own convictions and expectations increase continually; *that*, you will say, is because I become more and more familiar with the idea. It may be so and in some measure[1] *must* be so; but I always tried to be very critical on myself before I gave anybody else the opportunity, and even now I think I could say much stronger things against my notions than any body else has. Still the old views are so utterly untenable *as a whole,* that I am clear they must be wrong, whatever is right.

I had forgotten that Wiedemann was in Basle; give my kindest remembrances to him. I think I received a paper on electrolysis from him, but out here cannot remember, and cannot refer. Our sincerest remembrances also to Mrs. Schœnbein and the favourable family critics. I can just imagine them, hearing you read your MS., and flattering you up, and then giving you a sly, mischievous, mental poke in the ribs etc. They cannot think better of you than I do. Ever my dear Schœnbein   Your attached friend,

M. Faraday.

[1] Bence Jones, who has made several alterations, reads "manner," and further on "kindest" for "sincerest".

Schœnbein to Faraday.

MY DEAR FARADAY

How could I employ the leisure hour of a fine May morning better, and more agreeably, than by devoting it to an epistolary conversation with my dear Friend Faraday, whom I besides owe an answer to his last amiable letter; and to-day let me talk a little of Science.

As you cannot avert your mind from the contemplation of that mysterious agency, called Magnetism, I am unable to let Oxigen out of sight and of late I have been actively working again on that curious subject, not, I think, without some little succes. You know that these many years I have entertained the notion, according to which not only free, but also Oxigen being chemically associated to some matter or other, is capable of existing in two different conditions: in the common, or inactive, and the exalted, or ozonic state, and to distinguish by signs those different conditions from one another I have given to ozonised oxigen the symbol $\overset{\circ}{O}$ denoting the inactive O by its usual sign $=$ O. Considering the peroxides of hydrogen, nitrogen (hyponitric acid), Barium, Manganese, Lead etc as compounds containing both sorts of oxygen, I have given them the formula $HO + \overset{\circ}{O}$, $NO^2 + 2\overset{\circ}{O}$, $BaO + \overset{\circ}{O}$, $MnO + \overset{\circ}{O}$, $PbO + \overset{\circ}{O}$ etc and, as you are well aware, made these last six years, many experiments with the view of separating from the oxycompounds mentioned, and other similar ones, their ozonised oxigen, without obtaining however satisfactory results.

Some time ago Mr. Houzeau [1] communicated to the french academy a paper, in which he suggested ideas on the different states of the oxigen,[2] being contained in compounds, being

---

[1] Auguste Houzeau was born in 1829 at Elbœuf, Seine-inférieure and is professor of Chemistry at the École Superieure at Rouen.

[2] Recherches sur l'oxygène à l'état naissant. Comptes rendus T. 40. 1855. p. 947.

exactly the same which I for the first time ventured to express in Poggendorff's Annals seven or eight years ago and have since more fully developed in the publications of the Phil. Society of Bâle, notably so in the last number of the proceedings of that learned body. The views recently put up by Mr. Houzeau are therefore rather old acquaintances of mine, but that Chymist has ascertained a novel fact, and as I consider it, a very interesting one. On adding peroxide of Barium to the monohydrate of sulphuric acid, he obtained oxigen, enjoying all the properties of Ozone. I have arrived at the same end, but in a somewhat different manner. You know, Silver, being exposed to the action of ozonised oxigen at the common temperature is transformed into the peroxide of that metal, and you will recollect that I sent you a small quantity of that compound, some years ago.[1] Now it is from this peroxide of Silver, which I consider to be $AgÖ^2$, that I succeeded to eliminate some Ozonised Oxigen.

On throwing the said peroxide into the monohydrate of sulphuric acid a most lively disengagement of a gaseous substance takes place, conjointly with the formation of sulphate of Silver. The gas obtained in the manner indicated, enjoys the following properties: its smell strongly resembles that of Ozone, but minute quantities being inhaled produce a sort of asthma, as Ozone does; its electromotive power is strong, and like that of Ozone or Chlorine, plates of Platinum or Gold becoming negatively polarised in the gas; it eliminates Jodine from the jodide of potassium and therefore turns instantaneously my test-paper dark blue; it rapidly transforms the yellow ferrocyanuret of potassium, even in its solid state, into the red one; it suddenly oxidises sulphurous acid into sulphuric acid, and sulphuret of lead into sulphate; it energetically and chlorinelike discharges the colors of organic matters, such as Indigo, Litmus etc; it colors blue the alcoholic solution of guajacum etc.

[1] vide p. 180 and p. 184.

Now all these reactions being exactly those produced by Oxigen as modified by Electricity or phosphorus, i. e. Ozone, I think, we may be allowed to conclude, that the gas being disengaged out of the peroxide of Silver is, or contains at least, the same principle, i. e. Ozone.

Having but very minute quantities of that peroxide at my disposal, I, to my great regret, was forced to perform my experiments on a very small scale, but I had enough of the matter, as to ascertain, that the gas obtained was a mixture of $\overset{\circ}{O}$ and O, in which the latter very much prevailed. Although there is no doubt to me, that all the oxigen eliminated from the peroxide does, in the moment of its being set free, exist in the ozonic state, there are some obvious causes, that account for the mixt nature of the gas i. e. for the transformation of $\overset{\circ}{O}$ into O. One of them is the heat being disengaged at the points of contact between SO^3 and AgO^2 and the other the peroxide itself. As to the latter, you know perhaps that last year I ascertained the curious fact that a number of substances exert the same influence upon the ozonised oxigen, as heat does, i. e. destroy at the common temperature the ozonic condition of that oxigen without taking up a particle of it. The metallic peroxides enjoy that strange property in a very high degree, and notably so that of Silver, compounds, as you see, which to my opinion contain ozonized oxigen themselves. Now if a particle of peroxide of Silver, not yet decomposed, happens to come in contact with a particle of ozonised Oxigen, being disengaged from another portion of the peroxide, that particle must become desozonised. There are perhaps some other causes, unknown as yet, that tend to change $\overset{\circ}{O}$ into O in the case before us. I hope you still possess some of the peroxide of Silver, I sent you some years ago, and if so, you may even with that small quantity ascertain the correctness of my statements above made. In case you repeat my experiments, I advise you to put a little peroxide into comparatively much oil of vitriol, and do the thing at a low temperature, from reasons that are obvious enough. To give you some visible proofs of the great chemical power of the oxigen, having been eliminated from the peroxide of Silver, by the means above indicated, I join three strips of paper, one of them being impregnated with sulphuret of lead, another with indigo solution, a third one with the coloring matter of litmus and you will perceive part of each of them to be bleached.[1]

This was effected within a few instants by immersing a moistened end of the strip into the said oxigen.

From more than one reason I cannot help attaching some importance to the result of my experiments, and believing that, if properly worked out and philosophically interpreted, it will lead to others of still greater consequences. And pray, let me reason and conjecture a little about it.

If it be allowed, that the oxigen being contained in the peroxide of Silver, exists in the ozonic condition, and it being a fact, that free $\overset{\circ}{O}$ is by heat transformed into O, does it not appear very likely that the same agency has the power of changing the $\overset{\circ}{O}$ of the peroxide into O, and that this very change of condition is the proximate cause of the decomposition, which the peroxide undergoes when sufficiently heated? And if this conjecture should happen to be founded, are we not permitted to account in the same manner, for the decomposition of all the other oxycompounds being effected by heat and yielding free inactive Oxigen? I am inclined to think that we are, and in a paper of mine printed last year I have given detailed reasons for entertaining such an idea.[2] Now supposing my hypothesis to be true, I am afraid many of our present notions, on the

---

[1] The strips of paper referred to have been mislaid and are no longer attached to the letter.

[2] For further details on this subject a paper in the Gelehrte Anzeigen (Munich) should be consulted Bd. 41. 1855. p. 108: "Über die Darstellung des ozonisierten Sauerstoffes aus Silberoxyd."

phenomena regarding chemical analysis, synthesis, affinities, etc, cannot be maintained, and must sooner or later be essentially modified. Stating that peroxide of Silver, for instance, consists of one Eq. of Silver and two Eq. of Oxigen, and carbonic acid of one Eq. of Carbon and two Eq. of Oxigen, is telling, if I may say so, but half the truth, as regards the chemical constitution of the compounds named, for it implies the assertion, that the oxigen being contained in those compounds is the same thing, an admission which according to my opinion cannot be allowed to be true, for $\overset{\circ}{O}$ is not O, though the one may be transformed into the other.

But if the oxigen, being chemically associated to other matters, be capable of existing in different states and the bearings of the oxycompounds be so much influenced by the peculiar condition, in which their Oxigen exists in them, are we not permitted to suspect, that other elementary matters may also enjoy a similar capacity of assuming different conditions and be able to exist within compounds in those various states? May it not be presumed, that the chemical behaviour of such compounds essentially depends upon the peculiar condition of their constituent parts? Is it to be believed that carbon exists in the oil of turpentine exactly in the same state as it does in charcoal, and is it not possible that the decomposition of all the organic substances is effected by heat, because this agency has the power of transforming carbon from one state into another? To condense these questions, and others, that easily suggest themselves, into one, I ask, is it not very likely that, what they call "allotropism" acts a much more important and general part in Chymistry than it is thought of as yet? I for my part think it to be so.

Now no more of Science, theories and such like! We descend to daily life and my family. Being all of us highly in love with nature, we are very fond of rambling in fields, and woods, on hills and dales, to admire the unfathomable riches of beauties being displayed there. May is called in German "Wonnemonat", which means month of joy, and well meriting that poetical denomination, it is of course a favorite of ours, and we indulge during its reign as often as we can in our rambling propensities by taking trips in the neighbouring country. The Jura mountains are a particular point of attraction to us, with their rich woodland, limpid rivulets, green valleys, bold rocks and fine views. I preface thus to tell you, that some days ago, on a fine morning, a motley army consisting of big and small Children, male and female, and old folks too, were seen marching out of the old gates of Bâle tending their steps towards the "Gempenstollen", the highest and most prominent point of the Jura in our neighbourhood. Mr. Schœnbein, well acquainted with all the recesses, and by-ways, round about us, and his family making up good part of the army, was unanimously elected commander-in-chief, which important charge he accepted and filled it up to the best of his powers. The day turned out a glorious one, nature exhibiting all her charms. By a great and gradually rising round about way, leading through meadows covered with flowers, green fields, flowering orchards, beautiful beechwoods crowded with singing birds, we reached, after a four hours walk the summit of our favorite hill. A little fatigued, the army desired to camp here, and it was allowed to do so. The delicately green foliage of fine beeches, and the crowns of stately firtrees, formed a splendid canopy, and the mossy ground yielded soft resting places. Carrying our victuals with us, the dinner was soon ready and I can assure you that we enjoyed our cold morsels infinitely better, than we should have done, had we sat down at a sumptuous royal table. Our camp being placed upon the top of a gigantic projecting rock, it commanded a most extensive and glorious view: to the south at some distance, we saw the snowy heaventowering Alps of the Berner Oberland, nearer and to the west a great part of the Vosges and Alsatia, to the north the Black Forest and Baden, nearest us, the many valleys and summits of the Jura mountains. Being enchanted by that glorious sight, we could not but most reluctantly break up our camp, but Mr. Schœnbein gave orders at last to march home again, on a road however, different from that we had come, beautiful also beyond description. Having reached the foot of the hill the gypsy host was allowed to halt again, for taking refreshments, and by eight o'clock we approached the walls of the good town of Bâle, where the commander-in-chief discharged his troops, not without having received before, the thanks from high and low, old and young. I am sure you yourself and Mrs. Faraday, would have highly relished the gypsy party; but come over to us and we shall repeat it. Next midsummer we go to Langenbruck, a village in some pass of the Jura, intending to stay there for a month. It would be a high treat to me and us all, if we could spend that time with you and Mrs. Faraday.

The gentleman who will deliver this letter to you is Mr. Schweitzer of Bâle, an old pupil of mine and whom I take the liberty to recommend most friendly to your kindness.

Mr. Wiedemann charges me with his best compliments to you, he is very actively occupied with electrolytical researches and has received some interesting results.

Should a parcel be directed to you under my address, pray take and keep it until you find an occasional conveyance for Bâle. There is no hurry for it.

Excuse my immoderately long letter, let me soon have the favor of a letter and believe me

Your's
most truly

Bâle Mai 26th 1855.   C. F. SCHOENBEIN.

Don't forget to remember me friendly to Mrs. Faraday.

Faraday to Schœnbein.

Royal Institution 6 Novr. 1855.

MY DEAR SCHOËNBEIN

It is quite time I should write you a letter, even though I may have nothing to say, and yet I surely have something to write, though it may not be philosophy, for I trust affection will last out philosophy, and indeed were it not so, I should fear that I was indeed becoming a worn out worthless thing. But your last letter abounded in *all* matter, both the *philosophical* and also the *domestic* and *kind*, and I thank you heartily for it. That one day in the country — how I wish I had been with you, — but I could not now walk in Switzerland as I have done in former years. — All things suffer a change. May your changes be long deferred, for you must be very happy as you are. — And so am I; but my happiness is of a quieter kind, than it used to be and probably more becomes a man 64 years of age; and as we, i. e. my wife and I, go on our way together, our happiness arises from the same things and we enjoy it together, with, I hope, thankfulness to the Giver of every good and perfect gift.

I tried an experiment or two with the oxide of silver and obtained some results, but not equal to those you sent it, nor was it to be expected that I should reach the results of a Master in this subject. Your accounts and observations are most interesting and exciting, but I dare not try to pursue the subject, for even the matter I have in Magnetism is often too much for me and I am obliged to lay it by for a while, so that I am forbidden by nature to take up any new series of thought. But that ozone, that oxygen, which makes up more than half the weight of the world, what a wonderful thing it is, and yet I think we are only at the beginning of the knowledge of its wonders.

By the bye your letters often contain much that I should like others here to see and I want to ask you whether there is any objection to my shewing them to Tyndall and letting him, as one of the Editors of the Phil. Mag, print any of the philosophical parts, that he may select, in the Magazine. There are full three pages of your last which, if I were an Editor, I should have selected: — at the same time you must not in any way alter the pleasant tone and current of your epistles, — or else I shall be a great loser.

I cannot now remember how I received your letter and whether I saw M. Schweitzer, — I rather think not; but whether I was out of town, or whether he *sent* me the letter by some one, I am unable to call to mind. — I have received no parcels for you as yet, — but will take care of any that come. — I sent you Vol. III of Experimental Researches by Mr. Twining and have no doubt it has reached you — but I have not seen Mr. Twining since his return from your country.

The General board of health here published a report on the Cholera epidemic of 1854 and since that, a thick 8vo volume of Appendix. In the latter I am glad to see they refer to Ozone in several places p. p. 71. 89. 103 and of course to you, but whether the observations (by Dr. Moffat) are well made, and considered, I do not know; — in any case it indicates that ozone is gaining a growing attention amongst medical men.

My kindest remembrances to Madame Schœnbein and to those, whom, by a stretch of imagination, I strive to see around here, i. e. to the party of the day's excursions, and my very kind remembrances to M. Wiedemann also. It is delightful to see thinking workers rise up in Science. Believe me to be, my dear Schœnbein

Your faithful friend

M. Faraday.

Schœnbein to Faraday.

MY DEAR FARADAY.

Having these many months heard any thing neither from, nor of you, I had already begun growing anxious about the state of your health, when to my great satisfaction I was released from my anxiety by your kind letter of the 6th instant, which has made upon my mind the impression that you are a perfectly well doing man. May it please kind providence to preserve you, both to your friends, and Science for many years to come! This is one of my most ardent wishes, which I cannot help expressing you, over and over again; for I see that you have as yet much work to do, many a problem to solve, and more than one mystery to divulge to the philosophical world. Indeed, we cannot yet do without the seer and prophet of nature. —

Since I wrote you last, we, for the first time had here the most unwelcome visit of the Cholera, but thank God, its stay was short, and my family, as well as my friends, were left untouched by it. During the summer Mrs. Schœnbein and the girls spent a couple of months in the Jura mountains, where I joined them now and then to their great satisfaction, the father's disposition for rambling on green and wooded hills being their's too, and certainly we did not fail gratifying it to a great extent, walking very often for six or eight consecutive hours together. You will perhaps smile, when I tell you, that Miss Schœnbein has of late become a very zealous english scholar, reading, writing and speaking away your native tongue in rather a fluent and elegant style. But pray, do not imagine the father to have any part in the proficiency of the daughter, for you must be aware that a parent always proves a very bad master to his children. Certainly, on being sometimes called upon to look over the tasks of the young scholar's, I have an occasion to make some use of the little bit of English I am as yet master of. Number 2 and 3, having caught that liking from her eldest sister, have become pupils of her's and are going on well enough in their studies. As to me, I can, of course, have no objection to that taste for an outlandish tongue and litterature, being myself somewhat suspected of "Anglomanie", Once speaking of my daughter's accomplishments, I may as well add that she is a partly good musician too, playing the piano, not only with facility, but I think also with some taste. Being myself a great admirer of the heavenly art of music, and after my morning's schoolmastering sometimes feeling inclined to take a little rest on the sopha, I, in a half dozing state of mind, listen to Beethoven's, Mozart's, Weber's etc. delightful compositions being performed by Miss Schœnbein. Having for half on hour or so enjoyed that dreaming pleasure, and taken a cup of coffee, served up to me by my second daughter, I rise again quite refreshed, light my segar and go to my laboratory or to some other business. If you should once mark two o'clock, after noon, you will hardly miss the truth, if you imagine your friend lying on his couch, and listening to music, an attitude not very picturesque indeed, but nevertheless, proving to be an agreeable one to him, that assumes it. Now to finish with my talking of Miss Schœnbein, I will tell you, that she is very desirous of visiting England, and seeing the wonders of your country, but I am afraid, that her wishes will never be fulfilled, i. e. that she will never prevail upon her father to carry her there. Now before speaking of philosophy, for I cannot help talking to you of my bride, allow me to make a proposal to you, but pray, do not be angry about it. I cannot bear the Idea of seeing you no more in this world, and it being very unlikely, that I shall be able to cross once more the water, and you, in comparison to your friend, being an independent i. e. moveable man, could you not make up your mind to come over to us with Mrs. Faraday next year, and spend a month or two, I won't say, in Bâle itself, but in our fine hilly neighbourhood? where I should try to find out for you a quiet snug corner, in which you might carry on a sort of life quite congenial to your taste, and Mrs. Faraday's too. You were, as I hear, in Glasgow some months ago; now a journey to Switzerland is not a bit more, than a trip to Scotland, and in two days, sleeping included, you may be here with ease, by the way of France. Pray, take that proposal into serious consideration, and believe me that nothing in the world could prove to me and my family more gratifying, than a visit of your's and Mrs. Faraday's would do. —

The book, of which I once talked to you,[1] has been out these last three months and as soon as a proper opportunity will offer itself, you shall have it. Being written in german, you will declare it to be a sealed book to you, but you may easily find out a friend of your's being capable of opening it to you and, indeed, I should like you would acquaint yourself at least with some part of its tenor, as they contain a sort of profession of faith of a friend of your's. — The third volume of your Researches has as yet not reached me, and putting a high value upon its possession, I beg you to be kind enough, as to inquire a little after the fate of that volume.

Now let me talk a little of philosophy, and what should, or could I begin with, but with my favorite subject oxigen, the mere name of which is hated by Mrs. Schœnbein, having become jealous as well as afraid of that seducing and mighty body. Being not quite sure, whether I have written you since I got some very remarkable results, even on the risk of telling you the same story twice, I give you a short account of them. You know that I hold oxigen, both in its free and bound state, to be capable of existing in two allotropic modifications: in the ozonic or active and the ordinary or inactive condition. All the oxy-compounds, yielding common oxigen at a raised temperature, I consider to contain ozonized oxigen, and I am further

[1] "Menschen und Dinge" vide p. 239.

inclined to believe, that the disengagement of common oxigen from those compounds depends upon the transformation of their ozonized oxigen into inactive one, or as I use to denote that allotropic change of $\overset{\circ}{O}$ into O. Now a general fact is, that the oxigen, thus set free, always contains traces of $\overset{\circ}{O}$, more or less, according to the degree of temperature at which the oxigen happens to be disengaged from those compounds. The lower that degree, the larger the quantity of $\overset{\circ}{O}$ mixt with O, though I must not omit to state, that in all cases that quantity happens to be exceedingly small in comparison to that of O, obtained at the same time. The best means of ascertaining the presence of $\overset{\circ}{O}$ is the alkoholic solution of guajacum, recently prepared. You know that O does not in the least change the color of that resiniferous liquid, whilst free $\overset{\circ}{O}$ or $PbO + \overset{\circ}{O}$ etc. have the power of coloring it deep-blue. The blue matter is, as I think I have proved it, nothing but guajacum + $\overset{\circ}{O}$. Now if you heat the purest oxide of gold, platinum, silver, mercury, the peroxides of manganese, lead etc., in fact any substance yielding oxigen, within a small glass tube, into which you had previously introduced a bit of filtering paper, being impregnated with the said guajacum solution, you will see that bit of paper turning blue, so soon as the disengagement of oxigen begins to take place. And all the circumstances being the same, you will farther perceive that the paper is colored most deeply and rapidly by the oxigen being eliminated from that oxycompound, which requires the lowest temperature for yielding part or the whole of its oxigen. Thus the oxigen, being disengaged from the oxides of gold, platinum and silver, acts more energetically upon the guajacum solution, than the oxigen does, being eliminated from the oxide of mercury, the peroxide of manganese etc. I trust these results will be obtained in the Royal Institution just as well as I get them in the laboratory of Bâle, or else my discovery shall be a very poor thing. As there cannot, I should think, be any doubt, that all the oxigen being contained for instance in the oxide of silver, previously to that compound being decomposed by heat, exists but in one state, be that state what it may, how then does it happen, we may ask, that at the same time two different sorts of oxigen, O and Ŏ, are disengaged from the compound named? The answer to this question seems to me to be, that one of the two kinds of oxigen eliminated, must be engendered at the expence of the other, or to speak more correctly, that during the act of the elimination of oxigen from the oxide of silver, part of that oxigen suffers a change of condition. Now the oxides of gold, silver etc., enjoying the power of coloring blue the guajacum solution, just so as free Ŏ does, I draw from that fact the conclusion, that the condition of the oxigen being contained in the oxides of gold, silver etc., is the ozonic one, and farther infer, that by far the greatest portion of that Ŏ, under the influence of heat, is transformed into O. Why not the whole of the oxigen, being disengaged from those oxides, happens to be O, I certainly cannot tell, but I think that the very fact of the mixt nature of the oxigen in question, is, in a theoretical point of view, highly important and speaks in favor of my notions rather than against them. Although I have already heavily taxed your patience, I am afraid, I cannot yet release you from farther listening to my philosophical talkings, for I have still to speak of a subject that has of late deeply excited my scientific curiosity and taken up all my leisure-time. But to give you an Idea of what I have been doing these last two months, I must be allowed prefacing a little. You know that I entertain a sort of innate dislike to touch any thing being in the slightest way connected with organic Chemistry,[1] knowing too well the difficulty of the

---

[1] In one of the chapters of his "Menschen und Dinge" (vide sopra p. 239) he gives the following description of himself: "The other" — he had been comparing himself with Liebig — "the other entered the lists of scientific research somewhat timidly; if anything, he avoided all intricate subjects, rather than

subject, and the weakness of my powers to grapple with it, but in spite of this wellgrounded disinclination, I have of late and as it were by mere chance been carried in the midst of that field upon the intricacies and depths of which I have been used all my life to look with feelings of unbounded respect and even awe. The picking up of a mushroom has led to that strange aberration of mine, and you will ask how such a trifling occurrence could do that. The matter stands thus: What the botanists tell me to be called "Boletus luridus", with some other sorts of mushroom, has the remarkable property of turning rapidly blue, when their hat and stem happen to be broken and exposed to the action of the atm. air. On one of my ramblings, I found a specimen of the said Boletus, perceived the change of color alluded to, and being struck with the curious phenomenon, took the bold resolution to ascertain, if possible, its proximate cause. I carried home the part, set to work, and found more than I looked after, a thing which luckily enough happens now and then. By the short space being allowed, even to the longest letter, being prevented from entering into the details of the subject, I confine myself to stating the principal results, obtained from my mushroom researches. — Boletus luridus contains a colorless principle being easily soluble in alkohol, and as to its relations to Oxigen, bearing the closest resemblance to Guajacum, as it appears from the fact, that all the oxidizing agents having the power of blueing the alkoholic solution of guajacum, also enjoy the property of coloring blue the alkoholic solution of our mushroom principle and all the desoxidizing substances, by which the blue solution of guajacum is uncolored, also discharge the color of the blued solution of the Boletus matter. From this fact, and others, I infer that this mushroom principle, like guajacum, is capable of being associated to $\overset{\circ}{O}$ and

that he searched for them; on principle and to his own liking he as much as possible examined plain phenomena only, and stood in almost unconquerable awe of everything bordering on organic life."

is not affected by O. Now the occurrence of a matter, being a true brother to guajacum, in a mushroom, is a fact pretty enough of itself, but as to scientific importance far inferior to what I am going to tell you. The fact that the resinous Boletus principle, after having been removed from the mushroom (by the means of Alkohol) is not able to color itself spontaneously in the atmospheric air, whilst it seems to have that power, so long as it happens to be deposited in the parenchyma of the Boletus, led me to suspect that there exists in the Boletus luridus, besides the guajacumlike substance, another matter, being endowed with the property of exalting the chemical powers of common oxigen, and causing that element in its $\overset{\circ}{O}$ condition to associate itself to the resinous principle of the mushroom. And Mr. Schœnbein conjectured correctly, for I found, that in the juice, being by pressure obtained from a number of mushrooms belonging to the genera of Boletus and Agaricus and notably from Agaricus sanguineus (upon which I principally worked), an organic matter is contained, enjoying the remarkable power of transforming O into $\overset{\circ}{O}$, and forming with the latter a compound, from which $\overset{\circ}{O}$ may easily be transferred to a number of oxidable matters, both of an inorganic and organic nature and I must not omit to state that the peculiar Agaricus matter, after having been deprived of its $\overset{\circ}{O}$, may be charged with it again, by carrying through its solution a current of air. The easiest way of ascertaining the presence of $\overset{\circ}{O}$ in the said Agaricus juice, is to mix that liquid with an alkoholic solution of guajacum, or the resinous matter of the Boletus luridus. If the juice happens to be deprived of $\overset{\circ}{O}$, the resiniferous solutions will not be colored blue, but if it contains $\overset{\circ}{O}$, the solutions will assume blue color, just so as if they were treated with peroxide of lead, permanganic acid, hyponitric acid etc. From the facts stated, it appears that the organic matter in question is a true carrier of active oxigen, and therefore, when charged with it, an oxidizing agent. Indeed, that matter may in many respects be compared to NO₂, which as it is well known, enjoys to an extraordinary extent the power of instantaneously transformig O in Ŏ and forming a compound (NO₂ + 2 O) with that Ŏ, from which the latter may easily be thrown upon a multitude of oxidable matters. Now in a physiological point of view, the existence of such an organic substance is certainly an important fact, and seems to confirm an old opinion of mine, according to which the oxidizing effects of the atmospheric Oxigen (of itself inactive) produced upon organic bodies, such as blood etc., are brought about by the means of substances, having the power both of exciting and carrying oxigen. Before dropping this subject I must not omit to mention a fact or two more. The peculiar matter being contained in the juice of Agaricus sanguineus etc., and charged with Ŏ, gives up that oxigen to Guajacum and the latter to the resinous matter of the Boletus luridus, so that different organic matters, capable of being associated to O as such, exhibit different affinities for that oxigen, a fact not without physiological importance. Another fact worthy of remark is the facility, with which the nature of our agaricus matter may be changed. On heating its aqueous solution, that has the power of deeply blueing the guajacum solution, to the boiling point, it not only looses that property, but also the capacity of becoming an oxidizing agent, i. e. carrier of oxigen again, however long it may be put in contact with atmospheric air. I am very sorry to be prevented from entering more fully into the details of the subject, but from the little I have said about it, you may easily understand, why that mushroom affair has of late so much engaged my attention. As to the little bit of philosophical matter, which now and then my letters to you may happen to contain, you have, of course, full liberty to do with it what you think fit.[1]

[1] Printed under the following title: "On ozone and ozonic action in mushrooms" in Phil. Mag. Vol. 11. 1855. p. 137.

Before I conclude I must not omit to tell you, that the Swiss Association, which as you know, has become the mother of all rambling societies of Europe,[1] will meet at Bâle next mid-summer, under the presidency of Peter Merian a most intimate friend of mine. Now, if you should comply with my wishes above expressed, it would be very easy to leave your retreat in our neighbourhood and join us for a day or so. I have no doubt, you would like our meeting, which being a more familiar and much smaller one than that of the british or german association, is for that very reason more comfortable and agreeable. On coming here, you will see many of our Swiss philosophers, amongst others our friend de la Rive. I promise you a day in Bâle, which shall please you and remain, I trust, in your memory all your lifetime. If it fall to my lot to see such a day, I shall be the happiest man in the world.

And now I have done, my dear Faraday and ask your kind indulgence for the unusual length of my letter. Pray do not keep so long your silence, as you did the last time and believe me

Your's

most faithfully

Bâle Nov. 30. 1855.   C. F. SCHOENBEIN.

All the members of my family beg to be kindly remembered to you, and in doing so, I ask you the favor to present my best compliments to Mrs. Faraday.   S.

Mr. Wiedemann also charges me with his compliments to you.

---

[1] The Swiss Association was founded in 1815 and held their first meeting at Geneva. Then followed the corresponding German Society founded in 1822 at Leipsic and finally the British Association for the Advancement of Science, which met for the first time at York in 1831.

Faraday to Schœnbein.[1]

Royal Institution 21 March 1856

MY DEAR SCHOENBEIN

The heartiest and the kindest wishes to you and the best thanks for your last letter. I have it not here (Norwood, for I am resting a head like a sieve) but I know it was very pleasant, and I think contained some family details, which made me long to be with you, — but the fact is, that when I am with a friend, I soon need to get away again, because of the labour of conversation and its strain upon recollection. That which induces me to write just now is the fact, that a letter has been sent to me addressed: Dr. Schœnbein, Royal Institution, Albemarle Street and then in a corner, care of Dr. Faraday. I have waited a little while to see if any instructions would arrive, but have heard no more. Now what would you wish me to do with it? It is a heavy letter, and if sent by Post would cost about ten shillings, and yet I cannot help suspecting that it is only a pamphlet. So I thought it best to write and ask you what you would wish me to do and whether you know of and are expecting it.

I do not recollect any news, and shall be glad to lay my head down again, so with kindest remembrances to Madame Schœnbein and your damsels

remain as ever

Your Affectionate friend

M. FARADAY.

[1] Bence Jones gives this letter (vol. 2. p. 369) but with several omissions.

Schœnbein to Faraday.

MY DEAR FARADAY

I hasten to tell you that there is not the slightest occasion for your being in a hurry regarding the parcel you talk of in your last letter. I do not know what it contains, nor who sent it to you. Any opportunity therefore, an early or a late one, will do for sending the thing over to Basle.

I think I told you some months ago that the friend whom you charged with delivering the third volume of your researches to me last year, has not performed his task, and not liking at all the idea of losing your valuable gift, I repeatedly ask you the favor of looking a little after the miscarried book.

This time I shall keep my peace on scientific matters from the simple reason that I could not tell you much, even if I had the inclination to do so. It is true, I was not quite lazy, nor did I work quite for nothing last winter, but the exploits I performed are, as we Germans use to say, but half-laid eggs and of such embryonic things it is not safe to talk.

I have however a mind to entertain you of another matter more interesting, at least less dry, than that never ending subject of Oxigen.

Yesterday it was Easter-Monday and you must know that in our teutonic lands it is a great day to the whole juvenile world. I consider it as one of our specific national qualities, that we are very fond of children and have marked out a number of days and times of the year round, for the enjoyments of our little ones. Now such a time is Easter-time, and such a day easter-Monday. Many, many weeks before it comes, the little prattlers talk of nothing, but of the Easter-hare (Osterhaase in german) and the gifts he may chance to bring, and what that Easter-hare means you will easily infer from what passed in the garden of Mrs. Wiedemann[1] yesterday afternoon. A host of children were invited by that Lady (having herself a little boy[2] of four years of ago) to make their appearance at her house at three o'clock punctually. Mothers and elder sisters conducted the little guests to the appointed place, at the fixed time, and being assembled in a room they anxiously and impatiently expected there the announcement of "The hare has laid his eggs." No sooner had these words been finished than the rogues were seen running down the stair case into the garden, dispersing themselves in all directions and eagerly seeking for the eggs, being put in hidden places: within hedges, behind bushes etc. The discovery of each egg was hailed with joyful exclamations and never failed proving both to the happy finders and the unsuccessful seekers a fresh stimulus, to continue their searches. But you must not imagine those "hare eggs" to have been ordinary ones; they were beautifully colored: blue, red, yellow, lilac, brown, even variegated, and bearing all sorts of inscriptions: the names of the Children invited, the drafts of hares, foxes and other animals.

The eggs found by the boys and girls were put in a basket placed in the centre of the garden, as property of the little common-wealth, to be equally divided at the end of the festival and carried home by the Children as the trophies of the day.

Such like fêtes there were hundreds in our town yesterday, and I dare say millions all over the german lands. Great a philosopher as you are, sure am I, that such a sight would give you more pleasure than all the scientific institutions and

---

[1] Gustav Wiedemann who was professor of Physics at Bâle from 1854—1863 resided in a house in the Hebelstrasse, with a large garden attached to it.

[2] Now Prof. Eilhard Wiedemann, of Erlangen, wo was born in 1852 at Berlin. He was professor of Physics at Leipzig and Giessen before he was appointed to Erlangen in the same capacity.

all the curiosities of the whole civilized world together. Now I am at the end of my letter and have nothing more to say than that I shall ever remain

Your's
most faithfully

Easter-Tuesday 1856.[1]   C. F. SCHOENBEIN.[2]

Faraday to Schœnbein.[3]

Royal Institution 11 April 1856

MY DEAR SCHOENBEIN

My dear wife purposes answering your kind letter herself; so I leave her pp. 1 and 2 and shall only say most hearty thanks for your very pleasant, interesting picture of juvenile life. I could have enjoyed it very much indeed. I suppose you were about the biggest child there.

The Volume I sent, was by Mr. Twining, and I dare say it will make its appearance some day; for he was not going to Bâle but perhaps near it. Now, however, I have committed another copy, and also the letter I wrote you about, to Mr. Roscoe,[4] a student under Professor Bunsen at Heidelberg. He was to leave London, this week for Heidelberg, and I trust you will soon have the volume; — which receive favourably for my sake

Ever Yours
M. FARADAY.

[1] According to the postmark the letter left Bâle on March 29. 1856.

[2] At the end of the letter Faraday has added these words: Sent by Mr. Roscoe about April 6th.

[3] Passages from this letter are given in Bence Jones vol. 2. p. 371.

[4] Sir Henry Enfield Roscoe F. R S. emeritus Professor of Chemistry at Owens College Manchester, was born in 1833 in London. He also studied at Heidelberg under Bunsen, with whom in 1857 to 1863 he published his Photochemical Researches.

Mrs. Faraday to Schœnbein.

Royal Institution April 11th 1856

MY DEAR Dr. SCHOENBEIN

The receipt of your letter was an unexpected pleasure and honour and I hasten to thank you for it, and all the kind expressions it contains.

It would indeed be a great treat to me to visit Switzerland with my husband and to spend a little time quietly, as you propose, in the midst of your magnificient scenery, if I had the power of walking any distance, but that I have not, and I fear I should only be an incumbrance to my companions, if I attempted it.

I am disabled by a Rheumatic affection (I believe it is), but happily with little pain, so that our home continues to be a cheerful and a happy one, as, if you come to London we should be glad to show you; Mr. Faraday too, I am thankful to say, is in better health than he was years ago, when I think he suffered from too much study.

Pray present my best remembrances to Mrs. Schœnbein and your daughters and believe me, dear Dr. Schœnbein,

Yours very sincerely
S. FARADAY.

Schœnbein to Faraday.

MY DEAR FARADAY

I have to acknowledge the receipt both of your letter and that of Mrs. Faraday's and grateful as they have proved to me, I could not help being very sorry for their contents, which have at once annihilated my hopes of seing you here this summer.

I ardently wish and confidently hope that your excellent wife will before long be restored to her full health.

The third volume of your researches reached Basle a few days ago, and I am very much obliged for that repeated piece of kindness of Your's. I trust I shall live to see a fourth volume coming out, containing detailed proofs of the Identity of Magnetism and Gravity. How I would rejoice if such a Glory should fall to your lot! You have however performed scientific exploits enough, and if there has been any philosopher who legitimately merited to enjoy the "Otium cum dignitate", you are that privileged man.

This letter will be delivered to you by Professor Merian[1] of Bâsle, a most intimate friend of mine and with whom I am quite sure, you will down-right fall in love at the very first sight. To his eminent intellectual powers (he is a profound mathematician) he joins a heart full of the "milk of human kindness", such as I know no better one. If possible, make his personal acquaintance and that of his wife too, who happens to be a pretty good english scholar and a member of the celebrated family "Bernoulli".[2]

[1] Rudolf Merian, a brother of Peter Merian, was professor of Mathematics at Bâle. He was born at Bâle in 1797 and died there in 1871.

[2] The renowned mathematicians of this name came from the Netherlands. Jakob Bernoulli, who died in 1583 had to quit Antwerp and settled down at Frankfort. A grandson of his, also called Jacob and born about the year 1598, settled down at Bâle and died there in 1634. His eldest son Nicolaus, a merchant, was born in 1623, died in 1708 and left eleven children, of whom the fifth, Jacob, and the tenth, Johann, became the eminent authorities on mathematics. In addition to these no less than nine Bernoullis were more or less famous mathematicians. "New days of glory in the history of the services, rendered by the Swiss people to the advancement of science, commenced with the arrival of the first of the Bernoullis" writes Mr. Merian (in the Verhandl. der Schweiz. Naturf. Gesellsch. 1838. p. 16). "The transmission of a specific disposition of mind from generation to generation and the conferring of honour upon several members of the same house in the same sphere of human knowledge, is by no means rare. Scarcely however could one cite an instance which we might liken to that of the Bernoullis. For a full century the members of this family were the foremost among the mathematicians of Europe."

I send you some papers of mine treating of mushrooms and ozoniferous organic substances,[1] subjects of which I wrote you some time ago. If you cannot read them give the trifles to some of your young chemical friends, who may happen to learn a little bit of German by them, if nothing else.

I returned last night from a beautiful walking trip made into the Jura mountains and the valley of the Aar. Nothing could be finer than the landscape I saw, spring being out in its fullest bloom.

From the fact that I walked 24—30 miles a day you may draw some inferences regarding the constitution of the legs of your old friend.

Pray, present my best compliments to Mrs. Faraday, thank her in my name for her kind letter and believe me, my dear Faraday,

Your's
most faithfully

Bâle April 26th 1856.   C. F. SCHOENBEIN.

Schœnbein to Faraday.

MY DEAR FARADAY

Are you still alive or have you entirely forgotten your friend on the Rhine? It is indeed an age since I have seen a line from you and I think it is time to break your long silence. To induce you to do so I send you this letter conjointly with a paper of mine, which I desire very much that

---

[1] "Ueber die nächste Ursache der spontanen Bläuung der Pilze". München. Abhandl. Bd. 7. 1855. p. 723.

Some papers in other journals treat of the same subject: Erdmann Journ. Bd. 67. 1855. p. 496. Annal. de Chim. et Phys. T. 48. 1855. p. 193.

you should acquaint yourself with its contents. It treats of a matter being, as I believe, full of interest i. e. of the connexion that, to my opinion, exists between allotropic and catalytic phenomena.[1]

During our midsummer vacations I took a trip into the north of Germany, to me a "Terra incognita", rambled about in Holstein, visited Hamburg and Berlin, saw many scientific and other friends, made new ones, paid my respects to the Senior of the European philosophers at Potsdam in the Royal Castle, had a very interesting and long conversation with that eminent old man, touched a little the Thuringian Forest, mounted the Wartburg, where the great Reformer Luther fought against the Devil, passed a couple of agreeable days at Frankfurt, returned home highly satisfied with what I call my "North-pole expedition", and met my family in good health. Before I set out to my journey, I had worked a good deal and have done so ever since my return, not quite for nothing I trust, for I have succeeded in finding out a number of novel "phenomena of contact"[2] which I hope will add, if not much, at least something to our stock of knowledge regarding the Chemistry of Oxigen.

I have already drawn up a voluminous memoir, in which the results of my experiments are described and knowing that you take some interest in this kind of researches, I am very sorry to be prevented (by the smallness of the space allowed to a letter) from entering into details about my late doings. But to give you at least a slight Idea of the nature of those researches let me tell you that they refer to what they call catalytic actions so far as these concern oxidation. One of the

---

[1] "Ueber den Zusammenhang der katalitischen Erscheinungen mit der Allotropie." Basel 1856. See also Poggend. Annal. Bd. 100 1857. S. 1 and Phil. Mag. Vol. 12. 1856. p. 457.

[2] "Ueber einige neue Reihen chemischer Berührungswirkungen" München. Abhandl. Bd. 8. 1857. p. 37.

principal results obtained is the fact that in a number of cases two substances, "toto coelo" differing from each other as to their chemical nature: Platinum and the red globules of the blood [1] — produce the same effects i. e. determine oxidizing actions, which either would not take place at all or but very slowly without the presence of the substances named, and some others. I need not point out to you the probable importance of such a remarkable fact to physiology.[2]

Another fact not quite void of scientific interest is this, that in some instances I can show, as it were, steps which the oxidation of certain matters passes: first ozonisation of inactive oxigen, then a sort of loose combination of that ozonised oxigen with the oxidable substance, and finally actual oxidation of the latter. I have reason to believe that on looking a little closer into that matter, we shall discover a great number of similar cases and it is not impossible that any oxidation is a sort of chemical drama, consisting of different acts, the last of which is real oxidation. Shakespeare says, that there are many things, between heaven and earth, which the philosophers do even not dream of, and Schœnbein maintaining that between the moment on which two isolated elementary bodies meet, and that of, their chemical associating being finished, there lies a whole world of phenomena and is very much of which the Chemists of the present day have as yet not the slightest notion. There is even within inorganic Chemistry something which I might call Physiology, and the most interesting and truly scientific object of chemical research lies, to my opinion, within the short interval of time alluded to, and hence the great difficulty of such an investigation.

[1] In 1857 a paper was published in the Basl. Verh. Bd. 2. p. 3 entitled: "Über die Gleichheit des Einflusses, welchen in gewissen Fällen die Blutkörperchen und Eisenoxydulsalze auf die chemische Thätigkeit des gebundenen Sauerstoffs ausüben."

[2] Vide Vierordt. Arch. für physiol. Heilkunde. 1856. p. 1: "Über Sauerstofferreger und Sauerstoffträger in der organischen Welt."

Less interesting but pretty enough is a third fact which I must mention to you, namely that out of free ozonized oxigen and olefiant gas, formic acid is readily and directly formed, a result easily accountable by the chemical equation $C_4H_4 + 8O = 2 C_2 H_2 O_4$. But now enough of Chemistry and Oxigen.

If you should happen to have a friend in the country being blessed with girls and desirous to receive for a time in his family a grown up girl, pretty well versed in the german, french and english litterature, being a tolerably good musician, carefully educated and of an excellent moral character, I know one, whom I should venture to recommend. I must however not omit to tell you that the girl in question is very far from wishing to become a paid governess, she desires to be considered as a friend and member of the family, and make herself at the same time as useful as possible in the education of the children. That girl is my own eldest daughter, who is very anxious to pass six or twelve months in an English family. I do not much relish those wishes of her's, for I love her too tenderly, as readily to allow her going to a foreign country, but if it be possible to place her in a good family I shall not prevent her from crossing the Channel. Pray let me know, what you think about the plan of my adventurous, silly, sweet girl.

Mr. Wiedemann charges me to present to you his best compliments, he is at this present moment actively engaged in magnetic researches, which seem to lead to interesting results.

My friend Mr. Merian and his wife were highly gratified with the friendly reception they met with at the Royal Institution, and send the kindest remembrances to its amiable Master and Mistress.

In closing my letter I ask you the favor te remember me most friendly to Mrs. Faraday and tell her that Mr. Schœnbein had not yet entirely given up his hopes of seeing once more her Ladyship and her Lord on this side of the water.

Believe me my dear Faraday

Yours
most truly

Bâle Septbr. 20. 1856.   C. F. SCHOENBEIN.

Pray be kind enough as to send the inclosed paper to Dr. Whewell as soon as you can.

Faraday to Schœnbein.

Royal Institution 14 October 1856.

MY DEAR FRIEND

Hearty and healthy, and occupied, and happy, as you are, let me congratulate you, for every letter of yours brings me evidence of the existence of a healthy mind in a sound body. How you have been running about! and you go home as if you were refreshed, rather than tired by it. I do not feel so any longer; even if I go away for a little general health, I am glad to return home again for rest in the company of my dear wife and niece. But as the wise man hath said, there is a time for all things, and my time is to be quiet and look on, which I am able to do with great content and satisfaction. — I expect one of my nieces here very soon, who will let me into the knowledge of your last paper; in the mean time I have sent the other copy and your letter to Dr. Whewell. What you tell me of your paper makes me long to hear the whole of it; though the very pleasure of getting knowledge is now mingled with some thoughts of regret at the consciousness that I very quickly lose it again; — well — a time for all things.

S

I have been occupying myself with gold[1] this summer; I did not feel head-strong enough for stronger things. — The work has been of the mountain and mouse fashion; and if I ever publish it and it comes to your sight, I dare say you will think so:[2] — the transparency of gold — its division — its action on light. etc etc etc.

Now with regard to Miss Schœnbein's desires. — I am sorry that my unsocial habits have left me unacquainted with any such family as that which I think would suit your view. Not one name occurs to me; but Grove and to Mrs. Grove I shall show your letter as soon as they come to town. — It so happened that two or three years ago Tyndall shewed us a letter very much to the same purport, regarding a daughter of one of his German friends; that letter we shewed to a lady (Miss Hornblower) and it led to Tyndalls friend coming to London and being with Miss Hornblower for, I think, two years and it is not very long ago since she went back, very happy in the thoughts of her residence here. I have shown *your* letter to Miss Hornblower in hopes she might know of some family: and her note to me in reply, is such, that I send it on to you. Miss Hornblower is a very dear friend of ours, and in her character and all that is about her, all we could wish; — but then she keeps a school. It is an excellent establishment, with many masters, and the pupils who have been with her all love and respect her. If what she says induces you to write to

---

[1] "Experimental relations of gold (and other metals) to Light (Bakerian Lecture)." Phil. Trans. 1857. p. 145.

[2] In 1816 Faraday, then in his 24th year, gave six lectures at the City Philosophical Society; of these the fourth was upon radiant matter, the subject being the transparency of gold and the colour of the light transmitted through it. "Forty years after this lecture was given", says Bence Jones in a foot note (p. 195, vol. 1), "Faraday published *his last paper*, full of experiments, in the Philosophical Transactions, upon this subject." This statement is not quite accurate. His last paper was printed in 1859, being a note on regelation. Roy. Soc. Proc. vol. 10. 1859—1860. p. 440.

her, do so directly and without hesitation. For your private thought, I may say she is about 50 years of age, very active, though not very strong, and has sustained her establishment of 15 or 20 pupils at Stamford Hill for full 30 years[1].

Pray remember me to Wiedemann; — and us most kindly to Madam and Miss Schœnbein and also to the Merians and above all to Yourself.

Ever My dear Schœnbein
Yours Most truly
M. Faraday.

Schœnbein to Faraday.

Bâle November 10. 1856.

My dear Faraday

Many, many thanks both for your own letter and that of your Friend's. When you happen to see her again, pray tell her that from many reasons my daughter desires to stay here during the winter. When spring comes and we live then, we shall see, whether a move over the water may be effected. In the mean while your friend will perhaps be kind enough to let you know her views on the subject in question. All I can say is this: Miss Schœnbein knows well and speaks fluently french and german and is considered to be a pretty good musician, in which accomplishments she is very willing to make herself useful in the establishment of your friend. As to the moral character of my daughter, I am too partial to judge about, but I do not hesitate to qualify her as a modest, good natured and rather high-minded girl, and the purest Swabian blood running in her veins she partakes a little of the poetical spirit said to belong to the native land of her forefathers.

[1] Miss Schœnbein in fact did in the end come to Miss Hornblower's house.

Since I last wrote to you[1] I have actively continued my researches on the phenomena of contact, and obtained some results which are curious enough. You know perhaps, that according to my former experiments ozonised oxigen, at the common temperature, oxidizes both the elements of Ammonia, forming with that compound nitrate of Ammonia; whilst, as you are well aware, common oxygen under the same circumstances does not at all affect either gazeous or aqueous Ammonia. The same oxigen however, on being put in contact with certain matters, acquires the power of engendering with Ammonia nitrous acid i. e. nitrite of Ammonia. Platinum and copper are such matters. Moisten the former metal (being in that state *called platinum black*)[2] with a strong solution of Ammonia, leave for a short time those substances exposed to the action either of common oxigen or atmospheric air, treat then the metallic powder with some distilled water and you will easily detect in that liquid the presence of nitrite of Ammonia. The simplest way of doing so is to *add*[3] to that water some dilute sulphuric acid and paste of starch containing a little *of* pure jodide of potassium (free even from the slightest trace of jodate). Nitrite being present the mixture will become dark blue.

Assisted a little by heat, even compact platinum is capable of causing common oxigen to engender a nitrite with Ammonia. Put some drops of a strong solution of Ammonia *into a bottle, containing air*[4], introduce into the vessel the heated coil of

[1] Beginning from "I have actively continued" this letter is reprinted in Phil. Mag. vol. 12. 1856. p. 457, under the following title: "On the Oxidation of the Constituents of Ammonia by porous Media with some Remarks on Nitrification. By Professor Schœnbein of Basle."

[2] Respecting these italics, which are ours, we are following th esame rule indicated on p. 117, note 1.

Schœnbein had written "Ethiops", an expression at that time current on the continent, but long obsolete in England; it was formerly applied to various preparations of a black or very dark colour.

[3] put.   [4] into an airholding bottle.

a thick platinum wire, hold over that coil a strip of filtering paper, to which sticks paste of starch containing some jodide of potassium and being acidulated by dilute sulphuric acid, and you will perceive that paste instantaneously turning dark blue. Whilst the hot platinum coil rests within the bottle, whitish vapours *make*[1] their appearance, which, on being taken up by some distilled water, give to that fluid all the properties of a nitrite solution. *On acidulation with*[2] dilute sulphuric acid it deeply and instantaneously blues the *starch paste containing the iodide*[3], and such a strong reaction will be obtained, though the heated coil may have remained in the bottle but for a few seconds. The platinum coil does not require *being heated to redness*[4] to produce that effect, but those of iron wire etc. must have that temperature to enable oxygen to engender a nitrite with Ammonia. I above mentioned copper as another substance *which was capable*[5] of causing ordinary oxigen to oxidize both the elements of Ammonia at the common temperature, and I may add that its action even surpassed that of platinum. To convince yourself of the truth of my statement, put about 50 grammes of minutely divided copper (such as is obtained *by reducing*[6] oxide of copper by the means of hydrogen) into a *bottle containing oxigen or air*,[7] moisten that metallic powder with a solution of Ammonia, close or cover the bottle and you will soon see *the vessel fill*[8] with whitish fumes, which are nitrite of Ammonia; for if you introduce into the bottle a strip of paper being covered with acidulated paste of starch that contains some jodide of potassium, it will rapidly be colored blue. Or if you suspend for a short time strips of filtering paper being impregnated with distilled water, they will contain perceptible quantities of nitrite of Ammonia, as you may easily satisfy yourself by applying the test above men-

---

[1] are making. [2] Being acidulated by. [3] the iodide holding paste of starch. [4] red heat. [5] being capable. [6] from heated. [7] an oxigen or air-containing bottle. [8] see filling the vessel with.

tioned. Even a moistened glassplate or watchglass, *used to*[2] cover the vessel of reaction, will *do, to* receive within a very few minutes so much of the nitrite formed as to enable you to ascertan its presence by the most striking reactions.

To complete my statements I must not omit to mention that the copper powder soon after having been moistened with liquid Ammonia, exhibits a rise of temperature, no doubt resulting from the formation of the nitrate of Ammonia. The blue liquid obtained on shaking copper powder with aqueous Ammonia and oxigen or atmospheric air, besides oxide of copper, also contains nitrite of Ammonia, for if you put some soda to it and boil it *up,* to drive off the Ammonia and throw down the black oxide of copper, a solution is obtained which after being evaporated to dryness, leaves behind a yellowish salt *which consists*[2] principally of nitrite of Soda. This substance being mixt up with powdered charcoal and heated, burns that combustible matter, yields with sulphuric acid strong fumes of nitrous acid, *and* rapidly discharges the colour of indigo solution being strongly acidulated by oil of vitriol, colors brownish a solution of *protosulfate*[3] of iron containing free sulphuric acid etc. Common pure, or atmospheric oxigen on being put in contact with copper powder and aqueous Ammonia is so rapidly *absorbed,*[4] that I succeeded in depriving completely a whole cubic foot of atmospheric air of its oxigen within a few minutes. Copper and Ammonia may therefore be used as eudiometric means and for preparing nitrogen *from*[5] the common air. The facts above stated appear to me to bear closely upon the important question of nitrifications, and proving beyond any doubt that under the influence of *the* contact of some ponderable matters, inactive oxygen is empowered even at the common temperature to oxidize both the *constituents*[6] of Ammonia. Before long I hope to be able to give you some

[1] by which you. [2] being. [3] vitriol. [4] taken up. [5] out of.
[6] constituent parts.

more details on nitrification, a chemical phenomenon which at this present moment deeply enjoys my attention.[1]

(*Pray present my best compliments to Mrs Faraday and*) believe me

my dear Faraday
Your's most faithfully
C. F. S<small>CHOENBEIN</small>.

(*Mrs. Schœnbein and the young ladies charge me to offer to you and Mrs. Faraday their kindest regards.*)

Faraday to Schœnbein.

Royal Institution 23 January 1857

M<small>Y DEAR</small> S<small>CHOENBEIN</small>

I wished to write to you, and therefore wrote to my friend Miss Hornblower whose former letter you have. After a few days she wrote me enclosing a letter to Miss Schœnbein which I now send — it will explain itself and say more than I can. Your last but one letter I also laid before Mrs. Grove and some others, but nothing has come of it so far. Mrs. Grove was anxious to aid the course but could find no opportunity. You will see that the philosophic part of your last has appeared in the Phil. Mag. and I trust will aid by degrees in doing the work of science, but the work is slow. Look at Ozone, how beautiful it is and yet how its progress has been resisted and how little it was thought of at first. — I do not know that I am doing any thing — I forget — I have been subduing gold and other metals, but probably

---

[1] By this list the alterations are however not completely exhausted; "oxigen", for example has invariably been changed to "oxygen", words have frequently been transposed and so forth.

told you about that — I cannot say, and I must not say more just now, than to wish all happiness to Miss Schœnbein and the rest with you and the kindest thoughts to yourself from

Your friend
M. FARADAY.

Schœnbein to Faraday.

MY DEAR FARADAY

Not knowing exactly the direction of your friend at Stamford Hill, I take the liberty to inclose a letter, addressed to her, by my eldest daughter and beg you to forward it to its place of destination. If the plan of Miss Schœnbein should happen to be realized, I am very glad to know her placed with an intimate friend of your's and in your neighbourhood, being sure that in Stamford Hill she will find a second home, and in you and Mrs. Faraday a father and mother.

As to the girl herself, being good-natured, cheerful, healthy, active, and I may add well-informed and well-bred too, I trust she will please and suit your friend.

During our late crisis and warlike preparations I was very busy too, but in a very quiet and harmless way. I worked very hard upon oxigen (for what else should or could I do) and think to have succeeded in ascertaining a series of novel facts such as to my opinion at least, leave no shade of doubt about the correctness of an old notion of mine, according to which common oxigen must be considered as a chemically inert body and any oxydizing action apparently being brought about by O is invariably, and as a conditio sine qua non, preceded by an allotropic modification (change of chemical condition) of that elementary substance.

The facts alluded to appeared to me so simple and striking, when I saw them first, that looked for as they were, I felt an infantine joy, to which I could not help giving utterance, although I was quite alone in my laboratory. You shall know the details in my next letter, for at this present moment I have no leisure-time to write an epistolary memoir.

Amongst other little things I have found out that under given circumstances even strong acids may be chemically associated to metallic peroxides, such as PbO_2 and MnO_2, yielding, as you may easily imagine, highly energetic oxydizing solutions, such indeed, as act like free ozonized oxygen.

So you see, every day a little step is made onward in my favorite study and I hope progressing still farther for some time to come, for in the Ozone business much work is yet left to be done. We have hardly begun the "magisterium".

I don't know, whether you have been told that a great and wholly unexpected honor was bestowed upon Mr. Schœnbein some months ago. A gold medal[1] conjointly with a prize of about 3500 francs has been awarded to him (by the king of Bavaria) for his investigations on ozonised oxygen. Liebig being quite intimate with his Majesty, I suspect that our friend has not been quite strange to the matter. Be that however as it may, I cannot deny that I was highly gratified by that Royal munificence, less on account of the monay than of the meaning of the gift. The existence of the little baby, christened "Ozone", has been at last acknowledged even by a monarch; now the schoolmasters must follow the Royal example.

I intend to spend the easter holidays at Munic a place which from several reasons I am exceedingly fond of and visit more than any other town. In the first place I have got there many friends of a very motley description, artists, poets, philosophers etc. and there is even a Nimrod found amongst them. Varietas delectat. And then the Bavarian capital teems with master pieces of the fine arts, which, unartistical as I am, I

[1] The then king of Bavaria in November 1856 presented Schœnbein with the Maximilian Medal.

nevertheless relish very much. It is indeed a great treat to me now and then to shake off from my shoulders the dust of the laboratory and store up my mind with the Images of exquisitely beautiful objects, creations certainly belonging to an order of things infinitely superior to that under which we range physical phenomena and philosophical truths. And I will not conceal it from you, that on returning to the earth from the lofty regions, where Imagination reigns and rules, I feel myself a better philosopher and matter of fact dealer, for even on the prosaic ground of palpable matter, we cannot do without that enchantress who conjures up Ideal worlds.

New being at the end of my stories and sheet I beg you to pardon the loquacity of

Your

old and affectionate friend

Bâle Febr. 9. 1857.   C. F. SCHOENBEIN.

P. S. Pray present my best compliments to Mrs. Faraday.

Schœnbein to Faraday.

Basle April 25th 1857

MY DEAR FARADAY

I write you these lines to ask you the favor of letting occasionally know your Friend at Stamford-hill, that, about the time indicated by her, my daughter will keep herself ready for her projected journey to England and hope that some proper travelling companions will in the right season make their appearance at Basle, under whose guidance Miss Schœnbein may safely be carried over to London. — The last holidays

I passed at Munic and as you may easily imagine in a very agreeable manner, though in consequence of having sprained my leg I was kept in bed there for nearly a week. Liebig and many other scientific and artistic friends were at home, so that there was no want of rational enjoyments in the bavarian capital. Amongst the curiosities seen there, there was a specimen of the poisoned chinese bread sent to Liebig for chemical analysis. He found considerable quantities of Arsenic in it. Of late I (have) worked again a good on my favorite subject and ascertained a number of facts which seem to me to put beyond doubt the correctness of that old notion of mine, according to which oxigen, such as it exists in the atmosphere, is in a chemical point of view an entirely inert body and any oxidation being apparently brought about by it, is preceeded by its allotropic change of condition. The essential oil of bitter Almonds (Benzule) has become to me a beautiful object of research, which substance, being assisted by solar light, enjoys the power of rapidly taking up common oxigen and transforming it into that state, in which it produces all the oxidizing effects of ozonised oyigen[1] decomposition of jodide of potassium, coloring blue the solution of guajacum etc. Leaving that oxigen associated to the oil, it rather rapidly oxidized that matter into hydrated benzoic acid. In presenting my best compliments to Mrs. Faraday and begging you to drop the inclosed into a letter box I am my dear Faraday

Yours

most truly

C. F. SCHOENBEIN.

[1] The results of these investigations Schœnbein sums up in a paper entitled: "Über das Verhalten des Bittermandelöles zum Sauerstoff." Basl. Verh. Bd. 2. 1857. p. 3.

Faraday to Schœnbein.

Royal Institution 7. May 1857.

MY DEAR SCHOENBEIN

On receipt of your last I spoke to Miss Hornblower who said she had written fully either to you or Miss Schœnbein and had indeed been expecting an answer, as she was obliged to keep her own arrangements open until she heard from you; she seemed glad to learn how the decision went, but you must judge from her letter whether it requires a direct answer. — I think she said that in it she had spoken of time etc. etc., and I think she mentioned the time, but whether it was September or any other month I cannot now tell — I forget every thing and I am obliged to be content to forget, and this makes me anxious that no point of the arrangements should depend upon what I may say. But that direct communication should convey the necessary information. I should almost certainly introduce some blunder — I am daily occupied in making and repairing mistakes even in the very house I live in.

I have every conviction that Miss Schœnbein will like Miss Hornblower and when she knows her will soon highly esteem her. She is a woman of business, but she has always left a strong and kind impression on the minds of those ladies who have been with her from abroad, and I have no doubt it will be so with Your daughter. It can be no slight thing for you to part with her for a while, but you may be sure that at Miss Hornblower's she will have a safe home. We shall see what we can of her, though our residence here and the circumstance of our having *no house* cuts short our means of seeing friends as we could wish — but all that must be left. — Let me say a word of sympathy on our part to Mrs. Schœnbein under the coming circumstances: for the mother cannot but be anxious on the matter. My wife is an invalid at present and not yet out of her room or I am sure she would join me in kindest thoughts to you all.

Ever My dear Schœnbein
Yours
M. FARADAY.

Schœnbein to Faraday.[1]

Basle, Septbr. 17th 1857.

MY DEAR FARADAY

The moment is fast approaching, which will separate my eldest daughter from her home, parents and friends, and as you may easily imagine, all of us, and Mrs. Schœnbein most particularly, are looking for that painful hour with feelings appropriate to the case. The girl herself, however, exhibits on that occasion more courage than I thought she could command and though being fully conscious of what she is about to undertake, the wicked woman does not seem to have lost any of her wonted spirits. If I were not fully convinced that my daughter should find a second home with your friend, I certainly would not have given my consent to her emigrating there; and, besides, my knowing, that you and Mrs. Faraday are near her, gives me confident hopes, that she will be well off in every respect and meet with good counsel as often as she will happen to stand in need of it. Pray be kind to the girl, for though my child, I am allowed to assure you, that she is a good and excellent creature, who, I have no doubt, will please you, Mrs. Faraday and Miss Hornblower.

Within a month my second daughter Sophia, who by the bye was intended to be a philosopher, also will leave me to

[1] The chemical part of this letter is published in the Phil. Mag. for 1857. S. 4. vol. 15. p. 24.

go to the far North and stay over the winter with some friends of mine at Altona. Though she will be placed in very good hands, still to be deprived of two daughters at once, who have these many years given so much life to our little domestic circle, is rather hard to their parents and younger sisters; but we cannot help and must suffer the girls to go their own way. To Mrs. Schœnbein those separatings will cost floods of tears in spite of her stoical maxims.

In the course of this summer I have been travelling and working. I saw once more my favorite town "Nuremberg", that splendid and interesting monument of the middle ages, where every house, court and street puts you back to times and a state of things long gone by. At the same time I visited old intimate friends, (and that was the principal end of my journey) who thirty some years ago were my fellow students at the University of Erlangen. I need hardly tell you, that I enjoyed my trip very much and spent most delicious days with those old cronies of mine, one of whom happens to be one of the most extraordinary and amiable men, I know, being highly poetical, therefore full of imagination, rich of original ideas, of a matchless humor, teeming with wit and what I do not consider as the least of his many excellent qualities, full of the milk of human kindness, in short a genuine man every inch. In the little book[1] which will be presented to you by Miss Schœnbein, the author has tried to depict the man in the chapter entitled 'Der Freund".[2] Having once touched that "opusculum", the

---

[1] cf. Schœnbeins letters to Faraday of Feb. 27 and Nov. 30 1855. pp. 238 and 254; and also Faradays letter to Schœnbein of April 6. 1855. p. 242.

[2] Schœnbein here alludes to his friend A. von Zerzog, who unquestionably was an unusually erratic person. He was born in 1799 at Coburg, studied at Erlangen, Würzburg and Jena; together with Schœnbein he was a member of the patriotic students association (Burschenschaft), for which reason he was prosecuted, and punished with a year's confinement in a fortress; in 1848 he sat as a member for Frankfurt in the German parliament and died in 1880 as owner of a large estate at Prufeningen Castle near Regensburg. Schœnbein very

authorship of which I leave you to guess, I beg you to accept that trifling as a keepsake. It it sort of "quodlibet" and hardly worth while to be read. But if you should feel inclined to know a little what curious notions a friend of your's is entertaining on "Men and things", get some chapters of the little work translated to you. I see that the author has taken the liberty to talk even of yourself, but have reason to think, that in doing so he was actuated by the most friendly motives.

I have continued my researches on oxygen, that inexhaustible source of investigation, and ascertained a series of novel facts which seem to be not altogether void of scientific interest. One of those facts is queer and paradoxical enough. What do you say to a desoxidation of an oxycompound being effected by the means of oxygen itself? You are perhaps aware, that some years ago I found out a number of substances enjoying the power to transform free $\overset{\circ}{O}$ into O i. e. to act like heat. The oxides of the precious metals and the metallic peroxides such as that of manganese, lead etc. belong to that category, and which are oxy-compounds containing either all or part of their oxygen in the ozonic condition. Now it appears, that the action taking place for instance between free $\overset{\circ}{O}$ and $PbO + \overset{\circ}{O}$ is reciprocal; for not only the former happens to be converted into O, but the peroxide of lead is at the same time reduced to PbO, which seems to show that the $\overset{\circ}{O}$ of $PbO + \overset{\circ}{O}$ also becomes desozonized and on that account eliminated. The same desoxidizing effect is produced upon PbO_2 by the ozonized oil of turpentine and the peroxide of hydrogen (to me = $HO + \overset{\circ}{O}$). To show those remarkable effects in a simple manner, I employ a test-paper being impregnated, i. e. colored with minute quantities of peroxide of lead. If moist

---

properly says of him, if he would only take upon himself to write but a few sheets, they would teem with Shakespearean humour and be of greater value than half the books of the Leipsic exchange. (Vide "Menschen und Dinge" p. 173.)

be turned deep blue, just so as if free ozonized oxigen had acted upon the paste. The same color will make its appearance, if you treat in a similar way a recently prepared solution of guajucum. To show that even Silver is oxidized, put some drops of our oil upon a plate of pure silver and having the essence moved about in direct sunlight for a minute or two, aqueous sulphuretted hydrogen, being poured upon the spot of reaction, will cause a rather abundant precipitation of sulphuret of silver, a proof of the presence of oxide of silver. I need not expressly state, that the hyduret of Benzule is oxidized along with the metals, in consequence of which benzoates are formed: benzoate of lead, cadmium, copper, silver etc. A very pretty experiment may be made with metallic arsenic. Lay round a glass tube a ring of that metal (according to Marsh's methode), drop some oil of bitter almonds upon it, turn the tube, being held in horizontal position, round its axis, no action in the dark, whilst in the direct solar light that ring will rapidly disappear under the circumstances indicated, arsenic acid being formed, just so as it is the case in ozonized oxigen. Rings of antimony being not acted upon, or a least but very slightly under these circumstances, both the metals may be easily distinguished from each other by the means of hyduret of Benzule. The details of my researches on the oil of bitter almonds will be published by the academy of Munic.[1]

You know, that nitrification has been, these many years, a matter of interest and research to me and of late I have increased our knowledge about that subject by some novel facts. Some years ago, I found out, that ozonized oxigen transforms Ammonia into the nitrate of that base; last year I ascertained, that inactive oxygen on being put in contact with platinum or copper acquires the power of oxidizing even at the common

---

[1] "Über des Verhalten des Bittermandelöls zum Sauerstoff." München. Abhandl. Bd. 8. 1857. S. 159. In the München Abhandl. 1857. Bd. 8. p. 383 he has a supplement to the above paper.

temperature the elements of Ammonia into nitrous acid and water, nitrite of Ammonia being formed under these circumstances.

Now I have discovered that HO_2, Mn_2O_7 (permanganic acid), or the salts of that acid, for instance permanganate of potash, on being mixt up with aqueous Ammonia produce nitrites.[1] A singular fact is, that free ozonized oxigen alone seems to be capable of oxidizing the nitrogen of Ammonia into nitric acid, the ozonized oxigen of oxy-componds or the oxigen being rendered active by the influence of copper or platinum produces nitrous acid. Are we to infer from those facts, that the formation of a nitrite is the first stage of a nitrification?

One gambol more on my hobby-horse and I shall descend from the animal. I have of late succeeded in ozonizing the oil of turpentine so strongly that one equiv. of that essence is associated to one equiv. of oxigen, and you may easily imagine the great oxidizing power of that oil. By shaking it with peroxide of lead it becomes desozonized, PbO_2 being reduced to PbO, a fact, which according to the statements above made, is a matter of course.

Now you are released, my dear Friend, from listening to the talkings of a loquacious philosopher to whom, I hope, you will prove indulgent, as you have already so often done him that favor.

Now nothing more than the request to remember me friendly to the most gracious She-Sovereign of the Royal Institution, whom you will beg in my name to take my girl under her high protection.

In hoping that you and Mrs. Faraday are doing well. I am my dear Friend

Your's most faithfully

C. F. SCHOENBEIN.

[1] "Über das Verhalten des Wasserstoffsuperoxydes und der Übermangansäure zum Ammoniak." Erdm Journ. prakt. Chem. Bd. 75. 1858. p. 99.

I must add a remark or two on my peroxide-testpaper. I prepare it by drenching strips of this filtering paper with a solution of PbO_2 and that solution is produced by shaking together (for abount 15 minutes or so) two volumes of strongly ozonized oil of Turpentine and one volume of Extractum Saturni (subacetate of lead). On filtering that mixture I get a transparent liquid being colored like portwine which in fact is oil of turpentine holding some peroxide and oxide of lead dissolved. Upon the filter remains a yellow substance, being a mixture of PbO_2 and PbO. Within 24 hours a similar mixture is deposited out of the colored essence. It is a remarkable fact, that the test-paper is rapidly bleached in strongly insolated atmosph. air, as you will see from a strip laid by, which in a good sun was completely bleached within an hour's time.[1] For that reason my test-paper must be kept in the dark.[2]

Faraday to Schœnbein.

Royal Institution 25. Septr. 1857

MY DEAR SCHOENBEIN

I cannot leave my desk without telling you that yesterday I saw your daughter and received your letter. I went as soon as possible to Stamford Hill and found Miss Schœnbein very well, though not yet recovered from her fatigue — looking cheerful and happy and, as far as I could

---

[1] These strips have been lost.

[2] Instructions for preparing another form of test papers are given in the Verhandl. der Schweiz. Naturf. Gesellsch. for 1850. p. 44, which we give by way of comparison: Schœnbein dips writing paper in water in which is dissolved $\frac{1}{100}$ pt of lead nitrate or sugar of lead, and after drying them, brings them under a bell jar, containing some hydrogen sulphide. So soon as the paper has become perceptibly brown in colour, it is removed and kept in the dark. Two hours' exposure to a July sun proved sufficient to bleach it to a pure white, indicating that the lead sulphide had been transformed into lead sulphate.

judge, she and Miss Hornblower mutually pleased with each other. You need not doubt that she will find a most kind and careful friend in Miss Hornblower, a woman of method and discipline, but who by her tenderness and care makes all about her love her. You know one cannot judge of results in a hurry, but the first appearances are most favourable. I dare say Miss Schœnbein will find enough to do, but a good moral atmosphere to do it in and hearty good will on all sides. — We shall learn by degrees what opportunities the routine supplies and we shall hope to see her at our house when that is proper, after our return home.

I can easily imagine Madame Schœnbein's anxiety, but except from what may be founded on difference of habits in our two countries she need have none. — It so happens that I have three nieces with Miss Hornblower at this time and I hope they will make a friend of Miss Schœnbein and that you will hear a word or two about them now and then. — Two of them are sisters to Jeannie whom I think you have met here.

As to the philosophy of the letter I must enjoy and talk about that another time or else I shall lose the post

Ever My dear friend
Your's
M. FARADAY.

Our kindest thoughts on this occasion to Mrs. Schœnbein and the Sisters   M. F.

Faraday to Schœnbein.[1]

Royal Institution 24 Novr. 1857

MY DEAR SCHOENBEIN

I dare say you have plenty of letters with the London post mark now from Stamford Hill, and hardly require

[1] Portions of his letter are printed in Bence Jones vol. 2. p. 376.

to have your English associations stirred up by one from me, so soon after the last; — but we leave town on Friday for a little renovation, and I want to relieve myself by writing to you before we go. I expected you would have seen much of your last in the Philosophical Magazine before now but Dr. Francis[1] told me, a day or two back, that he was writing for some new type $\oplus$ and $\ominus$; for that nothing they have at present will serve the same purpose: — then I trust it will appear as it ought to do.. What a wonderful thing oxigen is, — and so I suppose would every other element appear if our knowledge were more perfect.

Sir James Clarke[2] applied to me the other day, to know if you had been able to draw up a set of practical directions for the observation of Ozone in the atmosphere; obviating such difficulties as arise at first, connected with the time of exposure, the continued exposure, the moisture or dryness of the test paper, etc. He seemed well aware of the general state of he subject, but thought that you would know sooner than the world at large, of any perfectionment. His object is to consider the medical effects of Ozone in nature, where without doubt it must have some, and perhaps, very important effects. Probably when you feel that there is any improvement in the mode of observing you will let us know. I think he said that Ozone seemed to be abundant about our Queens residence, Balmoral, in the North.

I ventured to send you a paper[3] the other day by the post. I was assured it would go free and shall be very sorry if, unaware, I have put you and other friends to post expence, but I find that the information I obtain by enquiry is often

---

[1] William Francis Ph. D. F. C. S. He was born in 1817 in London and is partner in the printing firm of Taylor & Francis in London.

[2] Sir James Clarke Bart., late Physician-in-Ordinary to the Queen, was born in 1788 at Cullen and died in London in 1870.

[3] "Experimental relations of Gold and other metals to light. Phil. Mag. S. 4. vol. 14. 1857. p. 401.

very uncertain in its nature, though positive in its form. The paper was about Gold, and the relation of it and other metals to light. Many facts came out during the enquiry which surprized me greatly; especially the effects of pressure and also those relating to polarized light. Lately I have been working on[1] the relation of *time* to actions at a distance; — as those actions which class as magnetic. But the subject is very difficult, — the requisite apparatus requires to be frequently remade, each time being more perfected; and whether I shall catch the $\frac{1}{800\,000}$ part of a second (if required) seems very doubtful. In the mean time I am for the present tired and must lay the research on the shelf.

Since I wrote to you we have had Miss Schœnbein here: — but since that I have not been able to see her or my old friend Miss Hornblower either, at Stamford Hill: Probably when the Christmas Holidays come on, we shall have the opportunity; but my wifes health is so infirm and our capabilities so limited at the Institution, that I dare not think of what we should like, before the time comes: I have undertaken to give half a dozen juvenile lectures after Christmas; — whether they will come off (as we say) or not, is doubtful. Patience —

I hope that Madame Schœnbein is cheered by her daughters letters. Miss Schœnbein assured me that there was a great deal of correspondence going on, and from the manner in which I heard of it, I should trust that it was cheerful. Remember me in the kindest manner to the anxious mother.

I do not think we have much scientific news, at least I do not hear of much; but then I do not go within reach of the waves of sound, and so must consent to be ignorant. Indeed too much would drive me crazy in the attempt to hold it.

Ever My dear Schœnbein
Yours most truly
M. FARADAY.

[1] Bence Jones prints "at".

Faraday to Schœnbein.[1]

MY DEAR SCHOENBEIN

I got as far as Stamford ..... day (which I very rarely do) and cam ..... a better reminder of the fitness of writing to you. Poor as I may be in subject matter yet a daughter, and your daughter, is surely quite enough. She looked very well and I was very glad to see her so contented, happy and cheerful. When she first came to this country I was very much frightened, least the experiment should fail, for that would have been no trifle; but now all anxiety of that kind is over. It was impossible, but that all her views of life, society, and manners should have been formed upon her experience and habits of home, and her own country, and I felt sure that much of what is good amongst us, must have been hidden from her for a time by the novelty of the customs, manners, and occupation she would find here. But she is a girl of sense and I think was not long in passing through the show and form of things to the reality beneath. As far as I can see the reality has not been ..... her and of ..... Englishman feel proud and as ..... very glad. However I dare say you know her mind in all these things far better than I can do. What I can see is that she seems happy in things as they are and growing in the estimation of those around her. Indeed there are many points in which I, who am at a distance, can see she is an example to all around her, such as her judgment, her steadiness of purpose, her conscience of things, her toleration of the judg-

[1] This letter has been partly destroyed by some corrosive acid, with it the date. The clue by which we were guided in ascertaining the approximate date, is the fact that he speaks of his intention of proceeding with his investigations on action at a distance. In the letter to Schœnbein dated Nov. 24. 1857 he informs him that he has been working on the relation of time to action at a distance. Hence these two letters presumably belong to the same period, and as he speaks of Miss Schœnbein having already been some time in England we would fix the date at about November, 1857.

ments of others, her truthfulness, and her propriety and many others which make the bases of a good mental character. She appeared to be very well. I wish I could see more of her amongst us, but the bad and uncertain state of my wife's health, and her little strength is a great barrier to our desires.

I cannot just now remember what were the last points of philosophy which you sent me or even those of my own which are worth speaking of to you. I work very slowly now I want to proceed with action at a distance and from ..... forgetting .... over I hope ..... exertion ..... we shall see.

Commend me to Mrs. Schœnbein: even the poor talk I have given you about her daughter will incline her a little towards me. Say I hope, she will receive her back some day or another, and find reason to be not less proud of her, than she ever has been: — *even when she was a baby*

Ever My dear Schœnbein
Very affectionately Yours
M. FARADAY.

Schœnbein to Faraday.

MY DEAR FARADAY.

I am afraid you will be dissatisfied with Mr. Schœnbein and think him to be a very lukewarm friend, if not even a forgetful one, and I must allow, appearances are strongly speaking against him; but I can assure you at the same time, that coldness of feelings has nothing to do with the silence he has been keeping these many months.

You know perhaps that in our commonwealth I have become a sort of a political and public character i. e. a member of our little parliament and as such I have got duties to fulfill. Now, of late, a party having sprung up amongst us, that attempted to change some fundamental principles of our constitution and your friend being a staunch conservative, he conjointly with his political friends of course opposed that tendency, and the consequence was, that in our senate we had some battles to fight, in which I could not help taking some active part, both within and out of doors.

You will no doubt smile at Mr. Schœnbein's acting a political part and you are quite right in doing so, for I will and cannot deny myself, that he is by no means the proper man for dealing in politics and may add, that the bias of his mind does not go that way neither. You must be aware, however, that the citizens of a small republic, such as our's is, are not always allowed indulging their private taste; they are now and then, as it were, forced to handle things, which they have not the slightest mind to touch, and such is Mr. Schœnbein's case. Our many-headed sovereign (the people) proves in general to be more imperious and exacting than your monarchs even, so that very often very little choice is left us between following and disobeying his pleasure and commands.

I tell you all these things, indeed very insignificant in themselves, to account for and justify my long taciturnity, for you may easily imagine, that the mind being seriously occupied with such matters, is little apt for any thing else, even not for letter-writing.

Now, after having carried a most signal and decisive victory over our antagonists, we belong again to ourselves, so that nothing prevents us from re-assuming our wonted peaceful work and I hasten to make use of the very first moment of the leisure-time regained to pay old debts to my friends.

First of all permit me to express you my most grateful thanks for the very numerous proofs of kindness and benevolence which you have of late been pleased to bestow upon my daughter. She was really overhappy in having been favored so much as to enjoy the enviable privilege of passing some days at the Royal Institution and getting introduced into the amiable family of your near relations. And I need not add, that the juvenile lectures, which you kindly allowed her to attend, highly pleased and interested the girl. I do not wonder at all the great pleasure and gratifications she has derived from such favors, and in reading the girl's lively descriptions of what she saw, heard and felt on the occasion, I could not help envying Miss Schœnbein and being a little jealous of her. The girl looks on the new world of wonders, in which she has been placed, with open eyes and all the freshness of youth, and, even at the risk of being taxed with partiality, I tell you, that the young maid now and then surprises me by the justness of remarks, which she makes upon men and things.

According to her often repeated assurances, my daughter feels quite happy in England and has (to me the most important point) become so exceedingly fond of her sphere of activity there, that the Idea of soon returning to Bâle is far from being a flattering one to her. Her truly filial attachment to Miss Hornblower is daily growing stronger and deeper and every letter of her's bears ample evidence of the feelings both of the deepest affection and highest veneration she entertains towards your excellent friend. You may easily conceive, how much gratifying such news must prove to myself, as well as to Mrs. Schœnbein and as it was by your kind interference, that our beloved Child has been so happily placed, both of us feel ourselves laid under the deepest obligations to you and you may rest assured, that this great piece of friendship will never be forgotten by us. Mrs. Schœnbein charges me to offer you in her name the most heartfelt thanks for your kindness.

From the very same reasons, that forced me to be neglectful to my friends as a correspondent, I have for some time very little worked, though it would not be quite true if I said to have been entirely idle. Now and then I took up some little piece of work, but without doing any thing being worth while of speaking about. I entertain however the hopes, that the forthcoming spring, in renewing all nature around us, will also call forth some dormant powers of my mind and stir me up again to scientific activity. At this present moment there is some dullness, I had almost said, sleepiness about me and it is full time to get rid of that drowsy disposition of mind. I saw the other day my last letter to you in the Philosophical Magazine; the epistolary production hardly merited the honor of being printed, be that however as it may, there is at any rate no harm in publishing such trifles and queer Ideas. I will not let pass unnoticed a little misprint, which is singular enough. Whilst from several reasons I have made it a point never to communicate any thing to the french academy, the printer has put "Academy of Paris" instead of Munic. Or have I perhaps made the mistake myself in my letter?[1] Errare humanum est; I do not think it however worth while, that the error should be corrected. From what you told me in your last letter, it appears that you are at present engaged in researches of the highest importance, for the problem to be solved is really of a transcendent nature. You only could think of undertaking such a bold enterprize and I wish you from all my heart full success. How does Mrs. Faraday fare? I confidently hope and ardently wish, that she is going better. Pray present my best compliments and kindest regards to her. In begging you kindly to excuse the emptiness of my letter I am, my dear Faraday for ever

                        Yours
                            most faithfully

Bâle Febr. 15th 1858.   C. F. SCHOENBEIN.

[1] vide p. 290 from which it will be seen that he wrote Munich and not Paris.

Schœnbein to Faraday.[1]

MY DEAR FARADAY.

These last six months I have been rather busily working on oxygen, and flatter myself not to have quite in vain maltreated my favourite; for I think I can now prove the correctness of that old idea of mine, according to which there are two kinds of allotropic modifications of active oxygen, standing to each other in the relation of + to —, i. e. that there is a positively-active and a negatively-active oxygen, — an ozone and an antozone, which on being brought together neutralize each other into common or inactive oxygen, according to the equation $\overset{+}{O} + \overset{-}{O} = O$.

The space allotted to a letter being so small. I cannot enter into the details of my late researches, and must confine myself to some general statements, which I hope, however, will give you a clear notion of the nature of my recent doings. Having written a paper on the subject, that will before long be published in the transactions of the Academy of Munich, I shall not fail to send it to you as soon as possible.

Ozonised oxygen, as produced from common oxygen by the electrical spark or phosphorus, is identical with that contained in a number of oxy-compounds, the principal ones of which are the oxides of the precious metals, the peroxides of manganese, lead, cobalt, nickel and bismuth, — permanganic, chromic and vanadic acids; and even the peroxides of iron and copper may be numbered amongst them.

The whole of the oxygen of the oxides of the precious metals exists in the ozonic state, whilst in the rest of the oxy-compounds named, only part of their oxygen is in that condition. I call that oxygen negatively-active, or ozone *par excellence,*

[1] This letter is reprinted from Phil. Mag. S. 4. vol. 16. p. 178 in which it had been inserted under the following heading: "Further observations on the allotropic modifications of oxygen, and the compound nature of chlorine, bromine etc."

and give it the sign $\overset{\circ}{\ominus}$, on account of its electromotive bearing. Though generally disinclined to coin new terms, I think it convenient to denominate the whole class of the oxy-compounds containing $\overset{\circ}{\ominus}$ "ozonides". There is another, less numerous series, of oxy-compounds, in which part of their oxygen exists in an opposite active state, i. e. $\overset{\circ}{\oplus}$ or antozone, wherefore I have christened them "antozonides". This class is composed of the peroxides of hydrogen, barium, strontium, and the rest of the alkaline metals; and on this occasion I must not omit to add, that what I have hitherto called ozonized oil of turpentine, aether, etc., contain their active oxygen in the $\overset{\circ}{\oplus}$ state, and belong therefore to the class of the "antozonides". Now, on bringing together (under proper circumstances) any ozonide with any antozonide, reciprocal catalysis results, the $\overset{\circ}{\ominus}$ of the one and the $\overset{\circ}{\oplus}$ of the other neutralizing each other into O, which as such, cannot be retained by the substances with which it had been previously associated in the $\overset{\circ}{\ominus}$ or $\overset{\circ}{\oplus}$ condition. The proximate cause of the mutual catalysis of so many oxycompounds depends therefore upon the opposite states of the active oxygen contained in these compounds.

I will now give you some details on the subject.

1. Free ozonized oxygen = $\overset{\circ}{O}$, and peroxide of hydrogen = HO + $\overset{\circ}{\oplus}$, or peroxide of barium = BaO + $\overset{\circ}{\oplus}$ (the latter suspended in water), on being shaken together destroy each other, HO + $\overset{\circ}{\oplus}$ or BaO + $\overset{\circ}{\oplus}$ being reduced to HO or BaO, and $\overset{\circ}{\oplus}$ and $\overset{\circ}{\ominus}$ transformed into O.

2. Aqueous permanganic acid = $Mn^2 O^3 + 5 \overset{\circ}{O}$, or a solution of permanganate of potash mixed with some dilute nitric acid, is almost instantaneously discoloured by peroxide of hydrogen or peroxide of barium, the nitrate of the protoxide of manganese being formed in the first case, and in the second, besides this salt, the nitrate of baryta. It is hardly necessary to state, that in both cases the $\overset{\circ}{\ominus}$ of the permanganic acid and the $\overset{\circ}{\oplus}$ of the peroxide of hydrogen or barium are disengaged as O.

3. An aqueous solution of chromic acid containing some nitric or sulphuric acid and peroxide of hydrogen, are rapidly transformed into the nitrate or sulphate of oxide of chromium, HO, and inactive oxygen, which is of course disengaged. A solution of chromic acid mixed with some nitric acid and BaO² gives a similar result, nitrate of baryta and oxide of chromium being formed, and O disengaged.

4. If you add to a mixture of any peroxide salt of iron and the red ferro-sesquicyanuret of potassium (both substances dissolved in water) some peroxide of hydrogen, prussian blue, will be thrown down, and inactive oxygen set free. On introducing into a mixture of nitrate of peroxide of iron and the ferro-sesquicyanuret of potassium the peroxide of barium a similar reaction takes place, prussian blue, hydrate of baryta, etc. being formed, and inactive oxygen eliminated. From these facts it appears that, under certain conditions, even peroxide of iron and HO² or BaO² are capable of catalyzing each other into FeO and HO, or BaO and O.

5. Under certain circumstances PbO² or MnO² are soluble in strong acetic acid, as you may see in one of my papers joined to this letter; now if you add to such a solution HO² or BaO², the peroxides will be reduced to HO or BaO and PbO or MnO, inactive oxygen disengaged.

6. It is a well known fact that the oxide of silver $=$ Ag $\overset{\circ}{O}$, or the peroxide of that metal Ag $\overset{\circ}{\oplus}{}^2$, and the peroxide of hydrogen $=$ HO $+$ $\overset{\circ}{\oplus}$, catalyze each other into metallic silver, water and inactive oxygen. Other ozonides, such as PbO $+$ $\overset{\circ}{\Theta}$ or MnO $+$ $\overset{\circ}{O}$, on being brought in contact with HO $+$ $\overset{\circ}{\oplus}$, are transformed into PbO or MnO, HO and O. Now the peroxide of barium $=$ BaO $+$ $\overset{\circ}{\oplus}$, acts like HO $+$ $\overset{\circ}{\oplus}$. If you pour water an intimate mixture of AgO, or AgO² and BaO², a lively disengagement of inactive oxygen will ensue, AgO, AgO² and BaO² being reduced to metallic silver and baryta. In concluding the first part of my letter, I must not omit to state the general

fact, that the oxygen disengaged in all cases of reciprocal catalysis of oxy-compounds, behaves in every respect like inactive oxygen.

There is another set of chemical phaenomena, in my opinion, closely connected with the polar states of the active oxygen contained in the two opposite classes of peroxides. You know that a certain number of oxy-compounds, for instance the peroxides of manganese, lead, nickel, cobalt, bismuth, silver and also permanganic, chromic, and vanadic acids, furnish with muriatic acid chlorine, whilst another set, such as the peroxides of barium, strontium, potassium etc., are not capable of eliminating chlorine, either out of the said acid or any other chloride. This second class of oxy-compounds produces, however, with muriatic acid, the peroxide of hydrogen; and it is quite impossible in any way to obtain from the first class of the peroxides HO^2, or from the second chlorine. You are aware that, from reasons of analogy, I do not believe in the doctrine of chlorine, bromine, being simple bodies, but consider those substances as oxy-compounds, for instance the peroxides of manganese, lead, etc., in other terms, as "ozonides". Chlorine is therefore to me the peroxide of murium $= MuO + \overset{\circ}{O}$, hydrochloric acid $= MuO + HO$, and, as already mentioned, the peroxide of barium $= BaO + \overset{\circ}{\oplus}$, that of hydrogen $= HO + \overset{\circ}{\oplus}$, and the peroxide of manganese $= MnO + \overset{\circ}{O}$. Proceeding from these suppositions, it is very easy to account for the different way in which the two sets of peroxides are acted upon by muriatic acid.

From reasons as entirely unknown to us HO can be chemically associated only with $\overset{\circ}{\oplus}$, and with no other modification of oxygen, to constitute what is called the peroxide of hydrogen; and in a similar way MnO (the hypothetical anhydrous muriatic acid of older times) is capable of being united only to $\overset{\circ}{\ominus}$ to form the so-called chlorine, which I denominate peroxide of murium. If we cause $MnO + HO$ to react upon

BaO + $\overset{\circ}{\Theta}$, MnO unites with BaO, and HO with $\overset{\circ}{\Theta}$; but if you bring together MnO + HO with Mn + $\overset{\circ}{\Theta}$, part of MnO is associated to MnO, another part to $\overset{\circ}{O}$, water being eliminated, according to the equation 2 (MnO, HO) + MnO + $\overset{\circ}{\Theta}$ = MnO, MnO + MnO, $\overset{\circ}{\Theta}$ + 2 HO.

As you will easily perceive, from these views it would follow that, under proper circumstances, two opposite peroxides, on being intimately and in the right proportion mixed together and acted upon by muriatic acid, could yield neither chlorine nor peroxide of hydrogen, but mere inactive oxygen. If somewhat dilute muriatic acid be poured upon an intimate mixture of five parts of peroxide of barium and two parts of peroxide of manganese, the whole will be rapidly transformed into the muriates of baryta and protoxide of manganese, the active oxygen of both the peroxides being disengaged in the inactive condition, and not a trace of free chlorine making its appearance. The same result is obtained from dilute hydrobromic acid.

Another consequence of my hypothesis is this: that an intimate and correctly proportionate mixture of two opposite peroxides, such as the peroxide of barium and of lead, on being acted upon by any oxy-acid, cannot produce the peroxide of hydrogen; or, to express the same thing in other terms, muriatic acid must act upon the said mixture exactly in the same way as the oxy-acids do; and that indeed is the case. Mixtures of the peroxides just mentioned and acetic, or nitric acids, are readily converted into the acetates or nitrates of baryta and protoxide of manganese, the active oxygen of both the peroxides being of course disengaged in the inactive condition.

Before I close my long story I must mention one fact more, which, in my opinion, is certainly a very curious one. If you mix an aqueous and concentrated solution of bromine with a sufficient quantity of peroxide of hydrogen, what happens? A very lively disengagement of inactive oxygen takes place, the liquid becomes sour, and on adding some aqueous chlorine to it, bromine reappears. From hence we are allowed to conclude, that, on bringing bromine in contact with peroxide of hydrogen, some so-called hydrobromic acid is produced. The hypothesis at present prevailing cannot account for the formation of that acid otherwise than by admitting that bromine takes up the hydrogen of HO^2, eliminating the two equivalents of oxygen united to H. I, of course, take another view of the case, bromine is to me an ozonide like peroxide of lead, etc., i. e. the peroxide of bromine = $BrO + \overset{\circ}{O}$. Now $HO + \overset{\circ}{\ominus}$ and $BrO + \overset{\circ}{\ominus}$ catalyze each other into HO, BrO, and inactive oxygen, BrO + HO forming hydrobromic acid, or what might more properly be called hydrate of bromiatic acid.

You see that I am growing more and more hardened in my heretical notions, or to speak more correctly, in my orthodox views; for it was Davy who acted the part of a heretic in overthrowing the old, venerable, true creed. Indeed the longer I compare the new and old doctrine on the nature of chlorine, etc. with the whole material of chemical facts bearing upon them, the less I am able to conceive how Davy could so lightly and slightly handle the heavy weight of analogies which, in my opinion, speak so very strongly and decisively in favour of Berthollet's views. There is no doubt Sir Humphry was a man of great genius, and consequently very imaginative; but I am almost inclined to believe that, by a certain wantonness, or by dint of that transcendent faculty of his mind, he was seduced to conjure up a theory intended to be as much out of the way and "invraisemblable" as possible, and serve nevertheless certain theoretical purposes; and certainly, if he entertained the intention of solving such a problem, he has wonderfully succeeded. But what I still more wonder at is both the sudden and general success which that far-fetched and strained hypothesis met with, and the tenacity with which the whole chemical world has been sticking to it ever since its imaginative author pleased to divulge it: and all this could happen in spite of the fact that the new doctrine, in removing from the field of chemistry a couple of hypothetical bodies, was, for analogy's sake forced to introduce fictitious compounds, not by dozens only, but by hundreds, — the oxy-sulphion, oxy-nitrion, and those "nonentia". But enough of this subject, upon which I am apt to grow warm and even angry. Although the results I have obtained from my recent investigations cannot but induce me to begin another, and I am afraid, endless series of researches. I shall for the present cut short the matter and indulge for some time in absolute idleness.

I am, my dear Faraday

Yours most truly

Bâle, June 25. 1858.
C. F. SCHOENBEIN.

Schœnbein to Faraday.

MY DEAR FARADAY

I take the liberty to introduce to you Professor Vischer[1] of Basle, an intimate friend and colleague of mine, who intends to make a stay at London for some time and is kind enough as to take charge of a parcel containing voluminous letters, scientific papers and something else destined for the Sovereign of the Royal Institution. It will perhaps interest you to learn on this occasion, that my friend, being an excellent greek scholar, acted the part of a god-father, when I christened my Child "Ozone" 19 years ago.

Mr. Vischer does, of course, not meddle in any way with chemistry, but is in every other respects a true "savant",

[1] Wilhelm Vischer was born in 1808 at Bâle, where he also died in 1874. He was Professor of Greek there. It was he, it will be remembered, who named ozone, deriving it from the Greek word ὄζειν, smelling. Vide also p. 174 and p. 184.

whose personal acquaintance, I trust, will afford you much pleasure.

I am my dear Faraday

Your's most sincerely

Bâle Jun. 28. 1858.

C. F. SCHOENBEIN.

Faraday to Schœnbein.

Royal Institution 28 July 1858.

MY DEAR SCHOENBEIN

Though I date as above yet I am residing in the country and that has caused me to miss your friend M. Vischer, which I was very sorry for. I called in Golden square — and wrote a letter in hopes he might return there but have heard nothing yet, direct from him.

But I saw Miss Schœnbein last Sabbath day and she gave me the papers and letters from you and your portrait, all of which I was very glad to have. I like the portrait very much and was vastly glad to have it. It is very like my old friend, but I perceive he is getting a little, a very little older; when you see my photograph, which Miss Schœnbein has, you will see that is my case, but then I have the advantage of you by eight or ten years — and am getting not merely older but *idler* and that is a worse thing.

I like your summary, brief as it is, of your views, very much and was just on the point of sending it off to Messrs. Taylor and Francis for the Phil. Mag. when I doubted a little about the latter end, and as the date was too late for this month, thought I would write to you. It is the part about Davy and the criticism on his view, and those of chemists generally. I have no objection to them, for I think all hypotheses unwholesome, unless accompanied by criticisms — but I was not sure whether you might object, intending it for me only. As there is time, tell me so in a short note before I send the MS. to the Editors for their acceptance or judgment.

Miss Schœnbein seems quite well. — So are we generally and so must you be considering your intentions. I have no philosophy for you I am idle

Ever truly your's
My dear friend
M. FARADAY.

Schœnbein to Faraday.

Speicher on the heights of the Canton of Appenzell Aug. 4th 1858.

MY DEAR FARADAY

I won't let wait you long for an answer to your very kind letter, with which you favored me some days ago, and first of all permit me to tell you that I felt much gratified at learning from it, that you have not altogether condemned my heretical views. You are aware that I have these many years entertained them and tried on more than one occasion to combat Davy's doctrine on the nature of Chlorine etc. I can therefore see no harm in making known those views to the scientific public of England, though I am quite sure that they will be but slightly relished by the majority of the british Chymists. I am even prepared to see Mr. Schœnbein declared to be half if not an entire fool, but being very little ambitious and caring far more for what I consider to be true, than for earning applause and eulogies from others, I shall take very cooly any strictures made upon my old-fashioned notions.

If you think my last letter to you worthy of being published in the Philosophical Magazine I give you full liberty to modify and curtail it, where and in what manner soever you please to do so. Getting more and more out of practice to speak and write your native tongue, I have no doubt, that my epistolary production will teem with all sorts of grammatical blunders and if your kindness is not too much taxed by the demand, I ask you the favor to correct the most palpable faults of my letter in order to render it less grating to english ears.

These last three weeks Mrs. Schœnbein, my two youngest daughters and myself have been residing upon the heights of the canton of Appenzell, that spot of Switzerland, I am most particularly fond of. It is the greenest land I know and I doubt very much, whether Ireland, emphatically called "the Emerald Island" can compete with Appenzell, the whole country about looking like an immense carpet of the softist velvet and being broken up into numberless hills, chasms, valleys, dales, which here and there are patched with fir-woods and covered with neat and snug little houses, the mere sight of which conveys comfort to the eye. Add to all these beauties a most extensive view on a great part of Switzerland, Swabia, Bavaria and the Tyrol, between which the "swabian sea", the stately lake of Constance is expanding its broad and blue sheet of water, you will readily allow, that such a seat and sight deservedly merit to be called glorious.

All of us, as you may easily imagine, fully enjoy the charms of the country, the peculiar nature of which seduces us to lead a truly gipsy life, to-day making this, to-morrow another hill our temporary laager. As often as I discover new beauties, I cannot help saying to myself: how should my friend Faraday enjoy such a sight! That under such circumstances Chymistry and every sort of philosophy are entirely forgotten, I hardly need assuring you.

In the beginning of next week we shall leave our alpine abode, Mrs. Schœnbein and the girls returning to Basle and Mr. Schœnbein going to Jena.

Pray present our best compliments to Mrs. Faraday and believe me

Your's

most truly

C. F. SCHOENBEIN.

Schœnbein to Faraday.

MY DEAR FARADAY [1]

As Doctor Bernoulli, a former pupil of mine is going to London and from there to Guatemala, I make use of this opportunity to send you through my young friend amongst other memoirs that paper, in which I have treated the reciprocal Katalysis of a number of oxycompounds.[2] You may give the "fasciculum" to a scientific friend, who happens to be master of the german tongue. The little parcel joined, you will be good enough to forward it to its place of destination.

It is not long since I returned from a journey undertaken to the south-west of Germany, which has turned out highly pleasant and interesting to me. First I attended the meeting of german philosophers held at Carlsruhe in the middle of September last, which was the most numerous and brilliant one, I have as yet had the good luck of attending. With a very few exceptions all the leading scientific men of Germany were

---

[1] This letter bears no date from the context however it follows that it must have been written in September 1858.

[2] Über die gegenseitige Katalyse einer Reihe von Oxyden, Superoxyden und Sauerstoffsäuren. Basl. Verh. Bd. 2. 1858. p. 139.

present: Liebig, Woehler,[1] Bunsen, Magnus,[2] Dove[3] and a host of others. Under such "auspiciis" the meeting could not but be excellent. All sorts of honors and attentions were showered down upon us from the grand duke and his young amiable duchess (the sister of the husband of your princess), the government and magistrates, down to the very lowest inhabitants of the capital. I think indeed, that science has very seldom been so much honored in its representatives, as it was the case at Carlsruhe some weeks ago.

Both their Royal Highnesses, all the Ministers, a number of political notabilities and the chief Magistrate of the Metropolis attended all the general meetings, holding out from the beginning to the end. No less than three times we enjoyed the hospitality of the reigning duke, supping, dining and taking tea with the court. Of other festivities there was no want: the finest plays were acted before the learned audience, splendid balls given in honor of the philosophers, the town of Baden-Baden, in the beautiful ruins of the magnificently situated old castle, treated the association in a sumptuous style, and the good people of Durlach invited us to enjoy their delicious grapes in their vine-yards, celebrating, what we call a "Wintzerfest" (vintage-feast) in which beautiful young Ladies of the town, clad in white, offered in a graceful and highly engaging manner the choicest fruits of the Land to the philosophers present, the number of whom was very great indeed, at least five or six hundred. In music-loving Germany nothing can be done without songs and other musical performances, and certainly we had plenty of them, along with patriotic toasts and

---

[1] Friedrich Wöhler M. D. was born in 1800 at Eschersheim near Frankfort. He worked under Berzelius for a short time and was professor of Chemistry at Göttingen where he died in 1882 He received the Copley medal.

[2] Heinrich Gustav Magnus Ph. D., professor of Physics at the University of Berlin, was born in 1802 at Berlin where he also died in 1870.

[3] Heinrich Wilhelm Dove Ph. D. .was born in 1803 at Liegnitz. He was professor of Physics at Berlin till his death in 1879.

other manifestations of joy at Carlsruhe, Baden and Durlach. The people on the other side of the water have hardly a notion of the teutonic enjoyments and the comfortable ease, in which those things are done. Am I right or not, if I say, that pleasure is a sort of business to the majority of the English and the enjoyment of it too much ruled by the codex of "bienséance", and the statutes of which are too much in favor of formalities and ceremonies. But every nation may have its own ways and whims, and after all "de gustibus non est disputandum". After having been fully satiated by intellectual and bodily pleasures at Carlsruhe, I took a trip with Liebig, Rose[1] and some other philosophers to see some interesting establishments in the country, and then, tempted by the glorious weather of antumn and the seducing neighbourhood of the finest scenery of the Rhine, I lounged about in the classical regions of the history of the Rhine, visiting many an old friend and drinking more than a glass of old Hock. One Excursion was most particulary beautiful: With a couple of friends I descended from Mayence to Bingen and arrived there, all of us, devout reverers of father Rhine, went up to the chapel Saint Rochus, emptying there in honor of his Majesty a bottle or two of his most generous and incomparable nectar. Those heights afford one of the most picturesque views along the Rhine. I won't tell you any more about my idle ramblings, suffice it to know, that they proved delicious, and that Mr. Schœnbein was "joliment" scolded by Mrs. Schœnbein on account of his very long outstayings. By this time I have entered the career of every day life and shall, before long, live again in the consortium of my chemical hero, whose interior nature I want to know much better, than I do now. You have no doubt enjoyed a tranquil and pastoral country-life at Hamptoncourt and I confidently

---

[1] Heinrich Rose Ph. D. studied Chemistry under Berzelius and was professor of Chemistry at the University of Berlin. He was born in 1795 at Berlin and died there in 1864.

hope, that Mrs. Faraday's health has been much benefitted by it. Miss Schœnbein is, as far as I know, doing well at Stamford Hill and continues to like her stay in England.

Expecting to hear soon of and from you, and asking you the favor to present my humble respects to Your Lady I am, my dear Faraday

for ever your's

(Sept. 1858) C. F. SCHOENBEIN.

Pray be kind to the bearer of this letter, written in a hurry.

Faraday to Schœnbein.

Royal Institution 13. Novr. 1858[1]

MY DEAR SCHOENBEIN

Daily and hourly am I thinking about you and yours, and yet with as unsatisfactory a result as it is possible for me to have. I think about Ozone, about Antozone, about the experiments you showed Dr. Bence Jones, about your peroxide of barium, your antozonized oil of turpentine, and it all ends in a giddines and confusion of the points that ought to be remembered. I want to tell our audience what your last results are upon this most beautiful investigation, and yet am terrified at the thoughts of trying to do so, from the difficulty of remembering from the reading of one letter to that of another, what the facts in the former were. I have never before felt so seriously the evil of loss of memory and of clearness in the head; and though I expect to fail some day at the lecture table, as I get older, I should not like to fail in ozone, or in any thing about you. I have been making some

[1] Printed in Bence Jones vol. 2. p. 403.

of the experiments Dr. B. Jones told me of, and succeed[1] in some but do not succeed in all. Neither do I know the *shape* in which you make them, as (I understand) good class experiments and telling proofs of an argument. — Yet without experiments I am nothing. If I were at your elbow for an hour or two, I would get all that instruction (as to precaution) out of you, which might bring my courage up. I remember in old times (at the beginning of Ozone), you charged me with principles and experiments. I wonder whether you could help me again? Most likely not, and it is a shame that I should require it; but without such help and precautions on my part, I am physically unable to hold my place at the table. And without I justify my appearance on a Friday Evening I had better withdraw from the duty.

What I should want, would be from *ten* to *fifteen*, or at most *twenty*, table experiments, with such instructions as to vessels, quantities, states of solution, materials, and precautions, as would make the experiments visible to all, and certain and ready. Also the points of the general subject, in what you have found to be the *best order* for the argument and its proof.

I have sought for the old bottle of *antozone oil of turpentine*, but believe I have used it all up. I fear it is of no use trying to make it by the end of January, next year: — yet about that time I must give the evening if I give it at all. If you encourage me to give the argument (and I can only try if you help me), have you any of the substance you could spare? and could you find conveyance for it by rail or otherwise? I fear there is no other substance that will represent it: — i. e. that approaches so near to isolated antozone, as that body does.

Now do not scold me. I am obliged to speak as I do. Perhaps you had better tell me that I must *give up the subject*, for that I can hardly succeed in telling it properly by the way I propose. Do not hesitate to say so, for I am well pre-

---

[1] Bence Jones (P. 404) reads "succeeded".

pared by my inner experience in other matters, to suppose that may be the case. But then tell me so at once, that I may think *over* my position here for January.

Now for a more cheery subject. I saw Miss Schœnbein a few days ago (after a long interval) and was glad to see her looking well and happy. I am sure you will not think the worse of us for the effect England has had upon her, when you see her again. She will make you, her mother, sisters and all happy. But I know she tells you all about herself and as to her state of contentment or happiness that will breathe in her letters. I have more to say, but cannot bring it to mind. Believe me to be as Ever My dear Schœnbein

Your true and obliged friend

M. FARADAY.

Faraday to Schœnbein.

Royal Institution 25 Novr. 1858[1]

Warmest thanks, my dear friend, for your last kind letter:[2] it has given me courage, and yet when I look into the journals about ozone and see how many things there are, which have been said by different men, and how thoroughly I have forgotten most of them: it makes me very doubtful of myself, for I cannot hold many points in hand at once, as I used to do, but I shall trust in your strength and kindness. I have repeated, as I said, some of your results. The peroxide of barium, which I have, seems to do pretty well, but it is vesi-

---

[1] A few passages from this letter are included by Bence Jones in his Life of Faraday (vol. 2. p. 405).
[2] This letter also has been lost.

cular and gray and so unlike what Brodie[1] made with great care and called the right peroxide,[2] that I doubt it, but I shall know better when I receive your instructions. I have forgotten the preparation of HO⊕ by the fluor salicic acid — where is it described in French, or where is it? — What strength do you prepare HO⊕, strong or dilute? — The peroxide of manganese, do you employ the natural or of the artificial? what is your process of preparation for solution in A. A. and do you use it wet or dry?

I have had the paper on reciprocal catalysis (23 June 1858) translated, so have, with the letters etc, obtained possession of part of your thoughts. But it is the experimental proofs and the method of making them perfectly, about which I am anxious and none but the discovering philosopher himself knows how best to make their value evident. For that reason I desire to work with your tools, and in your way and if the chemical [preparations] you refer to are to be *bought* in Bâle, in what you know to be the right state, send them to me, but if not, do not waste your time personally. I shall prepare them from your instructions.

I had your letters etc by Dr. Bernoulli on the 17th instant. I did not see him for he sent them by post and was to leave London the next day. He had been ill and detained in Berlin. But I could not tell when you had written, for your letter had *no* date and strange to say neither had his, except the Postmark. Yours by him and mine to you must have passed in the road.

Kindest remembrances to the household from one always under obligation to you and ever yours   M. FARADAY.

---

[1] Sir Benjamin Collins Brodie professor of Chemistry at Oxford, from 1855 to 1873. He was born in 1817 in London and died in 1880.

[2] Notice on further experiments as to the reduction of metallic oxides by the peroxide of barium. Chem. Soc. Journ. vol. 7 1855. p. 304.

Faraday to Schœnbein.

MY DEAR SCHOENBEIN

I have received the packet safe from M. Rumpf and write instantly to acknowledge it, with all thanks. But I have not any thing for Miss Schœnbein; I think M. Rumpf means to deliver, what you have sent, himself. Your daughter was very well and happy last Friday evening, when I had the honor to be in their company at Stamford Hill

Ever Yours

2 Dec. 1858 M. FARADAY.

Faraday to Schœnbein.

Royal Institution 19 Jan. 1859

MY DEAR FRIEND

I have received your last of the 13th instant.[1] You will be weary of my thanks nevertheless I send them. The peroxide of barium I have, has been very good in all former experiments. I hope tomorrow it will prove as good in those, I shall report from your last. I do not at all doubt it. The evening does not come off until the 25th of next month, but I have sent the tickets to Hampstead to Mr. Rumpf — and Miss Schœnbein — also to Miss Hornblower and others whom you know more or less. I have had some of the German papers translated and hope I have get hold of the subject thoroughly, if I can only keep it; but memory is most treacherous and I am obliged to look at every reading to see whether ozone is $\ominus$ or $\oplus$. I stick it before my eyes, but that is a clumsy way.

[1] This letter referred to by Faraday has been mislaid.

You seem to me to be leading a very gay life. Well, I am happy you have health, strength and spirits to do so: — that they may long continue with you is the earnest wish of

Ever Yours
M. FARADAY.

Faraday to Schœnbein.

Royal Institution 16 Feby. 1859

MY DEAR FRIEND

I must write, not knowing but that you may walk in during the act. I have delayed thus long, thinking that possibly when my letter got to Basle you might be here: — but whatever may be the case I must write. If you do not get my letter, Mrs. Schœnbein will and though Miss Hornblower wrote off to her on Monday, immediately that she knew the cause of your dear daughters death and I can say nothing in the way of information more than she can, still my letter will not be wrong. Last Thursday, I think, they had sent to us to learn Dr. Bence Jone's hours, intending to see him on the Saturday perhaps. On Sunday morning as I was dressing about $1/2$ p. 7 o'clock, a messenger brought me a note which telling me of Miss Schœnbeins very serious state, sent me first to Dr. Bence Jones and then to Stamford Hill: but I was too late to see the poor girl alive. She died at $1/2$ p. 7 o'clock. Dr. Bence Jones came in very soon after and then we telegraphed off to you the first time. In the evening of the same day, Sunday, I sent off the second telegraph message — On Monday Morning an examination took place, Dr. B. Jones being present and he tells me it was perforation of the stomach, a matter which could neither be foretold nor distinguished during life (for there was no sickness), nor aided if known, and so her end came and, as I understand with great peace of mind as to the future, though with much present pain of body.

We de not know what to expect, whether you are coming or not. Perhaps even now there is news of you at Stamford Hill, but we are some miles apart and unfortunately I have been ill and am confined to this house. I expect to hear from Miss Hornblower in the course of a few hours. You will either by letter or in person instruct her what to do, but if nothing is heard from you the burial must take place on Friday next. Miss Hornblower told me she had had a telegraphic message from you, but they are of necessity very brief. I left word with Miss Hornblower that if you come, and it suited you, we should be very glad to make your home *here* for the time. There are some friends of Miss Schœnbein at Hampstead, and I think also in Warwickshire where she spent her holidays. They have been informed and I believe one of them, a Clergyman from Warwickshire, purposes being at the funeral. But I am very imperfectly informed of these matters, which are all held doubtful until it is known what you will do.

I write to you, though I think you may not be at Basle and once I thought of writing to her Mother. This letter indeed is as much to Mrs. Schœnbein as to you. Your good daughter had made unto herself friends, who thought very much of her and I grieve to think she will not return to you to be a comfort to you both in future years. But God's will be done. You may think of her with great, though melancholy pleasure. She was full of thought latterly about you and the Ozone evening. I send you a note of hers to me only five days before her death.

My dear Wife and Niece, as knowing Miss Schœnbein, join with me in all sympathy with you both and your children. My niece's sisters have been indebted to her care for them at Stamford Hill. Associations in every way have risen about her, poor girl, and she will be mourned by many and for some time.

My dear friend — I can write to you about nothing else and I can do no good in writing — I simply grieve again and again for your loss and ours.

Most affectionately Yours

M. FARADAY.

The note from Miss Schœnbein referred to above is still preserved among Schœnbein's letters to Faraday, so that we are in the position to reprint it here. The time and date of her death have been added by Faraday.

Miss Schœnbein to Faraday.

Stamford Hill Feb. 8th 59.

DEAR MR. FARADAY,

Emboldened by your great kindness, I venture to take advantage of your offer of one more ticket in my father's name. This subject of Ozone being one that seems particularly interesting to medical gentlemen, I make this request in behalf of one of them.

I must add that my father is quite envious for this great privilege that is in store for me, of hearing your lecture.

Believe me, dear Mr. Faraday
very truly yours
EMILIE SCHOENBEIN.

Died at half past 7 o'clk A. M. on the 13th Feb. 1859 —

M. F.

Schœnbein to Faraday.[1]

Bâle Febr. (25.) 1859.

MY DEAREST FRIEND,

I enclose a few lines to acknowledge the kind letter of Mrs. Faraday's and your nieces, which really produced a soothing effect upon our harrowed minds and bleeding hearts; and it is particularly Mrs. Schœnbein that feels most thankfully for that proof of friendly and sympathizing feelings. Mr. Crowdy of Winchester and Miss Mayo of Hampstead, friends of mine and Emilia's, have most kindly and spontaneously offered to me to put a tombstone upon the grave of my deeply lamented daughter and ask my permission to do so as a favor. We were deeply touched by the delicate expression of their friendly feelings and gratefully accept of their kindness offered; but nevertheless I should consider it as the most grateful deed of yours if you would join your dear name to their's. Mrs. Schœnbein's bodily health is, thank God, nearly reestablished, but the sadness of her heart as yet very great; there are however intervals of tranquil resignation to the inscrutable decree of heaven. I have begun my lectures again, but in what state of mind I leave you to imagine. The whole world has become stale and insipid to me, has even assumed a sad appearance.

Pray offer my most grateful thanks to Mrs. Faraday and your niece and pity

your deeply mourning

friend.

---

[1] Faraday's letter of February 24th appears to be an answer to the above note from Schœnbein, which is therefore misdated and probably written about ten days earlier, for Faraday says in his letter (vide p. 323): "I am glad you would receive mine" (i. e. the one dated Feb. 16) "about the same time." In the original the date is undoubtedly Feb. 25th, nevertheless we have for the above reasons placed it before Faradays letter.

Faraday to Schœnbein.

Royal Institution 24 Feb. 1859

MY DEAR DEAR FRIEND

I received your touching letter, and I am glad you would receive mine about the same time. Your cry of anguish may well pierce our hearts here, for if the effect of the blow was stunning to us how much more would it be so to you. And that you should at the same moment be burdened with the heavy weight of Mrs. Schœnbeins illness! I do indeed grieve for you, but I hope you are by this time somewhat relieved in respect of that heavy home anxiety. Do tell her how we feel for her, and the two poor sisters. I am glad you did not come here, for your first duty was at home, to succour and support those dependent on you. You could well trust Miss Hornblower, for she had learnt to love your daughter. I have no doubt she has written of all things personal to you and Mrs. Schœnbein, and will fulfill all your possible wishes. I expect too that by this time you will have had letters from Dr. Bence Jones, Grove and others for I have shown your letters to me and Miss Hornblower unto them.

You mentioned the matter of a tombstone in your letter to me and affectionately desired to have my name by yours on it. I suppose this is usual with you, but with us it is very rare, or even unknown, and would excite much remark. That would be of no consequence, if the remarks were indifferent in their nature, but they would here be sure to carry a religious feeling or meaning with them, and as I am known to be a dissenter, strongly differing from the Episcopal church here, would give rise to much remark among those who know me. I understand too, that a dear friend of your daughter (I think the name is Crowdy) has written to you direct about the inscription on the stone. I believe he performed the funeral service, but as I know it would be a Church of England service, in which I could not conscienciously join, I was not there. However his letter with Miss Hornblower's communications will bring about the fulfilment of the proper arrangements.

Poor girl — (happy girl I well may say considering her strong hope in death) — we were hoping to have her with us tomorrow evening, but how vain are all our plans. Instead of a glad and buoyant heart I shall go to my work, as work indeed. I was desiring to put it off, but when I began to look about for the purpose, I found so many engagements had been made contingent upon the evening, and that even the Prince Consort was coming, that I could not properly change the date. I only hope that I shall not break down. I know I shall not be able to forget for the hour, and an overpowering thought may break in.

I hope that you are beginning to turn a little to occupation. I know how distasteful it will be, but you must be drawn away at times from the heavy thought; even though the exertion may be painful, it will be healing. Do think of this for the sake of yourself and your family and your friends and may God give you that grave and gentle consolation by degrees, which you ask for in your letter to me

Ever My dear Schœnbein
Your Affectionate friend
M. FARADAY.

Faraday to Schœnbein.[1]

Royal Institution London 25 April 1859

MY DEAR SCHOENBEIN

I have just seen your letter to Miss Hornblower, and so write knowing you will be at home again. I am glad

[1] Portions of this letter are printed in Bence Jones vol. 2. p. 422.

you went out, for though all things would be distasteful to you still they work out the transition back again from sudden and deep grief to a more collected, healthy, and necessary state of mind. For the same reason, I am very glad that Mrs. Schœnbein has left home for a little while, and trust that it may calm her spirits and do her good. It is impossible for me to write to you, or do any thing connected with you without thoughts of your dear daughter entering in. I have a volume of my collected experimental papers on physical and chemical matters to send you by the first opportunity. It was ready when Miss Schœnbein's box was sent to you from Stamford Hill, but I felt as if I could not intrude the book into so sacred a deposit as that box was, and so retained it for some fitter opportunity. I gave a Friday Evening on Ozone and Antozone for which only a few weeks before I had given tickets at her request to some friends of hers, but I could not, and cannot, talk to you about it. I did my best, though with thoughts often pressing in; still let me thank you for what you had, before the sad event, done to help me.

Your letter to Miss Hornblower spoke of a cypress tree; and I went yesterday to see the state of such trees as are on the ground and how they are likely to grow. — Those that are up, do not look well; but if Miss Hornblower will let me, I shall do what I can to plant such a tree on the spot. At present I cannot see her on the matter, for you will be sorry to hear that we are in trouble and anxious on her account. She fell some four or five years ago and hurt her knee; it has never ceased to be painful, and from falls since has become worse, and at last an operation was decided upon. This was performed the day before yesterday under the influence of chloroform, and by a very clever surgeon. He removed part of the bone which had become injured and unhealthy, and we hope for good results; but time and patience will be required. The accounts last night were favourable, but the time since the operation is as yet too short to allow of any thing beyond a hasty and imperfect judgment.

I sent your letter to Grove. He has been suffering from a sharp attack of rheumatic gout, which confined him to the house, but he is now getting better. — All your friends think of you and feel for you.

For a little on the other side, I may say that we are pretty well. My wife joins me in kindest remembrances and thoughts; and so too does my niece Jeannie for though she is not much known to you yet she was to Miss Schœnbein. — Extend these sympathizing thoughts to the children who remain to comfort you, Ever, My dear Schœnbein

Your's

M. FARADAY.

Schœnbein to Faraday.

MY DEAR FARADAY

The long silence I have kept to you is, I am afraid, the most palpable proof of your friend's having become a poor man indeed. Formerly it was a real treat to me to write you a letter, now I have to make the greatest effort to take up my pen, and fulfill even the most urgent duties of a correspondent and it is hardly necessary to tell you the cause of that change. My mind is no more what it was a short time ago; its former cheerfulness is gone and melancholy feelings and sadness have taken possession of it, weighing the more heavily upon me, that Mrs. Schœnbein is very far from being comforted and consoled about our grievous loss. Indeed time has as yet proved to us all a very poor healer of the deep wound, which was inflicted upon us four months ago. To distract a little my mind from domestic sorrow, and to forget the highly deplorable state of the affairs of Europe, I have these last three months shut up myself in my laboratory and I may say turned my back upon the rest of the world, avoiding even to touch a newspaper or to hear a syllable spoken about politics. Dry and stale as the subject must be to a mind grievously affected, I mean oxigen, I have taken it up again and worked upon it harder than I ever did. And I think not quite for nothing. First I ascertained the hypochlorites, manganates and ferrates (or rather the acids of those salts) to be "Ozonides", i. e. decomposable by the Antozonides: HO_2, KO_3, BaO_2 etc. Then I tried to show, that the nascent state of oxigen as such has nothing to do with the oxidizing powers of that element, and during the last six weeks I have almost exclusively occupied myself with what I call "the chemical polarization of neutral oxygen".[1] After having once ascertained a number of facts (known to you) from which I drew the inference, that there are two active kinds of oxigen standing to each other in the relation of $+$ to $—$, I thought it possible, even likely, that both kinds of active oxigen are at the same time produced out of inactive O, as often as one of them makes its appearance. Proceeding from those notions I first looked for $HO + \ominus$ as a production of the slow combustion of phosphorus, during which process, at it is well known, ozonized oxigen $= \ominus$ is engendered. My conjecture proved fully correct, peroxide of hydrogen being produced and contained in the sour fluid called phosphatic acid. And so closely are the two facts connected with one another, namely the ozonisation of inactive oxigen and the formation of HO_2, that you will never obtain the one substance without the other. Being once sure of that important coincidence, I extended my researches to the productions of the slow combustion of Ether and found to my no small satisfaction, that in this case too

[1] cf. "Über die chemische Polarisation des Sauerstoffs." Poggend. Annal. Bd. 108. 1859. p. 471.

notable quantities of peroxide of hydrogen (the type of the Antozonides) are engendered, conjointly with another compound containing Θ (or Ozonide). After having ascertained those facts, my attention was directed to the electrolysis of water and I think, there can be entertained no doubt, that not only Θ but also HO_2 i. e. $\oplus$ makes its appearance at the positive electrode. Under proper precautions I have reduced permanganic acid to MnO, CrO_3 to Cr_2O_3 etc., in fact desoxidized a number of bodies at that electrode. Reducing oxy-compounds at the electrode, where oxygen is disengaged, seems to be paradoxical enough. As to the small quantities of ozonized oxigen disengaged, and HO_2 formed during the electrolysis of water at the positive Electrode, I think, they must be considered as the surviving witnesses of the chemical polarization of the O of HO_2, which O is transformed by the current into $\oplus$ and Θ. The inactive Oxigen disengaged during the Electrolysis of water is most likely a secundary production, proceeding from the depolarisation or neutralization of $\oplus$ and Θ. Before long my papers on those queer subjects will be published, and you shall have them as soon as possible, as I flatter myself, that the matter will interest you. If I have correctly accounted for the novel facts lately discovered by me, i. e. if neutral oxigen be capable of being chemically polarized, or thrown into opposite states of chemical activity at the same time, well, I should think, I had done something to advance a little our knowledge of that mysterious and important element.

Our Midsummer-holidays having commenced I intend to go one of these days to the "Berner Oberland" to fetch my two eldest girls, who have for some weeks been staying at a watering-place for the use of a mineral spring there and returned, we have a notion to visit a retired part of the Black Forest.

I confidently hope you, Mrs. Faraday and your Niece are doing well and as to Miss Hornblower, I was very sorry indeed to learn from you, that she had been obliged to undergo a painful operation. I ardently wish that by this time, she will be entirely cured and enjoy perfect health. Pray remember me most friendly to all of them, excuse my poor, stale and insipid letter and write soon to

Your
poor friend

Bâle July 19th 1859.　　　　　　　　　C. F. SCHOENBEIN.

Faraday to Schœnbein.

Royal Institution 23. September 1859

MY DEAR SCHOENBEIN

The state to which you consider that grief has reduced you, must, I think be mine by course of nature and years; for I am just as you describe, weary, unwilling to write, and have nothing to say, really nothing to say; or else, surely I should have written sooner to you. Yesterday was my birthday and I then completed my 68th year. Well! many men are at that time of life far stronger than I am, either in body, memory, or mind; but surely I ought to remember how many pass away *before* that age, — and how plentiful and wonderful have been the mercies and goodness I have enjoyed during this long series of years. Indeed, I think it is only when I have to fulfill some expectation, as in giving a discourse, or writing to a friend like you, that I wish my powers were more than they are: and yet the very wish is ungrateful and brings to my mind a reproach. —

I was very glad to hear of you, and I hope the journey you were about to undertake to fetch your daughters home, with the intended little episode in the Black forest, will have done you all good. I have just had a little piece of enjoyment amongst fine scenery, for I have been in Scotland for a fortnight, and passed a few days among the lochs and mountains in the western parts. I have also been *two* days at the British Association at Aberdeen; but was glad to leave it quickly, and before the visits to Balmoral came on: for pleasant and happy as the occasions are, they are by their excitement a weariness to me: yet I was for the 48 hours with very kind friends. The whole matter would have suited you better than me.

Our friend Miss Hornblower continues in great pain; and I think we may consider the operation as a failure. Certainly it has failed to give the relief that was hoped for. She cannot move without crutches, nor without great pain. My wife and niece are pretty well: — the former desires her kindest remembrance to you, the latter is still in Scotland.

Very many thanks for Your scientific news. I see you will carry oxygen much farther yet, and expect, with every letter, some new point. As for me I am barren; the best I have are some negative results about electricity, heat and gravity.

Good bye My dear Schœnbein
Ever faithfully Yours
M. FARADAY.

Schœnbein to Faraday.

MY DEAR FARADAY

My having spent the autumnal vacations partly at Neuchâtel, partly at Presinge, the seat of our friend de la Rive, on the frontiers of Savoy, and returned to Basle but a few days ago, must excuse this late answer of mine to your last kind letter. Hard working had made such a temporary relaxation quite necessary to my mind. First of all, allow me to offer my most heartfelt congratulation to you on account of the celebration of your 68th birthday, and let us hope, that it may please Him, who is the sovereign Lord of our life, to grant the return of many more. Generally speaking a long age is rather an equivocal gift and in the most favorable case accompanied with many evils, which human flesh is heir to, amongst which not the slightest one is the feeling and consciousness that we have lost the buoyancy of youth. But there are some privileged men, whose mind, in spite of carrying a heavy load of years upon their back, remain elastic and green, continuing to take the liveliest interest with every thing, regarding the higher and nobler aims of mankind. Either I am entirely mistaken, or you are such a man. May your body be a little broken down, your hairs have turned grey or white, your countenance be furrowed by wrinkles, perhaps even your walk and step somewhat tottering, what is that to you, who are still soaring in the highest regions of philosophy, whilst youngsters, replete with bodily powers are crawling upon the lowest ground. A little more or less of memory, precious as this gift is, does not matter much, and after all, according to what you have accomplished during your career of life, you are more than any other man entitled to enjoy the "otium cum dignitate". There is a german saying "Fünfzig Jahre Stillestand, sechzig Jahr fängt's Alter an" and according to it, your friend must now also be called an old man, having the eighteenth of this month accomplished his sixtieth year. It is certainly with some reluctance, that I acknowledge myself to be a "senex", but my grey hairs give but two obvious an evidence in favor of the truth, and I must submit to what I cannot change. Although far advanced in the career of life, I nevertheless feel still rather youthly and have not yet lost to a perceptible degree my ancient love for science and philosophical research, and that I consider as an invaluable boon, received from Him, who is the Giver of all good things, and as calculated to cheer up the evening of my life. Like you, I have every reason to be most grateful to kind Providence for what fell to my lot, modest as it has been and not always made up of smiles and sunshine. But now enough of birthday reflections. During the summer gone by I have been rather active in my laboratory and trust my doings will not have been quite useless. Pray, listen now a little to my random talkings about philosophical matters. First of all know, that I continued to work upon what I have called "the chemical polarization of neutral Oxigen"[1] of which subject I communicated you something in my last letter and from it you will recollect, that during the slow combustion of phosphorus and aether, as well as the Electrolysis of water, both kinds of active Oxigen ($\oplus$ and $\ominus$) make their appearance, the former in the shape of HO + $\oplus$.

Having these many years considered the said slow combustion of phosphorus as the type of all the slow oxidations, which inorganic and organic bodies undergo in the moist atmospheric air, or pure common oxigen, I suspected, that the peroxide of hydrogen might be produced, if not in all (from secondary reasons), at least a great number of cases, and directed therefore my attention first to the slow oxidation of the more readily oxidable metallic bodies. My conjecture proved correct, having already found out that half a dozen of metals, during their slow oxidation, give rise to the formation of very appreciable quantities of HO_2, as you will perceive from the statements to follow. To ascertan with full certainty small quantities of that compound, I first wanted proper i. e. most delicate tests for HO_2 and I fully succeeded in finding out more than one of that description, in corroboration of which I may tell you, that by the means of them I am able

---

[1] Beginning at this point the remainder of the letter, so far as it does not concern private matters, was printed in the Phil. Mag. under the following title: "On the polarisation of oxygen." Vide Phil. Mag. Vol. 18. 1859. p. 510. The alterations being but trifling we did not deem it essential to take them into account.

to detect the millionth part of the said peroxide contained in water and even less than that. These tests depend upon the oxidizing and reducing effects produced by HO_2 upon certain substances. Dilute paste of starch containing some jodide of potassium, if it be mixt up with water containing but half a millionth of HO_2 is within a very short time colored darkblue on adding some drops of a weak dissolution of any protoxide salt of iron to the mixture. The dilute dissolution of HO_2 slightly acidulated by SO_3 discharges the red color of an acidulated dissolution of the permanganate of potash (by reducing the acid of that salt to the protoxide of manganese). HO_2, even in a most dilute state, throws down prussian blue out of a mixture of most dilute dissolutions of the red cyanide of potassium, and any peroxide-salt of iron (by reducing Fe_2O_3 to FeO). Most dilute HO_2, colored blue by some Indigosolution, is rapidly discolored, on adding some drops of a dilute solution of iron vitriol to the mixture. A dilute solution of chromic acid is certainly a less delicate test for HO_2 than the mentioned ones are, but its property of being colored azureblue by water, containing but $\frac{1}{20000}$ of HO_2 makes it in many cases a valuable and practical test, which I always use when I have to deal with water somewhat rich in HO_2. Now by the means of those tests I have of late ascertained, that during the slow oxidation of Zinc, Cadmium, Lead, Tin, Bismuthum and Copper (effected by moist common oxigen or atmospheric air), perceptable quantities of HO_2 are always formed conjointly with the oxides of those metals. To produce HO_2, some of the metals being in a state of mechanical division as Zinc, Cadmium and Lead, have but to be put in contact with pure water and atmospheric air for a very short time, but I find it more convenient to amalgamate first the metals with mercury. Take for instance 100 grammes of Zinc filings, and the same quantity of Mercury, put them into a tumbler filled with dilute sulphuric acid, stir up the metals by a glass rod and you will soon have a grossly powdered Amalgama. Now, after having that metallic mixture washed with water, put it loosely into a funnel, set upon a bottle, let a very thin vein of distilled water run over the amalgama, and by the means of dilute paste of starch containing Jodide of potassium, you will already detect peroxide of hydrogen in the water having passed (in the manner indicated) only once over the amalgama, if you add to a mixture of both some drops of a solution of ironvitriol etc. — If you shake for a few seconds the said amalgama together with air and 100 grammes of distilled water, the latter will have the property of striking blue the paste of starch, on adding to it a couple of drops of a dilute solution of any protoxide salt of iron. Water containing 1% of SO_3, all circumstances being the same, produces more HO_2 than pure water does. You may satisfy yourself with one instance. Take 100 grammes of a still liquid amalgama of Lead, shake it with 100 grammes of the mentioned acidulated water and atmospheric air for five to six minutes, separate, by filtering, the sulfate formed from the water, add to the latter some drops of a dilute solution of Chromic acid and your liquid will be transiently turned azureblue, a proof of the presence of HO_2. If you shake one volume of the said acidulated water, two volumes of pure Ether and some drops of a dilute solution of CrO_3 together, the ether assumes a still deeper blue color. The same acidulated water of course discharges the color of the permanganate solution etc. In saying so much about this matter, I must not omit to add that the quantity of HO_2 formed under the circumstances reaches soon its maximum, which does not go beyond $\frac{1}{6000}$ of the quantity of acidulated water employed. The reason of this fact is obvious. I shall not enter into any more details about the subject, hoping to find soon an opportunity for sending you a paper containining all the particulars about this highly interesting formation of HO_2. From the facts above stated and others not mentioned I am led to conjecture, that all the slow oxidations taking place in the moist atmospheric air depend upon what I call "the chemical polarisation of neutral oxigen" i. e. that this act always precedes that of real oxidation. The oxidable matter being eager to combine with $\ominus$ and water with $\oplus$ to produce $HO + \oplus$, determine that mysterious polarisation of O in a similar manner, as HO_2 is sometimes decomposed, if placed between two substances, one of which attracts the oxigen, the other the hydrogen of the compound. But be that as it may, perfectly sure is now the fact, that in a number of cases of slow oxidation the counterpart or antipode of $\ominus$ makes its appearance in the shape of $HO + \oplus$ and that the latter compound also acts an important part in those slow oxidations. I am inclined to suspect, that the chemical polarisation of O is deeply concerned in animal respiration and many other chemical actions going on in nature, but I will not yet talk about these matters. It seems that the late results of my researches tend to increase a little our insight in the workings of our chemical Hero, and you may therefore easily imagine, that I pursue my investigations on that really wonderful body with a zeal bordering upon mental excitement.

Mrs. Schœnbein and my children are, as to body, tolerably well, but the severe loss of our dearest Emilia still presses very heavily upon us all and most particulary upon the mind of my poor wife. That great physician Time has not yet healed much.

With the deepest regret I learn from you, that poor Miss Hornblower is far from having obtained the desired result from the painful operation she was obliged to undergo some months ago. Pray, remember me most kindly to her and express to the suffering Lady my fullest sympathy. It requires certainly an uncommon degree of moral strength and before all a most absolute submission to the will of God, to maintain herself in a tolerable condition of mind and spirits. Before closing my long letter, I ask you the favor to present my kindest regards to Mrs. Faraday, your Niece and relations, who were so very kind to my beloved daughter, who is now no more.

Pray, don't be too long in writing me and be assured, that every word coming from you is of the highest value to

Your
most attached friend

Bâle Oct. 26. 1859.   C. F. SCHOENBEIN.

Faraday to Schœnbein.[1]

Royal Institution 27 March 1860.

MY DEAR SCHOENBEIN

It seems to me a long while since we haven spoken together, and I know that the blame is mine, but I cannot help it, only regret it, though I can certainly try to bring the fault to an end. When I want to write to you it seems as if only nonsense would come to mind, and yet it is not nonsense to think of past friendship and dear communions. When I try to write of science, it comes back to me in confusion. I do not remember the order of things, or even the facts themselves. I do not remember what you last told me, though I think I sent it to the Phil. Mag., and had it printed; and if I try to remember up, it becomes too much, the head gets giddy and the mental view only the more confused. I know you do not want me to labour in vain, but I do not like to seem forgetful of what you tell me and the only relief I have at such times is to correct myself and believe that you will know the forget-

---

[1] This letter Bence Jones prints in his Life of Faraday vol. 2. p. 433 leaving out however some parts of it.

fulness is *involuntary*. After all, though your science is much to me, we are not friends for science sake only, but for something better in a man, something more important in his nature, affection, kindness, good feeling, moral worth; und so in remembrance of these I now write to place myself in your presence, and in thought shake hands, tongues, and hearts together.

We are all pretty well here. We get on well enough, in a manner, and are very happy and I cannot wish you better things; though I have no intention, when I say that, to imagine you without your memory or your science. Long may you be privileged to use them for the good of human nature.

Our friend Miss Hornblower suffers very much from an affection of the knee of which I spoke before to you. Lately she has seen Sir Benjamin Brodie, who does not make himself responsible for advising an amputation; he says it is a case so serious that the profession ought not to be made responsible for the results of an operation. Whilst going there, I have several times gone into a place of rest in that neighbourhood, to look at a stone you know of, and think of you all. Such places draw my thoughts much now, and have for years had great interest for me. They are not to me mere places of the dead, but full of the greatest hope that is set before man, even in the very zenith of his physical power and mental force. But perhaps I disturb you in calling your loss to mind; forgive me. Yet remember me very kindly to the mother and sisters.

Ever, My dear Schœnbein,
Yours Affectionately
M. FARADAY.

Schœnbein to Faraday.

MY DEAR FARADAY

I have been expecting letters from you these many months, but up to this moment quite in vain. I trust, that nothing is wrong with you i. e. that not ill health, or any other of the evils "which human flesh is heir to" has been the cause of your long silence. Now Professor Wiedemann and Dr. Hagenbach[1], intimate friends of mine going to London, I send you some lines through them, to give a sign, that, at least your friend is still alive. Mr. Wiedemann will tell you, that I have strictly followed up your very wise advice and worked rather hard all the year round. The remedy has not been without its salutary effects, though I cannot say, that the deep wound inflicted upon us last year is healed. As to Mrs. Schœnbein, she certainly at intervals seems to be composed and resigned, but the feelings of deep mourning and distress darken her mind again.

To give you a notion of my late scientific doings, I send you some papers on what I call "the chemical polarisation of the neutral oxigen",[2] of which highly interesting subject Mr. Wiedemann, who has seen the experiments, will give all the details you may desire to know. I am inclined to believe, that it is now a matter of fact, that any oxidation, apparently effected by common or inactive oxygen, is always preceded by the polarisation of that element. I know now three or four dozens of cases of slow oxidations, in which that mysterious act takes place; for instance in that of Phosphorus, Zinc, Iron, Lead, Copper etc., Ether, and a number of other organic matters: pyrogallic acid, desoxidized indigo etc.

[1] Jakob Eduard Hagenbach, professor of Physics at Bâle, where he was born in 1833.
[2] cf. note 1. p. 332.

In presence of such a numerous body of matter-of-fact evidence, I think, very little doubt can be entertained about the correctness of the new doctrine, that Oxigen is capable of being chemically polarized.

How is poor Miss Hornblower? Pray write in your next letter, how she is doing and remember me most friendly to your friend.

In entertaining the confident hope, that all is well with you and yours, I beg you to offer my kindest regards to Mrs. Faraday, your Niece and Brother.

For ever
Your's
most faithfully

Bâle March 29. 1860.   C. F. SCHOENBEIN.

Schœnbein to Faraday.

MY DEAR FARADAY

If I am not mistaken, the last letter, I wrote to you was that, by which I introduced to you Mr. Wiedemann, about six months ago and having ever since not heard any news from you, and being very anxious to know, how you are doing, I take up once more my pen to ask you the favor of a letter, so much the more, that I am at this present moment laid up by the gout, a condition of body entirely new to me and on that very account by no means agreeable. Indeed, up to the last wednesday a fortnight, I had known that of the ills "which human flesh is heir to" only by name and from english novels; you may therefore easily imagine, how much I was surprized at finding at once my legs, hitherto so loyal and obedient, in a state of open rebellion. No other choice was left to the poor sovereign, than to let his subjects rage and go their own way. To tell you the truth, I am afraid, that I have not been entirely blameless and it is perhaps, partly at least, my own fault, that such a catastrophe has occurred. I have carried on a savage war of conquest these last four or five months, and to arrive at my end, I was rather reckless, drawing very largely on the forces of my subjects and caring very little about their welfare. I certainly carried the point, but as it seems at the expence of the loyalty of the inferior classes of my realm; I entertain however the flattering hopes, that better times are approaching and a full restoration of my royal authority will take place before long. But why waging such a war? Oxigen, as you well know, is my hero as well as my foe, and being not only strong but inexhaustible in strategies and full of tricks, I was obliged to call up all my forces to lay hold of him, and make the subtle Being my prisoner. Now to drop the metaphor, I will tell you, that I have been working very hard these many months to get the "Antozone" or ⊕ in its insulated state and I flatter myself to have succeeded in that undertaking, at least to a certain extent.[1] You are aware, that from a number of facts, notably from the reciprocal desoxidizing influence exerted by many oxy-compounds upon each other, I drew the inference, that there exist two series of oxides, one of which contain ⊖ the other ⊕: "the Ozonides and Antozonides." The mutual desoxidation of those compounds I made dependent upon the depolarisation or neutralisation of ⊕ and ⊖ into O. Now ⊕ and ⊖, being able to be transformed into O, I thought it possible, even likely, that the contrary might be effected, i. e. the chemical polarisation of O into ⊕ and ⊖, and you know that in the course of the last and present year, I have ascertained a great number of facts, that speak, as far as I can see,

---

[1] Faraday sent this letter to the Phil. Mag. where the philosophical part of it was inserted under the following heading: "On the insolation of antozone". See Phil. Mag. vol. 21. 1861. p. 88.

highly in favor of that Idea. As the typical or fundamental fact of this chemical polarisation of O, I consider the simultaneous production of $\ominus$ and HO + $\oplus$ taking place during the slow combustion of phosphorus. This simultaneity is such, that ozone never makes its appearance without its equivalent HO + $\oplus$. All the metals slowly oxidizing themselves, HO being present, such as Zinc, lead, iron etc, give rise to the formation of HO + $\oplus$ and the same do a great number of organic substances, such as ether, the tannic, gallic and pyro-gallic acids, hiematoxiline etc. and even reduced Indigo, being associated to potash etc., makes no exception to the rule. The same simultaneity takes place during the electrolysis of water: never Ozone without peroxide of hydrogen. I admit therefore, that O, on being put in contact with an oxidable substance and water, undergoes that change of condition, which I call "chemical polarisation" i. e. is turned into $\ominus$ and $\oplus$, of which the latter combines with HO to form HO + $\oplus$, whilst $\ominus$ is associated to the oxidable matter, such as phosphorus, Zinc etc. In the preceding statements you have only a very rough outline of my late researches on the chemical polarisation of neutral Oxigen; the details on that subject are contained in a number of papers lately published,[1] and of which your english periodicals have as yet not taken any notice. Having gone so far, I could not but be very curious to try, whether it was not possible to obtain $\oplus$ in its insulated or free state. I directed of course my attention to that set of peroxides, which I call "Antozonides" and tried in different ways to eliminate from them that part of their oxygen, which I consider to be $\oplus$. Already years ago I remarked, in accordance with an observation made by Mr. Houzeau[2] that the oxigen disengaged from the peroxide

---

[1] He wrote an extensive series of papers on these researches; they were chiefly printed in "Gelehrte Anzeigen" and "Sitzungsberichten" of the Munich Academy of Science, also frequently in "Erdmanns Journal für praktische Chemie".

[2] See Schœnbeins letter dated May 26. 1855. p. 245.

of Barium by the means of the monohydrate of SO_3, exhibits an ozonelike smell and the power of turning my ozone testpaper blue. Having at that time not yet a notion of two opposite active conditions of Oxigen, I was inclined to ascribe those properties to the presence of minute quantities of Ozone in the said gas, but on examining it more closely, I found it to be neutral oxigen mixt up with a very small portion of Antozone or $\oplus$. A most important and distinctive property of Antozone is the readiness, with which it unites with water to form peroxide of hydrogen, whilst Ozone (alike neutral oxigen) is entirely incapable of doing so. Hence it comes, that the oxigen disengaged from $BaO + \oplus$ under certain precautions, becomes inodorous on being shaken with water, and that this fluid contains HO_2. The simple cause of the minute quantities of Θ obtained from $BaO + \oplus$ is the heat disengaged during the action of SO_3 upon the peroxide by which most of the $\oplus$ eliminated is transformed into Θ.

Now, what do you say to the extraordinary fact, that the antipode of ozone has these many thousand years been ready formed and incarcerated, only waiting for somebody to recognize and let it loose out of its prison. A darkblue species of Fluorspar has for years been known by the german Mineralogists, being distinguished by its property of producing a peculiarly disagreeable smell on being triturated. Many conjectures were put up as to the chemical nature of the odorous matter emitted from the spar: Chlorine, Jodine and even Ozone were spoken of, but it turned out to be a different thing. Mr. Schafhaeutl[1] of Munic sent me a month ago some hundred gramms of the said Fluor-spar (occurring within the veins of a granitic rock at Wœlsendorf a bavarian village near Amberg), asking me to try my luck in ascertaining the nature of the smelling matter, and I think I have fully succeeded in making

---

[1] Karl Emil Schafhæutl Ph. D. M. D. professor of Geology and Palaeontology at Munich, where he died in 1890. He was born in 1803 at Ingolstadt.

out what it is. Surprizing as it may sound to you and unique as the fact certainly is, that matter happens to be nothing but my insolated Antozone. But how do you prove that? will you ask me. In the first place it exactly smells like ⊕, disengaged from BaO₂; but smells are fallacious tests. They are; you shall have another proof, that will irresistibly carry conviction with it: on triturating the Fluorspar with water, peroxide of hydrogen is formed, not in homoeopathic but very perceptible quantities. When I found out first this extraordinary fact, I think it was on the 17th of Nov. last, I could not help laughing aloud, though I happened to be quite alone in my laboratory. I laughed, because I strongly suspected my foe to be hidden in the spar and broke his mask under water with the view of catching it by that fluid. Indeed, it was to me, as if I had caught a very cunning fox, long sought after, in a trap put up for him. To show you, that in saying this I have neither been joking nor dreaming, I shall send you as soon as I can, a sample of that wonderful spar, with which you may easily satisfy your curiousity and convince yourself of the correctness of my statements.[1] I must not omit to tell you, that, according to some previous experiments of mine, the Fluor-spar of Wœlsendorf contains $1/5000$th part of Antozone, a quantity, as you see not at all homoeopathic. How that subtle matter got into the spar, I cannot tell. Being once more upon my legs, I shall, as you may easily imagine, make a new attack upon my foe, with the view and hope of conquering him entirely. The price to be gained by such a fight is not too dearly paid, even by another fit of gout. Having already been too prolix about that matter, I must now drop it; before long you shall read a paper containing the details

[1] Wœhler writing to Liebig, September 25. 1861 says: "I have repeated some experiments with the fluorspar from Wœlsendorf, but have failed to satisfy myself of the accuracy of Schœnbein's results. The odour may turn out to be free fluorine; it certainly differs greatly from the smell of electrical ozone."

about insulated $\ominus$. Having also worked a good deal on nitrification and obtained a number of novel facts relative to that interesting chemical process, I could fill up another letter with a summary statement of them, but there being no space left, I am forced to give you an account of those researches another time and confine myself to the simple remark, that in a number of cases the formation of a nitrate passes through that of a Nitrite and ozonised oxigen only is capable of oxidizing a nitrite into a nitrate.

Mrs. Schœnbein and the girls are, thank God, pretty well and charge me with their kindest regards to you. The deep wound, caused by the severe loss of our beloved daughter is, of course not yet healed and we cannot think of it but with painful feelings, but upon the whole our minds are more composed and resigned. The sad mishap of Miss Hornblower's caused us much sorrow and we fully sympathize with the suffering, excellent Lady, confidently hoping, that her present state is at the least tolerable. Pray, express her our kindest regards.

Now my dear Faraday excuse kindly the immensurate length of a badly written letter and don't be long to acknowledge it.

For ever

Your's

most faithfully

Bâle Dec. 11. 1860.　　　　　　　　　C. F. SCHOENBEIN.

Don't forget my best compliments to Mrs. Faraday and your Niece.

Faraday to Schœnbein.

Royal Institution 11 January 1861

MY DEAR FRIEND

Whether this letter be long or short, I will write to you, for I see by my book of dates (I date and enter all the letters I receive from abroad) that I have neglected you too long. But all things slip out of my mind, I have nothing else to say. Do not estimate my esteem and affection for you by any such measure, as you might draw from my letters, but value it by the length and quality of your own. As for your last, I received it so near the end of the month that I sent it off at once to Dr. Francis, in hopes of seeing it within three days in the Philosophical Magazine. It did not however appear, but I have seen a proof since and it will be given to our men next month.

You really startled me with your independent antozone. What a wonderful thing oxigen is and to think of the $\oplus$ being included in a solid body. I suppose you do not despair of separating it from the fluor spar in its own proper from, whatever that may be; for I hope it can exist by itself. Does heat reduce it to O as it does Θ? Surely you must hold it in your hand like a little struggler for if I understand you rightly it must be a far more abundant body than the *Caesium* of Bunsen[1] and Knoblauch.[2] — For the hold you have already obtained over it, I congratulate you, as I would do if you had obtained a crown, and more than for a new metal.

[1] Robert Bunsen late professor of Chemistry at Heidelberg where he died in 1899. He was born in 1811 at Göttingen.

[2] Karl Hermann Knoblauch was professor of Physics at Halle. He was born in 1820 at Berlin and died in 1895 at Baden-Baden.

In associating Knoblauch's name to Bunsen's Faraday is labouring under a misapprehension. It is Bunsen and Kirchhof to whom we owe the discovery of cæsium in 1860.

But, surely, these wonderful conditions of existence cannot be confined to oxygen alone. I am waiting to hear that you have discovered like parallel states with iodine, or bromine, or hydrogen, and nitrogen. What of nitrogen? is not its apparent quiet simplicity of action a sham? not a show, indeed; but still not the only state in which it can exist. If the compounds which a body can form show something of the state and powers it may have when isolated (as in your Θ O $\oplus$), then what should nitrogen be in its separate state?[1]

You see I do not work — I cannot — but I fancy, and stuff my letter with such fancies (not a fit return) to you — Well, any thing to get a letter back from you.

Now I come to a dead stop; for this cold weather has laid hold of me, and I have either an attack of sciatica, or perhaps something more serious; we shall see in due time.

My dear Wife also feels the infirmity of years and of winter; but we cheer each other up. Miss Hornblower is pretty well, just now. My kindest regards to M. Wiedemann (to whom I wrote the best I could) and our sincere remembrances to Madame Schœnbein

      Ever My dear friend
         Yours
          M. FARADAY.

Faraday to Schœnbein.

19 April 1861

MY DEAR SCHOENBEIN

I had a note from Dr. Shuttleworth, and in due time called on him and received your very precious packet and letter very safe. I write solely to thank you for it. At

---

[1] For this passage, beginning at "But, surely, these wonderful conditions" see also Bence Jones vol. 2. p. 441.

the same time I may say, that I have verified your results, having repeated the experiments you described in the first part of your letter. I used as little as possible of the fluor spar, but I hope more will be found, or that you will discover how to prepare such a combination, for I am sure that having proceeded so far, and obtained Antozone in the free state with that concentration, which it must have, as it leaves the bruised spar, you cannot stop until you obtain it in the concentrate and separate state. But take care you do not poison yourself.

Your nitrification results are most interesting, and important, and I trust that you will lead them on to a full development and application. You deserve some reward for your labour; and though you have that which consists in the respect, praise, and honour, which philosophers award to you, yet there would be no objection to some of the money power, which ordinary men value and which is so often obtained by them in applying the thoughts of the thinkers.

I am still dull, stupid, and forgetful. I wish a discovery would turn up with me, that I might answer you in a decent, respectable way. But it will not.

Ever My dear Schœnbein
Yours
M. Faraday.

Schœnbein to Faraday.

My dear Faraday

Mr. P. Merian, the well know Geologist and one of the most intimate friends of mine at Bâle, going to England, I send you through him some bits of the antozoniferous Fluorspar of Wœlsendorf, which I hope will prove acceptable to you.

Last easter I went to Munic in search for that interesting material, and was lucky enough to find some there. It is true, the spar I got is not so richly charged with antozone as that was, of which I sent you a small specimen some time ago, but contains enough of it as to enable you to repeat all the experiments, I described in one of my former letters.

Part of the last midsummer holidays I, with my two youngest daughters, spent at Seelisberg near the lake of Lucerne, part of them at Combe Varin a quiet green spot on the heights of the Jura mountains, and returned to Bâle, but last Wednesday, refreshed in body and mind, both of which were rather tired and lame by hard working. Later I shall give you a summary account of my recent doings and the results obtained, which are rather curious and out of the way facts, not deficient, as I should think, of scientific interest. They refer to the so called simple halogenous bodies, principally to Jodine, which substances, as you well known, I consider to be oxy-compounds, i. e. Ozonides. The novel facts ascertained are by no means contradictory to that heretical notion; on the contrary, I think them to be highly in favor of it. At any rate, by that hypothesis I was led to the discovery of the facts alluded to.

Mrs. Schœnbein and my daughters are, thank God, doing pretty well and charge me with their best complements to you and in begging you to remember me most friendly to Mrs. Faraday

I am
    my dear Faraday
      Your's
       most faithfully

Bâle August 17th 1861.   C. F. SCHOENBEIN.

Faraday to Schœnbein.

Royal Institution 19 Septr. 1861

MY DEAR SCHOENBEIN

I lost the sight of Mr. Merian, for when he came to town I was at Newcastle; — when I came to town he was at Manchester (where I was not); — and when he returned I was away: — I am sent out of town a good deal now; — sometimes a little Trinity business,[1] more generally for rest and health. But I have the Fluorspar and thank you very sincerely for it — and I have tried a few of your experiments with it.

When you send me such things, I long for the power I once had, of taking possession by reading, of all new facts and making them my own; always in honourable trust for the discoverer. Now that is changed, and when I tried to compare former experiments with the more recent, I became confused: and so either in reading such papers as yours, or in trying to lay their matter before others I become confused, — forgetting the facts. So you must bear with me, yet not forgetting me; for I long to know all you do. No wonder that my remembrance fails me, for I shall complete my 70 years next Sunday (the 22); — and during these 70 years I have had a happy life; which still remains happy because of hope and content.

I look forward (?) to your new results with great interest; but I am becoming more and more timid when I strive to collate hypotheses relating to the chemical constitution of matter: I cannot help thinking sometimes whether there is not some state or condition of which our present notions give us very little idea, and which yet would reveal to us a flood, a world of real knowledge, — a world of facts available both by practical applications and their illustrations of first principles:

---

[1] In 1861, Bence Jones tells us, Faraday gave ten reports to the Trinity House and was much occupied with the adjustment of the illuminating apparatus to the lamp flames in the lighthouses (vol. 2. p. 437).

and yet I cannot shape the idea into a definite form or reach it by any trial facts that I can devise; and that being the case, I drop the attempt, and imagine that all the preceding thought has just been a dreaminess and no more; and so there is an end of it.[1]

Good bye My dear friend — Our kindest thoughts to Mrs. Schœnbein and the girls. I pass now and then the place where one of them reposes and go in and look at the place.

Miss Hornblower is deeply subjected to physical pain — We scarcely expect her to survive from week to week.

Ever My dear Schœnbein
Your's
M. FARADAY.

Schœnbein to Faraday.[2]

MY DEAR FARADAY

I have been busily occupied with my favorite study, and have found out several new facts regarding the allotropic states of oxigen, their changeability one into another, and nitrification, and I am inclined to believe that the results obtained are not quite void of scientific interest.

After many fruitless attempts at isolating ozone from an "ozonide", I have atlast succeeded in performing that exploit; and have also found out simple tests for distinguishing with the greatest ease ozone from its antipode, "antozone". As to the production of ozone by purely chemical means, the whole secret consists in dissolving pure manganate of potash

---

[1] Among the letters written by Faraday during the period of his decline this passage is quoted by Bence Jones (vol. 2. p. 442).

[2] This letter is reprinted from Phil. Mag. S. 4. vol. 23. 1862. p. 466 to which Faraday sent it under the following title: "On the allotropic states of oxygen and on nitrification." It is not dated, but as Faraday received it "a week or two ago", it was written in April 1862.

in pure oil of vitriol and introducing into the green solution pure peroxide of barium, when ozone mixed with common oxygen will make its appearance, as you may easily perceive by your nose and other tests. By means of the ozone so prepared, I have rapidly oxidized silver at the temperature of — 20^0 C., and by inhaling it produced a capital "catarrh".

Regarding nitrification, the most important fact I have discovered is the generation of nitrite of ammonia out of water and nitrogen, i. e. atmospheric air, which is certainly a most wonderful and wholly unexpected thing. To state the fact in the most general manner, it may be said that the salt mentioned is always produced if water be evaporated in contact with atmospheric air. This may be shown in a variety of ways. Let, for instance, a piece of clean linen drenched with distilled water dry in the open air, moisten it then with pure water, and you will find that the liquid wrung out of the linen and acidulated with dilute sulphuric acid (chemically pure) will strike a blue colour with starch-paste containing iodide of potassium, by the by, the most delicate test for the nitrites. It is therefore a matter of course that shirts, handkerchiefs, table-cloths, in fact all linen, etc., must contain appreciable quantities of nitrite of ammonia; and if the chemistry of England be not entirely different from that of Switzerland, you will find the same thing at the Royal Institution. The purest water, suffered to evaporate spontaneously in the open air, will after some time have taken up enough nitrite of ammonia (continually being formed at the evaporating surface) to produce the nitrite reaction. If you make use of water holding a little potash, or any other alkali, in solution, the same results will be obtained, i. e. the nitrite of that base will be formed (of course in small quantity). The most convenient way of performing the experiment is to moisten a bit of filtering-paper with a dilute solution of chemically pure potash etc., and to suspend it for twenty-four hours in the open air. On examining the paper it will be found to contain a perceptible quantity of a nitrite, which by a longer exposure of course increases. But you may still more rapidly convince yourself of the correctness of my statements, if you heat pure water to a temperature of 50° or 60° C in a porcelain basin, and suspend over the evaporating surface bands of filtering-paper soaked with a weak solution of potash, soda, or the carbonates of these bases. Within a very short time (in ten minutes or 20) there will enough of the nitrite accumulate in the paper to produce the reactions of the salt. I enclose a bit of paper treated in that way for a couple of hours, and by laying it upon a watchglass and pouring over it acidulated starch-paste containing iodide of potassium, you will perceive the effect produced. The fact which I have ascertained, that the purest water mixed with a little chemically pure sulphuric acid or potash and kept for some time evaporating in the open air at a temperature of 50° or 60° C (the loss of the liquid being now and then restored) contains, in the first case a perceptible quantity of ammonia, and, in the second case, of nitrous acid, may now he easily accounted for. You know that about eighteen months ago I found that, during the slow combustion of phosphorus in moist atmospheric air, very perceptible quantities of nitrite of ammonia are formed, and drew from that fact the inference that the salt is engendered by 3 equivalents of water combining directly with 2 equivalents of nitrogen. Now there is to me hardly any doubt that the production of that nitrite is due to the evaporation of water taking place about the phosphorus, whose temperature, in consequence of its burning state, proves to be higher than that of the surrounding medium, and the fact alluded to must therefore be considered only as a particular case of a general rule. The same remark applies to the formation of nitrite of ammonia which takes place during the rapid combustion of charcoal, etc. in atmospheric air; combustion, as such, has, I believe, nothing to do with that formation. I must not omit to tell you that by means of a large copper still, properly heated, and taking care not to introduce too much water into the vessel at once, I can prepare in a very short time several pints of water with which the reaction of nitrite of ammonia may be produced in the most striking manner. I hope before long to have an opportunity of sending you some of this water.

I cannot finish my letter without saying a word or two about nitrification in general, a fact hitherto so much enveloped in obscurity. I think the matter is now clear enough. The evaporation of water is continually going on in the atmosphere, and along with it the generation of nitrite of ammonia. Now, this salt being put in contact with the alkaline bases or their carbonates, nitrites of potash and the other alkalies are formed, which afterwards gradually become oxidized into nitrates. In our rainy countries these salts are washed away almost as soon als formed, and carried into the springs, rivers, etc.; and there is therefore no accumulation of them as in the East Indies, etc.

That the formation of our nitrite out of water and nitrogen is a fact highly important for vegetation need hardly be stated. Indeed each plant, by continually evaporating water into the atmosphere, becomes a generator of nitrite of ammonia, preparing, if not all, at least part of its nitrogenous food, and the same thing takes place in the ground on which it stands. I am therefore inclined to think that our friend Liebig is right in asserting that no plant wants any artificial supply of ammonia, or of matters producing that compound, there being enough of it offered by natural means. Having communicated the results of any researches on the subjects mentioned above to the Academy of Munich, I hope they will soon be published.

I am, my dear Faraday,
Your's most truly
C. F. SCHOENBEIN.

(April 1862)

X

To this paper Faraday added the following note:

(In relation to the peculiar circumstances under which oxygen and nitrogen combine, it may be worth while here to refer to the results obtained by Dr. Bence Jones (Phil. Trans. 1851, p. 407, etc.), where the direct union of these gases in all cases of combustion in air is described.[1] Schœnbein's results depend upon evaporation. — M. F.)

Faraday to Schœnbein.

The Green Hampton Court 22 April 1862

MY DEAR FRIEND

I received yours a week or two ago and was so much struck with the philosophic matter in it, that I sent it off at once to the Phil. Mag., so that I have not your letter with me, nor have I the power of ascertaining (being here) when I wrote to you last. I did not think it had been long ago, but I know that after a month or five weeks, I lose all count of the interval of time. I am glad you do not forget me and I thank you heartily for reproving me, but alas that does not mend the matter, i. e. the memory, and you must just bear with me whilst I go on failing.

I have not made Nitrite from the atmosphere yet, by your method, but the paper you sent me astonishes me by its power, when tested. I think that discovery very great. You are indeed a wonderful man and a great encouragement to all

---

[1] Dr. Bence Jones in 1851 published his researches on nitrification which we can summarize as follows: 1. That the action of oxygen takes place in the body, not only on hydrogen, carbon, sulphur, phosphorus, but also on nitrogen. 2. That in all cases of combustion, if ammonia be present, it will be converted partly into nitric acid. 3. That the nitrogen of the air is not indifferent in ordinary cases of combustion, but it gives rise to minute quantities of nitric acid (see also Phil Mag. 1851. p. 726).

philosophers, young and old, to persevere. In *continuing to think* you remind me of Newton and his results and reward.

For myself I am well and happy, but unproductive. Whilst I struggled against nature, I often made myself ill and weary, but since I resign myself I am far better and quite contented. It would be strange, if I were not — for though I fall out of the routes of the philosophers, I do not lose my friends. Ever My dear Schœnbein

Your friend

M. FARADAY.

Schœnbein to Faraday.

MY DEAR FARADAY.

Professor Eisenlohr[1] of Carlsruhe a most intimate friend of mine is going to London and wishing to get introduced to you, I write these few lines to recommend him to your kindness. You will, I am quite sure, be highly pleased with the personal acquaintance of that most excellent and amiable man, who by the bye, is a great admirer of you. Within a few days I shall leave Bâle for Goettingen, where I intend to spend part of our Midsummer holidays with my friends there: Woehler, Weber,[2] Wagner[3] etc. Having worked rather hard these last eight or ten months, I feel myself a little tired and my mind now wants some rest and relaxation. I trust, you have put yourself out of the way during the

[1] Wilhelm Eisenlohr, professor of Physics at the Polytechnic Institute at Carlsruhe. He was born in 1799 at Pforzheim and died in 1872 at Carlsruhe.

[2] Wilhelm Eduard Weber, was professor of Physics at Göttingen, Leipzig and again at Göttingen (1849) He was born in 1804 at Wittenberg and died in 1891 at Göttingen.

[3] Johann Rudolph Wagner, professor of Physics at the Polytechnic Institute at Nürnberg, later at the University at Würzburg. He was born in 1823 at Leipzig and died in 1880 at Würzburg

monster exhibition, not to be trodden down by the crowds of the foreign visitators invading the Royal Institution.

Before long you shall have another letter from me telling you something about my late scientific doings, which will perhaps be interesting to you.

In begging you to give my kindest regards to Mrs. Faraday, I am my dear friend

Your's most faithfully

Bâle July 18th 1862   C. F. SCHOENBEIN.

Faraday to Schœnbein.

DEAR SCHOENBEIN [1]

Again and again I tear up my letters, for I write nonsense. I cannot spell or write a line continuously. Whether I shall recover — this confusion — do not know.

I will not write any more. My love to you

ever affectionately yours

M. FARADAY.

When collecting letters and material for the purpose of writing a life of Faraday Dr. Bence Jones was anxious to have the original copies of Faradays letters to Schœnbein. He therefore, at Mrs. Faradays suggestion, expressed a wish to that effect in a note to Schœnbein dated June 19. 1868. Schœnbein very readily complied with this request, and in so doing wrote a reply which characterizes him so well, and once again embodies the ties of attachment by which he was bound to Faraday, in such touching terms, that we cannot refrain from reproducing it here.

[1] This is Faraday's last letter to Schœnbein and is included in the second volume of Bence Jone's Life p. 450.

Schœnbein to Dr. Bence Jones.

MY DEAR SIR

Agreeably to the wishes expressed in the lines with which you favored me the other day, I send you 34 letters written to me by our deeply lamented friend, during the course of many years. Certainly the collection is not complete; some of the letters may be lost, and a number of them mixt up with letters from other friends, which I cannot find out at this present moment.

The last letter I received from Faraday consists of only a few lines, hardly written, and written with a trembling hand; it is dated Septbr. 18th 1862 and laid by. From its contents you may easily imagine that, from delicacy of feelings, I did not dare answering that letter; for what could I say or write to our poor friend? and so our correspondence, kept up for a quarter of a century, dropt, not to be taken up again. Being so deeply attached to him, I need not tell you, that the interruption of our epistolary intercourse grieved me to the innermost of my heart.....

It is a matter of course, that you may keep the letters as long as you like, and I should be very happy, if Wheatstone happened to be Your "tabellarius".

Pray present my kindest regards to Mrs. Faraday and believe me

Your's
most faithfully

Bâle June 27. 1868.　　　　　　　　　　C. F. SCHOENBEIN.

CONTENTS

———•·———

		PAGE

1. *Schoenbein to Faraday.* Bâle. May 17. 1836.

   Inactivity of iron and other metals and their relation to nitric acid. Schœnbein apologizes for his poor English . . . 1

2. *Schoenbein to Faraday.* Bâle. Sept. 12. 1836.

   Insufficiency of Faraday's attempt to explain passivity of iron by a film of oxide. Schœnbein's and Herschel's theories of molecular change . . · 7

3. *Schoenbein to Faraday.* Bâle. Nov. 26. 1836.

   Inactivity of iron: Mousson's theory of a film of nitrous acid is wrong. Schœnbein unwilling to assume new force. Faraday an honorary member of Phil. Soc. of Bâle. Enquiries about an electrical machine 13

4. *Schoenbein to Faraday.* Bâle. Dec. 26. 1836.

   Transference of active and inactive state of iron from wire to wire   17

5. *Faraday to Schoenbein.* London. Jan. 28. 1837.

   Schœnbein's paper sent to Phil. Mag. Faraday not yet satisfied with his own explication. Expresses thanks for his election   21

6. *Faraday to Schoenbein.* London. Feb. 6. 1837.

   On publication of papers by Roy. Soc. Price of electrical machine   22

7. *Schoenbein to Faraday.* Bâle. April 27. 1837.

   Voltaic condition of iron produced by peroxide of lead. Noad's observations and Nobili's colours 23

8. *Faraday to Schoenbein.* London. May 2. 1837.

   Electrical machine and Phil. Mag. paper sent off 27

PAGE

9. *Faraday to Schoenbein.* London. May 4. 1837.
Schœnbein's letter sent to Phil. Mag. 29

10. *Schoenbein to Faraday.* Bâle. July 9. 1837.
Schœnbein dedicates: "Das Verhalten des Eisens zum Sauerstoff" to Faraday. Berzelius has written to Schœnbein. Crosse's insects. 29

11. *Faraday to Schoenbein.* London. Sept. 21. 1837.
Thanks for dedication of book. Crosse's insects 32

12. *Schoenbein to Faraday.* Bâle. Nov. 5. 1837.
First meeting with Faraday. Close examination of inactivity of bismuth: Andrews' work. On inactivity of nickel and cobalt, with Degen. Preservation of iron against sea water by Hartley 34

13. *Schoenbein to Faraday.* Bâle. Dec. 31. 1837.
Voltaic relation of peroxides, platina and inactive iron. Definition of chemical action. Peroxide of silver and iron . 42

14. *Faraday to Schoenbein.* London. Jan. 22. 1838.
Letter sent to Phil. Mag. Faraday's views. Unfortunate letter to Hachette 47

15. *Schoenbein to Faraday.* Bâle. June 14. 1838.
Fechner's attacks on contact theory 49

16. *Faraday to Schoenbein.* London. July 30. 1838.
Anything from Schœnbein is worth printing. Poggendorff in England. Fechner 50

17. *Schoenbein to Faraday.* Bâle. Aug. 12. 1838.
Fechner and Pfaff are voltaists. Rosenschöld on voltaic piles. Change of colour and voltaic currents 52

18. *Schoenbein to Faraday.* Bâle. Sept. 15. 1838.
Polarisation of fluid compound bodies 55

19. *Schoenbein to Faraday.* Bâle. Oct. 20. 1838.
Becquerel's theory of secundary currents is erroneous. Voltaic polarisation of fluid and solid bodies. Controversy on source of current electricity on the continent 55

20. *Schoenbein to Faraday.* Bâle. Feb 18. 1839.
Polarisation. Chlorine is like a peroxide. Hydrogen peroxide and passivity of iron 59

21. *Faraday to Schoenbein.* London. April 8. 1839.

 Approval of Schœnbein's conclusions. Moll's "Decline of Science in England". Induction. Marianini 61

22. *Schoenbein to Faraday.* Bâle. April 21. 1839.

 Voltaic researches and their bearing on organic chemistry. Chemical theory of galvanism 64

23. *Schoenbein to Faraday.* Bâle. July 3. 1839.

 Electrical state does not influence chemical behaviour. Berzelius' fundamental idea is wrong. De la Rive's and Becquerel's views on galvanism also. Schœnbein's French pamphlet at the Brit. Ass. Grant of money 65

24. *Faraday to Schoenbein.* London. Aug. 17. 1839.

 Brit. Ass. and granting of money. Becquerel's pile of acid and alkali 68

25. *Faraday to Schoenbein.* London. Sept. 24. 1839.

 Schœnbein returning to Switzerland 69

26. *Schoenbein to Faraday.* Bâle. Dec. 17. 1839.

 Schœnbein on importance of Faraday's papers on induction. Views on difference between magneto-electrical and voltaic induction. Definition of static electricity. Jacobi shows that intensity of a current is independent of its quantity . . 70

27. *Schoenbein to Faraday.* Bâle. April. 4. 1840.

 Phosphorous smell developed by electricity and its relations to chlorine. Faraday's and Grove's latest researches . . . 72

28. *Faraday to Schoenbein.* London. April 24. 1840.

 Faraday's observations on electrical smell, and on Grove's transfer of matter. Hare's criticism of his induction. Origin of electricity in voltaic pile 80

29. *Schoenbein to Faraday.* Bâle. Dec. 20. 1840.

 Flattering letter from Berzelius. Schœnbein asks about battery, to continue his researches on ozone 83

30. *Faraday to Schoenbein.* London. March 27. 1841.

 Faraday feels permanently worse. Schœnbein should apply to Grove for battery 84

31. *Schoenbein to Faraday.* Bâle. April 8. 1841.

 Lectures have kept him from working on ozone. His battery yields 15 cub. inches of gas per minute 86

PAGE

32. *Faraday to Schoenbein.* London. June 4. 1841.
    Faraday is to spend some time in Switzerland, avoiding all scientific thought 88

33. *Faraday to Schoenbein.* Zug. Sept. 7. 1841.
    Faraday hopes to see Schœnbein at Bâle. The stay has done him good 89

34. *Schoenbein to Faraday.* Bâle. Sept. 27. 1841.
    Schœnbein did not see Faraday at Bâle 90

35. *Faraday to Schoenbein.* London. Oct. 14. 1841.
    Faraday exceedingly well in health. Has not yet looked at a scientific journal 90

36. *Schoenbein to Faraday.* Bâle. April 9. 1842.
    Schœnbein cautions Faraday not to overwork himself. His "Reisetagebuch". Is working on electrolysis and peculiar condition of iron 91

37. *Schoenbein to Faraday.* Bâle July 8. 1842.
    Schœnbein prevented from attending the Brit. Ass. at Manchester. Hydroelectric currents are due to chemical action. Is working on peculiar state of iron. Voltaic pile out of mere cast iron 93

38. *Faraday to Schoenbein.* Tynemouth. Aug. 10. 1842.
    Faraday pretty nearly excluded as a workman of science. Author of "Mittheilungen" 95

39. *Schoenbein to Faraday.* Bâle. Aug. 22. 1842.
    Inactive iron more and more inexplicable. Moser's breath-images. "Reisetagebuch" and the Germans 97

40. *Faraday to Schoenbein.* London. Feb. 18. 1843.
    Faraday feels himself unworthy of picture drawn by Schœnbein in "Reisetagebuch". Herschel on inactive iron. Moser's images. Faraday working on electricitiy of high pressure steam. Peltier on space 101

41. *Schoenbein to Faraday.* Bale. April 26. 1843.
    Translation of "Reisetagebuch". On Faraday's induction and steampaper. Grove's gaseous battery. De la Rive's and Martens' researches 104

42. *Schoenbein to Faraday.* Bâle. May 11. 1843.
    Influence of one ingredient part of a binary compound upon the other 107

PAGE

43. *Faraday to Schoenbein.* London. May 16. 1843.
Translation of "Reisetagebuch". De la Rive in England . . 109

44. *Faraday to Schoenbein.* London. Aug. 8. 1843.
Mr. Vincent willing to translate "Reisetagebuch" 111

45. *Faraday to Schoenbein.* London. Sept. 6. 1843.
Armstrong's steam electric apparatus. "Reisetagebuch" in Athenaeum 113

46. *Schoenbein to Faraday.* Bâle. Feb. 17. 1844.
Schœnbein and Faraday on atomic theory. Grove receives degree of Bâle University 113

47. *Schoenbein to Faraday.* Bâle. March 30. 1844.
Should ozone be isolated Schœnbein will go to York . . 115

48. *Schoenbein to Faraday.* Bâle. March 30. 1844.
Production of Ozone by chemical means 116

49. *Faraday to Schoenbein.* Brighton. April 12. 1844.
Schœnbein's letter on ozone sent to Roy. Soc. Faraday's memory a bad indicator of scientific news 122

50. *Schoenbein to Faraday.* Bâle. April 19. 1844.
Identity of three odoriferous principles. Ozone an halogenous body resembling chlorine. Azote is ozonide of hydrogen . 123

51. *Faraday to Schoenbein.* London. April 29. 1844.
Production of ozone by chemical means is one to surprize and delight his friends 128

52. *Schoenbein to Faraday.* Bâle. May 29. 1844.
Ozone isolated. Nature of azote. Book on ozone . . . 130

53. *Schoenbein to Faraday.* Bâle May 31. 1844.
Schœnbein's ozonide of potassium was not pure 134

54. *Faraday to Schoenbein.* London. June 19. 1844.
Introduction for Dr. Holland 135

55. *Schoenbein to Faraday.* Bâle. Aug. 27. 1844.
Book on ozone. Schœnbein cannot be at York. Does the Brit. Ass. give grants of money? 135

		PAGE

56. *Faraday to Schoenbein.* Dover. Sept. 14. 1844.
   Accident to Faraday's brother. Faraday is reviving his health at Dover. Grove is to report on Schœnbein's book on ozone at York 137

57. *Faraday to Schoenbein.* London. Oct. 25. 1844.
   Faraday at inquest at Durham. Brit. Ass. and paper on ozone. Faraday says: "I am working but cannot get on" . . . 139

58. *Schoenbein to Faraday.* Bâle. Nov. 25. 1844.
   Meeting at Milan: Piria says ozone is nitrous acid. Ozone is not nitrous acid 140

59. *Faraday to Schoenbein.* London. Feb. 20. 1845.
   Faraday's memory becoming more and more treacherous. Condensation of gases: oxygen 143

60. *Schoenbein to Faraday.* Bâle. June 4. 1845.
   Schœnbein will read his paper on ozone at Cambridge himself 145

61. *Faraday to Schoenbein.* London. June 14. 1845.
   Faraday hopes to see Schœnbein in town . , . . . 146

62. *Schoenbein to Faraday.* Bâle. Oct. 20. 1845.
   Relation of ozone to nitrogen. Nitrification. Bleaching by means of ozone 146

63. *Faraday to Schoenbein.* Brighton. Nov. 13. 1845.
   Faraday working very hard: direct relation between magnetism and light, also electricity and light 148

64. *Schoenbein to Faraday.* Bâle. Dec. 30. 1845.
   Schœnbein on Faraday's discovery. Schœnbein on the oxides of nitrogen. Dr. Neef's discovery of relation of light to electricity 149

65. *Schoenbein to Faraday.* Bâle. Feb. 27. 1846.
   Schœnbein's water proof paper 151

66. *Faraday to Schoenbein.* London. March 5. 1846.
   Schœnbein's paper sent to Mr. Dickenson 154

67. *Schoenbein to Faraday.* Bâle. March 18. 1846.
   Transparent substance from common paper. Explosive cotton. Electrical properties of his prepared paper 155

68. *Schoenbein to Faraday.* Bâle. March 23. 1846.
   Preliminary experiments with his explosive cotton 158

		PAGE
69.	*Schoenbein to Faraday.* Bâle March 24. 1846. Bell made from Schœnbein's transparent paper	159
70.	*Schoenbein to Faraday.* London. Aug. 22. 1846. Schœnbein in England. Death of Faraday's brother	159
71.	*Faraday to Schoenbein.* London. Aug. 24. 1846. Faraday suggests experimenting with Schœnbein at the Royal Institute	160
72.	*Faraday to Schoenbein.* Tunbridge Wells. Aug. 25. 1846. Guncotton. Experiments at Woolwich	160
73.	*Faraday to Schoenbein.* London. Dec. 18. 1846. Faraday on guncotton-Schœnbein. Accident to Mr. Lancaster. Brande to lecture on guncotton. Faraday prevented from working through an affection of the knee	162
74.	*Schoenbein to Faraday.* Bâle. Dec. 26. 1846. Schœnbein's nitrate formulae. History of guncotton and French claims. Analyses. Resinous matter from sugar	164
75.	*Schoenbein to Faraday.* Bâle. July 1. 1847. Written in sympathetic ink. Test for ozone	171
76.	*Faraday to Schoenbein.* London. Oct. 23. 1847. Faraday overworked. On Schœnbein's test for ozone	172
77.	*Schoenbein to Faraday.* Bâle. Nov. 19. 1847. Action of charcoal on chlorine etc., which he still regards as oxycompounds. Change of colour of starch-paste by means of solar rays	173
78.	*Faraday to Schoenbein.* Brighton. March 17. 1848. Faraday can no longer remember anything of the past. Note by Mrs. Faraday	178
79.	*Schoenbein to Faraday.* Bâle. Sept. 1848. All metals oxidized by ozone. Test for arsenic and antimony. Oxidation of phosphorus in ozone	179
80.	*Faraday to Schoenbein.* London. Dec. 15. 1848. Faraday's memory worse than ever. Has worked on crystalline polarity of bismuth. Plückers work	182

PAGE

81. *Schoenbein to Faraday.* Bâle. March 27. 1850.
    Schoenbein wishes paper to be read on ozone at the Royal Institute 184

82. *Faraday to Schoenbein.* London. May 11. 1850.
    Faraday will give lecture on ozone himself. Would like a list of suitable experiments 185

83. *Faraday to Schoenbein.* London. Nov. 19. 1850.
    Bleaching by means of ozone. Faraday says oxygen is cause of the variations of terrestrial magnetism 186

84. *Schoenbein to Faraday.* Bâle. Nov. 25. 1850.
    Schœnbein's sulphuret paper, even in the dark, becomes brown again 189

85. *Faraday to Schoenbein.* Brighton. Dec. 9. 1850.
    Faraday has received ozonometer etc. Approval of Schœnbein's theory of atmospheric electricity. Speculation on nature of insulated oxygen 189

86. *Faraday to Schoenbein.* Brighton. Dec. 13. 1850.
    Testing of Schœnbein's ozonometer at Brighton 192

87. *Faraday to Schoenbein.* London. March. 5. 1851.
    Schœnbein's papers sent to the Chem. Soc. and the Medico-Chirurgical Society. Gaseous oxygen, says Faraday, looses its magnetic properties in compounds 193

88. *Faraday to Schoenbein.* Hastings. April 19. 1851.
    Faraday poor in health. Lecture on ozone in six weeks. Atmospheric magnetism 195

89. *Schoenbein to Faraday.* Bâle. July 25. 1851.
    Portrait of Euler brought by Mr. Sarasin 196

90. *Faraday to Schoenbein.* Tynemouth. Aug. 1. 1851.
    Faraday's ozone evening went of wonderfully well, and excited great interest 198

91. *Faraday to Schoenbein.* London. Dec. 16. 1851.
    Faraday working away at magnetism. On experiments . . 199

92. *Schoenbein to Faraday.* Bâle. May 7. 1852.
    Schœnbein's views on oxygen: "Jove of the philosophical Olympos" 200

		PAGE
93.	*Faraday to Schoenbein.* London. June 2. 1852.	
	Faraday sends three papers on lines of magnetic force. Rev. Mr. Sidney on ozone in vegetables	203
94.	*Schoenbein to Faraday.* Bâle. Aug. 29. 1852	
	A brief note delivered by Dr. Whewell	204
95.	*Schoenbein to Faraday.* Bâle. Oct. 17. 1852.	
	Schœnbein's memoir on oxygen. Working on colour of oxy-compounds. On modern chemists	205
96.	*Faraday to Schoenbein.* Brighton. Dec. 9. 1852.	
	Faraday quite worn out with work. Schœnbein's colour theories quite excite him. Their relation to Stokes' researches. Organic chemistry is a sealed book to Faraday	207
97.	*Schoenbein to Faraday.* Bâle. Dec. 18. 1852.	
	Connections between Stokes' researches and Schoenbein's. On the optical action of nitrous gas upon solutions of protosalts of iron	210
98.	*Schoenbein to Faraday.* Bâle. July 11. 1853.	
	Nature of ozone settled in Bunsen's laboratory by Baumert. Schœnbein sceptical	212
99.	*Faraday to Schoenbein.* London. July 25. 1853.	
	Faraday on table turning. Has lectured on ozone	214
100.	*Schoenbein to Faraday.* Bâle. Sept. 24. 1853.	
	Schœnbein at Munich. Met Liebig, who asked him to read a paper on ozone	216
101	*Faraday to Schoenbein.* London. Jan. 27. 1854.	
	Faraday working on telegraph wires. On Schœnbein's meeting with Liebig	219
102.	*Schoenbein to Faraday.* Bâle. Feb. 10. 1854.	
	Schœnbein's views on chemical action of light, heat, and electricity. Disapproves strongly of Davy's views	221
103.	*Schoenbein to Faraday.* Bâle. April 9. 1854.	
	Schœnbein, at Liebig's request, has compiled a book on ozone	226
104.	*Schoenbein to Faraday.* Bâle. May 4. 1854.	
	Letter of introduction for Dr. Stehlin	228

PAGE

105. *Faraday to Schœnbein.* London. May 15. 1854.
Repetition of Schœnbein's experiments with Dahlia colours. List of letters written and received 229

106. *Schœnbein to Faraday.* Bâle. July 4. 1854.
Catalytic action and other changes referable to allotropic modification 232

107. *Faraday to Schœnbein.* London. Sept. 15. 1854.
Faraday hesitates publishing Schœnbein's views on chemists. Dr. Drew and Airy on ozone observations in England . . 236

108. *Schœnbein to Faraday.* Bâle. Feb. 27. 1855.
Passage on Faraday in Schœnbein's "Menschen und Dinge". Wiedemann on electrolysis 238

109. *Faraday to Schœnbein.* Hastings. April 6. 1855.
Faraday says: "The imperishable marble of your book will surely flatter." Working on lines of magnetic force . . 242

110. *Schœnbein to Faraday.* Bâle. May 26. 1855.
Attempts to separate the two forms of oxygen from peroxides. Houzeau's work. Separation of some ozonized oxygen from peroxide of silver. Wiedemann on electrolysis. Picnic to the Gempenstollen 245

111. *Faraday to Schœnbein.* London. Nov. 6. 1855.
Repetition of Schœnbein's experiments. Different effects. Faraday's high opinion of Wiedemann 252

112. *Schœnbein to Faraday.* Bâle. Nov. 30. 1855.
Schœnbein at home. Cholera at Bâle. Allotropic forms of oxygen. Transformation of oxygen into ozone in mushrooms 254

113. *Faraday to Schœnbein.* London. March 21. 1856.
Faraday cannot recollect any news 263

114. *Schœnbein to Faraday.* Bâle. March 29. 1856.
Easter-Day at Mrs. Wiedemann's house 264

115. *Faraday to Schœnbein.* London. April 11. 1856.
Faraday sends a volume of his researches by Mr. Roscoe Note by Mrs. Faraday 266

116. *Schœnbein to Faraday.* Bâle. April 26. 1856.
>Schœnbein hopes to live to see Faraday's proof of the identity of magnetism and gravity 267

117. *Schœnbein to Faraday.* Bâle. Sept. 20. 1856.
>Schœnbein's trip to North Germany. Working on catalysis, and formation of formic acid. Miss Schœnbein is anxious to spend a year in England. Wiedemann's investigations. Mr. Merian in England 269

118. *Faraday to Schœnbein.* London. Oct. 14. 1856.
>Faraday not headstrong enough for much work. Paper on relation of gold to light. Miss Schœnbein and Miss Hornblower . 273

119. *Schœnbein to Faraday.* Bâle. Nov. 10. 1856.
>Miss Schœnbein's plans. On nitrification 275

120. *Faraday to Schœnbein.* London. Jan. 23. 1857.
>Miss Schœnbein. Faraday working on gold 279

121. *Schœnbein to Faraday.* Bâle. Feb. 9. 1857.
>Miss Schœnbein. Schœnbein on oxidizing effects. Awarded the Maximilian medal 280

122. *Schœnbein to Faraday.* Bâle. April 25. 1857.
>Miss Schœnbein's visit to England. Schœnbein in Munich: poisoned bread from China. Transformation of oxygen into ozone by oil of bitter almonds 282

123. *Faraday to Schœnbein.* London. May 7. 1857.
>Miss Schœnbein's visit to England 284

124. *Schœnbein to Faraday.* Bâle. Sept. 17. 1857.
>Miss Schœnbein's visit to England. Schœnbein on his researches on oil of bitter almonds, nitrification and his peroxide test paper 285

125. *Faraday to Schœnbein.* London. Sept. 25. 1857.
>Miss Schœnbein at Stamford Hill 292

126. *Faraday to Schœnbein.* London. Nov. 24. 1857.
>Clarke on ozone in atmospheric air. Faraday working on relation of time to actions at a distance 293

PAGE

127. *Faraday to Schoenbein.* London. No date.
    Fragment of letter partly destroyed by acid. Faraday on action at a distance. Miss Schœnbein. From context date about November 1857 296

128. *Schoenbein to Faraday.* Bâle. Feb. 15. 1858.
    Schœnbein as a politician 297

129. *Schoenbein to Faraday.* Bâle. June 25. 1858.
    Further observations on the allotropic modifications of oxygen, and on the compound nature of chlorine, bromine etc. . . 301

130. *Schoenbein to Faraday.* Bâle. June 28. 1858.
    Letter of introduction for Prof. Vischer, the "god father" of ozone 307

131. *Faraday to Schoenbein.* London. July 28. 1858.
    Faraday doubtful about sending Schœnbein's letter to the Phil. Mag. owing to his criticisms of Davy's views 308

132. *Schoenbein to Faraday.* Speicher. Aug. 4. 1858.
    Schœnbein sees no harm in giving his views on Davy to the British public. Staying at Appenzell 309

133. *Schoenbein to Faraday.* Sept. 1858.
    Meeting of German Association at Carlsruhe 311

134. *Faraday to Schoenbein.* London. Nov. 13. 1858.
    Faraday practically unable to lecture on ozone without Schœnbein's help. Feels loss of memory seriously. Miss Schœnbein . 314

135. *Faraday to Schoenbein.* London. Nov. 25. 1858.
    Information wanted for preparation of hydrogen peroxide . . 316

136. *Faraday to Schoenbein.* London. Dec. 2. 1858.
    Receipt of some packets acknowledged 318

137. *Faraday to Schoenbein.* London. Jan. 19. 1859.
    Peroxide of barium and lecture on ozone on 25th of Feb. Note by Miss Schœnbein applying for some tickets for Faraday's lecture on ozone. Miss Schœnbein died on the 13th of February 318

138. *Faraday to Schoenbein.* London. Feb. 16. 1859.
    Particulars of Miss Schœnbein's death 319

139. *Schoenbein to Faraday.* Bâle. (Feb. 25.) 1859.
    Schœnbein touched by expressions of sympathy at Miss Schœnbein's death. Has begun lecturing again 322

140. *Faraday to Schoenbein.* London. Feb. 24. 1859.
    Faraday anxious to put off his lecture on ozone, owing to Miss Schoenbein's death. Unable to do so 323

141. *Faraday to Schoenbein.* London. April 25. 1859.
    Faraday's lecture on ozone 324

142. *Schoenbein to Faraday.* Bâle. July 19. 1859.
    Schœnbein again working in his laboratory: slow combustion of ether, and the reduction of oxy-compounds 326

143. *Faraday to Schoenbein.* London. Sept. 23. 1859.
    Faraday's 68th birthday. Negative results in electricity, heat, and gravity 329

144. *Schoenbein to Faraday.* Bâle. Oct. 26. 1859.
    Chemical polarisation of neutral oxygen. Tests for hydrogen peroxide 330

145. *Faraday to Schoenbein.* London March 27. 1860.
    Faraday rather poorly and unable to remember things . . 336

146. *Schoenbein to Faraday.* Bâle. March 29. 1860.
    Wiedemann going to England 338

147. *Schoenbein to Faraday.* Bâle. Dec. 11. 1860.
    Minute description of isolation of antozone from Bavarian fluorspar 339

148. *Faraday to Schoenbein.* London. Jan. 11. 1861.
    "You really startle me by your independent antozone," writes Faraday, who himself is unable to work 345

149. *Faraday to Schoenbein.* London. April 19. 1861.
    By repeating Schœnbein's experiments with the fluorspar, Faraday gets his antozone 346

150. *Schoenbein to Faraday.* Bâle. Aug. 17. 1861.
    More antozoniferous fluorspar sent from Wölsendorf . . . 347

151. *Faraday to Schoenbein.* London. Sept. 19. 1861.
    Further experiments with fluorspar 349

PAGE

152. *Schoenbein to Faraday.* Bâle, April 1862.
    Allotropic states of oxygen. Isolation of ozone from an ozonide. General remarks on nitrification. Dr. Bence Jones . . 350

153. *Faraday to Schoenbein.* London. April 22. 1862.
    Schœnbein's nitrite paper sent to the Phil. Mag. Schœnbein and Newton 354

154. *Schoenbein to Faraday.* Bâle. July 18. 1862.
    Letter of introduction for Prof. Eisenlohr, a great admirer of Faraday 355

155. *Faraday to Schoenbein.* London. Sept. 18 1862.
    Faraday's last letter to Schœnbein. Reference to it in a letter to Dr. Bence Jones 356

INDEX

A.
Airy, 238.
Andrews, 35.
Arago, 35.
Armstrong, 113.

B.
Bachofen, 72.
Bancalari, 187.
Barnard, Miss, 293.
Baumert, 223, 311, 317.
Becquerel, 67, 71, 86, 87, 216.
— on Ritter's secondary piles, 56.
— on galvanism, 66.
Bence Jones, 193, 199, 203, 314, 319, 323, 354.
— on nitrification, 355.
— Life of Faraday, 48, 148, 173, 215, 274.
Bernoulli, 268, 311, 317.
Berthollet, 306.
Berzelius, 33, 223.
— on iron, 30, 102.
— electrochemical theory of, 66.
— on ozone, 82, 127, 134
— on water proof paper, 152.
— on guncotton, 158.
— in "Menschen und Dinge", 240.
— to Schœnbein, 30, 40, 83, 134, 153, 158, 163.
Bolley, 193, 196.
Böttger, 164.
Brabant, 49, 50.
Bracconnot, 169.
Brande, 163, 164.
Brodie, 317, 337.
Buch, 240.
Buckland, 61.
Bunsen, 266, 312.
— on ozone, 213, 215.
— on caesium, 345.
Burckhardt, 64, 179, 197.

C.
Cailletet, 144.
Charpentier, 87.
Christie, 73, 81, 116, 122, 129, 143.
Clarke, 294.
Cockerill, 41.
Congreve, 156
Cooper, 69.
Crosse, 31, 33.
Crowdy, 322, 323.
Cuvier, 240.

D.
Daniell, 61, 138, 151.
Davy, 105.
— Schœnbein on, 60, 224, 225, 306, 308, 309.
Degen, 40.
de la Rive, 30, 35, 82, 218, 223.
— on chemical action, 45, 51, 106.
— on Pfaff, 53.
— on galvanism, 66, 67.
— in England, 35, 111.
— book on ozone, 133
— Schœnbein's papers, 137.
— Faraday's discovery, 149.
— to Schœnbein, 53, 137, 149.
Deville, 174.
Dickenson, 154
Dove, 312.
Draper, 191.
Drew, 212, 214, 238.

E.
Eisenlohr, 265.
Euler 196, 198, 199.

F.

Faraday, member of Phil. Soc. of Bâle, 13, 22.
— memoir on iron dedicated to, 29, 32.
— in Schœnbein's book, 101, 104, 109, 204, 242.
— Crosse's insects 31, 33.
— passivity of iron, 7, 21, 28, 62.
— chemical and voltaic action, 45, 48, 51, 82.
— action at a distance, 295, 296.
— magnetism, 194, 199.
— magnetism and light, 148, 149, 150.
— lines of magnetic force, 203.
— polarity of bismuth, 182.
— induction, 48, 52, 63, 70, 105.
— electricity of steam, 103, 105, 110.
— condensation of gases, 144, 203
— diamagnetism of gases, 178, 187.
— oxygen, 187, 190, 191, 194.
— ozone, 81, 185, 188, 191, 192, 194, 195, 197, 198, 315, 317, 318, 320.
— magnecrystallic forces, 183.
— gold, 274, 279, 294.
— ice, 230.
— crystals, 52
— telegraph wires, 221.
— table turning, 214.
— experiments, 199.
— Schœnbein's letters, 33, 50.
— — papers, 51, 185.
Faraday, Mrs. letter to Schœnbein, 179, 267.
Faraday's brother, 137, 143, 159.
Fechner, 49, 51, 52.
Forbes, 90.
Francis, 294, 308, 345.
Frémy 216.

G.

Gould, 227.
Gould, Benjamin, 227.
Graham to Schœnbein, 209.
Grove, 18, 78, 81, 84, 85, 110, 111, 119 138, 229, 274, 323, 326.
— gaseous battery, 106.
— degree at Bâle, 115, 129.
— name for ozone, 124

Grove, gun cotton, 161, 164, 169.
— to Schœnbein, 79, 111, 113, 114, 115, 119, 133, 150, 153, 159, 161, 162, 209.

H.

Hachette, 48, 59.
Hagenbach, 338.
Hare, 82.
Hartley, 39, 40.
Henry, Prof., 32.
Henry, 185.
Herschel, 11, 12, 96, 162.
Hofmann, 210.
Hogg, 162.
Holland, 135.
Hornblower, Miss, 274 ff
Hunt, 103.
Houzeau, 245, 341.

I.

Iselin, 59, 61, 62.

J.

Jacobi, 72.

K.

Kirchhof, 345.
Knoblauch, 345.
Kohl, 101.

L.

Lancaster, 163.
Liebig, 206, 216, 258, 283, 312, 343, 353
— meeting with Schœnbein, 216, 217.
— on ozone, 227, 228, 237.
— to Schœnbein, 227.
Louyet, 161, 169.

M.

Marianini, 63.
Marignac 223.
Martens, 106, 107.
Magnus, 312.
Mayo, Miss, 322.
Merian, Peter, 227, 347, 348.
— his son, 226.
— Rudolf, 268, 272.
Moffat, 252.

Moll, 62.
Moser, 98, 102.
Mousson, 13, 14, 21.
Munk af Rosenschöld, 54.
Murray, 110.

N.

Neef, 151.
Newman, 27.
Newton, 355.
Noad, 27.
Nobili, 24, 27, 43, 48.

P.

Pasteur, 288.
Pelonze, 169.
Peltier, 103, 105, 106.
Pettenkofer, 168.
— to Schœnbein, 174.
Pfaff, 53, 58.
Phillips, letters from Faraday, 7, 62.
Pictet, 144.
Plücker, 183.
Poggendorff, 41, 51, 52, 84, 154.
— becomes voltaist, 50.
— to Schœnbein, 41, 154.
Prater, 103.
Prévost, 159.

R.

Ritter, 30.
— secundary piles, 56, 59.
Roscoe, 266.
Rose, 165, 166, 313.
Rumpf, 318.
Ryhiner, 108, 112.

S.

Schœnbein, an alchemist, 42.
— description by Faraday.
— England etc 6, 30, 34, 66, 69, 70, 114. 116, 145, 159, 160.
— nature and mankind, 99.
— Mittheilungen 92, 94, 96, 99, 101, 105, 109, 113, 243.
— Menschen und Dinge, 217, 239, 241, 256, 258
— Maximilian medal, 28 h.
— Atomic theory, 114.
— Chemistry 64, 187, 188, 190, 206, 225, 258.

Schœnbein, passive iron 1, 7, 10, 23, 30, 36, 60, 94, 98.
— book on, 29, 32, 41.
— gun cotton, 155, 156, 158, 161, 165, 169, 173.
— discovery, 162.
— analysis, 168.
— ozone, 121, 124, 134, 142, 146, 167, 174, 213, 238, 259, 269, 294.
— — first mentioned, 83, 124, 174, 184, 307.
— — formation, 116, 125. 128, 134, 180, 242, 305.
— — tests, 127, 171, 180, 290.
— — book on, 133, 135, 137, 138, 140.
— — and nitrous acid, 140.
— — and antozone, 301, 315, 325, 341, 345, 347, 350.
— galvanisation of metals, 60, 62, 64, 66.
— nitrification, 127, 146, 150, 276, 290, 344, 347, 351, 353.
— electrolysis 98, 106, 114, 151, 223, 233, 341.
— book on Physical Chemistry, 113, 115.
— changes of colour, 54, 205, 208, 222, 230, 236.
— polarisation, 55, 327, 332, 338, 341.
— on Faraday's work, 101, 142, 149.
— meets Liebig, 217.
— to Berzelius, 1, 57, 102, 127, 152, 156, 158, 161.
— to Liebig, 206.
Schœnbein, Miss, 212 ff.
Schweitzer, 251, 253.
Shuttleworth, 346.
Sidney, 203.
Sorel, 41.
Stehlin, 228, 237.
Stokes, 209, 211.

T.

Taylor, 163.
— Richard, 50, 51, 138, 186.

Taylor, Scientific memoirs, 27, 102, 187, 208.
— and Francis, 208.
Thénard, 234.
Thompson, 62, 186, 215.
Twining, 244, 253, 266.

V.

Vincent, translation of Mittheilungen, 112, 243.
— librarian, 221.
Vischer, 174, 184, 307, 308.

W.

Wagner, 355.
Watkins, 111, 145.
Weber, 355.
Whewell, 204, 205, 208, 273.

Wiedemann, 240, 244, 251, 262, 272, 275, 346.
— in England, 338, 339.
— electrolysis, 240, 251.
— magnetic researches, 272.
— Faraday on, 253.
— Eilhard, 265
— Mrs., 265.
Wöhler, 312, 355.
— antozone, 343.
— to Schœnbein, 225.
— to Liebig, 343.
Worringer, 95.

Y.

Yates, 112.

Z.

Zerzog, 286.

CORRIGENDA

page	21 line 7 from bottom read *had*	for *hat*.
»	34 » 9 » » » *language*	» *langage*
»	53 » 9 » top » *consider*	» *osider*.
»	54 note 3 after *"unter"* insert *"dem Einfluss"*.	
»	62 » 2 read *view*	for *new*.
»	65 » 1 » *p. 64*	» *p. 81*.
»	73 note » *electricity*	» *electricity*.
»	73 » » *dependence*	» *dependencé*.
»	76 » » *prevent*	» *piece*.
»	76 » » *piece*	» *peace*.
»	80 » » *unusual*	» *anusual*.
»	130 line 9 from top *shall*	» *shalll*.
»	162 note 2 read *vent*	» *want*.
»	166 » 1 » *i. e.*	» *i. c.*
»	174 » 1 » *met*	» *wet*.
»	208 » 1 » *circumstances*	» *curcumstances*.
»	225 » 2 » *where*	» *whese*.
»	238 » 1 » *He was*	» *Hewas*.
»	320 line 3 from top *do*	» *de*.

BY THE SAME AUTHOR

Siedetemperatur und Druck in ihren Wechselbeziehungen. Preliminary studies. Leipsic, *J. A. Barth*, 1885.

Über normale und abnorme Dampf-Temperatur. Two treatises. Bâle *J. G. Baur*, 1887.

Aus der Vorgeschichte der Spektralanalyse. A lecture. Bâle, *Benno Schwabe*, 1888.

Studien über Dampfspannkraftsmessungen. Vol. 1. Bâle, *Benno Schwabe* 1893.

Die Siedekurven der normalen Fettsäuren von der Ameisensäure bis zur Caprinsäure. Adapted for lecture purposes. Leipsic, *Breitkopf und Härtel*, 1894.

Theophrastus Paracelsus. A lecture delivered in honour of Theophrastus of Hohenheim. Bâle, *Benno Schwabe*, 1894.

Eine Spitzbergenfahrt. Sketches. Leipsic, *J. A. Barth*, 1896.

Studien über Dampfspannkraftsmessungen. Section 2, part 1. Bâle *Benno Schwabe*, 1897.

Mythos und Naturwissenschaften unter besonderer Berücksichtigung der Kalewala. A lecture. Leipsic, *J. A. Barth*, 1898.

Die Entstehung der Dalton'schen Atomtheorie in neuer Beleuchtung. Translated from the English of HENRY E. ROSCOE and ARTHUR HARDEN. No. 2 of the Monographs from the History of Chemistry. Leipsic, *J. A. Barth*, 1898.

Zwanzig Briefe, gewechselt zwischen Jöns Jakob Berzelius und Christian Friedrich Schoenbein in den Jahren 1836—1847. Bâle, *Benno Schwabe*, 1898.

Wilhelm Eisenlohr. A lecture delivered to celebrate the centenary of his birth. Karlsruhe, *G. Braun'sche Hofbuchdruckerei*, 1899.

Christian Friedrich Schoenbein, 1799—1868. Ein Blatt zur Geschichte des Neunzehnten Jahrhunderts. Part. 1. No. 4 of the Monographs from the History of Chemistry. Leipsic, *J. A. Barth*, 1899.

By GEORG W. A. KAHLBAUM and AUG. HOFFMANN:

Über die Einführung der Lavoisier'schen Theorie in Deutschland. No. 1 of the Monographs from the History of Chemistry. Leipsic, *J. A. Barth*, 1897.

By GEORG W. A. KAHLBAUM and E. THON:

Justus von Liebig und Christian Friedrich Schoenbein. Briefwechsel 1853—1868. No. 5 of the Monographs from the History of Chemistry. Leipsic, *J. A. Barth*, 1898.

IN THE PRESS:

By GEORG W. A. KAHLBAUM and E. SCHAER:

Christian Friedrich Schoenbein. Ein Blatt zur Geschichte des Neunzehnten Jahrhunderts. No. 6 of the Monographs from the History of Chemistry. Leipsic, *J. A. Barth*.

Messrs. WILLIAMS & NORGATE, London, will shortly publish:

The letters of Berzelius and Schoenbein. By GEORG W. A. KAHLBAUM, translated by FRANCIS V. DARBISHIRE and NEVILLE V. SIDGWICK.